Signs
and
Cities

Signs and Cities

Black Literary Postmodernism

Madhu Dubey

The University of Chicago Press Chicago and London

Madhu Dubey is professor of English and African-American Studies at the
University of Illinois at Chicago. She is the author of *Black Women Novelists
and the Nationalist Aesthetic*.

The University of Chicago Press, Chicago 60637
The University of Chicago Press, Ltd., London
© 2003 by The University of Chicago
All rights reserved. Published 2003
Printed in the United States of America
12 11 10 09 08 07 06 05 04 03   5 4 3 2 1

ISBN (cloth): 0-226-16726-7
ISBN (paper): 0-226-16727-5

Library of Congress Cataloging-in-Publication Data

Dubey, Madhu.
      Signs and cities : Black literary postmodernism / Madhu Dubey.
        p.   cm.
      Includes index.
      ISBN 0-226-16726-7 (alk. paper) – ISBN 0-226-16727-5 (pbk : alk. paper)
      1. American literature—African American authors–History and
criticism.   2. American literature–20th century–History and criticism.
3. Postmodernism (Literature)–United States.   4. African
Americans–Intellectual life.   5. City and town life in literature.
6. African Americans in literature.   I. Title.
PS153.N5 D83   2003
810.9′113′08996073–dc21

                                                            2003001354

Contents

Acknowledgments   vii

Introduction   1

1. The Postmodern Moment in Black Literary and
   Cultural Studies   17

2. Books of Life: Postmodern Uses of Print
   Literacy   55

3. Urban Writing as Voyeurism: Literature in the Age
   of Spectacle   99

4. Reading as Listening: The Southern Folk
   Aesthetic   144

5. Reading as Mediation: Urbanity in the Age of
   Information   186

Afterword   235
Notes   243
Index   277

Acknowledgments

Many people contributed in various ways to the writing of this book. Claudia Tate seemed to know I was going to write this book long before I did and initiated it by urging me to overcome my resistance to the very idea of postmodernism. It gives me great pleasure to put in print my appreciation for Françoise Lionnet, Valerie Smith, Micaela Di Lionardo, and Zohreh Sullivan—exemplary senior scholars whose generous confidence in my work kept me going through a difficult time in the writing of this book. A very special thanks is due to Phil Harper, who read the entire manuscript with scrupulous care and understood what I was trying to say more clearly than I did. His response assured me that I had an audience for this book and pushed me to make my argument at once more bold and precise. I am deeply grateful to Alan Thomas and Randy Petilos at the University of Chicago Press and to copyeditor Kathryn Gohl for making the process of revising and publishing this book feel so unimaginably smooth.

A fellowship from the Alice Berline Kaplan Center for the Humanities at Northwestern University allowed me to begin work on this project, and feedback from my colleagues there, especially Carl Smith, helped me to focus and clarify it. I couldn't have asked for a more nourishing intellectual environment than Brown University, where the bulk of this book was written and revised. The women affiliated with the Pembroke Center, including Nancy Armstrong, Rey Chow, Wendy Chun, Mary Ann Doane, Ellen Rooney, and Elizabeth Weed, made me feel for the first time that I had found an institutional home. Discussions with sociologist José Itzighsohn and visiting anti-postmodernist Matthew Jordan led me to modify some of my claims. The students in my graduate seminars at Brown, in particular Yogita Goyal, Chris Lee, Cheryl Locke, Katherine McMorran, Asha Nadkarni, and Daniel Voloch, wrote papers and dissertation chapters that were immensely stimulating for my own work. Gene Jarrett deserves a special mention for his meticulous research assistance and his encyclopedic knowledge of African-American literature.

I presented portions of this book while it was in progress at various academic forums. Some of those colleagues whose questions and comments helped shape and sharpen my argument are Alvina Quintana at the University of Delaware; Saurabh Dube at El Colegio de México; Barbara Foley and Jerry Phillips at the MLG conference in Chicago; Jonathan Arac and Nancy Glazener at Pittsburgh University; Cyraina Johnson-Rouillier and Glenn Hendler at Notre Dame University; Marlon Ross, Arlene Keizer, and Sandra Gunning at the University of Michigan at Ann Arbor; Tricia Rose at New York University; Barbara Johnson at the Pembroke Center Roundtable at Brown University; Carlene Polite at SUNY Buffalo; Crystal Bartolovich, Priya Jaikumar, and Sudipto Sen at Syracuse University; Bill Gleason, Jeff Nunakawa, Valerie Smith, and Tim Watson at Princeton University; and Jamie Daniels, Judith Kegan Gardner, and Walter Benn Michaels at the University of Illinois at Chicago.

Many friends read parts of this manuscript and gave me invaluable suggestions for revision: Susan Andrade, Indrani Chatterjee, Laura Chrisman, Daniel Kim, Roopali Mukherjee, and Sumit Sarkar. Ken Warren was my most difficult reader. Kunle George didn't read a word of this book, but heated telephone arguments with him over the years contributed immensely to it. Gordon Karim researched the MOVE disaster for me on the Internet. Nalini Ayya tracked down and mailed me an afterword to *Stars in My Pocket Like Grains of Sand* that I couldn't find anywhere and that drew into focus my whole discussion of postmodernism and race. Archana Kumar and Hazel Rowley gave freely of their editing skills and moral support. Greg Diamond racked his brains to come up with a catchy title. Pheng Cheah gave hours and hours of his time serving as an honorary therapist, talking me through my doubts and anxieties about the book. Apu Sagar helped push me through the closing stretch.

On a more personal note, I thank Jim Donovan for the long walks and desultory conversations at the Kopi Café that helped keep me sane while I worked on this book; David Hilliard for his part in my romance with Chicago as well as for more mundane forms of sustenance; Dianna Stenzel for much-needed musical distractions; Daniel Kim for being my "prison culture" in Providence; and Anil Pal, Hazel Rowley, and Josie Saldaña for making life away from Chicago actually feel enjoyable.

Finally, I must acknowledge my intellectual debt to two city-loving novelists, Leon Forrest and Samuel Delany. Leon gave me the warmest encouragement at the initial stages of writing this book. His unfailing shit-detector and his (always civil) rants against literary messianism helped me to find my own polemical voice. Any interesting ideas there may be in this book are inspired by Samuel Delany's writing. The very best thing about writing *Signs and Cities* was that it gave me an alibi for the hours I spent steeped in the pleasure of reading Delany.

Sections of some of the chapters in this volume have been published in different versions. Part of chapter 1 was first published as "Postmodernism as Postnationalism? Racial Representation in U.S. Black Cultural Studies," *New Formations* 45, Lawrence and Wishart, London (winter 2001–2): 150–68. Sections of chapter 2 have been published as "Folk and Urban Communities in African-American Women's Fiction: Octavia Butler's *Parable of the Sower*," *Studies in American Fiction* 27, no. 1 (spring 1999): 103–28; and "Literature and Urban Crisis: John Edgar Wideman's *Philadelphia Fire*," *African American Review* 32, no. 4 (1998): 579–95. Sections of chapter 4 have been published as "Postmodern Geographies of the U.S. South," *Nepantla: Views from South* 3, no. 2 (2002): 351–71; and "'South to a Very Old Place': Toni Morrison's *Song of Solomon*," in *The Word and the World: Essays in Honor of A. N. Kaul*, ed. Sambudha Sen (New Delhi: Oxford University Press, 2003).

Introduction

Colson Whitehead's *The Intuitionist,* published in 1999, is a novel fasci-
nated by elevators and the principle of "verticality," which literally enabled
"the metropolis, summoning [it] into tumultuous modernity."[1] The plot
of the novel revolves around the search for a missing text—manuscript
notes believed to contain a blueprint for the black box, or the perfect
elevator that will usher in the cities of the future. The author of these notes
is the deceased James Fulton, who begins his illustrious career by codifying
the principles of "Empiricism," the canon of elevator knowledge guided by
the "light of reason" (27). Midway through the novel, Fulton is revealed
to be an African-American who had successfully passed for white. This
discovery demands a "new literacy" (230), initiating a critical reading of a
founding document of urban modernity—Fulton's Empiricist textbook on
elevators—and decoding its repressed racial subtext. After an intellectual
conversion, Fulton goes on to publish *Theoretical Elevators,* inaugurating
Intuitionist philosophy, which is derided by the reigning Empiricist regime
of elevator inspectors as voodoo and witchery. Fulton's *Theoretical Elevators* can be seen as a countertext of modernity, in its critique of scientific
rationality and its recovery of suprarational modes of knowing that have
been discredited by Empiricist ideology. But the unpublished third volume
of Fulton's oeuvre also remains strongly invested in the vertical and utopian
aspirations of urban modernity, with its quest for futurity and technological
perfectibility. Fulton's black box is to be a marvel of engineering that will
"deliver us from the cities we suffer now" (61). Fulton wishes to mold the
rigidly monumental modern city into a more resilient urban form: "The
shining city will possess untold arms and a thousand eyes, mutability itself,
constructed of as-yet unconjured plastics. It will float, fly, fall, have no need
of steel armature, have a liquid spine, no spine at all" (198–99). The malleability of Fulton's future city is prefigured by the form of his text, which

exists only as a set of fragmented notes. By the end of the novel, Lila Mae Watson, the first black woman employee of the New York City Department of Elevator Inspectors, becomes the custodian of Fulton's dream, as she finds and devotes herself to decoding his manuscript. In the course of this labor, Lila Mae develops from a "modern city girl" (189) to a "citizen of the city to come" (255). Recognizing that no text can be definitive in its grasp of a changing and open-ended reality, Lila Mae resolves to revise and update Fulton's text to make it more responsive to the needs of future cities.

I begin with Colson Whitehead's novel because it so vividly captures the nexus of texts and cities that forms the subject of my study. Since the 1970s—the period widely referred to as postmodern[2]—African-American fiction has teemed with tropes of the book-within-the-book, and with scenes of reading and writing, which probe the twinned inheritance of print literacy and urban modernity. Such texts, which I discuss in this book, include Octavia Butler's *Parable of the Sower,* Samuel Delany's *Stars in My Pocket Like Grains of Sand,* Trey Ellis's *Platitudes,* Charles Johnson's *Faith and the Good Thing,* Toni Morrison's *Jazz* and *Song of Solomon,* Gloria Naylor's *Mama Day,* Ishmael Reed's *Mumbo Jumbo,* Sapphire's *PUSH,* and John Edgar Wideman's *Reuben* and *Philadelphia Fire.*[3] Signaling a moment of critique and crisis within the modern, these novels actively contribute to the wider currents of postmodern culture. Although we would expect African-American literature to form a vital resource for debates about postmodernism, it is conspicuously missing, even when these debates are launched in the name of racial difference. Stepping into this gap, *Signs and Cities* stages a long-overdue encounter between theories of postmodern urbanism and African-American literary and cultural studies.

Dramatic transformations of U.S. urban order since the 1970s have rendered the idea of community increasingly abstract and experientially unknowable, feeding into the crises of representation associated with postmodern culture. At the heart of these crises lie doubts about the continuing potency of the modern print tradition. Michel Foucault remarked that the flurry of writing about writing during the 1960s "was doubtless only a swansong"—of the modern, adds Andreas Huyssen, and as such, "a moment of the postmodern."[4] In the wake of advanced electronic technologies, print culture seems to be on the verge of extinction. The uncertain fates of the printed book and of modern notions of urban community are closely coupled in postmodern theory. In media and technology studies, the artifact of the book is taken to be the very emblem of the modern city, with its uniform visual blocks of print seeming to mirror the grids of a rationalized urban space. More substantively, print technology supports a unique model of mediated yet knowable community befitting modern urban conditions.

As a commodity, the printed book cannot presuppose the immediately visible, face-to-face audiences of folk and oral forms of communication. Because books are subject to the spatial and temporal distancing of producers from consumers entailed in all commodity culture, print readerships are modern and urban in the sense that they are always "concrete abstractions" grasped through acts of technological and social mediation.[5] But although modern print culture cannot deliver organic community, it could nonetheless constitute imagined communities. Print readerships are dispersed in space and time but nonetheless are communities because, in Benedict Anderson's famous formulation, their members "will never know most of their fellow-members, meet them, or even hear of them, yet in the minds of each lives the image of their communion." This "remarkable confidence of community in anonymity," to quote Anderson again, begins to seem impossible in the postmodern era.[6] Whereas print culture could work as a medium of social integration, assembling scattered readers into a national public sphere, the processes of technological and social mediation assume newly disorienting proportions in the postmodern period. Spatiotemporal distances appear to shrink under the pressure of advanced technologies of information and telecommunications, but of course the resulting impression of simultaneity and copresence is virtual, made possible by the most sophisticated modes of mediation. In effect, the new technologies bring about the virtual urbanization of the entire social world, lending greater visibility to differences and raising in heightened forms the problem of knowable community.

In this "late age of print,"[7] it is not only the idea of coherent communities but also a political conception of culture that becomes increasingly difficult to sustain. With digital technologies, the referent itself seems to evaporate, threatening the foundation of politics, which always demands sure access to the real. The political promise of modern print culture rested on claims of its special purchase on social reality. Even as the printed book inaugurated the mass production of commodities, it simultaneously sponsored ideologies of literacy and literature as gateways to a cultural sphere defined by its critical distance from the urban marketplace. In a typical formulation of this modern promise, Ben Agger writes that "Reading sparks awareness of the world's insufficiency," and books cultivate this awareness by standing apart from the world. Agger goes on to declare, apocalyptically, that "*the autonomy of bookness itself* is at issue" in the postmodern world, where the fast-blurring distinction between reality and representation is eclipsing the possibility of social critique.[8]

Contemporary responses to the presumed crisis of print culture generally take one of two forms. The first might be characterized as the modernist defense of the print tradition—the effort to shore up the humanist and the putatively universal subject of modern culture and politics the splintering demands of new and diverse social constituencies. second—properly postmodernist—response is to welcome the impending technological and political obsolescence of print culture, having exposed its imagined community to be a false totality. These familiar positions are at play in a range of crisis-ridden debates about plural literacies, the "death of literature,"[9] and academic canon formation. Of course it is no coincidence that the crisis of print culture erupts soon after racial minority groups begin to demand and gain access to the canon and the curriculum, drastically overhauling the notions of community and national identity that might be represented through print culture.

Debates about the political efficacy of the modern print tradition bear special resonance for African-American writers. From its beginnings, African-American literature has been fueled by an immense faith in the egalitarian promise of print modernity. As Henry Louis Gates observes, the nineteenth-century slave narratives were "propelled by the Enlightenment demand that a 'race' place itself on the Great Chain of Being primarily through the exigencies of print." If the slave narratives equated "the rights of man with the ability to write,"[10] much of the subsequent African-American literary tradition was galvanized by the belief that print literature could effectively press the case for full black participation in national life. In this tradition, the political potential of print literacy has been intimately tied to the progressive possibilities of urbanity. Key works and movements, from Frederick Douglass's 1845 slave narrative, through the Harlem Renaissance and the naturalist era, and up to a text like Toni Morrison's *The Bluest Eye*, published in 1970, established a close equivalence between books and cities, associating both terms with modernization.[11] Writing during the 1920s, Alain Locke viewed the mass black exodus out of the rural South into the cities as a deliberate flight from "medieval America to modern."[12] Echoing Locke, two decades later Richard Wright described the black urban migration as a lunge "toward the future." The migrants heading toward industrial cities shared "all the glorious hopes of the West," convinced that "reason and freedom could lead to paradise on earth."[13] Wright also clarified the tight link between urban modernization and print literacy when, assuming the voice of a typical urban migrant, he declared: "We love books inordinately"; "print compels us."[14]

The 1970s marked a decisive turn in the African-American literary tradition, when the emancipatory promise of urban modernity was widely felt to have been exhausted. By the beginning of the decade, the century-long stream of black migration out of the rural South into the urban North began to reverse direction. Before the Civil Rights revolution, it had been possible to think of racial inequality as a regional aberration, restricted to the supposedly premodern social order of the South. But the success of the Civil Rights movement made it all the more apparent that the legal extension of modern citizenship rights to African-Americans would not in itself solve the racial problem. The Watts riot occurred a mere few days after the passage of the Voting Rights Act in 1965. Outbreaks of racial violence in numerous cities prompted the 1968 Kerner Commission Report on Civil Disorders, which drew attention to the prevalence of de facto racial segregation in northern cities, officially certifying that the racial problem had moved from the rural South into the cities, and in fact had become nationalized. In the next couple of decades, industrial restructuring of U.S. cities, aided by shifts in public policy and political rhetoric, deepened the immiseration of black urban populations, making it difficult to sustain a vision of the city as a promised land of opportunity. These decades also witnessed the emergence of alarmist accounts of urban crisis that were coded in decisively racial terms. Debates in the mass media and academia about the "underclass" ascribed the economic problems plaguing U.S. cities to a collapse of black cultural values and community. Given the severe pressure such discourses exert on black culture, it is scarcely surprising that claims to represent racial community have become highly fraught in postmodern African-American fiction as well as literary and cultural studies.

Signs and Cities offers a historicized account of why problems of racial representation take the specific forms they do in African-American fiction since the 1970s, why these problems are magnetized around issues of urban community, and why tropes of the book have become a chosen literary vehicle for exploring these problems. I draw on a wide range of materials from urban geography, history, sociology, political science, literary and cultural criticism, and media and technology studies to substantiate the claim, central to this book, that problems of racial representation are taking exacerbated forms in the postmodern era. During the 1970s, for the first time in their history, African-Americans became a predominantly urban people, whether living in the South or the North. With urbanity forming the given condition of black social life, claims to racial representation could no longer be objectively grounded on organic models of community. Moreover, several interlocking developments in the post–Civil Rights decades (including the end of legal segregation, expansion of the black middle class, and ascension of black elites to administrative and political power) have strained the idea of a cohesive and singular black community. A sense of crisis in the category of racial community is seismically registered across the disciplinary spectrum of African-American studies.

In response to this perceived crisis, literary and cultural critics are recalling and refurbishing models of community and of racial representation developed earlier in the century. For this reason, an encounter between postmodernism and African-American literary and cultural studies seems particularly urgent, and may at the very least occasion some rethinking of prevailing models of black literary production. In the two most influential critical paradigms that have governed African-American literary studies— revolving around uplift and vernacular tradition—print literature is imbued with broad-based representative powers. The uplift paradigm casts the writer as an agent of social advancement and cultural improvement, thereby affirming the tangible value of print literacy for the masses. In the vernacular paradigm, writers may speak for distinctively black communities insofar as they can inflect their texts with the accents and idioms of black oral culture. Even as postmodern African-American fiction attests to the abiding seduction of these prior models of racial representation, it also prompts a reconsideration of these models by frontally tackling the difficulties of imagining racial community within contemporary urban conditions. Tropes of the book serve as perfect vehicles for this endeavor, forcing to the forefront issues of class antagonism, technological mediation, and time-space distanciation. None of the novelists I examine in this study is able smoothly to project coherent racial community, an exact fit between the interests of the writer and the masses, or an instrumental political function for literature. African-American novelists in the postmodern era thereby convey not only the diminishing credibility of existing models of racial representation but also a keen suspicion toward the very category of print literature.

Indeed, one of the paradoxes of the postmodern moment is that it witnesses the greatest effusion ever of print literature by African-Americans, along with a disavowal of their chosen medium by some of the most celebrated of these authors. Toni Morrison, for example, has said that she imagines her ideal audience to be "an illiterate or preliterate reader."[15] One of my aims in writing *Signs and Cities* is to account for this paradox whereby the most prolific African-American authors feel compelled to present their works as something other than print literature. If, as Henry Louis Gates has argued, tropes of the book in earlier phases of African-American literature testified to the progressive political promise of print literacy, the betrayal of this promise haunts African-American writers in the postmodern period. As part of their assault on the modern legacy, postmodern literary and cultural theorists subject the printed book, along with the "modern literary system,"[16] to sharp critical scrutiny, construing it as a technology with a history rather than as a transparent medium for transmitting timeless human verities. Participating in this postmodern turn, recent African-American fiction pays heightened attention to the "technotype" of the book.[17] Through its proliferating tropes of the book-within-a-book, this fiction raises a host of doubts and questions about modern

notions of literary value and, in this respect, forms a crucial, though unacknowledged, component of the postmodern interrogation of the modern
legacy.

Dialogue between African-American and postmodern cultural studies
has been initiated (notably by Phillip Brian Harper, bell hooks, Wahneema
Lubiano, and Cornel West) but has foundered on several grounds. Theories
of postmodernism are generally developed without reference to the specificities of African-American life and history, even as they routinely invoke
the idea of racial difference. To some critics, the very category of postmodernism has been so insidiously racialized—assuming a white Western
subject as its normative center—that it bears little relevance for African-
Americans and other "others" of the modern West. Taking these caveats
seriously, I nonetheless argue for the salience of a periodizing concept of
postmodernism for African-American literary and cultural studies—an argument that requires a critical reinflection of David Harvey's and Fredric
Jameson's macrotheories of the postmodern. I also argue that even as
African-American culture is being reshaped by the changes associated with
postmodernism, it is in turn central to the way these changes are being
discursively processed in theories of postmodernism. Although this may
not be immediately apparent, these two arguments are closely intertwined;
the impetus behind both is a strong dissatisfaction with the ways African-
American culture is perceived in the postmodern period.

To be sure, globalizing theories of postmodernism, such as those of
Harvey or Jameson, rarely make mention of African-American culture.
But once we move away from high theory to more concrete discussions of
postmodernism in the U.S. context, we find that African-American culture
lies at the heart of discussions of postmodern crisis and is in fact pervasively summoned both to embody and resolve the sense of crisis. This
holds true across the gamut of disciplines, including urban history, sociology, ethnography, cultural studies, literary criticism, and media studies. At
the most obvious level, the notorious category of the black "underclass" is
deployed to fan public fears about the total disintegration of urban community in postmodern times. Even as black urban culture is exuberantly
exploited to feed global commodity capitalism, mass-media and academic
debates cast the black urban poor as the catalysts of social and cultural crisis. If we look farther afield, at technological or semiotic accounts of postmodernism, we still find African-Americans appearing as the flashpoints of
crisis. A random but telling example is Scott Lash and John Urry's book
Economies of Signs and Space, which argues the now-familiar thesis that
"economic and symbolic processes are more than ever interlaced" in the
postmodern era. Lash and Urry assert that the "real loser" in such a
context is "the single black mother in the Chicago ghetto," who lacks the

tural capital that increasingly mediates access to economic and political
wer.[18]

There are solid reasons for placing African-Americans at the core of
any discussion of postmodernism in the U.S. context. All the economic,
political, and technological changes that are taken to be formative of the
postmodern condition (detailed in chapter 1) have followed a racialized
logic of uneven development, disproportionately afflicting racial minorities in the United States. It would be difficult to dispute the claim that the
vast majority of African-Americans have suffered heavily from the material
processes distinctive of the postmodern era. Yet, or more precisely *because*
of this, African-Americans are fetishized as the guarantors of everything
that is felt to be at risk in the postmodern era—bodily presence, palpable
reality, political intentionality. If the referent has waned under the pressure of digital technologies, African-Americans have managed to maintain
a connection, at once mystical and visceral, to material reality. While the
hyperreality of postmodern urban existence attenuates bodily experience,
the black body alone continues to shimmer with the aura of presence. From
this follow claims about the oppositional political propensity of black culture. In academic fields such as cultural studies, hip-hop music is lionized as
a uniquely postmodern form of political resistance, at once technologically
hypermediated and directly expressive of raw urban realities.[19] Whereas
postmodern culture at large lacks the epistemological grounds needed for
political projects, African-Americans remain rooted in "a reality that one
cannot not know" and thereby become the political touchstones of the
postmodern condition.[20]

African-Americans can be cast in this double role—as both the worst
victims and the redemptive agents of the postmodern condition—because
material oppression often automatically translates into political opposition in postmodern cultural studies. Some striking examples, discussed in
the following pages, are bell hooks's strategy of "choosing the margins,"
the "third worldism" espoused by Fredric Jameson, or Edward Soja's notion of "Thirdspace." In these and other instances, possibilities of critical
resistance are situated in residual zones that somehow elude the dominant logic of postmodernism. This romance of the residual that beguiles
so much postmodern thinking about race forms one of my principal tar-
gets of critique in *Signs and Cities.* To perceive African-American culture
in residual terms is to exempt it from the contingencies of the postmodern condition. Locating black culture in pockets of sheer alterity within or
outside contemporary social conditions, we inevitably primitivize this culture. Although primitivism can support sharp critiques of modernity, it can
also all too easily slide over into fetishism of racial "others." Converting
a structural position of relative powerlessness into a desirable ontological

condition, we mine sites of material deprivation for their cultural capital. As cultural value increases in inverse proportion to political and economic power, aesthetic appreciation comes to compensate for and thereby mystify the realities of material suffering.

Not surprisingly, given the racialized logic of the residual, black culture in the postmodern era is persistently identified with oral and performance modes associated with the voice or the body and is often explicitly opposed to linguistic expression. For example, Cornel West contends that the "ur-text" of black culture is "neither a word nor a book" but instead the "guttural cry" or the "wrenching moan."[21] In one of the most widely read anthologies on postmodern culture, Andrew Ross's collection of essays, *Universal Abandon: The Politics of Postmodernism*, Anders Stephanson poses such questions as "Music is *the* black means of cultural expression, is it not?" or "The black community is more contestational than average America, is it not?"[22]—questions that are profoundly insulting, especially because they appear in the only piece treating black culture in a volume that otherwise applies the most discriminating forms of analysis to differences in postmodern culture.

It is not too difficult for cultural critics on the left to abjure the demonizing of African-American culture that lends force to accounts of postmodern crisis, such as, for example, in "underclass" or canon revision debates. But evidently it is much harder to resist romanticizing black culture as the last vestige of authenticity left in postmodern times, at once radically other and viscerally knowable. The obvious appeal of this approach is that it allows us to bypass the difficulties of mediation that are entailed in our intellectual work as cultural critics, to lay claim to political truths that are immediately apprehensible because they are said to inhere in the voice or the body, and thereby to certify that our theories have been honed on "the ragged edges of the Real."[23]

Cultural politics in the postmodern era might be better served by trying to grasp the racialized logic of uneven development that systematically links residual and dominant categories rather than through mystical evocations of the numinous reality, bodily presence, or sublime orality of African-American culture. By this logic, we would view black culture as an integral part of the postmodern condition, without for a second losing sight of its historical specificity. The structural interdependence between various spheres that is essential to the concept of uneven development would have serious implications for cultural studies, making it harder for us to remand black culture to a zone of opaque otherness, a pure elsewhere to contemporary social conditions.

Once black culture is admitted to be as subject to social and technological mediation as any other culture in the postmodern era, its political salience could not hinge on a primal connection to bodily experience or material reality. An emphasis on mediation would move black culture out of a prelapsarian into a historical sphere, but, as is obvious from current academic accounts of hip-hop music, this alone would not neutralize the powerful lure of racial primitivism. Organicism can be an effect of technological fetishism, just as dire claims about the irreality of contemporary life breed desires for absolute epistemological guarantees. Having resisted the romance of the residual, we would have to be equally wary of the other prevalent tendency in the postmodern era—of viewing technology as a surrogate for politics.

Technological determinism manifests itself as a revamped version of formalism in the sphere of postmodern literary studies. Texts that reflect on their own textuality, their own status as mediated representations, are often seen to militate against racial essentialism. In the following chapters I argue, to the contrary, that there is no straight line from form to politics and that aesthetic innovations do not inevitably produce politically subversive effects. Postmodern African-American literature is deemed to have shed the burden of racial representation simply by virtue of refusing narrative realism. But disruptive aesthetic strategies may actually render the romance of race more palatable in postmodern times. In a reading of Toni Morrison's *Song of Solomon* that is highly suggestive for my argument here, Lawrence Hogue notes that this novel rather than, say, David Bradley's *The Chaneysville Incident* or Sarah Phillips's *Andrea Lee,* has been canonized because, despite its "deconstructive" narrative strategies, it supplies a reassuring notion of black culture.[24] Tweaking Hogue's argument, I would suggest that postmodern literary theory most readily embraces those texts that give readers a secure handle on black racial difference while catering to sophisticated appetites for formal complexity. Indeed, a synthesis of aesthetic indeterminacy and racial essentialism, allowing us to have our cake and eat it too, may be defining of postmodern approaches to racial representation in literature.

To discern what is novel about racial representation in postmodern African-American fiction, we may have to snap the enduring link between narrative realism and politically naïve representation or, conversely, between formal experimentation and political contestation. A unique feature of the postmodern moment is that claims to representation can no longer proceed on the assumption that literary texts transparently reflect preexistent social realities but must squarely address the problem of formal and technological mediation. This is not, however, to say that postmodern African-American literary texts make no mimetic claims. They nearly always do, but the question of how exactly the literary text gains access to the real becomes an insistent preoccupation. As Brian McHale notes, the postmodern novel is an illusion-breaking genre that obtrusively calls attention to the materiality of its own medium.[25] Any effort to identify the distinctive elements of postmodern fiction, then, demands some consideration of form and technology, and this is one reason I organize this study around tropes of the book. At the same time, self-consciousness about the medium of representation in postmodern literary theory often verges on a new kind of formalism, which does not bracket political questions (as did earlier varieties of formalism) but instead tends to swallow politics into aesthetics. Such tendencies toward aesthetic solipsism can be avoided only by keeping in play the idea of referentiality as a crucial dimension of the problem of literary representation. But how exactly do we keep alive a notion of the real without resorting to metaphysics or mysticism? This is one of the toughest challenges confronting contemporary cultural critics.

This challenge seems all the more daunting in an intellectual climate in which poststructuralism and historical materialism are generally pitted against each other, and in which the very word *real* is rarely used without scare quotes—except, of course, with reference to African-American culture. Some idea of the real that eschews both organicism and technological fetishism, innocent mimesis and textual inflation, seems urgently needed in the postmodern era. In working toward such a notion in *Signs and Cities,* I take my cue from Samuel Delany, to whom I owe much more than the title phrase of my book.[26] Science fiction writer and theorist, and now also an urban historian, Delany styles himself a deconstructionist as well as a "die-hard, card-carrying materialist."[27] In his recent book on urban redevelopment, *Times Square Red, Times Square Blue,* Delany inserts a timely reminder, worth quoting at length:

> Some old-fashioned Marxism might be useful here: Infrastructure determines superstructure—not the other way around. And for all their stabilizing or destabilizing potential, discourse and rhetoric are superstructural phenomena. . . .
>
> Infrastructure makes society go. Superstructure makes it go smoothly (or bumpily).
>
> . . . In the field of human endeavor language is a stabilizing mechanism, not a producing mechanism—regardless of what both artists and critics would prefer. This in no way contradicts the notion that the world to which we have access is constituted entirely of language.[28]

These bald statements on infrastructure and superstructure will surely seem surprising to those familiar with Delany's writing, which is known for its finely tuned conception of the relation between words and world and has even been accused of a tendency toward boundless semiosis. It is instructive to ask what compels Delany to take what some would characterize as a vulgarly Marxist stance on culture and political economy. *Times Square Red* was written and published at a historical juncture marked by a "prodigious expansion of culture throughout the social realm."[29] Most of the blind spots of postmodern cultural studies as well as of contemporary projects of racial representation arise from the inflation of culture at the expense of political economy. The category of culture is overworked in each of the several overlapping fields of discourse I survey in this book. In recent urban studies, semiotic approaches to cities as cultural texts are occluding the material vectors of urban form.[30] Although signs of racial difference circulate ubiquitously in the realm of commodity culture, racial segregation in U.S. cities intensifies at the level of built environment. Likewise, public debates on urban crisis place an enormous explanatory and redemptive burden on the category of culture, displacing the problems of urban poverty onto claims about the poverty of black urban culture.

Delany's old-fashioned Marxist position is explicitly directed at influential accounts of U.S. urban life that, because they are skewed toward superstructure, are pathologizing minority urban cultures. In the postmodern era, arguments about the causative role of culture are palpably shaping political choices and public policies affecting various constituencies—such as the black urban poor—that are structurally excluded from participating in these debates. Intellectuals only exacerbate this situation by centralizing the role of culture in debates on urban poverty, whether by endorsing dominant claims about the cultural deviance of the black urban poor or by contesting these claims through celebratory accounts of black urban culture. Either strategy perpetuates the absurd presumption that a group's cultural practices should have some bearing on the question of its right to public resources and social justice.

In such a context, a more effective *discursive* tactic for intellectuals might be to place questions of political economy squarely at the center of our debates and to interrogate the cultural capital we accrue by claiming to write on behalf of underrepresented social groups. As Delany points out, this sort of position will go against "what both artists and critics would prefer," because it circumscribes the ambitions of those of us who work in cultural studies. But at the present moment, our best hope of exercising our optimal role as cultural critics—to make society go bumpily rather than smoothly—may lie in deflating the exorbitant political value of culture in postmodern U.S. society.

Culture remains a valuable object of study precisely because it seems to operate as a causative mechanism in the postmodern era. But currents in postmodern theory and culture cannot be fully grasped without reference to the political economy of contemporary U.S. society. To give some concrete examples, the cultural politics of difference cannot be properly understood without simultaneously keeping in view the urban redevelopment programs that have produced a specific material organization of class and racial divisions. Similarly, we miss the full implications of southern cultural regionalism without an account of the concurrent political and economic changes—notably the industrial boom and the Civil Rights movement—that have overhauled racial relations in the region. Strictly speaking, political economy is but one discourse among others: my knowledge of it derives from a reading of books about political economy, which carry the same epistemological status as books in cultural studies. But the recognition that all knowledge is textual need not provoke a disheartened retreat from any effort to know and understand the world. I am convinced that it is necessary to posit some notion of the real in order to make any claims about social life, while remaining fully aware that because human knowledge of reality is always discursively mediated, it is also always fallible and revisable.

Although this will surely seem counterintuitive, my focus on the sphere of literary culture, along with attention to political economy, has cautioned me against overstating the political valence of culture in the postmodern era. One of the hardest challenges of my intensive engagement with postmodern black literature for this book was that I had to reluctantly relinquish my assumptions—engrained through long disciplinary training—about literature as the most agile handle on social reality. Some modernist critics of postmodern culture, such as Ben Agger, have called for a "radical hermeneutic" modeled on the "literary" mode, because the peculiarly fictive truth-claims of literature maintain a distance between reality and representation, thereby nourishing political critique.[31] But far from being the monopoly of print literature, fictive truth-claims are staked in many other cultural media, including cinema and popular music. As my readings of novels in the following chapters testify, some literary texts do foster a richly critical perspective on social reality, but no more so than other cultural texts. For Agger, because of its unique conditions of credibility, literature always highlights its own "corrigibility" as a mode of apprehending the world.[32] Yet, as a product of institutionalized study and as the centerpiece of liberal education, print literature is deeply sedimented with ideologies of cultural value that shine forth as transcendent truths. It is difficult, in the postmodern era, to defend the idea that corrigibility—and, by extension, political critique—is an intrinsic or exclusive property of print literature.

Paradoxically, literature can be sharply illuminating of postmodern crises of representation precisely because it occupies a shrunken and embattled corner in the contemporary cultural domain. As an elite and exclusionary preserve, print literature cannot gratify ambitions for immediate or mass political relevance. If we honestly acknowledge its restricted audience, literary critics cannot but be modest about the political claims we make for literature and, hopefully, more alert to the mediations entailed in our work as academics. Of course, we should be equally restrained when we write about the political effects of more popular forms of culture, but because of the broader public appeal of these forms, academic cultural critics are more easily able to elide questions of intellectual/mass mediation. A focus on the sphere of print literature allows us to bring the populist claims of postmodern cultural studies under careful scrutiny. Problems of political scope and value are compounded in postmodern African-American literature for a number of reasons detailed in my first chapter. Because print literature is the sphere most severely in crisis, and because here claims to racial representation are particularly aggravated, it offers one of the most revealing points of entry into debates about postmodern culture.

In the first chapter of *Signs and Cities,* I spell out what exactly it means to speak of a postmodern moment in African-American studies. Selectively examining key texts from various disciplines, I sketch in this chapter the lineaments of a widely registered crisis in the idea of black community and specify the problems of racial representation sparked by this crisis. To distinguish postmodern from modern projects of racial representation, I look closely at exemplary efforts (by bell hooks and Cornel West, among others) to forge new forms of community suited to the changed realities of the post–Civil Rights period. These entail a shift from uplift to populist and from print to vernacular paradigms of black intellectual work. Even as they stress their critical distance from previous models of black community, I argue, postmodern cultural critics find it difficult to legitimize their own claims to racial representation without reanimating the cultural politics of 1960s black nationalism. In the domain of print literature, antirealism and textual self-reflection are generally identified as the unique elements of postmodern black fiction and said to disable essentialist constructs of black culture and community. I dispute such assumptions through a comparative analysis of Ishmael Reed's *Mumbo Jumbo* and John Edgar Wideman's *Reuben.* In their common effort to incarnate the black urban writer in the image of Thoth, Egyptian god of writing, these novels explicitly engage the difficulties of resolving postmodern problems of racial representation through the medium of print literature.

One reason so many African-American writers are skeptical about the political value of literature is that the very technology of print is felt to be obsolete in postmodern culture, which some characterize as hypervisual and others as a culture of "secondary orality."[33] The wider public reach of visual, aural, and electronic technologies, and their presumably greater sensitivity to the demands of diverse social constituencies, intensifies authorial

anxieties about the political provenance of print literature. In the rem
ing four chapters, I examine the problem of literary value in relation to a
distinct cultural medium or technology—print in chapter 2, visual media in
chapter 3, oral vernacular culture in chapter 4, and electronic technologies
of information in chapter 5. Each of these chapters is organized around a
particular trope of the book, or of reading and writing, that serves to distill
and resolve a problem peculiar to postmodern urban culture.

The hidden racial consequences of urban redevelopment since the 1970s
form the subject of my second chapter. I focus on three novels, Octavia
Butler's *Parable of the Sower,* Sapphire's *PUSH,* and John Edgar Wideman's
Reuben, that employ some variant of a "Book of Life" to test the utopian
promise of the modern print legacy in the dystopian conditions of postmodern cities. In chapter 3 I examine the visual regime of postmodern
urbanism, highlighting its contradictory subjection of African-American
bodies as objects of fear and desire. Tropes of urban writing as voyeurism
in Toni Morrison's *Jazz* and Wideman's *Reuben* and *Philadelphia Fire* crystallize the problems of finding knowable community in the hypervisual environment of the postmodern city. In chapter 4, I analyze the recent revival
of southern regionalism as a recoil from the highly mediated conditions
of postmodern urbanity into organic racial community. Toni Morrison's
Song of Solomon and Gloria Naylor's *Mama Day,* which strain unsuccessfully
to refigure reading as listening, betray the impossibility of sustaining folk
resolutions to postmodern crises of urban literary representation. My final
chapter deals with the dilemma of knowing "others" and reality specific to
the information age, as explored in postmodern theory and in Samuel
Delany's science fiction novel *Stars in My Pocket Like Grains of Sand.*
Delany's numerous tropes of reading defined as mediation, drawn from
emergent information technologies, model forms of sociality commensurate with contemporary urban conditions.

Reading African-American literature in conjunction with discourses on
postmodern urbanism can be a mutually illuminating enterprise. Attention
to the inescapably urban scene of contemporary African-American literary
production compels a revaluation of the claims to racial representation advanced in black literary and cultural studies, and helps explain why these
claims so often get inflated at this particular historical moment. The novels I discuss in this book directly confront a range of questions pivotal to
debates on postmodern urban culture, such as: What forms of knowable
community are available in the novel environs of postmodern urban life?
How, if at all, might we grasp as a whole the fragmented and polarized
spaces of postmodern cities, or map the lines of power that are increasingly
invisible from any one location? What possibilities of social critique exist
in an era in which all culture is subsumed by commodity capitalism? How

can we ground claims to cultural representation when emergent electronic technologies are unmooring signs from reality and thereby impairing the very notion of referentiality? Focusing such questions through the lens of race, the novels I consider here often stimulate incredulity toward overstated claims about the hyperreality, semiotic illegibility, or cultural pluralism of postmodern cities. In so doing, these novels make a vital, and thus far unrecognized, contribution to current debates on postmodern urban culture.

1.

The Postmodern Moment in Black Literary and Cultural Studies

It is difficult to write about late-twentieth-century U.S. culture without taking on the term *postmodernism,* which, without clear consensus about its meaning, circulates widely as a periodizing concept. Generally dated from the 1970s, postmodernism is believed to mark a decisive break from the modern era at the cultural, epistemic, and socioeconomic levels. In most theories of postmodernism, the modern period is identified with industrial capitalism, although its successor is variably characterized as a postindustrial society or a new stage of "multinational" or "disorganized" capitalism.[1] No account of which I am aware makes a convincing case for seeing the postmodern as a socioeconomic order radically discontinuous from the modern, although certain significant changes—such as greater global integration of capital or the spread of advanced information technologies—have undoubtedly occurred. At the cultural and epistemic levels, the novel elements associated with postmodernism, such as philosophical and aesthetic antirealism, heightened consciousness about representation, refusal of totality and closure, or fragmented and unstable subjectivity, have been persuasively shown to have modernist antecedents.[2] In fact, a strong impetus behind *Signs and Cities* is to dispute prevailing claims of thoroughgoing rupture between the categories of the modern and the postmodern in a number of fields, including urban studies, media and technology studies, and literary and cultural criticism.

Why, then, do I use the term *postmodernism?* Regardless of whether the term has any decidable referent, it has become a cultural fact, given that artists and intellectuals across a broad spectrum in the United States believe in the reality of a decisive shift that has thrown the category of the modern into crisis. Trying to account for this sense of crisis in the fields of African-American literary and cultural studies is one of the main intentions of this book. But I also use *postmodernism* in a stronger sense—as a content-laden term—to refer to a cluster of socioeconomic developments that have occurred since the 1970s and are best described in David Harvey's study *The Condition of Postmodernity*. In contrast to the postindustrial thesis or even to claims of a new stage of capitalism, Harvey views the 1970s as "a troubled period of economic restructuring and social and political readjustment,"[3] a moment of transition from the rigidly organized and massified system of postwar Fordism to a more flexible regime of accumulation. Harvey extensively details recent changes in production, labor markets, finance, and consumption, but he regards these changes as a new wave of modernization and global industrial reorganization rather than as fundamental breaks with industrial modernity or with the capitalist mode of production. Although Harvey's discussion of the distinctions between modern and postmodern culture is often dichotomous, his seems to me the most coherent and measured account of the material force-field of postmodernism.

Following Harvey, I treat socioeconomic developments since the 1970s as novel in significant respects yet part of an intense round of moderniza-tion. For this reason, I refrain from using the term *postmodernity,* which implies an epochal shift, a supercession of the modern era. I do, how-ever, make frequent use of phrases such as "the postmodern period" or "postmodern times" as shorthand references to the ensemble of political, economic, technological, social, and cultural transformations that have oc-curred in the United States since the 1970s. In the realms of art, culture, and intellectual discourse, I employ the term *postmodern* to describe a mo-ment of perceived crisis within the modern. Of course the term *modern* itself is a slippery category in postmodern discourses: depending on the particular polemical or aesthetic stakes involved, the term mutates to cover a range of different values, including instrumental rationality, scientific epistemology, progressive notions of time and history, unitary political agency, totalized conceptions of social order, centered and stable identity, and falsely universal definitions of the human.[4] The terms *modern* and *modernism* are often conflated, although aesthetic modernism more often than not sets itself at odds with many of the modern categories itemized above. But flattening of the categories that are under attack is a routine feature of polemical writings and is certainly not an infraction unique to postmodern discourses.

One of the most vexed issues in debates on postmodernism is the precise relation between socioeconomic and cultural levels of change. Nearly all the influential theories of postmodernism (in particular Fredric Jameson's) have been censured for succumbing to reductive models of reflection, homology, or expressive totality.[5] On this count, my approach is fairly straightforward: the racial crises associated with postmodernism are so emphatically understood in cultural terms that culture not only operates as a pressure point but also begins to feed back into political and economic policy decisions. To bluntly anticipate my argument in this chapter, I focus on two facets of late-twentieth-century political-economic and technological developments: their drastic alteration of U.S. urban space and community, and their severely damaging effects on the vast majority of African-Americans. These facets are linked in the sense that the deteriorating conditions of African-American life—hardening spatial segregation and high levels of poverty and unemployment—are taken to be the main indices of postmodern urban crisis. In addition to being decisively racialized, this crisis is explained in cultural terms, as a failure on the part of urban African-Americans to sustain healthy traditions and communities. With black culture so directly implicated in popular and academic accounts of socioeconomic crisis, African-American novelists and literary and cultural critics begin to play defining roles, registering as well as countering or stoking the sense of crisis. But before I enter into the specifics of this argument, some preliminary remarks seem necessary on why the category of postmodernism should even be considered relevant to African-American literary and cultural studies.

Periodizing Black Postmodernism?

In the most common usage of the term, derived from Jean-François Lyotard, the *postmodern* is understood as a posture of incredulity toward the "grand narratives" of the modern West, translated as "tall tales" by Jonathan Arac.[6] Although Lyotard names several such narratives, he reserves his strongest fire for the meta-narrative of the "emancipation of humanity" (51), which casts the human in universal and totalized terms. Two of Lyotard's utterances, from his appendix to *The Postmodern Condition,* have become the mantras of most variants of postmodernism: "Let us wage a war on totality" and "Let us activate the differences" (82). For Lyotard, the idea of "humanity as the hero of liberty" (31) has lost credibility in the postmodern era, when this unitary subject is seen to dissolve into a plethora of differences (40). Within the national context of the United States, Lyotard's pronouncements on the demise of the modern political subject seemed to be confirmed by the eruption, during the 1960s, of micropolitics of difference organized around race, gender, sexuality, and so forth. Importantly, however, even as they attacked the idea of a modern Western subject that arrogated the power to speak for all humanity, these movements sought to extend the modern political project of liberal democracy. Most versions of the politics of difference have modeled themselves on the Civil Rights and Black Power movements, suggesting the enabling centrality of African-American politics and culture to the emergence of postmodernism in the United States.

The politics of difference is greeted as a crisis by critics of postmodernism such as David Harvey because it splinters the putatively universal subject of modern (class-based) politics into a host of special-interest constituencies. In *The Condition of Postmodernity,* Harvey trenchantly argues that differences are reified and rendered mutually incommunicable in postmodern cultural theories, which generally neglect the political and economic systems that make differences mean in historically specific ways (116–17). Harvey's book has been rightly criticized by feminist geographers such as Doreen Massey for its often sloppy formulation of universalism and particularism.[7] In his attack on the "local" or "regional" bases of postmodern cultural politics, Harvey slides between literal and metaphorical uses of these terms, sometimes referring to place and at other times to particular political interest groups, especially women and racial minorities. When Harvey writes that "The 'othernesses' and 'regional resistances' that postmodern politics emphasizes can only flourish in particular places" (239) or when he describes political movements mobilized around race or gender as "localized struggles" (46), we have to assume that he is speaking in loosely metaphorical terms, for there is no basis for arguing (and Harvey never does actually argue this point) that feminist or racial politics are any more or less rooted in place than are class politics. Harvey's argument cannot be sustained, even if read metaphorically, to imply that the politics of difference is mired in particularity rather than that it is place-bound. The Civil Rights movement is but one obvious example of a politics organized around a particular racial issue that appealed to political principles of universal human rights.[8]

A further problem with Harvey's argument, identified by scholars from feminist and African-American studies, is its formulation of the cultural crises associated with postmodernism. In a multifaceted argument that I can only briefly summarize here, Harvey attributes current perceptions of cultural instability to an accelerated round of time-space compression brought about by the reorganization of global economic order during the 1970s. This capitalist restructuring has involved a new and intensified phase of modernization, rendering the meaning of time and space increasingly abstract, and sparking crises of representation across all levels of culture. In her critique of Marxist urban geography, which lumps Fredric Jameson and Edward Soja together with Harvey, Doreen Massey argues that their global theories of postmodern disorientation assume a modern, masculine, Western subject who once occupied a seemingly stable center. Invoking Toni Morrison and bell hooks as counter-examples, Massey contends that for most inhabitants of the world—those who were subjected to slavery and colonialism—the experience of place and time, home and history, has been fractured for centuries, so that what is being proclaimed as a novel feature of postmodernism has in fact been long familiar to the West's "others."[9] Toni Morrison makes a similar point in her remark to Paul Gilroy that, as a consequence of slavery, African-Americans have been confronting postmodern dilemmas long before the term was coined.[10]

If we take the discursive displacement of the modern Western subject as the sticking point of postmodernism, we would have to question the applicability of the modern/postmodern periodization to fields such as African-American studies. As Wahneema Lubiano points out in a rejoinder to David Harvey, the decentering of Western cultural authority can scarcely be regarded as a crisis for African-American literary and cultural studies, where skepticism about modern Western meta-narratives has a much longer history.[11] At least going as far back as the mid-nineteenth-century slave narratives, interrogation of the practices of modern humanism has been a driving force of African-American literature. Moreover, as Phillip Brian Harper persuasively argues, the fractured subject of postmodern culture has long formed a staple element of minority literatures. Harper's point is not simply that the experience of psychological fragmentation for minority writers has predated the postmodern moment but also that it is rooted in a social history of marginalization and that this history has been a founding, albeit repressed, condition of possibility for postmodern culture.[12]

Such arguments pose important cautions for any attempt to periodize postmodernism along unitary global lines, calling attention to discrepant and asynchronous tendencies within the categories of modernism and post-modernism. Once these categories are admitted to be internally differentiated, racial and feminist politics cannot so easily be dismissed as "local" and "subordinate" to the supposedly universal politics of the modern era. The far more difficult question, however, is what exactly we do with differences once we acknowledge their importance. If Harvey fails to reckon with the divergent histories of the West's "others," many postmodern theorists lock these groups into a relation of radical alterity to the West, and in this respect become vulnerable to Harvey's critique. In *Justice, Nature and the Geography of Difference*, Harvey argues that postmodern theories of political change bank their hopes on "residual" or "surplus" areas that are placed outside the prevailing system.[13] What's more, these residual and surplus zones are generally inhabited by people who epitomize racial difference from the West.

A perfect example is Fredric Jameson's influential theory of postmodernism as the "cultural dominant" of late capitalism. Jameson's use of this phrase calls to mind Raymond Williams's discussion of residual, dominant, and emergent cultural forces, which is meant to offer a dynamic and

internally contested model of periodization.[14] But in his magisterial study
of postmodernism, Jameson claims that a novel feature of the late capitalist
period is the elimination of all the residual elements that were still available
in the modern era: "the postmodern must be characterized as a situation in
which the survival, the residue, the holdover, the archaic, has finally been
swept away without a trace."[15] As a Marxist intellectual, Jameson wants to
be able to theorize the possibility of critical resistance to capitalism, and
here he is led to contradict himself. Advocating "third worldism" as the
most promising source of social critique,[16] Jameson ends up resurrecting
the very category of the residual that he had earlier banished as a viable
alternative in the present. Jameson's strategy of third worldism is only one
prominent instance of the logic of the residual that runs through much
contemporary cultural theory, which looks to places that have been most
conspicuously left behind by the processes of capitalist modernization as
spaces of greatest opposition. An overly totalized notion of the "dominant" almost always entails as its corollary a romanticized notion of the
"residual," with a sharply antithetical articulation of the two terms.

An instance of this romance of the residual from African-American
cultural studies is bell hooks's "Choosing the Margins as a Space of
Radical Openness," an essay that has been widely taken up by advocates of
postmodernism. The margin, or the space occupied by African-Americans,
operates at two levels throughout hooks's essay. First, the margin is identified with certain sites of material oppression—the racially segregated areas
to which African-Americans were confined in the rural South, and urban
ghettoes, where African-Americans are susceptible to "every postmodern
mode of dying" imaginable.[17] In the course of the essay, this "site of deprivation" is rhetorically converted into "a space of resistance" (149), which
hooks does not link to a particular kind of social order. Hooks traces her
journey from the margin, a physical place of oppression, to the center, here
equivalent to mainstream U.S. society. But in this process, hooks chooses
to continue inhabiting the margin, which must then refer to an epistemological standpoint rather than an actual place. Acknowledging the double
inscription of the term *margin* in her essay, hooks asserts that "spaces can
be real and imagined" (152). But what remains uncertain is the passage
from one kind of space to the other: how exactly are the material sites
of racial oppression transformed into spaces of resistance? The only clue
hooks offers is that spaces "can be interrupted, appropriated, and transformed through artistic and literary practice" (152), suggesting that critical
resistance is primarily conducted in the field of culture.

The elisions in this account of racial margins are even more clearly highlighted as Edward Soja appropriates hooks's essay in the service of his
elusive concept of Thirdspace. Railing against the exclusive emphasis on

time and history in modern social theories, Soja has long been trying to develop a postmodern theory of space. His most recent notion of Thirdspace is explicitly meant to transcend binary oppositions between margin and center, space and time, and most significant for my purposes, between real and imagined spaces. Soja claims that the category of Thirdspace opens up a new and nondualistic relation between material and discursive ideas of space.[18] The radically postmodern perspective offered by Thirdspace seems to be most accessible to racial minority intellectuals, as Soja exemplifies his concept through bell hooks's essay on the margins and through several literary passages on borderlands by Chicano/a writers. According to Soja, hooks enters Thirdspace by "deconstructing" binary modern conceptions of empirical and cognitive space (98)—in other words, through a discursive operation. Here again, as in hooks's essay, a situation of material deprivation is mysteriously transmuted into a position of cultural privilege, and notwithstanding Soja's claims about Thirdspace, it is precisely the mediation between these two realms that remains unexplained. Although Soja is ultimately interested in political change, at no point does he consider the kinds of collective political action that might be required to transform actual margins such as the urban ghetto or the segregated South into spaces of possibility. Consequently, whereas the sites of deprivation can be materially specified as actually existing places, the spaces of resistance remain strictly discursive and metaphorical realms.

Soja's and hooks's accounts are greatly revealing of the ways in which the difference of racial minorities is incorporated into theories of postmodernism. First, U.S. racial minorities are recognized to be disaffiliated from the dominant conditions of postmodern society as a result of the historical and geographical specificity of racial oppression. But somewhere along the way, the material particularity of their marginal location evaporates as they become prized carriers of epistemological or cultural difference. At this level, racial minorities become irreducibly other—not just to prevailing social conditions but even to theoretical discourse about these conditions. The condescension implicit in this move is manifest in the way Soja includes African-American and Chicano/a writers in his discussion of Thirdspace. In contrast to dense theoretical expositions of Lefebvre and Foucault, Soja restricts himself to extended quotations from hooks's essay and from literary works by Gloria Anzaldúa, Maria Lugones, and Guillermo Gómez-Peña. These writers, it seems, cannot be subjected to critical analysis or explication but can only convey lived experience through literary, lyrical expression. In this way, certain racial minority groups become the bearers of sheer, untranslatable difference.

Theorists like Edward Soja or Fredric Jameson routinely invoke the concept of uneven development but fail to apply it consistently to their accounts of postmodernism. As used by Marxist geographers such as Neil Smith, this concept posits social and economic inequality as a constitutive rather than incidental feature of capitalism, which is understood as a geographically and historically differentiated yet systemic global phenomenon.[19] Jameson, as suggested earlier, often describes the "dominant" system as a monolith, such as when he asserts that "the postmodern moment, as the cultural logic of an enlarged third stage of classical capitalism, is in many ways a purer and more homogeneous expression of this last, from which many of the hitherto surviving enclaves of socioeconomic difference have been effaced."[20] The concept of uneven development may yield a more supple and dynamic periodizing model, allowing us to grasp social differences as effects of the discontinuous spread of global capitalism and to conceive of dominant and residual trends as disparate yet systematically linked. By this logic, African-American life would not be wholly subsumed within the "cultural dominant" of postmodernism. Stemming from a particular history of political and economic exclusion, developments in African-American culture, such as the critique of modern Western humanism, will not always follow the same trajectory as trends in the dominant culture, as argued earlier. At the same time, however, African-American culture does not form a residual category that develops in complete autonomy from the dominant culture. I would claim that the postmodern *does* mark a moment of crisis in African-American studies, although this is not a crisis occasioned by the waning authority of modern Western meta-narratives.

The postmodern moment is characterized by a widely registered crisis in the category of racial community—a crisis rooted in the specificities of African-American history (notably the changed conditions of racial community after the political transformations of the Civil Rights movement) but also conditioned by the national and global developments (such as the shift from a Fordist to a flexible regime of accumulation, industrial restructuring, and the scaling down of the welfare state) that are said to be formative of the postmodern era. Even further specification is necessary when speaking of a postmodern crisis in racial community. Mike Featherstone and Zygmunt Bauman have correctly noted that what passes for the "cultural dominant" of postmodernism applies unevenly to certain class sectors and not others and that what is announced as a phenomenon of global proportions is essentially a crisis in the social role of elite intellectuals.[21] This also holds true for African-American studies, where problems of racial representation assume special magnitude for the elite class that had previously enjoyed a position of cultural authority as spokespeople for the race and who now feel this role to be in jeopardy.

This crisis of representation is overdetermined by a constellation of political, economic, and cultural developments since the 1970s. Because different dimensions of these changes are extensively detailed in the chapters that follow, here I provide only a summary account. Within the national context of the United States, processes of capitalist reorganization have clearly followed a racialized logic of uneven development, sharpening already existing inequalities and polarities. In response to heightened international competition and dwindling profits, capital relocated from its established bases in the Northeast and Midwest to less developed regions in the third world and the "Sunbelt" South, in search of higher tax incentives, lower wages, and weaker labor unions. The deindustrialization of the "Frostbelt," resulting in the loss of millions of manufacturing jobs, has severely harmed African-Americans, who were concentrated in those industries that suffered the greatest job losses. The shift from manufacturing to service has resulted in a bipolar employment structure, characterized by a small proportion of well-paid, high-tech jobs, a large pool of low-skilled and poorly paid service jobs, and an evisceration of the middle levels of skill and income. African-Americans are overrepresented in the lower rungs of this dual economy, holding low-waged service positions that pay much less than did the lost manufacturing jobs.[22]

These economic shifts have dramatically modified the spatial forms and social structures of deindustrializing U.S. cities. The core areas of the older industrial economy, largely inhabited by racial minorities, have undergone steep economic decline as the result of the relocation of capital to suburbs and to the South. At the same time, some of these core areas are being transformed from "centers of production and distribution of material goods to centers of administration, information exchange, and higher-order service provision."[23] Due to the combined effects of a spatial and skills "mismatch," African-Americans have not been able to access the new jobs opening up either in the suburbs or in revitalizing urban areas: the expanding employment sectors are either spatially remote from areas of African-American residence or, when they are located in urban cores, require levels of technical skill not possessed by most central-city African-Americans.[24] The conversion of cities from centers of manufacturing to hubs of finance, services, and upscale consumption has also caused the massive residential dislocation of lower-income African-Americans and deepened their isolation within segregated areas of concentrated poverty.[25]

Some social scientists, such as William Julius Wilson, see these economic developments as sufficient causes for the worsening plight of the African-American urban poor.[26] But rather than obeying an inexorable logic of their own, the structural changes noted above were actively enabled by political and public policy choices. Increased mobility allowed capital to demand a "good business climate," which local and state governments vied to create through business subsidies, tax breaks, increased discipline of the labor force, and reductions of the social wage. The greater willingness of local and state governments in the South to ensure such business conditions encouraged industrial relocation out of the Frostbelt into the Sunbelt.[27] In the deindustrializing cities of the Northeast and Midwest, federal highway construction and mortgage programs smoothed the way for suburbanization, which diminished urban tax bases and hastened the economic decline of center cities.[28] Drastic cuts in federal aid to cities spurred the privatized urban redevelopment programs that are reinforcing already existing patterns of racial segregation.

In the political arena, the decisive retreat from the redistributive policies of the welfare state during the post-1960s decades was justified by recourse to an often overtly stated racial logic. Wrongly perceived to be disproportionately draining welfare resources, urban African-Americans were stigmatized as the latest incarnations of the "undeserving poor."[29] The War on Poverty and community development programs of the 1960s, flawed as they were, had targeted the black urban poor as deserving recipients of public aid. These programs, enabled by the political climate established by the Civil Rights movement, could no longer garner public support by the end of the decade, when the short-lived national consensus on black civil rights dissolved into moral panic about African-Americans as the prime threat to urban security and national community. As Margaret Weir observes, by the 1970s, the idea of black political and economic integration "no longer evoked images of passive resistance to southern racists; it now called up troubling memories of urban riots."[30] The emergence and rapidly spreading popularity of the term *underclass* in mass-media and academic debates about urban poverty clinched the racialized logic of urban crisis discourses in the postmodern era. The term *underclass* was used to refer not to the multiracial population that actually formed the ranks of the U.S. urban poor but rather to a black subset of this population seen to be actively responsible for its impoverished situation.

"Underclass" rhetoric clearly reveals the centrality of black urban culture to accounts of postmodern social crisis. The mass media as well as social science scholarship typically portray the "underclass" as a recalcitrant mass situated utterly beyond the pale of mainstream American culture. A 1977 article in *Time* magazine described the "underclass" as "more intractable, more socially alien and more hostile than almost anyone had imagined," driven by values radically at odds with national norms.[31] In their widely publicized accounts, Nicholas Lemann and Ken Auletta concurred that it was a distinctive cultural ethos that posed the greatest obstacle to the betterment of the "underclass."[32] The most influential analysis came from sociologist William Julius Wilson, who, although he offered structural reasons and remedies for black urban poverty, gave ammunition to culturalist accounts in his extensive discussion of the "tangle of pathology in the inner city." Asserting that teenage pregnancies, out-of-wedlock births, welfare dependency, drug use, and violent crime had reached "catastrophic proportions" in black inner-city neighborhoods by the 1970s, Wilson fueled the alarmist perception that black urban America was in a state of unprecedented crisis.[33]

Wilson claimed that the grim realities of post-1970s ghetto life were a uniquely contemporary phenomenon. In earlier decades, black inner-city neighborhoods had exhibited high levels of "social organization" and intra-racial class integration (3). The presence of middle- and blue-collar residents in the ghetto had acted as a stabilizing social force, helping to acculturate the poor into mainstream (i.e., middle-class) behavioral norms such as the work ethic or the two-parent nuclear family. Following the expanded employment opportunities and the removal of formal barriers to residential integration made possible by Civil Rights legislation, a "black middle-class exodus" (7) from the inner cities during the 1970s removed much-needed "social buffers" and "mainstream role models," thereby hastening the cultural deterioration of ghetto life (56).[34]

Wilson's argument continues to compel belief even though it has been vigorously refuted in social science scholarship. As Michael Katz's collection of essays, *The "Underclass" Debate: Views from History,* demonstrates, only historical myopia can sustain claims about the unprecedented cultural collapse of late-twentieth-century black urban communities.[35] Several historians have recalled the existence of class friction within black urban communities earlier in the century, such as conflicts between recent working-class migrants from the South and established black urban elites.[36] In addition, historians have tried to temper the sense of novelty that attends current discourses of urban crisis, reminding us that debates about the cultural pathology of the black urban poor go all the way back to the publication of W. E. B. Du Bois's *The Philadelphia Negro* at the beginning of the twentieth century.[37] Drawing on Du Bois's study, Antonio McDaniel belies Wilson's idealized depiction of the black urban communities of the past. McDaniel argues that Du Bois, like Franklin Frazier and William Julius Wilson after him, overstated the beneficial role that the black middle class could serve for the black urban poor. Wilson harks back to the postwar period when the black middle class presumably played this role, yet Franklin Frazier (and, we might add, St. Clair Drake and Horace Cayton), writing in this era, scathingly depicts a black middle class indifferent to the plight of the poor. Frazier, in turn, idealizes a previous generation that Du Bois indicts for its failure to uplift the black urban masses.[38] A longer historical view reveals an infinitely regressing quest for a lost

n age of the ghetto, illustrating the "escalator" effect that Raymond
...ms found endemic to pastoral critiques of the urban present.[39]

For Wilson, the ultimate responsibility for ameliorating urban poverty
rests with public policy and not with the black middle class. Nevertheless,
his middle-class exodus thesis places undue weight on the role played by
culture in black urban poverty as well as on the role of the middle class
in buffering the poor from urban crisis. Wilson's argument reverberated
powerfully in the fraught debates about black middle-class accountability
to the poor that raged during the 1980s and 1990s. A 1989 *Time* magazine cover story on the black middle class fanned the flames, popularizing
Wilson's "persuasive theory that the worsening status of the underclass is
inextricably tied to the flight from the inner city of its upwardly mobile
population."[40] Various magazines geared to a general black readership, including *The Crisis, Ebony,* and *Essence,* featured stories during the 1980s
debating the extent of the black middle class's responsibility to the urban poor.[41] One reason for the suddenly increased media visibility of the
black middle class was that, as a consequence of the Civil Rights movement
and the economic boom of the 1960s, this class doubled in size, forming
nearly 30 percent of the black population by 1970.[42] Media focus on the
expansion of this class, concurrent with its phobic attention to an allegedly
growing black "underclass," further reinforced Wilson's picture of post-
1970s black America as more polarized than ever before along the schisms
of class.

Such discourses of communal crisis have left a sharp imprint on African-
American literary and cultural studies, even as the feeling of crisis has in
turn been stoked by literary and cultural critics. Writers of literary and popular fiction have also actively entered the public debate about the middle
class's proper disposition toward the urban poor, with Toni Morrison cau-
tioning against "intellectual slumming," James Alan McPherson lamenting
the alienation of the middle class from the vernacular idioms of the people, Ishmael Reed lambasting black academics "posing as experts on the
inner city, which for them is another planet," Toni Cade Bambara noting the linguistic gap between a "working-class sister from the projects
who . . . speaks in nation-time argot" and a "more privileged sister . . . who
speaks the lingo of postmodern theory," and Bebe Moore Campbell disputing Wilson's exodus thesis through her journalistic portraits of professional African-Americans who remained or returned to help the inner-city
poor.[43] Given the centrality accorded to culture in public debates on the
"underclass," it is not in the least surprising that the notion of community
is thrown into crisis in postmodern black literature, or that cultural critics
and writers of literature have become key players shaping current debates
on black urban poverty.

As Ishmael Reed bitterly remarked, the most "profitable" strategy for black intellectuals during the 1980s, one sure to bring prestigious grants, was to join the thriving "black-pathology industry."[44] Although many took strongly dissenting stances, the intellectuals who reaped the highest visibility (in middle-brow print journalism as well as television and radio) were those who complied with the terms set by dominant "underclass" discourses, polarizing the black middle class and the urban poor on cultural grounds. Orlando Patterson contrasted the "acculturated" black elite with the "hedonistic, sex-obsessed, nonfamilial, anti-intellectual, and pathetically macho" street culture of ghetto residents. Henry Louis Gates, calling attention to the existence of "two nations ... both black," declared, "It's time to concede that yes, there *is* a culture of poverty" blocking the material progress of poor urban African-Americans.[45] In the most influential account, Cornel West emphasized the "structural character of culture," identifying spiritual "nihilism" rather than economic deprivation or political impotence as the "most basic issue" confronting the underclass.[46] Echoing Wilson, West found a "qualitative fissure" in African-American urban history: the "trans-class character" of black urban communities disintegrated during the 1970s, directly precipitating the collapse of spiritual values and cultural traditions.[47] None of these intellectuals sought to disguise the conservative public-policy implications of their cultural portraits of the underclass. Cornel West worried that even "progressive social change" may not reverse "deeper processes of cultural decay." Henry Louis Gates exhorted the black urban poor to exercise individual responsibility. Glenn Loury, echoing Gates in his advocacy of self-help solutions, contended that the problems facing the black urban poor lie outside the scope of government remedy.[48]

Black intellectuals seeking to speak in the interests of the poor occupy a position of extreme contradiction in the postmodern era. Sharpening class divisions are highlighted by media and academic analysts as factors exacerbating the predicament of the African-American urban poor. Yet these discourses enjoin black intellectuals to transcend the very class divisions that are seen as crucial components of the crisis, in order to represent the interests of the poor. Projected panaceas for urban crisis hinge on reclaiming an ideal of trans-class racial community, just as the material conditions for such community seem all but inaccessible to black intellectuals in the postmodern era. Several political scientists, including Michael Dawson, Martin Kilson, Manning Marable, and Adolph Reed, have remarked that the concept of black political "community," assuming a unified set of common interests, began to seem like a "historical anachronism" by the 1970s.[49] Although conflicting political interests obviously existed during the era of segregation, as Reed argues, the "presumption of corporate racial identity was a rational expression" of the realities of this era, when African-Americans as a whole were formally excluded from participatory democratic politics.[50] But the conditions of black politics have been transformed in the post–Civil Rights era, as a result of legal desegregation, affirmative action legislation, increased black electoral participation, and incorporation of black elites into bureaucratic governance.

The ramifications of these developments for the notion of black political community are perhaps most clearly evident at the level of urban politics. Harold Cruse had pointed out, in his critique of Black Power militants, that they evaded the question of "Which class will benefit from Black Power when it arrives and control the economic and political power that's sought." The various antipoverty and community development programs instituted by the federal government in response to the black urban insurgency of the 1960s "paid out very well in middle-class salaries," as Cruse observed.[51] These programs set in place state-sponsored mechanisms of political participation, giving rise to a new black "regime of race-relations management."[52] By virtue of the very terms of its access to political power, such a regime was structurally incapable of representing the interests of its disadvantaged constituents. As Adolph Reed argues, newly elected black mayors and public officials could only gain access to city resources by aligning themselves with pro-growth economic agendas, which are invariably antithetical to redistributive goals and have been shown to reproduce class and racial inequalities.[53] The exercise of black political power over the last three decades makes undeniably clear that the political ascension of black elites will not automatically advance the interests of the lower strata of African-Americans. Consequently, the racial politics forged in the era of segregation as well as the nationalist politics of the 1960s, presuming a cohesive community of racial interests, begin to appear increasingly obsolete in the post–Civil Rights period.

A distinguishing feature of black politics in the postmodern era is that race no longer forms the singular axial principle of all political projects affecting African-Americans.[54] To argue this is not, however, to endorse William Julius Wilson's claim about "the declining significance of race" in post–Civil Rights America. Because racial status still significantly determines material life-chances for a vast majority of African-Americans, racial politics cannot be banished as the relic of a bygone era. But racial politics can no longer be premised on models of unmediated representation or of monolithic racial community. In 1992, Toni Morrison observed that it should be "clear to the most reductionist intellect that the time for undiscriminating racial unity has passed."[55] Morrison made this statement in the wake of the nationally televised confirmation hearings for Clarence Thomas's accession to the Supreme Court, which made dramatically

visible the gender and class conflicts striating black political community.
Morrison's remark has been widely cited as expressive of the postmodern
moment in black culture and politics, when differences within the race
seem more intractable than ever before. The question of how to build an
antiracist politics that gives due weight to intra-racial differences forms the
central challenge of the postmodern period in African-American studies.

Modern and Postmodern Projects
of Racial Representation

A useful point of departure for a discussion of postmodern approaches to
racial representation is offered by two well-publicized articles on the "new"
African-American intellectuals by Robert Boynton and Michael Berube,
published in the *Atlantic Monthly* and the *Village Voice*, respectively, in
1995. Berube contends that postmodern black intellectuals are "committed to rethinking forms of African-American collectivity" while rejecting
the identity politics of 1960s black cultural nationalism.[56] Both Boynton
and Berube differentiate this intelligentsia not only from the preceding
generation of nationalists but also from the "modern" generation of New
York intellectuals commemorated in Russell Jacoby's widely read book *The
Last Intellectuals*. Jacoby had argued that, with the academic institutionalization of intellectual work and the professionalization of the academy
since the 1960s, "public intellectuals" (a term coined by Jacoby) who
could reach an educated general readership had become extinct.[57] Boynton
and Berube refute Jacoby's claim by arguing that the black intellectuals
of the post-1960s generation in fact have access to a larger public than
did the New York intellectuals whom Jacoby had eulogized and elegized.
The wider public provenance of the new black intellectuals stems from
their refusal to restrict themselves to the print-literate and high-cultural
spheres privileged by the moderns. Black public intellectuals blur and cross
the boundaries between high and popular culture, observes Boynton, and
Berube elaborates that their "unique relationship to the vernacular of their
time" affords them an "unprecedented opportunity" to speak to and from
a variegated public sphere.[58]

The two key features, then, that are said to distinguish postmodern from
modern black intellectual and cultural production are its quest for a politics
of difference that eschews essentialist constructs of community, and a shift
from print to vernacular media. But these two tendencies often work at
cross-purposes in contemporary black cultural studies. The displacement
of print by vernacular forms of representation is motivated by the desire
to address a broad-based black community and entails claims about the
authentic culture of African-Americans. A lingering investment in the idea

of black cultural specificity, as well as in the very problematic of racial representation, generally winds up reinstating the essentialist notions of community that postmodern cultural critics strive to surpass. This is easily evident in the writings of bell hooks and Cornel West, who have gained the highest visibility as authorities on postmodernism in the sphere of black cultural studies.

Hooks and West figure centrally in Edward Soja and Barbara Hooper's essay, "The Spaces that Difference Makes," which boldly outlines the main distinctions between modern and postmodern cultural politics. Soja and Hooper describe identity politics as "modernist" and include within this category "most orthodox forms of modern Marxism and some forms of radical feminism and black nationalism."[59] Even as such politics challenge a hierarchical and dualistic ordering of differences, they remain caught within this order, seeking mainly to invert it and to centralize the subordinated term. Such movements earn the label "modernist identity politics" through their tendencies toward "master-narrative essentialism and binary totalization" (187). As an alternative, Soja and Hooper advocate a "radical postmodern politics of difference" (184) that aims to empower "a multiplicity of resistances rather than searches for that one 'great refusal,' the singular transformation to precede and guide all others" (187). For their definition of this brand of radical postmodernism, Soja and Hooper are indebted to Cornel West's essay "The New Cultural Politics of Difference," published three years earlier. By West's account, postmodern politics bases itself on the concrete and contextual rather than on the abstract and universal values of modern politics. Taking as its starting point a position of social specificity, the politics of difference aspires to new forms of affiliation, to "contingent, fragile coalition building" in place of "homogeneous unity or monolithic totality."[60]

Such accounts of the distinction between modern and postmodern politics capture important shifts in U.S. cultural studies that occurred during the 1970s. In academic fields such as feminist and African-American studies, the move toward postmodernism largely involved an emphasis on the intra-group differences suppressed in radical feminism and black cultural nationalism. Indeed, the postmodern moment in African-American studies is widely configured as the era of postnationalism. Greg Tate may have been the first to use the term "postnationalist" to describe currents in black culture since the 1970s.[61] In a manifesto for one such movement, Trey Ellis claims that the New Black Aesthetic (under which he encompasses recent trends in film, music, performing arts, and literature) takes a revisionist stance toward nationalist discourses of racial authenticity.[62] In the sphere of literature, Lawrence Hogue contends that postmodernism entails critical distance from the "unfragmented racial tradition" linked with nationalism.[63] However, sharp distinctions between "modernist identity politics" such as nationalism and the "new" postmodern politics of difference unravel under closer inspection. Despite claims to the contrary, it is not at all clear that most variants of postmodern cultural politics actually manage to avoid essentialist conceptions of social difference or that they succeed in balancing the claims of intra-group difference and solidarity more effectively than did earlier nationalist or radical feminist movements.

In their opposition between "modernist identity politics" and the postmodern politics of difference, Soja and Hooper draw heavily on bell hooks's formulation of these terms in her essay "Postmodern Blackness." Here, hooks labels 1960s black nationalism "modernist" on account of its "universalizing agenda" as well as its commitment to identity politics.[64] This is an arguable assertion: the black cultural nationalism of the 1960s might more persuasively be characterized as postmodernist in that it deployed identity politics to expose the spurious universalism of modern Western humanism. In *The Black Aesthetic,* a manifesto of sorts for the nationalist Black Arts movements of the 1960s, writer after writer railed against the way humanist universality is dichotomized against black racial particularity. For example, John Oliver Killens observed that "when Western man speaks of universality, he is referring to an Anglo-Saxon universality," whereas "the frame of reference of an American Negro is *ipso facto* [assumed to be] antiuniversal."[65] Postmodern critiques of modern humanism were anticipated (or perhaps more accurately initiated) by the cultural nationalist project, which, in James Emmanuel's words, sought "no less than the redefinition of man"—a redefinition necessitated by the assumption that "The West is humanity, humanity is the West."[66] Wanting "to see the idea of 'universal' laid to rest,"[67] nationalist intellectuals of the 1960s instead propagated an ideal of culture rooted in racially specific experience.

In speaking of the "universalizing agenda" of nationalism, what hooks probably has in mind is its unitary definition of racial identity and its centralizing of race as the sole axis of all emancipatory politics. This is what hooks suggests when she writes that postmodern critiques of essentialism are valuable because they compel recognition of multiple identities and divergent interests within the category of blackness. Hooks further elaborates her sense of the disjunction between black nationalism and postmodernism in her essay "The Chitlin Circuit: On Black Community." Here, hooks writes that African-Americans are experiencing a profound sense of loss and crisis, arising from the difficulty of constructing forms of racial community suited to the political realities of the post–Civil Rights era. Hooks reiterates that for several reasons, "neonationalist responses . . . no longer realistically address how we live as black people in a postmodern world."[68] In addition to raising the common postmodernist objection to nationalist politics—that it does not reckon with the heterogeneity of black experiences—hooks also discredits nationalism as a phenomenon linked with "black capitalism" and "patriarchy." Then, as hooks turns to the question of how African-Americans can reclaim an antinationalist model of community in the postmodern era, her argument takes a curious turn. Hooks draws her model of "beloved black community" from black folk life in the segregated South. This model is more inspiring than the nationalist one because, first, its agrarian rather than capitalist basis nourished an ethics of caring and sharing, and second, it epitomized "an organic unity between black women and men" that was eroded by the emergence of nationalism (36). Hooks concludes with the advice that African-Americans rebuild community in the post–Civil Rights era by renewing "rituals of belonging" associated with "traditional black folk experience" (39).

Hooks's proposal for recovering black community in the postmodern era is rife with contradictions. Her argument hinges on an opposition between nationalism and agrarian southern life that cannot be sustained on historical grounds, as is obvious from the fact that she can offer no evidence for her contentions that southern folk life was free of "male domination" and that black nationalism introduced gender divisions into black community (36). An important reason for hooks's rejection of nationalism is that its rhetoric of racial authenticity erases the differences within black experience, yet these differences are also wished away in her own idealized image of the "organic unity" of southern black life. Although hooks assumes a postmodern perspective to condemn nationalist paradigms of community, she subsequently distances herself from postmodernism in order to defend her own version of racial authenticity. In her opinion, African-Americans "cannot afford the luxury" of postmodern critiques of authenticity because they are already "coping with a sense of extreme fragmentation" (38). Hooks's cure for the fragmentation of black communal life in the post–Civil Rights era calls for a retrieval of the very conditions that she earlier admits to be irrevocably lost—the "organic unity" and "traditional black folk experience" of the days of racial segregation. These terms exactly restore the principles of nationalist community—separatism, racial tradition, organicism, and authenticity derived from vernacular culture. The only difference is that hooks's model of beloved community is rooted in the folk culture of the segregated and rural South rather than on urban vernacular culture, and in this respect it is even more inaccessible in the present than is the nationalist model.

A similar reversion to organic forms of racial community characterizes Cornel West's pronouncements on African-American life in the postmodern era. As noted earlier, West's writing adds fuel to crisis-ridden accounts of black urban community. Like hooks, West responds to this crisis by nostalgically recalling an earlier era when black cultural traditions were intact and when class differences within the race did not carry the divisive implications they do in the present. Even when explicitly addressing the state of African-American life in the postmodern era, West draws his own authority to speak on behalf of the race from essentialist constructs of black community. An egregious example of this tendency appears in West's interview with Anders Stephanson, included in Andrew Ross's collection *Universal Abandon: The Politics of Postmodernism*. Both Stephanson and West liberally make use of reductive phrases such as "the black community" or "the black political constituency."[69] In response to Stephanson's question, "What does it mean to a black American to hear that . . . we have lost the real?" West replies as follows:

> *There is a reality that one cannot not know.* The ragged edges of the Real, of *Necessity*, not being able to eat, not having shelter, not having health care, all this is something that one cannot not know. The black condition acknowledges that. It is so much more acutely felt because this is a society where a lot of people live a Teflon existence, where a lot of people have no sense of the ragged edges of necessity, of what it means to be impinged upon by structures of oppression. To be an upper-middle-class American is actually to live a life of unimaginable comfort, convenience, and luxury. Half of the black population is denied this, which is why they have a strong sense of reality. (277)

West's response is apparently materialist in its reference to class variations within American experiences of material contingency. But West goes on to elide these distinctions as he generalizes about "the black condition," which becomes synonymous with the experience of acute material deprivation. Most of the poor in the United States, who are not black, along with that "half of the black population" that is not poor, must disappear in order to permit West to speak on behalf of the race as well as the poor.

Although the postmodern cultural critic avowedly pays scrupulous attention to class differences within the race as well as to issues of intellectual/mass mediation, this is rarely borne out by practice. The claim that postmodern intellectuals more accurately represent the interests of the race as a whole than did their modern counterparts is secured through vernacular definitions of black cultural ethos. The vernacular forms the site where rifts arising from class and educational differences may be healed and an organic connection established between the intellectual and the people. The populist ambitions of postmodern projects of racial representation hinge on their critical distance from modern paradigms of the print-literate intellectual conversant in high cultural traditions. The best-known instance of this paradigm in African-American studies is W. E. B. Du Bois's early-twentieth-century ideal of the Talented Tenth, those elite intellectuals who would serve as "missionaries of culture among their people." Convinced that culture filters "from the top down," Du Bois hoped that the intelligentsia, fluent in Western high culture, would deliver the black masses out of their condition of ignorance and illiteracy.[70]

Several African-American intellectuals have assailed the Enlightenment inheritance of the Talented Tenth model from an explicitly postmodern perspective. In *The Future of the Race,* a book he co-authored with Henry Louis Gates, Cornel West faults Du Bois for his elitist condescension toward the black masses.[71] As "self-appointed agents of Enlightenment" (64), the Talented Tenth assume the task of civilizing the benighted masses by initiating them into high culture (64–65). Like a true postmodernist, West questions the assumption that highbrow culture is inherently humanizing, concluding that "we have little reason to believe that people who delight in the work of geniuses like Mozart and Beethoven or Goethe and Wordsworth are any more or less humane than those who dance in the barnyards to the banjo plucking of nameless rural folk in Tennessee" (68). Similarly, Ishmael Reed mercilessly indicts "talented tenth intellectuals" for embracing a supposedly "common culture" that is actually "Yankee or Anglo," for taking "the Enlightenment,... which introduced scientific racism" as their "intellectual model," and for "missionizing" less privileged African-Americans.[72]

Repudiating the uplift ambitions of the Talented Tenth, both Reed and West propose a countermodern model of the black intellectual authorized by vernacular rather than print or high culture. Reed's neo-hoodoo aesthetic aligns itself with the Afro-diasporic cultural traditions that have been suppressed by Enlightenment notions of a common human culture. Reed has long been singled out by literary critics as the exemplar of black postmodernism because of his incorporation of popular-cultural energies into his writing and his relentless attack on institutionalized high culture. In Reed's fiction, critique of modern Western aesthetics is indissolubly linked to celebration of a racially specific black culture. Andreas Huyssen is one of the few theorists of postmodernism to note that its challenge to the modernist cultural canon gained impetus from the self-assertion of minority cultures, which had long been relegated to the low-cultural margins.[73] In this light, 1960s black cultural nationalism once again emerges as a crucial constituent of postmodernism, with its stress on vernacular culture and racial particularity calculated to displace high modern ideals of universal culture.

Although this is seldom acknowledged, postmodern black intellectuals remain deeply in thrall to this nationalist legacy. Whereas Reed, whom West has labeled a political conservative, has been unwavering in his refusal of the Talented Tenth mission and has consistently drawn on popular culture to deflate the hubris of this mission, West advocates an incoherent amalgam of uplift and populism. Despite his scathing critique of the "service" ethic of Du Bois's Talented Tenth in *The Future of the Race,* West elsewhere calls for a revival of precisely this ethic of "sacrifice" and "service to the race," maintaining that it "created a moment of accountability."[74] West is equally contradictory on the issue of whether print or vernacular traditions should vouchsafe the cultural authority of postmodern African-American intellectuals. Du Bois's Talented Tenth ideal apotheosized print culture: as Henry Louis Gates remarks, black intellectuals in the Du Bois era strove to prove that they, "too, were a people of the Book."[75] West's ambivalence about the modern print legacy derives in part from apprehensions about the impending demise of book culture that he shares with many postmodern cultural theorists. Print culture is felt to be on the brink of social irrelevance because, wedded to an exclusionary notion of humanist culture, it is less amenable to pluralist cultural demands than are the electronic media of the postmodern age. These media are apparently sweeping away not only the technology of print but also the promise of critical autonomy from the given social world proffered by modern print culture.

In the spirit of the times, West is pessimistic about the viability of print culture, and consequently about the role of the literate intellectual in the age of electronic reproduction. Observing that there aren't that many "intellectuals of the book" anymore, West laments the fact that print literature is being sidelined by audio and video technologies.[76] West grants that the quest for print literacy is still a driving ambition among African-Americans but argues that the benefits of literacy are increasingly understood in "pecuniary" terms, thus accounting for the peripheral status of intellectuals in black culture.[77] In his well-known essay on the nihilism of contemporary black urban populations, West bemoans the full penetration of commodity capitalism into black life, citing the spread of market values as a primary cause of the moral decay of black community in the postmodern era.[78] The print tradition may have delivered on its modern promise of safeguarding critical distance from commodity culture, but this hope proves futile as African-Americans now seek print literacy mainly in pursuit of material gain.

When West decries the pecuniary incentives for print literacy among an unspecified black community, he probably means to refer to the middle class or to middle-class aspirants. (It seems unlikely that West would expect those who suffer material deprivation to value humanist intellectual work over the practical benefits of print literacy, such as expansion of employment opportunities.) But West's argument about the marginal status of print culture in African-American life fares not much better if we assume that he is referring to the middle class. The 1980s saw a dramatic growth in specialty black bookstores and in distributors and publishers catering to a specifically African-American readership, a trend that should, in one publisher's words, "lay firmly to rest the tired myth that blacks don't buy books." The highest demand, from this audience for commercially published books, was for "serious" nonfiction.[79] Even "intellectuals of the book" were poised to command a fairly good share of this new market by the beginning of the 1990s; as a university press editor remarked, "Black intellectuals who want to write for a wider audience will find one."[80] A significant proportion of this growing readership is drawn from the "new" black middle class, which saw its greatest moment of expansion during the post–Civil Rights decades.

The class basis of this audience discomforts many postmodern black intellectuals, as it did nationalist intellectuals such as LeRoi Jones/Amiri Baraka, who wrote of his own book, *Home: Social Essays,* that "Since this book is so expensive, it will fall into the hands of more MC Negroes than people out on the block. (MC meaning middle class)."[81] Postmodern intellectuals such as Cornel West and bell hooks aspire to serve the race but cannot stomach the modern idea of acculturating the lower classes into a print-literate tradition. Because hooks and West wish to reach a black audience larger than those who can afford to buy books, print seems to them a medium of restricted social scope. Consequently, hooks cautions that given the high levels of functional illiteracy among "black folks," intellectuals cannot hope to "spread the message by books alone."[82] Similar desires for connection with a mass black audience motivate West's laments about the poverty of black print culture. Asserting that "Black America has yet to produce a single literate intellectual, with the sole exception of Toni Morrison," West claims that the two "organic intellectual traditions" of African-American culture are both oral—the Christian tradition of preaching and the musical-performance tradition.[83]

In his effort to replace the literate Talented Tenth intellectual with an organic intellectual, West recapitulates all the founding moves of 1960s black cultural nationalism. His attachment to allegedly outmoded notions of racial authenticity is evident from his attempt to single out the "ur-text of black culture," which he defines as vocative, kinetic, and nonverbal.[84] What's more, West's definition of this culture reproduces the nationalist hierarchy of (elite, inauthentic) print and (popular, authentic) vernacular culture. West exactly echoes nationalist writers such as Amiri Baraka or Larry Neal when he pits the mediocrity of black print culture against the creativity of oral traditions. In "The Myth of a Negro Literature," published in 1966, Baraka had scoffed at the "agonizing mediocrity" of black print production and identified black music as the "profound contribution" of African-Americans.[85] Larry Neal concurred that black written poetry does not match the expressiveness of a "James Brown scream."[86] For both Baraka and Neal, black print literature was insufficiently expressive of racial ethos because it formed the exclusive province of the "Negro bourgeoisie," whereas black music, accessible even to "the lowest class of Negroes," more fully "represented the collective psyche."[87] In Cornel West's postmodern account, oral culture performs exactly the same function of populist legitimation as it did for the 1960s nationalists.

West's example reveals the difficulty of resisting essentialism while remaining invested in the project of authentic racial representation. This project cannot but reactivate claims of a transparent relation between the intellectual and the masses as well as reified models of black culture and community. The best reason for questioning postmodern projects of racial representation is not that they recall a supposedly passé modern era but that they fall short of their own stated goal of truly giving voice to the people. In his book *Yo Mama's Disfunktional*, Robin Kelley rightly excoriates prevailing social science scholarship on the "underclass" for its reductive view of black urban culture as an unmediated reflection of ghetto realities. One reason social scientists miss the complexity of this culture is that "they do not let the natives speak." Kelley presents his own work as an attempt to "give voice to those urban populations under siege," with his title meant to "represent what I imagine the very subjects/objects of reactionary social science and public policy might say if they could speak back to the critics and analysts."[88] Dominant discourses on the "underclass" pathologize black urban culture on the grounds of its aberration from a normative model of U.S. mainstream culture. Reacting against the uplift ideology implicit in such discourses, the postmodern intellectual assumes the vernacular voice of the cultural interpreter instead of the modern role of cultural legislator,[89] in the hope that this strategy will more accurately represent the black urban masses. But the continued silence of the "natives" is a precondition for the intellectual's attempt to speak for them. Whether deriding the nihilism of black urban culture (as do Gates, West, Loury, and others mentioned earlier) or celebrating its expressive richness, the intellectual cannot give voice to the urban masses as long as he or she claims to represent them. As Adolph Reed has eloquently argued, terms such as "masses" or "the underclass" are "homogenizing mystification[s]" in that both entities "exist only in the third person; no discernible constituency describes itself and rallies under either label." As such, these terms assume a "mute" referent that must be spoken for because it cannot be imagined as a subject of political discourse.[90]

The silence of the represented is a necessary condition of existing structures of racial representation. Claims to racial representation prove difficult to dismantle at the level of discourse because their roots lie in the structural conditions of African-American access to public culture. Anders Stephanson's interview with Cornel West shows that even in the most difference-sensitive postmodern contexts, black intellectuals are still expected to speak for the entire race. As Kobena Mercer and Joy James have argued, so long as institutionalized racism curtails full black access to public discourse, the part will continue to stand in for the whole, and in fact, the high visibility of a few token figures will serve to disguise a system that excludes the many. Within this kind of economy of cultural production, intellectuals engaged in racial representation will necessarily amass cultural capital at the expense of those non-elite groups that are "prohibited from a counter discourse."[91]

Print Literature and Racial Representation

The contradictory nature of the burden of racial representation imposed on African-American culture is perhaps most clearly apparent in the domain of print literature. With its origins in the era of slavery, the African-American literary tradition was launched to demonstrate the slave's membership in the human race through the agency of writing. For the earliest slave narrators, this enterprise was fraught with difficulty, as Henry Louis Gates has shown in his discussion of slave narratives published in the late eighteenth and early nineteenth centuries. Gates identifies recurrent scenes featuring a "Talking Book" in these narratives, scenes in which the narrators seek to make a Western printed text (usually the Bible) speak to the slave or in the slave's voice. Gates admits that what these scenes actually exhibit is the trope of the "un-Talking Book" (165), for in most cases the book remains silent.[92] The earliest use of tropes of the book in African-American literature registers the racial disqualification of slaves from print culture and, by implication, their categorical unfreedom. In the next phase of the tradition, nineteenth-century slave narrators stage scenes of reading and writing to prove their fitness for freedom. For authors such as Frederick Douglass, the act of writing itself becomes a "tacitly political gesture" (171). Gates's argument that print literacy retains its "implicitly political import" well into the twentieth century (171) is seconded and elaborated by Robert Stepto, who traces the sustained link between print literacy and political freedom for a range of African-American writers from Frederick Douglass to Ralph Ellison.[93]

In Gates's narrative, this tradition comes into its own with Zora Neale Hurston, whose novel *Their Eyes Were Watching God* exemplifies the first genuinely Talking Book or "speakerly text" of African-American literature (174). Hurston, along with subsequent writers such as Ishmael Reed and Alice Walker, succeeds where the eighteenth-century slave narrators failed—appropriating an alien print tradition by making it speak in a black oral voice (181). For Gates, then, the Talking Book, or the written text that achieves the condition of black vernacular speech, represents the "urtrope" or the culminating point of the African-American literary tradition (131). Robert Stepto is careful to clarify that he does not subscribe to this sort of progressive view of the black literary tradition, but he too sees print literacy and orality as the two motors driving the tradition. Unlike Gates, Stepto does not construe print as an alien technology that best serves black interests once it is oralized. In fact, in his 1991 preface to the second edition of *From Behind the Veil*, Stepto defends his focus on print literacy as a way of liberating black culture from the "essentialist thinking" that would have it "be exclusively a vernacular construct" (xi). Nevertheless, in identifying two broad generic types that obtain in African-American narrative across various historical periods, Stepto puts in place certain oppositions between print literacy and oral culture that still powerfully influence critical appreciation of this literature.

The first of these generic types is the narrative of ascent, which features heroes who become increasingly individualized and dissociated from racial community as they master print literacy. In this sort of narrative, literacy does initiate a movement toward social mobility and political freedom, but it also always fosters a stance of "solitude" or "alienation" (167). The protagonists of immersion narratives, in contrast, achieve "tribal literacy" in oral vernacular tradition (169), which, unlike print literacy, always works as a medium of communal fusion. In Stepto's opinion, only one African-American literary text, Ralph Ellison's *Invisible Man*, synthesizes both types of narrative, presenting a hero who ultimately acquires both print and tribal literacy, individual and group consciousness.

African-American literary texts from the period covered by Stepto's study, from the mid-nineteenth century up to the 1950s, do not readily bear out his account of print literacy as a force of alienation from racial community. Only Richard Wright's autobiographical narrative, *Black Boy*, exactly corroborates Stepto's argument. Even Frederick Douglass's 1845 slave narrative, the text that has taken on archetypal status as a literacy narrative and that is often said to exemplify the individualizing effects of print literacy,[94] on closer inspection reveals a strong concern with the benefits of literacy for the race as a whole. Not only was the publication of Douglass's narrative meant to further the political cause of abolition, but the most powerful image of collectivity in the narrative is of a slave community "linked and interlinked with each other" by the activity of book reading.[95] Numerous African-American authors during the decades covered by Stepto's book (including W. E. B. Du Bois, James Weldon Johnson,

Frances Harper, Pauline Hopkins, Jessie Fauset, Claude McKay, Richard Wright, and Ralph Ellison) were, like Douglass before them, intensely preoccupied with the question of the collective uses of print literacy and literature. Throughout the twentieth century, African-American literature has returned to variants of the ideology of racial uplift, which affirms print literacy as a vehicle of collective racial progress.

In a later work, "Distrust of the Reader in Afro-American Narrative," Stepto draws sharper contrasts between writing and orality, especially with regard to their differential capacity to represent racial community. Here, Stepto argues that African-American literature has been propelled as strongly by suspicion of literacy as by "abiding faith in it."[96] Because of their deep distrust of the racial protocols of U.S. print culture, African-American authors posture as oral storytellers rather than as writers, and they reimagine their readers as listeners, in an effort to inculcate more responsible and sympathetic habits of reading. Stepto substantiates this last claim through an opposition between the "competitive," "deconstructionist" readings encouraged by print traditions and the more "authenticating" procedures of oral traditions (201). Similar assumptions—about oral media as the most effective vehicles for representing racial community—circulate widely in criticism on African-American literature. Many of the most influential studies of African-American narrative have been organized around tropes derived from black oral tradition, such as specifying, signifying, conjuring, or the blues. Drawing on the oral dynamics of antiphony or call and response, black literary texts are said not only to activate participatory and communal conditions of reception but also to figure forth a uniquely black model of democratic politics.[97]

The impetus behind such oralized critical paradigms is to establish a seamless continuity between African-American literary production (including literary criticism) and a wider black cultural community. The chief limitation of such models is that they displace issues of political representation to the level of form so that, regardless of its readerships, the African-American novel represents black community insofar as it incorporates black oral culture into its narrative voice and structure. Because most vernacular theories of African-American fiction tend toward formalism or structuralism,[98] they fail to capture the dynamism of black literary production, or to explain how and why recurrent tropes and generic patterns are differently modulated in response to changing historical pressures. In earlier phases of its history, African-American literature was valued (and often perhaps overvalued) as a potent tool in the struggle for political freedom and equality. Since the 1970s, however, the category of print literature has been subjected to a thoroughgoing process of revaluation, under the conjoined impact of black cultural nationalism and postmodernism. Vernacular-based theories of African-American literature, which blossomed during the 1980s and still exercise considerable critical sway, are profoundly indebted to the aesthetic and political legacies of 1960s black cultural nationalism.

In the mid to late 1960s, the Black Arts movements initiated one of the most significant developments in the history of African-American literature—its institutionalization as an object of academic study. Efforts to extend the literary canon since the 1960s have assumed direct links between literary and political representation whereby the inclusion of a minority writer in the canon is seen as a gain in group representation. Yet this is least likely to be the case in the sphere of print literature. As John Guillory observes, the recovery of previously excluded traditions has proceeded on the premise that "the field of writing is a kind of *plenum,* a textual repetition of social diversity," whereas in fact "the most socially consequential process of exclusion occurs primarily at the level of access to literacy."[99] Keenly conscious of the privilege attaching to print literacy, proponents of black cultural nationalism undermined literature as insufficiently reflective of black experience even as they struggled to get it recognized as worthy of academic study. Reflecting the conflict between integrationist and separatist impulses endemic to cultural nationalism, Black Arts advocates both valorized those oral vernacular traditions that were excluded from the precincts of certified American culture and sought to expand these precincts to include African-American literature. In the postmodern period, African-American literature bears contradictory political valences that can be directly traced back to the nationalist legacy. Thanks to the efforts of the nationalists, African-American literature is now institutionalized in U.S. universities and, as such, subjected to the disciplinary methods of literary criticism. But precisely as an object of specialized academic study, print literature is also suspect for its alienation from the everyday life-world of African-Americans.

The nationalist attack on literature has been reinforced by postmodern cultural theory, which has sought to unseat literature from its prestigious position as the crowning achievement of the modern print tradition. The overt rationale for this postmodern move is identical to that of 1960s cultural nationalism—to replace the modernist canon of humanist culture with a more inclusive notion of culture. Notwithstanding this populist intention, contemporary doubts about the social legitimacy of literature may also reflect, as John Guillory argues, "a crisis in the market value of its cultural capital occasioned by the emergence of a professional-managerial class which no longer requires the (primarily literary) cultural capital of the old bourgeoisie."[100] Paradoxically, the combined nationalist and postmodern attacks on the literary institution seem to have been quite fertilizing for literature. Print literature by African-Americans has commanded its largest commercial as well as academic audience in the post-1970s decades.

With its academic institutionalization, African-American literature seems increasingly remote from generalized notions of "the black experience" yet continues to be freighted with racially representative value. Charles Banner-Haley laments that fiction by postmodern writers such as Clarence Major or Ishmael Reed has become so academicist and abstruse that it seems "emotionally out of touch . . . with the reality of Afro-America."[101] But even as it is deemed to be inaccessible and superfluous to the vast majority of African-Americans, literature is simultaneously charged with redemptive political hopes—so much so as to draw the ire of political scientists such as Joy James.[102] Literary and cultural critics increasingly dominate African-American political debates, and perhaps as a consequence, certain literary practices are upheld as forms of political activism. Illustrating this tendency, Cornel West, in his essay on the state of emergency in black urban America, suggests that only an ethic of love can arouse a sense of agency among the nihilistic poor.[103] The sole model of this love ethic that West can proffer is a scene from a literary text, Toni Morrison's *Beloved*. Yet in "Black Culture and Postmodernism," West justifies his neglect of literary artists and his focus on mass culture on the grounds that his main interest lies in "black resistance in the form of social movements." Presumably, popular cultural forms such as rap are more easily linked with social movements than is the elite medium of print literature.[104]

Political claims about African-American literature have always depended on realist aesthetics, from the documentary impulse of the slave narratives to the reflectionist principles prescribed by the cultural nationalist program. Black literature could best fulfill its political purpose of bettering the collective condition of the race by telling the truth about black experience. This durable link between realism and racial representation is widely believed to have snapped, finally, in the postmodern period. In an article on black science fiction, Walter Mosley notes that black writers have just begun to gain acceptance within popular genres such as science fiction and hopes that this trend will finally free African-American literature of its burden of representation, which Mosley describes as follows:

> Our writers have historically been regarded as . . . best suited to address the nature of our own chains. So if black writers wanted to branch out past the realism of racism and race they were curtailed by their own desire to document the crimes of America. A further deterrent was the white literary establishment's desire for blacks to write about being black in a white world, a limitation imposed upon a limitation.[105]

Mosley draws attention to the twin facets of the demand for racial representation in literature—the obligation to always and only write as a racially particular subject, and the expectation of mimetic realism. Mosley argues that African-American writers have largely been missing from popular genres such as science fiction because the logic of racial representation has trapped them within realist genres. Because black writers have finally begun to diversify into popular fictional genres, Mosley anticipates an explosion of black science fiction that will "break the chains of reality" and open up a "new world of autonomy."[106]

It seems logical to expect, as does Mosley, that representational demands would be relaxed for a popular genre that does not claim fidelity to things as they are. Surprisingly, though, this turns out not to be the case, as is clear from popular responses to Samuel Delany, one of the two well-known African-American writers of science fiction. In a piece published in the *Village Voice,* Greg Tate writes that he "figured Delany for an oreo" until he read a speech given by Delany at the Studio Museum of Harlem which referred to African-Americans as "our people." Although Delany informed Tate that all but one of the characters in his novel *Stars in My Pocket Like Grains of Sand* are black, this was not good enough for Tate, because the race of these characters was not at the core of their cultural identity. What Tate expected from "our one black SF writer" was fiction that imagined "the future of black culture from a more or less nationalist stance."[107] Clearly, even a popular genre known for its angular approach to social reality is still held accountable to nationalist imperatives of realism and race representation.

The links between mimetic realism and the assumption that any part can and must substitute for the whole—between the two meanings of representation as depiction and delegation, in Kobena Mercer's formulation[108]—have become firmly entrenched in popular and academic responses to African-American writers. As suggested by Walter Mosley's comments, the demand for verisimilitude imposes a racially particular position of enunciation on the African-American writer. A writer like Delany, who thwarts both of these demands, is censured for his "racially defused" vision.[109] This tight interlock of mimetic realism, racial particularity, and delegation is perpetuated even by those literary critics who wish to surpass the problematic of racial representation. In a reading of Samuel Delany exactly contrary to Tate's, Ross Posnock argues, at two intersecting levels, that Delany manages to shed the mantle of racial representation by writing avant-garde, antirealist fiction. Posnock contends that the experimental quality of Delany's writing militates against the entailments of racial representation, "both aesthetically and politically."[110] Posnock's argument against the aesthetics of racial representation is also a brief against postmodern identity politics, which requires the African-American writer to speak as a racially marked subject. In Posnock's view, African-American writers can be released from the "ghetto" of group identity only by recourse to a modern ideal of "cosmopolitan universalism" (20)—a deracialized sphere of "democratic culture . . . grounded in common humanity" (13).

Posnock's argument hangs on a set of dichotomies between the terms *modern* and *postmodern:* between the *politikos* of universal democratic ideals and the *ethnos* of racial particularity, and between the free-floating, cosmopolitan subject of modernism and the tribalism of postmodern identity politics (17). This opposition is based on the spurious presumptions that racial politics cannot bear universal implications and that modern political constructs have been free of race. Posnock's conception of modern and postmodern cultural politics is especially inapplicable to Samuel Delany's writing, which urges readers to reconsider precisely such dichotomies. Delany associates modern culture and politics with the "notion of a centered subject," which he describes as a "mirage" subtending the material oppression and ideological exclusion of racial and gendered "others."[111] This falsely universal subject (like Posnock's idea of the free-floating modern subject) inhabits a "dream outside of historical time," which Delany exposes as a delusion.[112] Delany advocates an alternate postmodern notion of the "subject-in-history" that can, in principle, "be denied to *no* one" (204). In Delany's clunky formulation, the postmodern subject is a "self-inseparable-from-the-material-universe-and-all-we-don't-know-about-it that is one with the notion of the self-in-history-that-is-all-we-do-know-about-our-universe" (199). In other words, the postmodern subject, as conceived by Delany, is consonant with the principles of historical materialism. This subject appears theoretically incredible only because modern and postmodern positions are so often pitted against each other. Posnock is critical of identity, which he claims is reified in postmodern discourse, but extols modern subjectivity, which he believes is a more fluid category. But polarized notions of modern and postmodern subjects are easily reversible, as Delany's remarks suggest: from certain polemical perspectives, the modern subject appears as a stabilizing ideological construct, and postmodern identity is persuasively seen as more vulnerable insofar as it admits its own historical contingency.

The real problem with Posnock's binary oppositions between modern and postmodern subjects is that these are grounded in a strictly formalist approach to ideology and politics. Posnock construes the modern political subject to be dynamic because he derives his account of this subject chiefly from the formal strategies of modernist literature, which unsettle realist categories and conventions. Posnock conflates aesthetic and political representation, as when he argues that Delany eludes the problem of racial representation by refusing narrative realism. I dwell on Posnock's argument at some length here because it exemplifies the formalist bent of so much contemporary literary theory. Texts that interrupt fixed aesthetic conventions are said to challenge ideological and political constructs as well, such as essentialist notions of identity, cultural tradition, or community.

Such formalist assumptions are nowhere more clearly evident than in the critical discourse surrounding Ishmael Reed's *Mumbo Jumbo,* generally regarded as the exemplar of black literary postmodernism. Reed's novel juxtaposes a variety of texts and signifying systems (including photographs, drawings, invitations, and newspaper items), calling into question its own truth-claims as a literary text. Because of this semiotic heterogeneity and formal self-reflexivity, critics have interpreted *Mumbo Jumbo* as a postmodern novel that deflates claims to racial representation. In the most influential of such readings, Henry Louis Gates argues that Reed displaces the representational methods of the black literary tradition through the stylistic techniques of pastiche and parody. Reed's stress on the materiality of the signifier serves, in Gates's view, to dissolve the notion of a "transcendent black signified" that guarantees the truth-claims of literary texts.[113] In a reading indebted to Gates, David Mikics similarly pits the idea of authentic racial tradition against postmodern ideals of interpretive indeterminacy, arguing that Reed frustrates demands for racial representation through his aesthetic subversion of totality, unity, and purity.[114]

Gates and Mikics configure nationalism and postmodernism, racial essentialism and self-conscious textuality, as necessarily incongruent categories. *Mumbo Jumbo* elicits such readings to the extent that its formal strategies are explicitly designed to thwart the realist demands of nationalist aesthetics. Whereas nationalist critics such as Addison Gayle saw literary form as the "delivery system" for a preexisting content,[115] Reed disturbs the long-standing expectation that black literary texts should smoothly mirror racial reality by showing, as Gates argues, that truths about black culture are produced through the very process of textual signification. Reed flouts the reflectionist imperative through his parodic use of documentary devices such as photographs, newspaper reports, and footnotes. Nationalist conceptions of politicized art are overtly satirized in *Mumbo Jumbo* on account of their unitary, purist, and repressive models of black culture. Abdul, a character who personifies nationalist aesthetics, squeezes black art to make it fit a particular racial ideology and burns the ancient Book of Thoth because of its uncertain political valence. As part of his reaction against cultural nationalism, Reed tries to liberate the aesthetic domain from the instrumental demands of politics, and he achieves this aim through his selective re-creation of the myth of Thoth, the Egyptian god of writing.

Reed incarnates Thoth in his ibis aspect, and the bird emblem gives rise to a series of word associations—ibis, bird, Black Birdman, Charlie "Bird" Parker, jazz, Jes Grew—that evoke the mutable, improvisatory, and resilient spirit of black culture. In a telling departure from mythical accounts of Thoth, Reed purges the god of writing of his judiciary and administrative functions, displacing these to Set, whom Reed polarizes against Osiris, god of nature, life, and fertility. As "the deity of the modern clerk" (162), Set uses law and government to bring popular culture under official supervision. This fictional revision of the myth of Thoth is critical to Reed's project of elaborating an antinationalist conception of black art. Whereas nationalist ideologues set out to legislate the proper political uses of art, Reed celebrates a text of black culture that cannot be "herded" or "rounded up" to serve any single political ideology (140). By severing Thoth and his book from the legal and administrative spheres, Reed opens the way for an affirmative notion of black art fully freed from political co-optation. Reed also abjures the totalizing ambitions of nationalist aesthetics by suggesting that no part can stand in for the whole because black culture is multifaceted and inexhaustible.

But in disavowing nationalist aims for art, Reed does not surrender all claims to racial representation. In fact, by refusing narrative realism Reed actually strengthens his claim to capturing the essential truth of black culture. Reed spurns verisimilitude because the stabilizing representational methods of realism cannot contain the volatile energies of black culture, and in this sense, the dynamic form of his novel lays claim to a higher-order realism. *Mumbo Jumbo* suggests that the variegated reality of black art is in fact distorted when it is bent to pragmatic political uses. The formal principles of postmodern aesthetics—internal heterogeneity, polyvalence, refusal of closure—are the very core of black culture as defined by Reed and thereby help render the real essence of this culture. Patrick McGee has argued that Reed's neo-hoodoo aesthetic, affirming as it does the syncretism of black art, offers an alternative to the purist master narratives of modern Western culture, and, we might add, of 1960s black nationalism.[116] Yet *Mumbo Jumbo* also contains its own grand narrative, its centuries-deep hermeneutic, about a mythical struggle between black and Western cultural forces. In this tall tale about the career of the Book of Thoth, recounted at the novel's climax by PaPa LaBas, black culture both changes and persists unchanged through the ages in that continual innovation forms the transhistorical essence of this culture. Through his

contrast between a spontaneous, popular black culture and an aridly rational, codified Western culture, Reed achieves a rapprochement of sorts with
1960s cultural nationalism. Reed's playful and parodic presentation of this
grand narrative is precisely what allows him to preserve a notion of black
art as primitivist as any to be found in 1960s nationalist discourses.

Contrary to the formalist assumptions of postmodern literary theory,
then, Reed's insistence on textual mediation is perfectly compatible with his
self-avowed ambition of "trac[ing] the true Afro-American aesthetic."[117]
As Reed's example demonstrates, disruptive formal strategies often leave
intact claims to racial representation, and it is possible to flout narrative
realism and yet purport to render authentic racial culture. The question of
referentiality stubbornly persists as a vexed problem in African-American
fiction as well as literary criticism in the postmodern period. In sharp contrast to Henry Louis Gates's formalist approach, Cornel West has argued
that Reed's fiction, like much black postmodern art, retains a political edge
because it is rooted in a "reality that one cannot not know."[118] As we saw
earlier, this is the reality of acute material deprivation, which West deems
representative of African-American experience as a whole. According to
West, postmodern black art maintains its political accountability to the
race by staying anchored in this bedrock reality of African-American life.
To be sure, most postmodern black novelists, even when they renounce
narrative realism, nonetheless seek to certify the political aims of their fiction by asserting its special purchase on racial reality. Attesting to the ways
in which crisis-ridden discourses on black community contour the postmodern black literary imagination, this reality is generally equated with
the predicament of urban poverty. Many of the novels I consider in this
book contain explicit representations of a racialized urban "underclass,"
such as Octavia Butler's *Parable of the Sower,* Samuel Delany's *Stars in My
Pocket,* Sapphire's *PUSH,* and John Edgar Wideman's *Philadelphia Fire*
and *Reuben.* Even in those novels that do not directly engage contemporaneous discourses on urban crisis, the question of the political salience of
literature hinges on its ability to advance some sort of referential claim.
This is the case even for those subgenres of postmodern black fiction that
shun mimetic realism, such as the marvelous realism of Toni Morrison's
Song of Solomon and Gloria Naylor's *Mama Day* or the science fiction of
Octavia Butler and Samuel Delany.

But the referential claims of postmodern African-American fiction take
more complex forms than is suggested by Cornel West's observation that
black postmodern art is political insofar as it fingers "the ragged edges of
the Real." Most contemporary African-American novelists remain severely
exercised by their own distance from the realities of material deprivation

and are far less certain than West about what reality with a capital R might mean. Doubts about the political value of literature for a wider black constituency are distilled through the tropes of the book that proliferate in postmodern black fiction—tropes that always self-reflexively grapple with the question of how the literary text can vouchsafe its referential claims. Closely entwined with the problem of referentiality are doubts about the restricted social compass of print literature. Forcing attention to the print modality of literature, tropes of the book raise in heightened forms the problem of elite/popular mediation. Most of the novelists I consider in this book strenuously disavow or stretch modern conceptions of print literature so as to make it respond to the demands of hitherto marginalized social groups. So, for example, Toni Morrison and Gloria Naylor seek to model their writing on oral vernacular traditions that are putatively more expressive of black cultural community than is print literature. Samuel Delany strives to distance the popular genre of science fiction from the institutionalized category of "Literature with a capital L."[119] Through such populist gestures, contemporary African-American novelists critically reappropriate the print legacy in an effort to extend the social and political provenance of their own representational medium.

The trope of the Book of Thoth, featured in both Ishmael Reed's *Mumbo Jumbo* and John Edgar Wideman's *Reuben,* vividly instantiates this attempted rehabilitation of the modern print tradition. Reed recasts Thoth as "the first choreographer" as well as the recorder of dance forms (164). Characterizing dance as a vital ancient ritual, Reed invokes and stretches the mythical Thoth's role as scribe of ritual formulae in order to imbue writing with performative dimensions. Accordingly, the Book of Thoth in *Mumbo Jumbo* epitomizes the dynamic text of black popular culture. Jes Grew, Reed's name for the spontaneous energies of this culture, manifests itself mainly through dance and music but is "seeking its . . . text" during the 1920s era in which the novel is set.[120] The Book of Thoth—a hieroglyphic anthology of dance forms and ritual formulae— is a quintessentially postmodern, that is to say, a countermodern text. Its format as an anthology militates against the modern convention of the singular author, holder of copyright and source of textual meaning. The hieroglyphic character of this text counters the abstraction of print technology, infusing it with pictorial possibilities as well as with numinous and hieratic value. Chafing against the silence and fixity of print, the contents of the Book of Thoth—ritual chants and dance movements—evoke the synesthetic, kinetic, and multimedia dimensions that are said to distinguish postmodern textuality. In the novel's present, the book circulates in "dispersed" fashion (69), in the form of a chain, in order to evade official capture.

Through the Book of Thoth, Reed profanes the fetish object of the printed book, opening it up to the volatile energies of black popular culture. Throughout the novel, Reed caricatures the administrative, political, and even military apparatus deployed to protect the exclusive and sacrosanct bastions of Western art. If the modern West mystifies art objects into fetishes that must be worshipped in special spheres removed from everyday life, black art recaptures the golden age of Osiris's reign, when "every man was an artist and every artist a priest" (164). Among postmodern African-American novels, *Mumbo Jumbo* stands virtually alone in its festive and carnivalesque portrayal of black urban popular culture, and in this sense, contrary to critical consensus, it does not really exemplify black literary postmodernism. The political nuance of Reed's aesthetic project in this novel inheres in his conviction that black popular cultural energies can exceed all forms of political and official co-optation. Epitomizing a symbiosis of literary text and popular culture, the Book of Thoth projects an unusually smooth resolution to postmodern problems of literary representation. In its affirmation of the oppositional potential of urban popular culture, *Mumbo Jumbo* owes much to the black nationalist and other countercultural movements of the 1960s, during which the novel was written.

Reed's celebration of the subversive energy of black urban popular culture seems to become increasingly unavailable to subsequent African-American writers for a variety of reasons, not least the rapidly spreading popularity of discourses pathologizing black urban culture. Another crucial factor is the shrinking credibility, in the postmodern era, of the idea that print or vernacular culture can maintain autonomy from capitalist commodity culture. Andreas Huyssen has argued that postmodern art in the United States failed to muster the critical edge of earlier avant-garde movements in part because it arrived on a popular cultural scene that was thoroughly incorporated into commodity capitalism.[121] Huyssen's observation rings true for much postmodern black fiction, which either discredits a degraded mass culture or posits a folk culture displaced backward in time as the only defense against commodity capitalism. Many postmodern black novelists continue to press claims to broad-based racial representation on the strength of their links with the vernacular traditions of the people, but they find this to be a far more difficult endeavor than does Reed. The problem of mediating between print and vernacular culture is compounded by a historically specific matrix of factors, including the transformed conditions of black politics in the post–Civil Rights decades, the sharpening intraracial class polarities resulting from structural economic changes, the sway of crisis-ridden discourses on black urban community, and the academic institutionalization of African-American literature.

The difficulties of resolving contemporary problems of racial representation through the medium of print literature form the central preoccupation of Wideman's novel *Reuben,* published in 1987. Whereas Reed's Book of Thoth symbolizes a print literary tradition regenerated by the countermodern energies of black popular culture, Wideman invokes Thoth in order to mourn the incapacity of the contemporary black writer to recapture the ritual dimensions of premodern writing or to represent the culture of his people. Wideman casts Thoth in the overlapping roles of court clerk, patron of scribes, mediator between deities, reckoner of days, officiator of sacred rituals, and guardian of the dead. In the Egyptian Books of the Dead, Thoth often appears in the judgment scenes held before the council of the gods as an advocate for the dead, overseeing their safe passage into the world beyond death. Reuben, the writer figure in Wideman's novel, aspires to this ritualistic function but in fact can only operate as a camera, freezing the dead. The writer in *Reuben* cannot reincarnate himself as a premodern figure in whom writing, law, administration, magic, and sacred ritual are all conjoined. The mythical Thoth was simultaneously a legal scribe who recorded divine decrees that he also often helped to decide, the author of the Book of Thoth, a collection of ritual formulae, and the writer of "the divine book," which recorded the details of the sun god Re's government.[122] But in Wideman's novel, these various functions are sundered into specialized domains that cannot be incorporated into any single figure.

If Wideman cannot sustain Ishmael Reed's "neo-hoodoo" conception of writing as a holistic domain of simultaneously secular and sacred dimensions, he can no more readily affirm a politically instrumental role for literature. In contrast to Reed, Wideman highlights Thoth's roles as legal mediator, court recorder, and administrative clerk in an effort to extend the pragmatic social scope of writing and to reinstate the postmodern writer as the "unacknowledged legislator" of his people. As Thoth mediated between Horus and Set, helping to settle their conflict, so the writer figure in Wideman's novel uses his knowledge of the law to mediate between the poor residents of Homewood and the powers-that-be downtown. Wideman's attempted vindication of writing in the postmodern era demands the reintegration of literary and political, symbolic and practical realms. Reuben practices legal mediation through magic: he performs rituals of empathetic identification with his clients, hoping that the force of his compassion will bring about favorable changes in their lives. Instead of actually taking his clients' cases downtown, Reuben conjures up imaginary resolutions to their legal problems. In this sense, the efficacy of Reuben's legal work depends on the saving power of fiction. His greatest service to the Homewood community is to provide its members the illusion that someone represents them and to offer them a species of justice they are unlikely to receive in real life. Its power to dodge reality and to entertain imaginary possibilities is what ultimately redeems the writing of literature in *Reuben*.

But this redemption remains tentative because Wideman can neither endorse a notion of politicized art secured by straightforwardly realist claims nor entirely banish the tricky question of literature's relation to social reality. Unlike Reed's Book of Thoth, which authentically captures the plenitudinous culture of the race, Wideman's Thoth-writer obsessively ponders the fragility of his claims to representing the black community of Homewood. The fictive terms of Reuben's legal representation of this community suggest that literary writing cannot serve immediate social uses or be wholly adequate to social reality. But for Wideman, wrestling with the question of literature's insufficiency to an extra-textual real becomes the only way of keeping alive a political conception of literature. Altogether suspending this question can encourage solipsistic and masturbatory notions of self-sufficient textuality, captured in *Reuben* through a vivid image of Thoth in his baboon aspect: "a baboon, brow furrowed in deep thought, middle finger searching his asshole, was a perfect emblem for the writer."[123] In *Reuben,* unlike in *Mumbo Jumbo,* questions of textual mediation are deliberately yoked to problems of social mediation: through heightened attention to the oblique relations between literary texts and reality, Wideman interrogates his own claims to representing the culture of the people.

Wideman's novel suggests how literature might offer a unique point of entry into postmodern debates about racial representation. Its peculiarly fictive conditions of credibility as well as its narrow social purview are a liability for literature, curbing claims of direct and mass political relevance. But this very liability can be valuable if it compels readers and writers to confront the risks and errors entailed in literary projects of racial representation. Exposing Reuben as an impostor at the end of his novel, Wideman implies that the writer's claims to representation can only proceed at a fictive level and are, therefore, necessarily caught in the meshes of mediation. An emphasis on mediation seems especially valuable in a postmodern situation where, as I argue in the following chapters, political projects either founder on dire claims about the total eclipse of the real or seek mystical fusion with pre-textual realities. The value of studying postmodern African-American novels in this context is that they treat the question of literature's relation to social reality as a problem that must be squarely addressed although it cannot be conclusively settled. Without surrendering political hopes for literature, these texts call for more scrupulous accounts than currently prevail of the political agency of black literature. Forcing attention to the fallible yet ineluctable nature of mediation, tropes of the book in postmodern black fiction provoke rigorously self-critical reflection about contemporary projects of racial representation. Despite widely varying uses, these tropes impart a keen awareness of the imposture always risked when writers claim to speak for those less privileged groups who are excluded from print culture.

2.

Books of Life: Postmodern Uses of Print Literacy

Thas the alphabet. 26 letters in all. Them letters make up words.
Them words everything.
—Sapphire, *PUSH*

Even some fiction might be useful.
—Octavia Butler, *Parable of the Sower*

The Book of Life exchanges hands. Who will read it next, kill for it next?
—John Edgar Wideman, *Philadelphia Fire*

The modern legacy of print literacy has come under fire in the postmodern era because of its presumed irrelevance to new social conditions and constituencies. The more powerful sway of electronic technologies has sparked a crisis for writers of print literature, which seems at best to occupy a residual space within the postmodern cultural domain. Proponents of electronic technology often validate their assault on the print tradition by citing its cultural elitism and racial exclusions. The postmodern attack on print culture is symptomatic of a wider disenchantment with the career of modern humanism, in which print literacy has been thoroughly implicated. Nowhere has the humanist legacy been interrogated as sharply or deeply as in African-American literature, which has long been demonstrating that the dehumanization of African-Americans was essential to the definition of universal humanity in print modernism. Yet the archive of African-American literature is never consulted in postmodern debates on modern humanism and print culture.

Were we to actually examine this archive, we would find a complex stance—of simultaneous demystification and adaptation—toward the modern print legacy. Sapphire's novel *PUSH,* published in 1996, features a protagonist, Precious, who embodies the very prototype of the black urban erclass" and whose narrative is propelled by a quest for print literacy. dered by the welfare bureaucracy's attempt to sabotage her quest, ous writes: "Ms Rain [her literacy instructor] say I am intellectually alive and curious. I am just trying to figure out what is going on out here. *How what happen to me could happen in modern days.*"[1] Precious's critical take on the spuriously universal promise of modern print culture speaks for itself, yet it is through the print medium that Precious believes she can most effectively conduct her critique. In this chapter, I focus on literary texts— *Philadelphia Fire* (1985) by John Edgar Wideman and *Parable of the Sower* (1993) by Octavia Butler, along with Sapphire's *PUSH*—that continue to be profoundly invested in the modern idea of print literacy as a vehicle of social critique and advancement. As the epigraphs for this chapter suggest, it is perhaps premature to proclaim the death of print culture. For some marginalized groups, especially African-Americans, who historically have been barred from participating in this culture, print literacy is not yet obsolete.

Butler, Sapphire, and Wideman deploy strikingly similar tropes of the book that encapsulate the utopian promise of the modern print legacy— "Earthseed: The Books of the Living" in *Parable of the Sower,* "Life Stories: Our Class Book" in *PUSH,* and "The Book of Life" in *Philadelphia Fire.* These Books of Life test the continuing uses of the modern print tradition and raise a cluster of interrelated questions about print literacy that seem especially urgent in the postmodern urban context, such as: What sorts of reading communities can the writer of print literature address? Can print literacy still serve its modern function of cultivating a critical understanding of society? Is acquisition of literacy tied to social mobility and progress, as was presumed to be the case in the modern era? What pragmatic and symbolic functions, if any, can literacy perform for the disadvantaged black population that obsessively preoccupies contemporary purveyors of urban crisis—the so-called black urban underclass? Can contemporary African-American writers of literature bridge the sharpening class divisions characteristic of the postmodern city and represent the interests of the black urban poor? Can print culture support the creation of imaginary alternatives to the dystopian realities of postmodern cities? Distilling such questions through their variants of the Book of Life, Butler, Sapphire, and Wideman try to rehabilitate the legacy of print literacy in order to make it serve the interests of the most disempowered sectors of postmodern U.S. society.

Reading the Postmodern City

PUSH, Parable of the Sower, and *Philadelphia Fire* depict highly fragmented urban scenarios that are proffered as texts to be assembled and interpreted by their characters and readers. All three novels extensively detail the racial effects of urban development since the 1970s. In what follows, I treat these literary texts not merely as illustrative supplements to social science scholarship on postmodern cities but as a valuable archive in themselves. These novels, by forcing the question of how to read urban texts and how to grasp them as interpretive wholes, take on a much-debated problem—of the semiotic legibility of postmodern cities—in contemporary urban theory. Butler, Sapphire, and Wideman all press the case for developing a critical literacy that can decode the manifest visual text of the postmodern city and grasp its repressed racial subtexts.

As a science fiction text, *Parable of the Sower* offers a unique point of entry for a critical analysis of postmodern urbanism. A character in this novel, which is set in Los Angeles County during the years 2024–27, wistfully recalls "What a blaze of lights cities used to be" in the not-so-distant past. In the novel's present, however, "lights, progress, growth" are bitterly dismissed as "all those things we're ... too poor to bother with anymore."[2] Although science fiction is presumed to project future societies, Butler has said that in this novel she "made an effort to talk about what could actually happen or is in the process of happening."[3] In keeping with the doubled temporality of much science fiction, Butler's novel presents a distorted yet recognizable portrait of her readers' present world as well as an extrapolation of future possibilities that are incipient in this world.

The remembered past in Butler's novel—the city of blazing lights—evokes the present of her contemporaneous readers. Glittering urban cores have been conspicuously visible emblems of U.S. urban development since the 1970s. The dystopia of the novel's present suggests the logical future consequences of these patterns of development, as the city of lights degenerates into "a carcass covered with too many maggots" (8). Cities in *Parable* consist of walled neighborhoods whose residents have armed themselves to protect their property against looting and arson. The streets outside these enclaves are occupied by an urban underclass made up of "the street poor—squatters, winos, junkies, homeless people in general" (9). The power of Butler's novel inheres in the fact that its dystopian urban future is so closely extrapolated from current trends that it creates a shock of familiarity rather than estrangement. Butler has identified the walling of communities as a process that is actually and already occurring in contemporary U.S. cities.[4] In fact, the novel's propertied neighborhoods walled against a menacing urban underclass uncannily resemble both John Edgar Wideman's journalistic sketch of Los Angeles as a city structured by "invisible walls" and Mike Davis's grim sociological account of "Fortress L.A." When Wideman writes, "The South Central ghettos, brutally cordoned and policed, and the barred, burglar-alarmed, security-patrolled enclaves of Hollywood Hills mirror one another obscenely, grotesquely. Who's locked in? Who's locked out?" he may well be describing the Californian urban areas we encounter in Butler's novel.[5]

The doubled temporality of *Parable of the Sower* graphically exposes the contradictory directions of U.S. urban development over the last quarter of the twentieth century. Juxtaposing growth and carcasses, blazing city lights and arson, gated communities and homelessness, guarded department stores and widespread looting, Butler's novel urges readers to grasp these polarities as interdependent features of the postmodern city. The urban redevelopment programs of the last quarter of the twentieth century were designed to stimulate economic growth by making cities more profitable for private capital investment, reflecting significant shifts in the urban policy goals of federal and city governments by the mid-1970s. Outbreaks of black urban violence in numerous cities during the 1960s had forced public attention to the entanglement of structural racism and urban poverty, and federal aid to cities had more than quadrupled by the end of the decade. The Model Cities and community action programs of the 1960s, underwritten by direct federal aid, were dismantled by the mid-1970s in favor of downtown revitalization by private developers. Public responses to the fiscal crises of the 1970s invalidated the claims of the poor and racial minorities who largely inhabited deteriorating central city areas and whose presence in these areas was seen as a deterrent to urban economic growth. With the decline in racial militancy as well as in federal commitment to redistributive policies during the 1970s, urban cores populated by racial minorities became sites of profitable capital investment. These core areas, once organized around industrial production, were converted into centers of privatized and upscale consumption, earning David Harvey's description of the postmodern city as "a consumption artifact."[6]

The increased role of private capital investment in urban downtown areas since the 1970s has been rationalized by pro-growth ideologies, based on the assumptions that economic growth can remedy urban decay and poverty, that growth can be best achieved by capital development unfettered by public control, and that the benefits of this growth will eventually trickle down to all urban areas.[7] The visible proof of this achieved growth are the gleaming city centers, described in *Parable of the Sower* as "a blaze of lights" or in *Philadelphia Fire* as "a circus of lights."[8] In the Philadelphia of Wideman's novel, the downtown area that used to be "stone slum" has been converted by the 1980s into "solid gold." The novel describes in detail the process whereby the city bought this devalued land "for next to nothing" and leased it to private developers, who transformed the area into a site of luxury residence and lavish consumption where "everything" could be "bought and sold" (78, 46). A character in the novel, Timbo, cultural attaché to the mayor of Philadelphia, hails these new developments as "progress, real progress." But *Philadelphia Fire* shows that "what's growing is garbage dumps" peopled by the poor, homeless, and racial minorities (79), whose expulsion makes possible the creation of the postmodern city into a "consumption artifact."

Wideman's Philadelphia is, of course, a fictional construct, yet the novel sharply delineates the aims and ends of urban development in this city since the 1970s. Various studies of the development of Philadelphia document that following the recession of the mid-1970s, private capital moved into the inner city, spurring its transformation from a declining industrial to a booming corporate center. The sense of economic and cultural vitality was restricted to Center City, where the new skyline visibly symbolized urban renewal. Yet this development entailed extensive demolition of low-income housing in neighborhoods predominantly populated by African-Americans. The massive dislocation of low-income African-Americans from Center City was one of the factors that earned urban renewal its notorious reputation as "Negro removal." Urban historians concur that these patterns of development disproportionately impacted the African-American poor and heightened racial and class polarities, resulting in the creation of a dual city.[9]

In Wideman's fictional Philadelphia, urban development has produced cities fractured along class and racial lines, exacerbating the spatial segregation and social isolation of the urban poor. The by-product of downtown development is a city of starkly widening inequality: "Rich richer and poor poorer" (79). The Harlem presented in Sapphire's *PUSH*, with its vacant lots, dilapidated housing projects, and "lifes of trash" (104), mirrors the "garbage dumps" occupied by the African-American poor in *Philadelphia Fire*. The exact obverse of the Harlem cityscape is downtown Manhattan, presented in *PUSH* as a center of consumption that is decisively racialized as "white." Harlem is mostly "usta be buildings," but as you travel downtown "it's a different city," with "bookstores/café/BLoomydales," "big glass windows/stores/white people" (128). Urban development in Manhattan has been fairly representative of national patterns, bringing about the economic resurgence of parts of the borough along with a sharp rise in homelessness and a reduction of low-cost housing.[10] If renewal projects helped maintain Manhattan's status as "the heart pump of the capital blood that sustains the free world,"[11] little of this economic vitality spilled over into Harlem, as Sapphire's novel makes clear. Neil Smith suggests, in his study of gentrification in Manhattan, that racial composition delayed the incursion of private capital into Harlem.[12] High capital investment in downtown Manhattan was matched by a corresponding decline in public social expenditures uptown. In *PUSH* we are shown Mayor Edward Koch, who was deeply indebted to private developers for campaign contributions, threatening to close down the Harlem Hospital—"say niggers don't need no hospital all to theyself" (74).

How different societies define and satisfy human needs is a question central to dystopian (and utopian) fiction. *Philadelphia Fire, PUSH,* and *Parable* explicitly raise this question of how the needs of rich and poor, white and black, are being redefined in a context of privatized urban development. In Butler's novel, economic power is concentrated in a few large corporations and the nation-state has all but disappeared except as an enabling mechanism for capital accumulation. Like Koch in *PUSH* and Mayor Wilson Goode in Wideman's novel, the fictional President Donner resorts to the language of waste and necessity to justify his capitulation to capital: the national government has sold off all public projects that will not "earn an immediate profit or at least promise big future profits. There's no mood now for doing anything that might be considered unnecessary or wasteful" (75). President Donner facilitates capital mobility by suspending "'overly restrictive' minimum wage, environmental, and worker protection laws" (24). These federal policies enable the privatization of Olivar. Formerly a well-to-do suburb of Los Angeles and home to an upper-middle-class, white community, Olivar sells itself to KSF, a multinational corporation, which offers the residents of Olivar steady employment, a "guaranteed food-supply," and security from the "spreading chaos of the rest of Los Angeles county" (106). The corporation pays workers wages that barely meet living expenses, forcing them into a cycle of debt slavery that perpetuates their financial dependence on the company.

Showing that increased privatization of cities results in a decisive shrinkage of human needs, *Parable* overtly challenges the assumptions of growth ideology. The novel also demonstrates that unchecked capitalist development is not race-blind and will not eventually spill over to disadvantaged social sectors. The Robledo neighborhood, which forms the primary setting of the novel, is, like Sapphire's Harlem, left behind by the processes of capital development because it is "too poor, too black, and too Hispanic to be of interest" (106). Lest we dismiss the severe social costs of private development in *Parable* as fanciful sci-fi images of an improbable future, Butler inserts a reminder that "none of this is new" and that much of it was already discernible during the 1990s (263).

Projecting widespread scarcity and escalating class and racial antagonism as the probable cul-de-sac of current patterns of urban development, *Parable of the Sower* thoroughly discredits the enduring image (revived in recent times) of the city as a marketplace of abundant consumer options.[13] It is the gated community rather than vibrant downtown sites of consumption that Butler presents as the epitome of postmodern urbanism. The novel's depiction of walled enclaves of consumption, on the one hand,

and urban violence motivated by unequal access to commodities, on the other, implicitly critiques a powerful contemporary ideal of urban progress—the ideal of unlimited economic productivity gauged by expansion of privatized consumer options. Similarly leery of this ideal, Wideman, in his 1988 essay "The Divisible Man," mourns the absence of "the alternative institutions we dreamed of creating in the '60s," inspired by a "dream of better, not more. Truly better. Not more pigs slopping at the trough, not a larger bite of the rotten pie, not more, but better."[14]

Wideman's novel reveals the runaway logic of conspicuous consumption in a grotesque scene in which Cudjoe, after partaking of the celebrated "restaurant renaissance" of Center City Philadelphia,[15] ponders the "possibility of excess made real by the city": "Accumulating. Bloating. Smiling and chattering while piles of bones, hunks of fat, discarded gristle and cores,... what was unconsumed and unconsumable, waste and rot and persiflage heaped up, the garbage outweighing him, usurping his place. Eaten by refuse faster than he can cram it down his throat" (92). Cudjoe's metaphor of the city as a monstrous machine that consumes and expels humanity as its waste product is complemented by the literal image of urban zones of scarcity inhabited by human beings who have no choice but to feed on waste. JB, a homeless man who narrates sections of the third part of the novel, is one such person who scavenges meals from garbage dumpsters. In a horrific twist, what Cudjoe sees as superfluous waste becomes a necessity for JB. If a conspicuous proof of the fetishism of postmodern consumer society is the proliferation of aesthetically pleasing methods of packaging commodities,[16] JB points out the entirely unexpected uses of this packaging for the hungry homeless: "You're grateful for boxes which keep the treats safe inside the Dumpster's rotten maw. You feel blessed because someone packages each morsel, each ingredient in its own individual container. Grateful for paper and plastic that protects each meal, that preserves and delivers leftovers a second time around" (176).

A person like JB belongs to the class of "surplus people" that Wideman discusses in his essay "Dead Black Men and Other Fallout of the American Dream." Describing surplus people as the casualties of an international restructuring of industrial economy, Wideman insists that the problem of "urban decay" cannot be understood in "strictly American" terms.[17] By means of frequent parallels between Philadelphia and "Third World" cities (79), *Philadelphia Fire* places urban areas such as the renovated Philadelphia downtown within a global economic order. The novel thereby offers a "way of seeing that unmasks the fetishisms" promoted by progrowth ideologies of urban development, which, as David Harvey argues, treat the spatial text of the city as a self-contained object immanent with meaning.[18] Other forceful critics of postmodern urban development, such as Rosalyn Deutsche and M. Christine Boyer, have also remarked on the ways in which ideologies of growth and consumption have fostered fragmented and fetishistic perceptions of the urban condition.[19] To sustain the appearance of growth, certain urban realities, such as vibrant downtown areas, must be viewed as discrete and disconnected from other urban realities, such as homelessness or racial segregation. Downtown areas come to stand in for the entirety and the representative directions of urban growth, and areas of poverty are either obscured from view or regarded as "lag-time spaces" that will eventually catch up with the inexorable logic of progressive development.[20] What we lack, Boyer laments, is a "map of the city linking together the poorer neighborhoods with the enclaves of the well-to-do," allowing us to comprehend these as interdependent phenomena rather than as "random disparities."[21] Both Deutsche and Boyer suggest that such a map might be found in the concept of uneven development, which allows us to grasp the city in its entirety and to discern the systemic elements that lend coherence to the visual text of the city.

The very idea of mapping is suspect in postmodern social and cultural theories, connoting as it does a will to totalizing vision. As I elaborate in chapter 5, discourses of postmodern urbanism draw on the metaphor of the network rather than the map as a means of highlighting the unstructured heterogeneity of contemporary cities. Countering such images of the postmodern city as a free and random interplay among differences, Butler, Sapphire, and Wideman painstakingly map out the rigid organization of urban space into racially segregated zones. Notwithstanding the current suspicion of maps and totalities, these novelists present mapping as a form of critical literacy that can disclose the concealed structural logic of postmodern cities. In the opening chapters of *Parable of the Sower,* the protagonist, Lauren Olamina, insists on the uses of print literacy in helping her community prepare for impending urban collapse. Lauren has assembled a survival kit containing only a few indispensable items, including a street map. When her neighborhood burns down and she is forced to flee the dangerous terrain of Los Angeles County, the map helps Lauren find her way in the absence of street signs. Here, the map literally helps her to negotiate an urban context of extreme dislocation, revealing directions that are not immediately visible to the eye. In *PUSH,* the functional illiteracy of Precious reinforces her sense of enclosure within the narrow and segregated space of Harlem. As she acquires literacy, Precious begins to understand her own restricted place within the wider urban system, an understanding focused through the image of a subway map pasted on her bedroom door. Studying this map, Precious assumes an imaginary mobility, tracing the different neighborhoods she might travel to on the subway. This exercise enables her to grasp as a whole the contradictory facets of

New York City—vacant lots in Harlem versus lustrous store windows in downtown Manhattan—and pushes her toward a sharper understanding of the unevenly developed and racialized order of her city.

Like Harlem in *PUSH,* or the walled enclaves of *Parable of the Sower, Philadelphia Fire* also depicts an urban order based on racial and economic segregation: "Everybody had zones. Addicts, prostitutes, porn merchants, derelicts. Even people who were black and poor had zones" (45–46). Cudjoe, one of the narrators of *Philadelphia Fire* who is also an aspiring writer, persistently poses the question of how the writer of fiction might integrate these discrete urban spaces into a single and whole vision. It is only by bringing into view spaces that are repressed by dominant narratives of urban growth that Cudjoe can grasp the uneven development of Philadelphia, and the map metaphor serves him well in this attempt. Cudjoe draws attention to what is not visible downtown but is essential to comprehending the meaning of downtown: the "pitiful bloods" who have been driven "off the map" of the city (79). To resist a myopic and fractured view of the city, Cudjoe resolves that "he must always write about many places at once." "Always moving," the contemporary writer must "travel through those other places" because no place contains its own meaning (23). City spaces, in *Philadelphia Fire,* are to be understood as "concrete abstractions" whose full meaning can only be explained with reference to structural processes that are not immanent in any one locale.[22] The novel treats urban space as part of an asymmetrical global system of linked locales whose meaning is "always everywhere at once" (184).

It is no wonder, then, that one of the narrators of the novel is a homeless man who "inhabits many places, no place" (184). In the third part of the novel, presented from the sharply conflicting points of view of a homeless man, a youth gang member, and a suburbanite, the narration itself strains to span and to force an encounter between the mutually incommunicable zones of the postmodern city. Unsurprisingly, this section culminates in the burning of the homeless man, which, notwithstanding its phantasmagoric depiction, captures a grim and increasingly actual feature of contemporary U.S. cities. Located in the heart of downtown Philadelphia, this scene of violence calls attention to the hidden costs of urban revitalization, forcing readers to recognize, in Rosalyn Deutsche's words, that "today there is no document of [urban] ascendancy which is not *at the same time* a document of homelessness."[23] Urban conflagration in *Philadelphia Fire,* as in *Parable* (which similarly presents widespread homelessness as a likely consequence of current urban development policies), highlights the potentially explosive contradictions of the postmodern city.

As Mike Davis has most famously argued, the economic and racial polarities of the postmodern city are reproduced at the level of built environment, with spaces of privatized consumption being architecturally designed to exclude "the underclass 'Other.'" Academic as well as mass media discourses "ceaselessly throw up spectres of criminal underclasses ... to foment the moral panics that reinforce and justify urban apartheid."[24] In recent discourses of urban development, the rhetoric of growth (focused on downtown areas) and the rhetoric of crisis (focused on the "underclass") seem to run along separate and parallel tracks, disabling recognition of how redevelopment policies themselves have contributed to urban immiseration. A key strategy in keeping perceptions of growth and crisis disconnected in the public imagination is to portray black urban poverty as the product of deficient cultural values and behavior rather than of flawed public policies. As Michael Katz points out, during the course of the 1970s, public understanding of poverty "slipped easily, unreflectively, into a language of family, race, and culture rather than inequality, power, and exploitation."[25]

To combat this sort of account of urban poverty, *Philadelphia Fire* astutely characterizes the "underclass" as a "surplus" population produced by shifts in public policy and global economic structure. *Parable of the Sower* also refutes current formulae about black urban poverty by presenting a multiracial underclass spawned by late-twentieth-century patterns of privatized urban development. *PUSH* contains the most scathing critique of public policies toward the urban poor, in particular recent welfare reforms, as part of its ambition to refute the "shit and lies out there" about urban poverty (4). During the 1980s, the decade in which Sapphire's novel is set, official poverty discourse began to center almost exclusively on the "underclass," a clearly racialized and feminized category. Michael Katz succinctly identifies the cluster of fallacies that have allowed public debates on welfare to represent poor black women as the core of the urban "underclass": teen pregnancy in the United States has reached epidemic proportions, this epidemic is proliferating most rapidly among poor urban African-Americans, and single black mothers consume most of the U.S. social welfare budget.[26] The idea of a "reproductive underclass" fans public fears that poor black women are profusely giving birth and transmitting a set of pathological behaviors to their offspring that will ensure the continuance of black urban poverty.[27] As *PUSH* shows, images of the black teenage welfare mother as a "vampire sucking the system's blood" (31) are used to rationalize the state's increasingly punitive approach to the black urban poor.

The victim-blaming strategy of current "underclass" discourses hinges on a rhetoric of normative family values. Brett Williams has argued that this rhetoric "rests on a hoax," painting the postwar era as a golden age when American families were nuclear and stable, and using this idealized model to measure the disintegration of family life among contemporary urban poor. As Williams shows, the African-American variant of this rhetoric

posits a postwar era of mythical black urban communities that were integrated by class because they were racially segregated.[28] Cohesive families
are staple features of these nostalgic portraits of the "golden age of the
ghetto."[29] Sapphire's novel militates against such discourses promoting
familial stability as a remedy for urban poverty. In *PUSH,* family is a site of
unmitigated trauma. Precious is raped by her father and subjected to both
physical abuse and economic exploitation from her mother. Although the
novel takes great risks in depicting a dysfunctional black family that might
appear to confirm current "underclass" discourses, it makes abundantly
clear that far from causing poverty, familial pathologies are produced and
perpetuated by stringent public policies.

In *PUSH,* it is never organic ties that supply psychological or cultural sustenance for the urban poor but instead contingent communities based on
specific interests and practices, such as a literacy class or an incest survivors'
group. After her first meeting with the incest survivors' group, Precious
marvels at "How Mama and Daddy know me sixteen years and hate me,
how a stranger meet me and love me" (131), affirming a specifically urban
ideal of sociality among strangers. Precious's experiences with families and
strangers suggest that constructive responses to crisis conditions must be
sought and found not within organic settings from the past but within the
terms of the contemporary city.

Books of Life: Utopian Elsewheres to the Postmodern City

PUSH is uncompromising in its refusal to entertain spatial or temporal
elsewheres as viable responses to dystopian urban conditions. The book
of "Life Stories" contained in *PUSH* is thoroughly urban in the settings
and problems it describes and the type of community it celebrates. "Life
Stories" is an anthology co-authored by the women in Precious's literacy
class—Puerto Rican Rita Romero, Rhonda Patrice Johnson of Jamaican
origin, Jermaine Hicks the "Harlem Butch," and Precious. Consisting of
autobiographical pieces written for the literacy class, "Life Stories" brings
together an interracial community of women from diverse geographical
origins. This group is bound not by ties of blood, place, or even common
culture but by shared class and gender oppression and by commitment to
the specific goal of acquiring print literacy. The authors of "Life Stories,"
all of whom would be categorized as members of the urban "underclass,"
spurn the solace of family, religion, golden past, or organic community.
To all these characters, the city offers enhanced educational and employment opportunities, the promise of independence from abusive families,
and provisional communities that supply support for a range of personal
and social problems. One of the authors of "Life Stories" briefly yields to

talgia, re-creating her homeland of Puerto Rico as a natural paradise, ... quickly rejects the idea of return: "Go back? To where you never been? I'm better off here" (n.p.).

Butler and Wideman take a more ambivalent approach to the problem of urban community. The Books of Life in *Parable* and *Philadelphia Fire* are authored by religious cults that pursue organic alternatives to their respective urban dystopias. In Butler's novel, "Earthseed: The Books of the Living" is written by Lauren Olamina, who founds her own religion in order to urge people to confront the collapse of urban order and to take action directed at establishing a new, utopian community. Strikingly parallel to the Earthseed group is MOVE, the back-to-nature cult in Wideman's novel, which deliberately sets itself at odds with the city administration as well as with contemporary ideologies of urban modernization and progress. MOVE's manifesto, "The Book of Life," is inspired by a pastoral model of community, just as the "Earthseed" text invokes agrarian ideals to guide its assault on recent patterns of urban development. Although Wideman ironizes whereas Butler seems to endorse such utopian movements, both authors admit even as they fight the seduction of organicist responses to urban crisis. Both grapple—unsuccessfully, as we shall see—with the difficulty of sustaining urban ideals of utopian community.

As suggested by its name, the Earthseed movement in *Parable of the Sower* exemplifies an agrarian alternative to the dystopian urban present. Because cities in the novel no longer function as rational systems of production and consumption, the protagonist seeks more viable economic and ecological alternatives, such as living off the land (52). This turn to a simple agrarian economy is certainly a logical consequence of the novel's refusal to equate current trajectories of urban development with progress. Yet the novel's critique of prevalent myths of urban growth is not supported by the age-old polarization of city against country (a polarization that is given renewed life in recent discourses of southern regionalism, detailed in chapter 4). As Raymond Williams warns, literary contrasts between urban and rural life tend to repress the realities of agricultural labor and thereby blind us to the functional interdependence of city and country in modern capitalist societies.[30] Butler is careful not to disguise the harsh facts of agricultural labor or to represent the rural sphere as an elsewhere to the urban capitalist economy. Emery, the only farm worker featured in the novel, has worked for an agribusiness conglomerate that paid wages in company scrip and practiced a form of exploitation through debt as pernicious as the debt slavery common in privatized cities such as Olivar. Through such exact parallels between conditions of labor in rural and urban areas, the novel resists constructing a pastoral fiction of the countryside as an Archimedean lever for its critique of urban capitalism.

Butler even more emphatically disavows the retrospective stance that typically characterizes agrarian critiques of urban conditions. Commenting on the pastoral method of creating an idealized rural past as a "stick to beat the present," Raymond Williams remarks on its tendency to turn "protest into retrospect," a tendency that curtails the radical reach of pastoral critiques of modern urban life.[31] *Parable of the Sower* explicitly repudiates the conservative (and conservationist) ideologies that tend to accompany retrospective critical stances toward the present. The adults in Lauren's community in Robledo are "still anchored in the past, waiting for the good old days to come back" (50); this backward vision prevents them from reckoning with the many changes that have already occurred and from imagining future social transformation. In deliberate opposition to the "dying, denying, backward-looking" posture of her community (22), Lauren searches for a belief system that can "pry them loose from the rotting past" (70). To this end, Lauren establishes her own religion of Earthseed. This name comes to her as she is working in the garden and thinking of the way "plants seed themselves, away from their parent plants" (68). Lauren envisions members of her utopian community as "earthseed cast on new ground" (160), far from the familiar spaces of home, family, and neighborhood.

Lauren's seed metaphor suggests a response to urban crisis that strikingly diverges from the metaphors of roots and ancestry that crystallize southern folk resolutions to urban problems. Exemplary of this folk resolution are Toni Morrison's essays "Rootedness: The Ancestor as Foundation" and "City Limits, Village Values," which affirm the figure of the ancestor as a bulwark against the putative fracture of black community in the wake of urbanization.[32] As a bearer of cultural memory, the ancestor helps displaced urban migrants to preserve their roots in the rural South; these roots sustain "village" models of community that alone can withstand urban dislocation.[33] In this conception of the ancestor as the foundation of urban community, a remembered rural past grounds a critique of the capitalist city as well as an alternate model of social order.

In contrast, the Earthseed movement in Butler's novel does not take its bearings from the past, whether real or imagined. If the roots metaphor points toward consolidation of past values as a positive response to current urban problems, in *Parable of the Sower* the attachment to the "apparent stability" of home, family, and neighborhood stymies action directed at change. Like the gated community, home, too, is imaged in this novel as "a cul-de-sac with a wall around it" (73). This is not to suggest that Butler discounts the emotional solace that can be drawn from family. Butler has said in an interview that family seems to her to make up "our most important set of relationships," and, in fact, other novels by Butler have been criticized for the heavy redemptive weight they place on family.[34] *Parable of the Sower* fully grants the sustaining value of "homeplace," which, as bell hooks famously describes it, has historically constituted one of the few sites of recuperation from public oppression for African-Americans. But Butler does not take the next step, as does hooks, of affirming that "the construction of homeplace" bears a "radical political dimension."[35]

As exemplified by the reactions of the adults in Robledo, people often react to perceived crisis by conserving familiar structures in an attempt to fend off change. The defense of traditional values associated with an idealized past often serves dubious political ends, as is obvious from the family values rhetoric of contemporary discourses on the urban "underclass."[36] The seed metaphor of Lauren's "Books of the Living" suggests a valuable corrective to such approaches, urging as it does the need to discard ideas and ideologies rooted in the past that aim only to stabilize, not to transform, present social conditions. Home and family in Butler's novel, as in Sapphire's, cannot escape or counter the systemic logic of urban poverty. *Parable* delineates the broad national and international economic processes that impinge on every home and every neighborhood, clarifying the futility (and impossibility) of constructing urban communities on "village" foundations. Lauren's aspiration to seed herself away from the shadow of home and family signals her readiness to relinquish available mirages of security and to embrace drastic change if this is the only means to future survival and growth. This readiness is expressed in the motto of Lauren's religious text: "When apparent stability disintegrates, as it must—God is Change" (91).

Both the name of Lauren's religion, Earthseed, and its governing metaphor of seeding suggest notions of community and place quite other than those inhering in the roots metaphor, which conserves cultural and ancestral traditions as mainstays against modern urban forces of displacement. The "Earthseed" text takes mobility across space as its enabling condition. Recognizing that all visionary schemes of social transformation require an imagined elsewhere to inspire action, Lauren writes that the "destiny" of Earthseed is "to take root among the stars" (74). By this Lauren literally means that the future of the human race lies in extrasolar space. The extraterrestrial direction of Earthseed, a common-enough science fiction device, hyperbolically conveys the expansive globalism of the novel's vision, far removed from the localism of roots-based metaphors of folk community.

I do not mean to imply that mobility in itself is a forward-looking urban value or that localism necessarily breeds nostalgia for organic community. In fact, urban community movements have often sought to defend the use values attached to specific locales against the instability of an urban space that is repeatedly reformed by the dictates of capitalist exchange value.[37] As Logan and Molotch have argued, contradictions between use and exchange values, between place as the site of lived community and place as commodity, are at the root of "truly urban conflict." Poor neighborhoods inhabited by racial minorities have been especially vulnerable to the rapid conversions of urban space over the last few decades; the forcible dislocation of these residents has been the invariable by-product of urban development projects intended to boost property values. In this light, mobility can hardly be affirmed as a more progressive stance than efforts to protect the use values of places and communities against the disembedding forces of capitalist spatial turnover.[38]

This conflict between urban use and exchange values is dramatized in a recent novel, *Tumbling,* by Diane McKinney-Whetstone, which depicts a low-income black residential neighborhood in Philadelphia that forms the site of a closely knit community modeled on the southern "village." Residents band together to protest and obstruct an urban renewal project undertaken by real estate developers and subsidized by the city administration, which threatens to raze the neighborhood. Despite the residents' efforts, their neighborhood church is bulldozed to clear the way for highway construction. *Tumbling* ends with the lines, "They would not be moved. No way, no way."[39] In the novel's closing scene, residents form a makeshift community on the debris of the church in a last-ditch and ultimately futile effort to preserve the use value of their neighborhood—futile because the community lacks the clout to overcome the pro-growth coalition jointly run by entrepreneurs, city officials, and political leaders.

It is because neighborhoods and communities are imbricated in wider and unequally structured webs of exchange value and political power that struggles to conserve local use value and communal integrity are almost always unsuccessful. For this reason, the author of the "Earthseed" text insists that readiness to move—to outer space, if need be—is critical for survival in modern capitalist cities. Like *Tumbling,* the first part of Butler's novel laments the inevitable defeat of movements to maintain local and communal self-sufficiency. The Robledo neighborhood cannot survive because its relative financial and social stability is structurally interconnected to the extremely unstable masses of the poor and pyromaniacs who throng outside the walls of Robledo and who eventually burn down the neighborhood.

Just before the destruction of Robledo, Lauren Olamina preaches a funeral sermon for her father, commemorating his attempts to preserve the integrity and durability of locale and community: "We have our island community, fragile, and yet a fortress. Sometimes it seems too small and too weak to survive. . . . But . . . it persists. . . . This is our place, no matter what" (120). This is, however, a funeral sermon, and Lauren is mourning the death of traditional conceptions of community rooted in a fixed and impermeable sense of place. At the end of her sermon, a member of the community begins to sing, "We Shall Not Be Moved," to which Lauren mentally responds, "We'll be moved, all right. It's just a matter of when, by whom, and in how many pieces" (121). Appropriately enough, then, the first half of the novel traces the literal destruction of Lauren's home, neighborhood, and community in Robledo, and the second half describes her journey north (with a band of fellow travelers she picks up on the way) toward a new community. The novel ends soon after the group reaches its destination. The entire action of the novel reveals the impossibility of maintaining "village" ideals of community in postmodern times. In this sense, even as it dramatizes the collapse of actual cities, the novel insists on an urban understanding of place and community as the inescapable basis for constructing alternate images of social order.

The journey section of the novel traces the formation of a contingent community on the move—"born right here on Highway 101," as Lauren puts it (200). This "crew of a modern underground railroad" (262) is distinguished by the fact that most of its members are racially mixed and therefore "natural allies" in a society that frowns on miscegenation (186). Most members of the group have suffered some form of injustice, whether caused by poverty, forced prostitution, child abuse, or debt slavery. The sole purpose that cements this group of diverse people is their resolve to move toward a better future. Despite the natural reference of its name, Earth-seed is not an organic community unified by collective memory, ethnicity, shared cultural heritage, or attachment to place. Like the urban community constituted by the book of "Life Stories" in *PUSH,* the Earthseed group is racially and culturally mixed, and demands constant efforts of transla-tion. The boundaries of the community, the porous lines between insiders and outsiders, allies and enemies, must be continually redrawn; they must "embrace diversity or be destroyed" (176). The process of finding unity in diversity is necessarily risky and difficult, requiring the ability to interpret unfamiliar cultural codes and the alert balancing of suspicion and trust typ-ical of urban social interactions. This group makes collective decisions by way of debate and persuasion rather than by appeals to tradition.

Given the novel's insistence on this decisively urban model of commu-nity, the settlement established by Lauren and her Earthseed group at the end of the novel surely appears puzzling. The journey that takes up most of the second half of the novel ends in Humboldt County in California, on a piece of property owned by Bankole, one of the group of travelers who journey north with Lauren. The economy projected by the Earth-seed community at the end of the novel is small in scale, primitive, and self-sufficient in the sense that farming, breeding livestock, and building shelters are expected to take care of basic production and consumption needs.[40] It is clear that jobs paying money are scarce in neighboring towns and, given that several members of the community are former debt slaves or throwaway laborers, working Bankole's land seems preferable to selling labor. One of the more valuable features of Bankole's land is its isolation; because it is "far removed from any city" (281), it is relatively immune to attack from outsiders. That the area's distance from cities is viewed as an advantage is not surprising considering that cities, as centers of asymmetrical accumulation, have been shown throughout the novel to be especially vulnerable to criminal violence targeting the scarce commodity. The Earthseed community plans to guard its settlement by assigning members to keep watch at night and later by training dogs to protect the property.

How is this settlement different from the walled community of the beginning of the novel? Robledo was destroyed because its goal of local self-sufficiency was unfeasible given its dependence on a wider, starkly inequitable economic order. The community at the end of the novel recognizes, though it cannot quite reckon with, these inevitable connections. Despite some affinities with Arcadian rural communities such as the island of Willow Springs in Gloria Naylor's *Mama Day* (discussed in detail in chapter 4), the Earthseed community cannot be regarded as Arcadian in that it does not presume the essential simplicity of human needs.[41] The potentially destabilizing desire to accumulate surplus, on the part of individuals and the group, is expressed in a member's remark that he wants a job outside the community that will pay money as well as in the community's plan to sell surplus produce in nearby towns. The members of the community insist on the provisional nature of their settlement; there are "no guarantees" (288), Lauren points out, and should their experimental community fail, they will have to be prepared to move on.

Yet the Earthseed community also aims impossibly to maintain local self-containment and stability. The novel's concluding image of community does not suggest a more viable balancing of use and exchange values, localism and mobility, than does its opening image of the walled "cul-de-sac" neighborhood. The Robledo section of the novel sounds the death knell for place-bound notions of community, and the journey section reaches for a different model of community that is not coextensive with place, and place that is conceived as a "concrete abstraction" rather than as a self-enclosed site of social meaning. Butler wrestles with the difficulties of writing a fiction adequate to this understanding of place and community, yet the novel ends with an insulated, agrarian, face-to-face model of community that is not so distinct, after all, from the walled community of Robledo. In this respect, the Earthseed settlement is symptomatic of the difficulty that limits the contemporary literary imagination seeking utopian urban alternatives.[42] The small-scale, self-sufficient, agrarian ideal established at the end of Butler's novel is rife with contradictions: even as the Earthseed group recognizes that any truly alternate social vision requires wholesale transformation of global economic order, they end up thinking small because the abstraction of this order makes it difficult to grasp and imagine large-scale change. Or, in Manuel Castells's expression, "When people find themselves unable to control the world, they simply shrink the world to the size of their community."[43] Perhaps the real utopian propensity of *Parable of the Sower* lies not in its achieved images of community but in its emphasis on the human agency required for social transition, and in its affirmation of the sheer will to change, even when this will can find no secure or satisfactory object.

Wideman's approach to the problem of urban community is similarly fraught with contradiction. Like *Parable*, *Philadelphia Fire* demonstrates the fragility of place-based notions of community in postmodern urban environments. Mobility and simultaneous occupation of several places are necessary conditions for postmodern urban writing because no place remains still long enough to permit a stable spatial or temporal perspective. When Cudjoe first returns to Philadelphia after a nearly decade-long absence, he searches for his old haunts preserved "like stage sets" in his memories, but these places are "gone," they have been "urban-removed" (85). As in Butler's novel, the longing for spatial permanence is couched in pastoral terms, as, for example, when Cudjoe sets out to find the "green oasis" of Clark Park, where he played as a child (28). Wideman, like Butler, refuses the nostalgic retrospective vision that often characterizes pastoral alternatives to the urban present: "Oh, it [the city] must have been beautiful once. Walking barefoot in green grass, the sky a blue haven, the deep woods full of life. Now the grit of old dogshit," along with drugs and guns, attests to the decay of the green ideal in the postmodern city (159–60). The novel derides this backward-looking stance as a prime example of what Raymond Williams famously terms the "escalator" effect of the pastoral mode, whereby every age harks back to a prior age of perfection and simplicity.[44] To illustrate this effect, Cudjoe reaches back to one of the earliest Western pastoral images, the Garden of Eden, and imagines Adam and Eve "missing the good ole days, how things used to be, and they ain't been in the garden five minutes" (130).

But the novel's approach to the pastoral is far more mixed than the simple mockery of the preceding passages might suggest. *Philadelphia Fire* remains strongly sympathetic to the pastoral when it operates as a means of direct engagement with contemporary urban problems. The novel's epigraph, quoting William Penn, governor of Pennsylvania and founder of Philadelphia, offers one instance of the pastoral mode used to envision an ideal urban order: "Let every house be placed, if the Person pleases, in the middle of its platt ... so there may be ground on each side, for Gardens or Orchards or feilds, that it may be a greene Country Towne, which will never be burnt, and always be wholsome." Despite its urban rather than agrarian setting, Penn's vision of a garden city is in keeping with the American pastoral tradition, which, as characterized by Leo Marx, idealizes cultivated landscapes located in the "middle ground" between nature and culture.[45] The garden city ideal presented in the epigraph is ironized by juxtaposition with the novel's action, which centers around the conflict between the city of Philadelphia and the MOVE community, and ends in the very calamity Penn wished to preempt—the burning of sixty-one houses. Although *Philadelphia Fire* stresses the distance between Penn's garden ideal and the realities of late-twentieth-century Philadelphia, as an ideal the garden image remains imaginatively compelling to the novel's narrator, even if only as a means of measuring the magnitude of contemporary urban decay.

The novel's assessment of the other garden ideal presented in the novel—MOVE's vision of the earth as a "peaceful garden" (11)—is equally mixed. MOVE (short for "The Movement") was founded in the late 1960s by Vincent Leapheart, later known as John Africa. The social and philosophical beliefs of MOVE were contained in a text titled "The Book of Guidelines," more commonly referred to by MOVE members as "The Book," which was a typed manuscript dictated by Leapheart and transcribed by a white community college professor named Donald Glassey. According to this book, MOVE stood for "life, natural law, which ... made pure air, clean water, fertile soil, ... and made the principle of freedom" against "man's law that has created and sanctioned industry that is polluting the air, poisoning the water, the soil." Leapheart identified "man's system" with all forms of technology and culture, including science, industry, medicine, electricity, and education. MOVE targeted the modern city as a concentrated manifestation of the evils of man's system and in particular as a social form built by technology and geared around consumption.[46] Like the Earthseed cult in *Parable of the Sower*, MOVE sought to expose capitalist society's failure to fulfill the needs it induces, and to opt out of this system by tailoring consumption to satisfy only the "natural" demands of health and survival. MOVE's practices, in keeping with its naturalist philosophy, of leaving open garbage to decompose in the yard, letting scores of unvaccinated dogs and cats run free on their property, and keeping their children uneducated and scantily clad even in winter, brought it into conflict with its neighbors, whose repeated complaints to the police and the city administration eventually led to the infamous siege and bombing of the MOVE house in West Philadelphia on May 13, 1985.

MOVE members also forced a confrontation with the city by refusing to pay utility bills and openly violating city health and housing codes. MOVE refused the city's compromise offer to relocate to an isolated spot in the country, where its back-to-nature practices would not offend neighbors. According to an untitled document written by MOVE women in prison, the group saw its location in the heart of the city as crucial to its purpose: "As long as the city exists, to move to the country would be to divert from the problem and not to correct it. . . . The city was once the country. But it is city now, because the sickness MOVE is talking about spread itself and will keep spreading if it isn't stopped. It is MOVE's work to stop this sickness."[47] As is clear from this passage, MOVE's back-to-nature ideology was intended to provide not an imaginary elsewhere but a vehicle of direct opposition to the city.

In *Philadelphia Fire,* Wideman alters some details (mostly names of members) but preserves the basic principles motivating MOVE's assault on city life. Wideman highlights MOVE's critique of urban progress tracked in terms of increased material comforts, rising levels of consumption, and technological advancement. To oppose this notion of progress, the leader of MOVE, whose name in the novel is Reverend King, deploys the rhetoric of an innocent human nature corrupted by urban society. Although King uses the image of the garden to evoke the inherent harmony between humanity and nature, MOVE's ideology diverges quite sharply from the classic American pastoral ideal encapsulated in the epigraph from William Penn. Distinguishing between pastoral and primitivism, Leo Marx writes that whereas the pastoral mode locates human well-being in a realm that mediates between nature and society, primitivism celebrates humanity's closeness to the pole of primal nature.[48] In *Philadelphia Fire,* Reverend King, described as a "nouveau Rousseau" (84), elaborates his primitivist conception of humanity through the parable of a "holy Tree of Life" being destroyed by "the rotten system of this society" (10). Like Butler's Lauren Olamina, King figures human beings as "seeds" destined to "carry forward the Life in us," so that when "society dies from the poison in its guts, we'll be there and the Tree will grow bigger and bigger till the whole wide earth a peaceful garden under its branches" (11). The Earthseed religion and the MOVE cult employ the common seed metaphor to vastly different ends: whereas in *Parable of the Sower* seeds symbolize the indeterminacy and mobility of a human nature subject to constant transformation, Reverend King's seed image serves a social project aimed at recovering an essential human nature.

In Wideman's novel, MOVE's naturalistic beliefs and practices are brutally suppressed by the city because, unlike Earthseed, which thoroughly endorses the achievements of modern science and technology, MOVE repudiates every aspect of modern urban life. As the cultural attaché to the mayor of Philadelphia explains to Cudjoe, the mayor had no choice but to snuff out the organization because they were "trying to turn back the clock. Didn't want no kind of city. . . . Wanted to live like people in the woods. . . . Mayor breaking his butt to haul the city into the twenty-first century and them fools on Osage want their block to go to the jungle" (81). Other references to the group as a bunch of "savages" (13) made conspicuous by their dreadlocked hair indicate that it is the racially coded primitivism of MOVE that is so menacing to the city administration committed to urban development.[49] Reverend King actively solicits this perception, calling himself "the funk king" (12) and encouraging his followers to embrace the dirt and smell of their naked "natural sel[ves]" (15). The critical dimensions of King's rhetoric of funk are strikingly reminiscent of Toni Morrison's *The Bluest Eye*, which evokes funk to figure a natural racial identity repressed in modern urban society. Both of these critiques of urban life ground themselves in an imagined past that guarantees their naturalistic definitions of human (and specifically racial) essence.

Philadelphia Fire clarifies the only partial effectivity of this kind of social critique through its paradoxical appraisal of King's turn to primitivism: "even though he did it wrong, he was right" (13). MOVE was right in discrediting consumerist notions of the good life promised by the postmodern city. But MOVE "did it wrong" because, although based in the city, it sought to reinstate an organic ideal of community that is not only impossible to maintain in modern times but is also suspect even as a hypothetical construct. King envisages the MOVE community as a "tribe" (13) and a "family" (10). Margaret Jones, a former member of MOVE, points out the hierarchical and authoritarian tendencies often implicit in communities modeled on families when she tells Cudjoe, "I was part of his family. One his slaves that quick" (13). Through a brief mention of coercive sex, the novel hints at the gendered power imbalances as well as the enforced heterosexual norms that are naturalized by familial tropes of community. For Wideman, as for Butler, a critique of familial models of community does not amount to an underestimation of the value of family as such. The crucial importance of familial bonds is repeatedly emphasized in *Philadelphia Fire*, but the many lost children in the novel demonstrate that families cannot transcend systemic socioeconomic conditions. Like *Parable of the Sower*, Wideman's novel rejects not family per se but the use of familial metaphors of utopian community.[50]

Uses of the term *tribe* as a trope for lost community are also indirectly undermined in a passage that seems to be mocking Afrocentric narratives of a golden age of ethnic purity: "Tall tales about . . . long ago . . . when our clan spoke with one voice and followed the ancient ways, . . . when our flesh was a fit vessel for the ancestral spirits. . . . Old sad stories because now we are fallen, laid low" (171). Extended beyond its immediate Afrocentric reference,[51] this barbed passage can be taken as a critical comment on so many recent reactions against postmodern urban life that deploy the tropes of family, tribe, and ancestry. Such tropes of racial community, because they are always moored to an idealized and irretrievable past, can only evade the difficulties of constructing community in present urban conditions. In this respect, both *Philadelphia Fire* and *Parable of the Sower,* even as they draw on the pastoral mode to reinforce their critiques of the contemporary American city, also emphatically disengage themselves from the pastoral (and the primitivist) tendency to locate alternate communities in a mythical golden age.

The contradictions in Butler's and Wideman's treatments of community are greatly revealing of the ways in which contemporary discourses of urban crisis contour the imaginative range of postmodern African-American fiction. Although both authors expose the inadequacy of organic notions of community, they also acknowledge the powerful appeal of such notions in the postmodern era. Moreover, neither Wideman nor Butler is able to imagine utopian models of community that are commensurate with postmodern urban conditions. To this extent, they concede some ground to urban crisis discourses that proclaim the collapse of community in the postmodern city and that measure this collapse by positing healthy black communities that are invariably removed in time or space—either to an earlier golden era of the northern urban ghetto or to the rural South.

Manuscripts and Print Commodities: Urban Reading Communities

The question of representing black urban community in literature has become deeply fraught for African-American writers over the last couple of decades for a set of interlocking reasons. As I argue in chapter 1, the idea of community is steeply inflated in discourses on urban crisis and the "underclass," which tend to displace the economic problems plaguing U.S. cities onto the sphere of black culture and community. It is hardly surprising in such a context that so many African-American writers feel obliged to represent cohesive black communities even (and perhaps especially) when they wish to refute current "underclass" discourses. But this endeavor is made difficult by the widely circulating arguments that the formations of the "new" black middle class and the "underclass" have been closely intertwined and that, in fact, black urban poverty has been exacerbated by a black middle-class exodus from the ghetto. Such theories place a severe burden of guilt and responsibility on African-American writers who identify with the middle class and who wish to address a wider black urban community.

Each of the novels I examine in this chapter contains some sort of fictional representation of an underclass and centrally explores the question of how the writer of literature might speak to as well as for disadvantaged black urban constituencies. Tropes of the book offer particularly apt vehicles for exploring this question, because, as producers of commodities, authors are necessarily separated in space and time from their readerships, which can only be known as abstract entities. The commodity status of the printed book has always impinged on questions about the value of literature, but these questions appear more pressing than ever in the postmodern era, when cities are restructured as "consumption artifacts" and when all cultural production is thoroughly incorporated into commodity capitalism. Within such a context, how (if at all) can print literacy serve its modern function of safeguarding a cultural sphere of autonomy and critical distance from the marketplace? It is surely telling that the postmodern African-American novels that remain invested in the modern print legacy all feature the trope of the manuscript rather than the commodity object of the printed book.

PUSH and *Parable* re-create unique circumstances of manuscript circulation that are meant to override the problem of time-space distanciation inherent to commodity culture and to project reading communities that are face to face but nonetheless urban in some key respects. These novels are rare postmodern texts that take dystopian cities as their settings but remain undaunted by crises of urban literary representation. Butler and Sapphire offer resolutions to these crises that are possible only at a fictive level, by imagining scenes of reading and writing that are removed from the sphere of commodity consumption. Such reception contexts help obviate authorial anxieties about the delocalized community of readers constituted by the printed book. Both novels synthesize silent reading and oral communication to project knowable reading communities that can validate the writer's social function.

"Life Stories" in *PUSH,* as noted earlier, is an anthology jointly written by women who would likely be identified as belonging to an urban "underclass." This typed manuscript is appended to the end of Sapphire's novel and represents the final group project of the literacy class as well as the culmination of Precious's quest for literacy. Because this manuscript embodies the end product of the literacy class and is placed at the very end of *PUSH,* questions about its circulation are not raised as significant issues in Sapphire's novel. It is, nevertheless, crucial that "Life Stories" is a typed manuscript with a clearly defined readership rather than a print commodity whose distribution escapes authorial control. The circulation of the manuscript is restricted to the students and teacher of the literacy class. As is clear from some of the contributions to the anthology, "Life Stories" has taken shape through a dialogic process, with members of the class reading and commenting on earlier drafts of each other's entries and often incorporating responses to each other's entries within their own.

Dialogue also characterizes the process by which Precious acquires literacy in the course of the novel. When Precious first enters the special education class, she is functionally illiterate. Her instructor, Blue Rain, teaches her to read and write using the method of "the dialogue journal":

> You know how you write to teacher 'n she write back to you in the same journal book like you talkin' on paper and you could SEE your talk coming back to you when the teacher answer you back. I mean thas what had made me really like writing in the beginning, knowing my teacher gonna write me back when I talk to her. (94)

If, as Marshall McLuhan and Walter Ong have argued, writing accentuates the distancing sense of sight and subordinates the immersing properties of sound,[52] sight and sound are inextricably fused in Precious's dialogue-journal. The trope of "talking on paper" mitigates the alienation of the subject endemic to writing, which entails abstraction from an immediate spatiotemporal context, yet this trope still preserves the dynamic of mediated expression involved in putting words down on paper. Sapphire's novel thus overcomes the polarization of book and oral tradition, of urban and organic communities, that prevails in much postmodern African-American fiction (analyzed in the next two chapters). For example, Toni Morrison's *Jazz* configures the book as a commodity object that mutely registers the urban author's distance from his or her audience, in contrast to southern oral tradition, which draws its listeners into a circle of intimate community. These polarities simply do not figure in *PUSH*, where the literacy class is described as a "circle" that first makes Precious aware that she belongs to a community (62). Although this reading and writing community is face to face, it is distinct from the folk communities associated with southern oral tradition in that it is not rooted in race, place, or cultural tradition. Refiguring writing as talking on paper, *PUSH* is able to affirm a literate community that is urban in the sense that it achieves intimacy by means of difficult acts of mediation among strangers.

Parable of the Sower takes a strikingly parallel approach to the question of how to imagine urban reading communities that are at once mediated and united by a common, contingent purpose. Lauren's sacred book consists of a collection of verses encapsulating the precepts of the Earthseed religion. This text is written by hand in one of Lauren's school exercise books and is passed around and read aloud among the members of the traveling Earthseed community. That the "Earthseed" text is not a commodity to be bought and sold is essential to Butler's redemptive vision of writing. Lauren's manuscript circulates freely among a select group of readers and so manages to address the immediately visible community that is typically associated with folk modes of communication. As in *PUSH,* the novel's fictional situation closes the gap between reading and listening, author and audience. Its author is physically present to oversee the text's reception by her audience, which is the delimited community of her fellow travelers. If the commodity object of the printed book often arouses authorial anxieties about the unknowability of urban community, in Butler's novel the processes of reading aloud and discussing the text of "Earthseed" bind the community together into a purposive whole.

The author of "Earthseed" is always present in person to explain and defend the book's contents, which are often contested by its audience of listeners and readers. Moreover, in contrast to the complete, autonomous, and static nature of printed books, "Earthseed" is a context-bound text rather than a finished product in that Lauren is engaged in writing throughout the course of the journey. Her writing bears a dialectical relation to the ongoing life of the group, drawing its subject matter from the group's experience and in turn shaping the group's understanding of this experience. In this sense, the book, as suggested by its title, is literally a book of and for the living. In another sense, however, the content of this book remains fixed and unrevised by its readers' contestations. Despite the group's vigorous arguments over the meaning of the book, the interpretation of "Earthseed" is never subject to crisis. Lauren dismisses Bankole's suggestion that readers of the text will transform it beyond recognition with the assertion, "Not around me they won't!" (234).

The authoritative status of "Earthseed" is further reinforced by the fact that although excerpts from it are occasionally included as quoted passages within the text of *Parable,* they most often appear as epigraphs to the novel's chapters. Typographically set off from the body of the text, these epigraphs visually summon up the transcendent authority of disembedded discourse and, indeed, actually function as sacred discourse. Lauren observes that sacred books such as the Bible, the Talmud, or the Koran help people in times of trouble to "remember a truth or a comfort or a reminder to action" (198). This is exactly how the text of "Earthseed" works, inspiring and guiding the novel's characters as well as framing and illuminating the action presented in the novel.

The "Earthseed" book exercises this sacred power even in its oral dissemination. When Lauren preaches from the book, one member of her audience mockingly responds with an "Amen" (197), but Lauren quite literally refers to her readers as converts (200). The only text other than

"Earthseed" that appears in the novel as decontextualized, framing discourse is a passage from another sacred book, the Bible. The parable of the sower, quoted from the book of Luke, supplies both the title and the epigraph for the novel. Figuring Jesus Christ as the sower, the seed as the sacred word, and varieties of soil as different types of listeners, this parable essentially addresses the problems of creating a spiritually responsive community. The typographically distinct appearance of the biblical parable and of excerpts from "Earthseed," as well as obvious parallels between the seed metaphor employed by these two sacred texts, encourages us to equate the written text of "Earthseed" with divine oral utterance. This equation appears truly remarkable in light of the fact that so much postmodern African-American fiction presents writing as a technology that desacralizes the organic community unified around oral utterance. Integrating the spoken and written word, text and interpretation, author and community, Butler's novel invests the writer with redemptive powers.

Unlike her fictional author, Octavia Butler clearly experiences some unease about the fact that her reading audience is shaped by the market imperatives of the book publishing industry. In a 1990 interview with Randall Kenan, Butler says that she dislikes generic labels such as "science fiction" because they are "marketing tools," "inhibiting factors" that predetermine and limit her audience. In a later interview, Stephen Potts asks Butler whether she would like to "break down some of the walls between generic marketing categories," to which Butler responds, "Oh, that's not possible.... They're there, ... and there's nothing you can do about it."[53] But in *Parable,* Butler creates a fictional situation in which the existence of money and commodity markets is a "hopeful sign" rather than a source of modernist dismay (52). During the course of their journey north, the Earthseed group periodically visits guarded supermarkets where they can buy commodities for survival, including some books. In the novel's dystopia, supermarkets provide the only secure places where consumption is ordered by the principle of exchange. In view of the looting that otherwise characterizes consumption in the novel's cities, the operation of money and commodity markets, ensuring the universal commensurability of exchange value, constitutes an essential condition for social order and signification. Yet the novel nowhere considers how the conditions of commodity exchange mediate the circulation of books or the construction of cultural value.

Both Sapphire and Butler are able to affirm the salvational power of literacy only by first dissociating it from the circuits of exchange value that govern all cultural production in the postmodern era. Tropes of the book as a manuscript rather than a print commodity allow for a peculiarly smooth resolution to postmodern crises of urban literary representation. *Parable* and *PUSH* refuse organic and folk notions of community, insisting instead on the need to forge contingent associations among strangers. But their unique scenes of reading and writing install face-to-face rather than abstract communities, exempting each novelist from frontally encountering the crises of knowability that preoccupy so much urban fiction. In *PUSH,* the literacy instructor thus describes the task of reading: "The author has a message and the reader's job is to decode that message as thoroughly as possible. A good reader is like a detective, she say, looking for clues in the text. A good reader is like you, Precious, she say. Passionate! Passionately involved with whut they are reading" (108). This account of good reading, expressed through the quintessentially urban metaphor of reading as detection, perfectly captures the special terms under which *PUSH* and *Parable of the Sower* rehabilitate modern literacy for postmodern times, conjoining as it does decoding and passionate involvement, immersion and mediation.

Wideman's approach to problems of urban literary representation is more pessimistic than is Butler's or Sapphire's, as is clear even from the novel's recurrent analogies among urban authorship, detection, and "sleaze control" (46). In *Philadelphia Fire,* urban writing cannot assume a cohesive community of readers or elude the conditions of commodity consumption, even when this writing takes the form of a sacred manuscript rather than a printed book. That urban reading communities can never be known in advance by their authors is illustrated by the bizarre movement of "The Book of Life" through the city of Philadelphia. "The Book of Life" is Wideman's title for the MOVE text, called "The Book" or "The Guidelines," which was disseminated in a variety of ways to an audience wider than the MOVE community. Donald Glassey, who transcribed, typed, and edited this text, taught it to his sociology classes at Philadelphia Community College. Passages from the book were also read aloud and broadcast, through an electrically powered bullhorn, to MOVE's neighbors on Osage Avenue.[54] Although "The Book" reached a larger audience than the immediate MOVE community, its dissemination was nevertheless controlled by MOVE members and served the unequivocal function of publicizing MOVE ideology.

In *Philadelphia Fire,* Wideman imagines a far more wide-ranging and indeterminate trajectory for "The Book of Life," highlighting its unpredictable appropriations as it exchanges hands in the city. We learn, in the third part of the novel, that "The Book of Life" is currently in the possession of Richard Corey (a character clearly based on Donald Glassey), who originally co-authored the book with the leader of MOVE. Corey wrote the book to propagate MOVE's visionary ideal of the Tree of Life that would regenerate the decaying city. But Corey finds that the seeds of hope the book was meant to nurture, embodied in the children of the city, have degenerated into terrible weeds that are poisoning urban life. This realization dawns on Corey after he is mugged by a gang of adolescents. Disillusioned by the perversion of his green ideal, Corey translates the "secrets, stored in the sacred Book of Life," into the "snarly pig tongue" of law and order (167). In other words, like his real-life counterpart Donald Glassey, Corey becomes an informer, betraying incriminating information about MOVE to the police. Corey's case illustrates a persistent logic whereby all efforts to imagine ideal social orders ultimately capitulate to the city's repressive system of law and order; Corey's conversion from visionary writer to police informant grimly confirms Cudjoe's analogy between urban authorship and sleaze control.

Corey retains possession of "The Book of Life" until his death by suicide, after which his briefcase, containing the book, is stolen by JB, the homeless man and occasional narrator of the third part of *Philadelphia Fire*. Unlike the actual MOVE book of guidelines, which was a typed manuscript, "The Book of Life" is here revealed to be a handwritten journal. We learn from the fragments read by JB that the book, written from the dismayed perspective of an adult, announces the arrival of "The Children's Hour," when disgruntled gangs of adolescents will take over the city and propagate their own violent misreading of the book. JB soon abandons the effort to decipher the tiny and barely legible script and nods off to sleep. He wakes up to find that a group of kids has stolen the book from him and has set him on fire. JB then imagines that he is preaching or singing to a multitude of people from "The Book of Life." But the book suddenly turns to smoke and ashes in his hands, in yet another reprise of the novel's symbolic pattern of the green ideal destroyed by urban conflagration. This particular stage in the book's travels is left deliberately vague. JB, along with readers of *Philadelphia Fire,* does not know whether the fire and the theft of the book have happened in fact, or in someone else's dream narrated in a book, or in an imaginary book that JB himself is writing. In a heavy-handed gesture intended to suggest the uncertain destiny of the book circulating in the city, Wideman informs us, "All were possibilities" (189).

Two interrelated aspects of the trajectory of "The Book of Life" through Philadelphia are especially striking—its shifting content and its mode of circulation by theft. Although the authorship of the book appears to remain fixed, its content, the parable of the tree of life co-authored by Reverend King and Richard Corey, undergoes dramatic transformations as the book changes hands. Its regenerative vision carries widely divergent implications for the various people who handle the book. To MOVE members, the Tree of Life symbolizes an Arcadian ideal of simple human needs that can be satisfied without violating the natural order. In Richard Corey's image of "the rainbow children of Life, all born to Life's bounty" (167), the book prefigures the possibility of racial and civic harmony, and of natural resources evenly distributed among all. Both King and Corey envisage the city's children as wholesome seeds containing the hope of genuine, not cosmetic, urban renewal.

When members of a children's gang seize the book, they use and misuse it to serve their own interests, preserving some elements of the book's original meaning but revising others beyond recognition. The children, who had formed the redemptive protagonists of "The Book of Life" but have now become its readers and authors, endorse the book's primitivist conception of children as embodiments of the purity of nature: "Our bodies are perfect and clean." Echoing MOVE's attack on education as an instrument of social repression, the children castigate the school system for treating them "like beasts who must be tamed." But they stretch this romanticist view of children into a rationale for usurping from adults the rewards of consumer society. Their assertion of their "perfect right to Money, Power, and Things" (91) is a far cry from MOVE's ideal of natural desires fulfilled by modest levels of consumption. An unspecified narrator announces and asks, in the third part of the novel, "The Book of Life exchanges hands. Who will read it next, kill for it next?" (160). The book wreaks havoc as it travels through the city. The children's interpretation of the book directs its life-giving vision toward violence, robbery, and arson, transmuting its green ideal to fire, smoke, and ashes. Obviously, the urban context, built on "Money, Power, and Things," constrains readings of the book, converting its green ideal into a pretext for arson and violence.

The transformations in the meaning of "The Book of Life" are abetted by the book's mode of circulation in the city. Like the "Earthseed" text in Butler's novel, "The Book of Life" is a handwritten manuscript, not a printed book distributed within a system of commodity exchange. In *Parable,* the noncommodity status of the "Earthseed" text limits its dissemination to a carefully chosen community of listeners. In *Philadelphia Fire,* even though the book is not technically a commodity, its meaning as well as its readership elude authorial control. The book is stolen by unforeseen readers, and its meanings are sometimes simply mislaid, as in the case of JB, who easily gives up the struggle to decode the text and falls asleep, allowing the children's gang to steal the book and redirect its message. The book's circulation by theft as well as its varying uses might be taken to suggest that *Philadelphia Fire* construes reading as an act that can disrupt the prevailing order of the postmodern city as a "consumption artifact." In his influential account of reading as a practice of resistant consumption, Michel de Certeau has questioned the hierarchical division of labor perpetuated by modern ideologies of writing, which cast authors as producers and readers as passive consumers. The "efficiency of production implies the inertia of consumption." But, in fact, de Certeau argues, "to read is to wander through an imposed system (that of the text, analogous to the constructed order of a city or of a supermarket). Recent analyses show that 'every reading modifies its object.'" De Certeau goes on to compare reading with poaching, a form of consumption that violates the laws of property and text.[55]

In *Philadelphia Fire*, the many thefts of "The Book of Life" result in willful misreadings that disobey the laws of property and text, but this does not necessarily make these readings instances of resistant consumption in de Certeau's sense. The "constructed order" of Wideman's city is a rigidly segregated and asymmetrical order of consumption. Theft draws attention to the inequalities of this system (as is clear from the "commodity riots" that have flared in American cities since the 1960s),[56] but theft also capitulates to the ideologies of consumption that ratify postmodern urban order. In *Philadelphia Fire*, the order of the city is analogous to the order of a supermarket in its relentless promotion of commodities as the sole repositories of value. This urban order channels readings of the book, transforming its anticonsumption message into yet another exhortation to consume by any means necessary, even theft. When the children's gang uses the book to sanction a violent seizure of "Money, Power, and Things," they may be flouting the laws of property and text but they are not thereby producing a reading that exceeds either the dominant urban ideologies of consumption or the socioeconomic structures normalized by these ideologies. Even when the book is not a commodity and when its principal message is to refuse the lure of commodity consumption, it is stolen and consumed as if it were a prized and scarce commodity. Although Wideman's novel acknowledges the plural and indeterminate readings made available in the city, it ultimately suggests that the oppositional potential of these readings is contained by the socioeconomic and ideological system of the postmodern city.

Postmodern Uses of Print Literacy

To say that *Philadelphia Fire* reveals the limited oppositional powers of reading is not the same as saying that the novel invests no social value in acts of critical literacy. To the contrary, Wideman, like Butler and Sapphire, remains strongly committed to defending the modern tradition of print literacy against the assault of electronic technologies. In the postmodern period, print culture is often deemed to be on the verge of extinction insofar as it is associated with individualist, elitist, and hierarchical ideologies, whereas the new technologies are said to be more amenable to the claims of diverse social constituencies.[57] Butler, Sapphire, and Wideman actively participate in these debates about the social legitimacy of print culture, specifically exploring the question of what use, if any, it may serve for those racial groups previously underrepresented in this culture.

Contrary to the claim that electronic technologies are sponsoring a pluralist culture that is more hospitable to minority groups than is its print counterpart,[58] Sapphire's novel suggests that print literacy can offer these groups a sense of agency denied them in electronic culture. At the beginning of the novel, when Precious is functionally illiterate, her mind is flooded with "TV set voices" telling her that, as a member of the "underclass," she is ugly, stupid, and invisible (38). Precious has internalized electronic media representations of the "underclass" so deeply that she cannot even identify herself as a subject: "Why can't I see myself, *feel* where I end and begin" (31). Once she joins the literacy class, Precious begins to acquire a sense of interiority and agency, and thereby to participate in the process of self-making that forms the hallmark of the modern tradition of print literacy.[59] The women in Precious's literacy class are required to keep journals expressing their feelings and giving narrative form to their experiences. Their instructor urges them to "Write what's on your mind" (60), because "feelin's is important" (64) and each individual "has a story to tell" (96). In these classroom scenes, print literacy is shown to be the most effective medium for instilling members of the "underclass," who are mute objects of representation in electronic media, with an awareness of their own subject status.

Further confirming the promise held out by print modernity, *PUSH* shows that acquisition of literacy equips individuals with the critical distance requisite to understanding their positions in society. It is only once she can read and write that Precious stops using television voices as metaphors for her own thoughts and is able to challenge formulaic media images of the black "underclass." Print literacy also offers Precious the power of choice, as the very name of her literacy program, Higher Education Alternative, suggests. At this point Precious does not "know what an alternative is" (16), but when she is told that "an alternative is like a choice, a different way to do something" (26), she makes her very first choice in the novel—to enroll in the literacy program. From this point onward, the novel develops in a clearly linear direction, tracing the stages in Precious's quest for literacy and culminating in the completed text of "Life Stories." Acquisition of print literacy is equated with "progress" (82) and is shown to lead to social distinction (Precious wins the mayor's Literacy Award for her outstanding achievement) as well as to an enhanced awareness of personal agency (to Precious, the award is "good proof . . . I can do anything" [88]).[60]

Sapphire's novel affirms literacy not only for its psychological and symbolic value as a medium of self-making but also for the pragmatic uses it can serve for disempowered groups. Before Precious learns how to read and write, she feels bewildered by official documents and institutions dealing with the urban poor, as illustrated by her fear of the "file" that she cannot decipher: "I wonder what exactly do file say. . . . pages the same for me, . . . I do know every time they wants to fuck wif me or decide something in my life, here they come wif the mutherfucking file" (28). Later in the novel, Precious steals her file from her social worker's office, and her literacy enables her to grasp the injustice of welfare policies and to challenge official discourses about urban poverty. This and numerous other examples exhibit the practical advantages of print literacy as a vehicle of social critique and advancement. Education in literacy offers Precious a means of moving out of dead-end jobs and of lifting herself and her children out of poverty.

Parable of the Sower is remarkably similar to *PUSH* in its affirmation of the pragmatic uses of print literacy in the crisis-ridden conditions confronting the poor in postmodern U.S. cities. Comparable to the figure of Ms. Rain, the literacy instructor in Sapphire's novel, is Butler's pedagogue Lauren Olamina, who is crucial to the novel's vision of social improvement. Widespread adult illiteracy is a striking feature of the urban dystopia presented in Butler's novel, which reaches back to a seemingly distant moment in the African-American literary tradition to press its case for the continuing value of literacy in postmodern times. The novel's overt allusions to the classic slave narrative scenario, in which the slave learns to read and write despite the master's prohibition,[61] suggest that the era of slavery is not so distant from our own and that unequal access to literacy and education remain serious impediments to the achievement of a democratic society. One of the main goals of the utopian Earthseed community is to provide education, and especially instruction in reading and writing, to illiterate adults. Lauren's profession of choice is to be a teacher, and in fact, while the group is on the road, Lauren uses the "Earthseed" book to teach the many illiterate members in the group to read and write. The Earthseed ideal of an equitable society hinges on universal extension of print literacy.

In Toni Morrison's *Song of Solomon,* the story of First Corinthians suggests that print literacy is a skill irrelevant to the restricted job market (offering mainly low-wage service employment) to which most African-American women have access. In *Parable of the Sower,* to the contrary, literacy is a highly marketable skill, as becomes clear when Lauren's brother is generously paid for reading instruction manuals to help illiterate adults operate their stolen, high-tech equipment. Lauren, too, hopes to get paid for her reading and writing skills, which, far from being the isolating attributes of an economically redundant intellectual class, are crucial to the very struggle for physical survival. Early in the novel, when Lauren first begins to realize that the future of her neighborhood is in jeopardy, she prepares herself for the impending catastrophe by reading her father's old books. From them, she gains practical information about handling medical emergencies, using plants for medicinal and nutritional purposes, building log cabins, raising livestock, making soap, and so forth. The skills Lauren learns from her reading pay off when Earthseed is on the road, in an area where water is scarce and exorbitantly priced, and Lauren is able to draw drinking water out of sand: "According to a couple of books I read, water is supposed to seep through the sand with most of the salt filtered out of it. . . . It might save our lives someday" (184). In this instance, as in many others, books possess an immediate use value that literally saves lives.

Butler's novel creates a fictional state of emergency so extreme that it credibly suppresses all the socially divisive implications of print literacy. The fact that some Earthseed members are literate whereas others are not never seems to provoke conflict within the group. Even the teacher-student relation between Lauren and the illiterate members of the group is free of its inherent power imbalance. The hierarchical specialization of roles that inevitably attends the introduction of reading and writing into a society is simply not raised as an issue in *Parable,* and in fact, this elision forms a necessary condition for the novel's salvational view of print literacy. Not coincidentally, Wideman's *Philadelphia Fire,* which offers a far more pessimistic evaluation of the practical uses of print literacy than does *Parable,* also presents literacy as "one of the most important axes of social differentiation in modern societies."[62]

Interviews as well as autobiographical and biographical sources reveal that Wideman is haunted by authorial anxiety and guilt about his privileged education. In the autobiographical *Brothers and Keepers,* Wideman describes his departure from home to the University of Pennsylvania as a flight "from poverty, from blackness": "To get ahead, to make something of myself, college had seemed a logical, necessary step; my exile, my flight from home began with good grades, with good English, with setting myself apart long before I'd earned a scholarship and a train ticket over the mountains to Philadelphia. With that willed alienation behind me, . . . guilt was predictable."[63] This guilt was apparently intensified by the many academic and literary distinctions that followed—a Rhodes scholarship, faculty appointment to an Ivy League institution, and two PEN/Faulkner awards for his fiction. Wideman says in an interview with Charles Rowell that one of the central aims of his fiction is to measure the distance between "the life of the black kid growing up in a predominantly black neighborhood" and "the life of a middle-class academic in a white world" and to "make some sense of the conflicts, contradictions, and possible resolutions" arising therein.[64]

Wideman's struggle to bridge the gap separating "the ghetto kid and the man of letters"[65] is dramatized in *Philadelphia Fire* through the dilemma faced by Cudjoe, a teacher, writer, and "Distinguished Negro Intellectual" (74), who, like Wideman, is plagued by the burden of representation placed upon him by his educational status. Cudjoe perceives his underprivileged black students in West Philadelphia as "his tabula rasas" (126), using the metaphor of writing to express his racial-uplift ambitions. Agonizing over the question of whether he is fit to be a "role model" to his students (128), Cudjoe (and perhaps Wideman) concedes too much ground to current "underclass" discourses, which attribute the persistence of black urban poverty to the absence of middle-class role models in the ghetto. Accordingly, Cudjoe regards his task as teacher and writer to be essentially that of uplifting the urban poor through the medium of print literacy.

However, in the urban context of the 1980s, Cudjoe finds the uplift ideal to be increasingly inaccessible to African-American intellectuals. One reason for this is that intra-racial class polarities appear to be sharpening as a result of urban redevelopment projects. In Wideman's fictional Philadelphia, these projects are designed to create the "University City" (79), founded on the ideal of "modern urban living in the midst of certified culture" (78). The notion of the University City has played a prominent part in earlier African-American literary ideals of urban order. Charles Scruggs, who traces the "trope of the university as a city upon a hill" in the works of early twentieth-century writers such as W. E. B. Du Bois and James Weldon Johnson, argues that this trope propagates an ideal of urban civilization based on the uplift of the black masses to elite cultural standards.[66] *Philadelphia Fire* exposes the difficulty of attaining this ideal in late-twentieth-century America, where the construction of the University City requires the forcible exclusion of the black urban poor.

Cudjoe is further paralyzed by the decline of the university's role as a public institution responsive to its urban environment. In the novel, the University of Pennsylvania shuts down its school of social work, the one institution that had earlier prepared African-American intellectuals to minister to "the immediate needs of the dispossessed urban proletariat surrounding the island of University" (112). The dismantling of the school, a gesture meant to quash "certain misconceptions about a university's role that had arisen in the sixties" (112), bears profound significance for Cudjoe, who is engaged in writing two books, one a study of the MOVE disaster and the other a novel about the sixties, a decade that has shaped his understanding of his social mission as an intellectual. With the debilitation of the sixties legacy of intellectual activism, Cudjoe feels crippled as a writer: he abandons the novel about the sixties, and we never find out whether the MOVE book ever gets written.

It is not through these projected books, however, but through a theatrical project that Cudjoe really tests the viability of the uplift ideal. Cudjoe plans to produce Shakespeare's *The Tempest* with a cast composed of his economically underprivileged and barely literate students in West Philadelphia. He describes the production of the play through an explicit image of black urban cultural achievement—"an ebony tower taller than Billy Penn's hat spouting to the stars" (132)—which, through its visual and symbolic suggestions of uplift, calls to mind the trope of the university as a city on a hill. In keeping with the University City ideal, Cudjoe's project casts the intellectual as the salvational agent who will uplift the black urban masses by teaching them literacy in high cultural texts. This stage production by poor black students of a canonical literary text forms the centerpiece of the novel, and the fact that a postmodern African-American novel so seriously considers this project as a means of social transformation surely appears odd. Postmodern literary and cultural theorists have assailed the canon of Western literature—the "great books" tradition—as the one product of print culture that most urgently needs to be overhauled.[67] In the modern print tradition, literature is privileged as a humanizing medium that can acculturate readers from diverse social backgrounds into a universal, timeless, and transcendent value system. By the 1960s, the widespread attack on the false universalism of Western humanist culture made the literary canon itself seem bankrupt. Instead of humanizing the reading subject, the study of literary classics was now seen to endow contemporary readers with "ideological blinders" that eased their accommodation to a hierarchical society.[68]

Antonin Artaud wrote, in his manifesto "No More Masterpieces," that "if the public does not frequent our literary masterpieces, it is because those masterpieces are literary, that is to say, fixed; and fixed in forms that no longer respond to the needs of the time."[69] In the United States during the 1960s, the attack on the literary canon came from racial minority groups and women, for whom "the Western literary tradition as taught in the universities exemplified the worst kinds of cultural arrogance, racism, and elitism—all masked under the mystifying clichés" of humanism and universal values.[70] Yet this is precisely the period—the late 1960s—when Wideman's fictional surrogate attempts to uplift his poor black urban students through a performance of Shakespeare. The ambitious hopes Cudjoe invests in this production appear absurdly inflated when he characterizes it as "Real guerilla theater. Better than a bomb. Black kids in the park doing Shakespeare will blow people's minds" (143). The play idea is obviously better than a bomb (though not in the sense meant by Cudjoe)—far better to perform Shakespeare in the park and blow people's minds than to blow up black children's bodies, as did the police when they bombed the

MOVE house in West Philadelphia. But what makes the black children's enactment of a literary text so politically subversive as to be called "guerilla theater"? More importantly, how can this literary project alter the course of the children's lives?

What Cudjoe's play project attempts is an adaptation of the modern print tradition, with the Western literary canon as its crowning achievement, to postmodern cultural demands. Cudjoe himself regards this project not strictly as uplift but as a synthesis of canonical literary and black vernacular traditions. Through his attempted fusion of "the Academy and the Street,"[71] Cudjoe seeks to bend the literary canon to make it "respond to the needs of the time," to borrow Artaud's words. Artaud's manifesto against the literary canon is also a defense of theater as a plastic medium that can more effectively capture the interests of the contemporary mass public. Artaud's preference for theater over print literature is perfectly in keeping with the drift of postmodern cultural theory, which tends to polarize the fixity of print against the malleability and performativity fostered by the new electronic technologies.[72] Cudjoe's project, which requires his students to first read and then enact *The Tempest,* aims to bridge print and performance media.

Cudjoe also presents his students with what he calls "an authentically revised version" of *The Tempest* as "a play about colonialism, imperialism" (127), thereby seeking to inculcate a critical literacy rather than an idolatrous posture toward the Western literary canon. Cudjoe's revision of the play bears the clear imprint of the "internal colony" model (applying the colonial model to the African-American situation) that was developed by black political thinkers and activists during the 1960s, thus illustrating Cudjoe's effort to update the canon to make it more responsive to contemporary political realities. Cudjoe's translation of Shakespeare into the sounds of black vernacular English exemplifies the parodic and playful propensities of postmodern cultural media. To quote Richard Lanham's memorable description of postmodern stances toward Western aesthetic masterpieces, Cudjoe's interpretation of *The Tempest* is akin to "calling the Mona Lisa out to play."[73]

Even Cudjoe's assessment of the precise manner in which the production will transform his students' lives suggests an attempted fusion of modern and postmodern, print and performative elements. Cudjoe believes that the play project—which he describes as his "gift to the community" (132)— can redirect the lives of the schoolchildren by teaching them "to be other than what they are" (127). Theatrical role-playing can expand the narrow horizons of the children's lives, enhancing their "capacity for make-believe" (149) and enabling them to imagine other possible selves and lives. Yet this imaginative potential inhering in performance forms is not so distinct from the modern idea of reading as a consciousness-expanding exercise, as suggested by the "alternatives" that print literacy makes available to Sapphire's protagonist. Both the reading and enactment of the play usher in "the moment when identities slip away" (149), and this transcendence of identity seems especially urgent for Cudjoe's students, whose class and racial status restrict them to a narrow range of possible future identities—as dishwashers, janitors, cooks, prisoners, sanitation workers, and housekeepers (117). In an ironic evocation of dominant discourses on the "underclass," Cudjoe writes that the play project will help counter "the inadequacy of your background, your culture. Its inability . . . to cast up . . . appropriate role models" (128). Despite the irony of this passage, however, Cudjoe's narration, along with Wideman's novel, seriously entertains the idea that the literate intellectual can perform a socially valuable function for the urban poor.

From the disillusioned perspective of the 1980s, Cudjoe himself retrospectively assesses the play scheme as a "harebrained project" (146) intended primarily to assuage his own sense of superfluity as a member of the privileged class. The play offers Cudjoe the delusory solace of active participation in the lives of the broader urban community from which he feels severed by class and educational achievement. Cudjoe's fantasy of social reconciliation betrays the excesses of his literary imagination as well as the self-justifying motives that drive his overestimation of the intellectual's redemptive role in society. The fact that the play never happens endorses this reading of Cudjoe's project as indeed harebrained, impractical, and far removed from the sphere of "real" social action. Significantly, it is during the late 1960s that Cudjoe's theatrical production is conceived and aborted. By setting the failure of the play project during this period, Wideman suggests that claims about the political efficacy of intellectual and cultural work were inflated even during the era that is widely considered to be the heyday of the politicized black academy.[74]

This harsh judgment of the play project is simultaneously asserted and ironized in a passage in which Cudjoe overtly comments on his own overvaluation of the literary imagination: "This is an irresponsible way of looking at things. . . . Better to light one little candle than to sit on one's ass and write clever, irresponsible, fanciful accounts of what never happened, never will. Lend a hand. Set down your bucket" (157). Read at face value, this passage devalues the writing of fiction as compared with concrete acts that serve tangible social functions. *Philadelphia Fire* clearly does not claim for intellectual and pedagogical work the urgent practical value it bears in *PUSH* and *Parable of the Sower*, where print literacy can literally save lives and bring about social advancement. But Wideman's novel does vest some social value in literature, although not a utilitarian value that can be measured through concrete material effects. In his interview with Charles

Rowell, Wideman insists that literary writing is not "instrumental" but "expressive." The fact that literature is not "totally task-oriented" forms the very core of its value for Wideman. Literature taps into the human "capacity for wonder, for play, for imagination," and because this is "the capacity that modern ... mass civilization is eroding," the literary artist can play "a crucial role."[75] The unique function of literature is to stretch reality, create illusions, entertain imaginary possibilities that must not be discredited because they do not directly fuel social change. It is in this sense that Cudjoe's project of staging Shakespeare's play is partially re-deemed. No practical social consequences follow from the play, which is in fact never staged. But during the 1980s, a decade acutely disheartening for politicized black intellectuals, the *idea* of staging the play is affirmed for the "endless circles of ... possibility" it opens up in the imagination (133). This modest social function is all that Wideman's novel can assign to liter-ature. Unlike Butler's novel, which attributes sacred as well as pragmatic powers to writing, *Philadelphia Fire* cannot cast the writer as "a cultural hero, or a priest," or even as a direct agent of social and political change.[76]

Not surprisingly, Wideman's non-utilitarian aesthetic entails a suspicion of social realism, long presumed to be the generic choice most suited to the task of racial representation. African-American literary texts treating urban experience have been held especially accountable to the demands of social realism: to cite only the most obvious instance, the nationalist aesthetic of the 1960s equated authentic racial representation in literature with ac-curate reflection of black urban realities. Even during the 1980s, when the influence of black nationalist aesthetics is presumed to have waned, such assumptions about realism and racial representation continue to ex-ercise considerable sway, as is clear from contemporaneous responses to *Philadelphia Fire*. Reviewers repeatedly pitted the literariness of Wideman's style against the urban realities he depicts, tacitly assuming that this subject matter requires a transparently mimetic style and, further, that literature that acknowledges itself to be literature is somehow incongruous with black urban realities. Jack Kroll, for example, remarked that the novel's "literary pyrotechnics" and its "linguistic brilliance" bleached out the urban reality that it sought to render. Even more telling was Darryl Pinckney's ob-servation that "the novel's literary ornamentation is unfortunate because Wideman has a genuine feeling for ghetto life."[77]

Given this horizon of reader expectations, it is no wonder that Wideman's novel evinces a strong ambivalence toward the category of liter-ature, paradoxically manifested through a hyperliterary style. *Philadelphia Fire* obtrusively calls attention to its own literariness, as if performing an aborted modernist mission to shore up literary value against the ruins of the postmodern city. Contrary to nationalist and other pragmatist aesthetics,

Wideman's novel suggests that causal links between literature and social change can never be precisely calculated. However, Wideman's acknowledgment of literature's tenuous relation to social reality stops short of a modernist celebration of aesthetic transcendence. *Philadelphia Fire* warily flirts with but ultimately rejects both realist and modernist assessments of literary value. As we read the novel, we are tossed between contradictory impulses to inflate and deflate the social importance of literature. This vacillation on the issue of literary value plays out at the level of narrative form, which is neither politically functional nor aesthetically gratifying. The narrator confesses, midway through the novel, that he feels his "narrative faculty weakening" (115), and his difficulty in maintaining formal order is clear through the rest of the novel, which contains several undigested quotations from other writers, short and broken paragraphs lacking sequential flow, and an assortment of disparate and often unspecified narrative voices and perspectives. The novel tries out and discards various generic options, including realist social commentary, self-reflexive meditations on writing, and autobiographical confession. This confusion is also manifest at the linguistic level, where the high literary and black vernacular styles do not quite mesh.

Jan Clausen, a rare critic to offer a charitable interpretation of the novel's schizophrenic form, writes that the "strategic disruptions" that occur from part 2 of the novel onward create "a layering of voices that represents not an organic community, . . . but a community of strangers."[78] Clausen accurately pinpoints one source of the novel's stylistic incoherence—its incapacity to locate, represent, and serve, even at an imaginary level, a fully knowable black urban community that might authenticate the social purpose of literature. *Philadelphia Fire* cannot achieve a narrative form that might bring the academy into the street or span the various urban communities divided along overlapping class and racial lines. Wideman's fictional persona, Cudjoe, wishes that literature could perform this socially mediating function, but his failure to do so is underscored by the novel's "anxious design."[79] Literature cannot legitimize itself by affirming tangible ties between the writer and the black urban community, and this inability produces extreme stylistic distress. Flaunting its literariness, *Philadelphia Fire* strains to grasp the modernist solace of a distinctive stylistic signature, but the illegibility of this signature conveys its author's strong suspicion of a literary language that is unreadable to the urban audience it wishes to address.

In sharp contrast to Wideman, Octavia Butler and Sapphire are able to affirm the pragmatic and representational value of their literary texts by insisting on the mimetic accuracy of their fictions. The very opening of Sapphire's novel declares that socially valuable fiction must "tell the truth, else what's the fucking use?" (4). A schoolroom scene in *PUSH* explicitly raises the question of how literature might best represent the experiences of the African-American poor. In this scene, Precious turns to Alice Walker's novel *The Color Purple* as an inspiring literary model for her own story. Her teacher informs her that "one of the criticizsm of *The Color Purple* is it have fairy tale ending. . . . Ms Rain love *Color Purple* too but say realism has its virtues too." Precious responds with, "Izm, smizm! . . . I don't know what 'realism' mean but I do know what REALITY is and it's a motherfucker, lemme tell you" (83). Although Precious here seems to reject her teacher's realist criterion, in fact she is reinstating it in heightened form by asserting that her own experience as a poor black woman constitutes reality in capital letters and is being communicated to readers entirely without the mediation of literary genres and conventions. *PUSH* pointedly sets out to counter the "lies and shit out there" about a black urban "underclass," and it gains mimetic authority from the fact that it is written in the first-person voice of Precious, a member of this so-called underclass. This narrative choice carries the obvious benefit of obviating the problem faced by so many postmodern African-American writers of how to bridge intra-racial class divisions and make literary writing commensurate with the realities of urban poverty. Sapphire's narrative choice also confers authenticity to the urban story presented in the novel; as implied by Precious's comments quoted earlier, the black urban poor experience the reality of the city in the most raw and direct ways and so are best positioned to tell the truth about this reality. The first-person narrator's innocence of literary conventions further enhances the immediacy of the urban reality presented in *PUSH*.

This type of resolution is more difficult for Octavia Butler, given that she writes science fiction, a genre generally assumed to bear an oblique relation to social reality. Butler's novel gets around this problem by prioritizing the category of "science" over "fiction" and by stressing its own reflective rather than imaginative dimensions. A striking aspect of the "Earthseed" book is its unqualified validation of scientific epistemology. As Lauren points out, the governing tenet of Earthseed—"God is change"—is compatible with scientific principles such as the second law of thermodynamics (195). It is Lauren's observation of natural processes of metamorphosis that gives rise to the principle of god as change. Lauren insists that the measure of Earthseed's legitimacy is "ongoing reality" rather than "supernatural authority" (197), claiming that her belief system reflects a reality that is immediately accessible to empirical observation:

> I've never felt that I was making any of this up . . . I mean, I've never felt that it was anything other than real: discovery rather than

invention, exploration rather than creation. I wish I could believe it was all supernatural, and that I'm getting messages from God. But then, I don't believe in that kind of God. All I do is observe and take notes. (69)

Early in the novel, Lauren voices some uncertainty about the truth-value of her religion, wondering, "Is any of this real? Dangerous question. Sometimes I don't know the answer" (23). But as the novel progresses, Lauren becomes increasingly confident that her religious text reveals the "literal truth" (22).

Although *Parable of the Sower* frontally engages with the social crises of postmodern urbanity, the novel's extremely dystopian setting paradoxically works to contain the problem of representation besetting so many postmodern African-American novelists. A crucial aspect of this problem is the question of whether writing, and in particular literary writing, can ever be wholly adequate to the real. The novel's creation of a state of social emergency gears all communal concerns toward the goal of physical survival, thereby suspending epistemological doubt. With her unqualified affirmation of scientific epistemologies, the writer of the "Earthseed" book can lay claim to truths that are easily verifiable and directly applicable to life. Its recourse to the supposedly transparent truth-value and instrumentality of science helps the "Earthseed" text to bracket all questions about the tricky relation between writing and social reality. Such bracketing forms a necessary support for the novel's redemptive vision of the writer as teacher, preacher, and literal savior of life.

"Even some fiction might be useful," says Lauren Olamina as she tries to persuade a friend about the importance of books to physical survival (56). But *Parable* does not invest any special redemptive power in the literary imagination as such. In fact, Butler's novel can infuse the writer with socially transformative power and present books as essential tools "of the living" only by effacing its own modality as literature. Lauren Olamina is not the only author in this book to insist that her writing is based on "discovery" rather than "invention." Octavia Butler, too, in interviews, underplays the inventive and fantastical dimensions of her novel, emphasizing instead its close reflection of actual social trends that she has observed. For example, in an interview with Jerome Jackson, Butler states that in her writing, she has "to say what I feel is true. Obviously, I mean verisimilitude as well as the literal truth,"[80] exactly echoing Lauren Olamina's claim that the "Earthseed" text reflects the "literal truth" (22). It is surely telling that *Parable of the Sower* and *PUSH,* two rare African-American postmodern novels to endow urban literature with representative and utilitarian value, can only do so by suppressing their own literary medium.

Robert Disch summarizes as follows the two main tendencies of the modern print legacy that is under attack in the postmodern period:

> One, essentially utilitarian, was committed to the functional uses of literacy as a medium for the spread of practical information that could lead to individual and social progress; the other, essentially aesthetic and spiritual, was committed to the uses of literacy for salvaging the drooping spirit of Western man from the death of religion and the ravages of progress.[81]

Taken together, Butler, Sapphire, and Wideman revive both of these facets of modern print culture—the utilitarian and the spiritual/aesthetic—to test their viability in the postmodern era. In *PUSH,* print literacy is affirmed for its functional uses as a vehicle of social mobility, with Precious's developing acquisition of literacy explicitly tracked as "progress." *Parable,* too, demonstrates that books contain practical information that can aid physical survival, but this novel also explores the spiritual dimensions of literacy through its sacred "Books of the Living." This religious text, like the "Book of Life" in *Philadelphia Fire,* is meant to supply spiritual sustenance against "the ravages of progress" visible everywhere in the postmodern city. Although, as Disch suggests, the spiritual/aesthetic components of print literacy have typically been conjoined and housed in the domain of literature, in Butler's novel the spiritual and the aesthetic are separated. In fact, *Parable* can affirm the utilitarian as well as spiritual uses of literacy only by minimizing its own aesthetic modality as a work of literary invention. *Philadelphia Fire,* in contrast, focuses its reassessment of modern print culture on the category of literature, and consequently, it is not surprising that this is the novel least optimistic about the practical efficacy of the print tradition. At the same time, however, Wideman cannot rest with a purely aesthetic evaluation of literature; the question of its material uses for disadvantaged groups persists to disturb his already tentative affirmation of the aesthetic value of literature as a means of enlarging the imagination.

Despite the ambivalence that marks all these novelists' approach to the modern print legacy, they all seek to adapt this legacy to make it responsive to previously excluded racial constituencies. In particular, three defining aspects of this legacy are reimagined in order to lend print culture use value in the present: the commodity status of the printed book; the solitary and private conditions that characterize the reading of books, along with the ideologies of individualism associated with the self-making function of print literacy; and the putatively universal humanist values that are apotheosized in the modern print tradition, especially in the canon of great literature.

It is no accident that the use value of literacy in these novels can only be affirmed under special conditions of reception and distribution that are entirely removed from the circuits of commodity exchange. A widely bemoaned feature of the postmodern era is the total incorporation of print (and all) culture into commodity capitalism. Only by way of a complete withdrawal from commodity culture can novelists like Butler and Sapphire invest writing and reading with communal value. The one novel that cannot posit a clearly knowable community that might legitimize the African-American writer's social function, *Philadelphia Fire*, is also the novel in which the book circulates as if it were a commodity. Butler's and Sapphire's novels are able to postulate reading communities that are proximate in time and space by re-creating the conditions of manuscript reading, which help mitigate the abstraction of print culture by infusing it with orality.

Through these communal situations of reading aloud, *PUSH* and *Parable* are also able to abrogate the solitary and silent conditions that attend the consumption of printed books. Although the self-making agency of literacy is affirmed, particularly in *PUSH*, where print literacy serves to extend subjectivity to members of marginalized social groups, the focus in both novels is on communal rather than individual uses of literacy. The culminating product of Precious's quest for literacy is a collectively authored anthology. The "Books of the Living" in Butler's novel are intended to bind the Earthseed group into a purposive community committed to common spiritual and material goals. In both novels, procedures of reading aloud within a group install communities that are cohesive and yet contingent, face to face and yet urban in that they are forged from diversity. This device permits Butler and Sapphire to overcome, at a fictive level, the crises of representation confronting postmodern African-American writers: an imaginary community of the urban poor bound together by the book helps validate the social function of the African-American writer.

It is only through a complex process of critical revision that these novelists are able to adapt the modern tradition of print literacy for postmodern times. One such act of critical appropriation is Cudjoe's attempt, in *Philadelphia Fire*, to re-accentuate the language of Shakespeare in a streetwise vernacular style. Another example are the "Life Stories" in *PUSH*, which seize the category of literature for those who have not yet gained access to literary representation because they have been considered unworthy of possessing their own stories and subjectivities. None of these novels suggests that the adaptation of the modern print legacy to serve the interests of marginalized racial groups will be smooth or easy. In fact, the tortuous difficulties of this project are visible on nearly every page of *PUSH*: atypical usages of typography, spelling, and syntax demonstrate the in which print standards have to be contorted to accommodate an ecedented literary subject.

each of these novels, affirmation of the continuing potency of the modern print tradition depends on critical distance from emergent technologies, which are shown to debilitate the possibilities of social critique nurtured by the print tradition. All three novels directly confront the fact that print literacy must compete with these other media that command a wider sphere of social influence. Butler is the most confident about the future life of print literacy in an electronic era. Showing that reading skills are necessary to operating high-tech electronic equipment, *Parable of the Sower* bears out Walter Ong's argument that the electronic media depend heavily on print literacy, contrary to widespread modernist fears that the new technologies are eroding print culture.[82] In *PUSH,* Precious's mother and social worker both discount the practical uses of her education in print literacy and argue instead for the more instrumental benefits of computer literacy (65, 89). The novel, however, proves them wrong through its repeated demonstration of the pragmatic value of print literacy. Questions about the viability of print technology in an electronic era are even more centrally raised in *Philadelphia Fire.* Print literature in Wideman's novel is shown to be under siege by other media and technologies that seem better suited to the times—a dimension of the novel that I examine in the next chapter. With the spreading reach of electronic visual media, oral vernacular cultures, and information technologies in the postmodern era, the power of the modern print tradition appears to be attenuated, raising doubts about the social value of literature that are explored in the next three chapters.

3.

Urban Writing as Voyeurism: Literature in the Age of Spectacle

How, here, could anyone *know* anyone?
—Samuel Delany, *Neveryóna, or: The Tale of Signs and Cities*

Sth, I know that woman.
—Toni Morrison, *Jazz*

In Samuel Delany's novel *Neveryóna, or: The Tale of Signs and Cities,* Pryn journeys from her village home to the city, where, bewildered by a profusion of unfamiliar visual signs, she wonders: "How, here, could anyone *know* anyone?" In the course of her travels through various towns and cities, Pryn is repeatedly mistaken for a spy because she is one of the privileged few in the land who can read and write. After several ineffectual denials, Pryn finally concedes the truth of this misrecognition: "To write for others . . . it seems one must be a spy."[1] The three novels I discuss in this chapter, John Edgar Wideman's *Reuben* (1987) and *Philadelphia Fire* (1990) and Toni Morrison's *Jazz* (1992), employ the metaphor of the writer as voyeur to explore the problem—of knowing others in cities—posed by Pryn when she first encounters the confusing visual text of Neveryóna. In these novels, writing (and in particular the commodity object of the printed book) is shown to be deeply implicated in the voyeuristic modes of knowing promoted by postmodern cities organized as commodity spectacles,[2] and, as a consequence, disabled in its efforts to represent community.

Accounts of postmodern urbanism often posit a sharp break between the visual regimes of modern and postmodern cities, celebrating the cultural heterogeneity and spatial fluidity of contemporary cities against the rigidly hierarchical structure of their modern variants. In what follows, I qualify such claims of rupture, arguing that the postmodern city reinforces the spatial divisions as well as the mechanisms of visual surveillance associated with the modern city. The visual semiotics of postmodern urban space look far less free-floating when viewed through the lens of race. Morrison and Wideman expose the contradictory presence of black bodies in modern and postmodern visual media—as objects of desire and fear, objects that are both fetishized as tokens of sexual presence and policed in order to secure normative notions of urban community. Linking questions of cultural visibility and urban spatial order, Wideman's and Morrison's novels disclose the continuing application of modern techniques of observation and discipline in the postmodern city.

Metaphors of urban writing as voyeurism reveal the debilitation of literary value by visual technologies. In *Reuben, Philadelphia Fire,* and *Jazz,* writing is shown to be thoroughly complicit in the objectifying dynamics of urban commodity spectacle. Identifying the writer with a camera, both novelists present voyeurism as a distinctly urban epistemology founded on distance and division. Photography, cinema, television, and other "machines of the visible,"[3] as depicted in these novels, disarm critical resistance by presenting themselves as direct traces of reality. The special role of the fiction writer is usurped by visual media, with their apparently superior power to create convincing illusions and to capture social reality. In response to this crisis of literary representation, Morrison and Wideman entertain possibilities of modeling writing on oral media. Both writers also strain to legitimize the fictive truth-claims of literature as a corrective to urban spectacle, which advertises itself as a veritable substitute for reality.

Modern and Postmodern Urban Regimes of Visuality

In their critical treatment of urban technologies of vision, Morrison and Wideman contribute to a strong antivisual current in African-American literary and cultural studies. If the question posed by Samuel Delany's Pryn—"How, here, could anyone *know* anyone?"—suggests the difficulty of attaining certain visual knowledge of others in the city, the opening sentence of Toni Morrison's *Jazz*—"Sth, I know that woman"—in stark contrast declares its narrator's confident knowledge of urban others in an oralized voice.[4] As Michele Wallace observes in "Modernism, Postmodernism, and the Problem of the Visual in Afro-American Culture," visuality is widely regarded with suspicion in African-American cultural studies and pitted against orality, which is valorized as the more authentic medium of black cultural production. Tracing the historical shifts in the staging of visuality as the "negative scene" of black literary production, Wallace argues that invisibility is the distinguishing trope of black literary modernism, epitomized by Ralph Ellison's *Invisible Man* (1952), whereas postmodern black literature (exemplified by Ishmael Reed's *Mumbo Jumbo,* published in 1972) is preoccupied with the problem of hypervisibility.[5]

The heightened visibility of racial difference is often identified as a notable political gain of postmodern culture. But African-American writers are leery of the peculiar terms of this visibility and of the very possibility of using visual technologies to create politically meaningful representations of African-American culture. An early and critically unremarked postmodern novel, Carlene Polite's *Sister X and the Victims of Foul Play,* published in 1975, clearly sets out the approach to visuality and orality taken in much subsequent African-American fiction as well as literary and cultural criticism. Obviously informed by Guy Debord's analysis of the "society of the spectacle," Polite's novel shows how capitalist commodity culture reifies black bodies into "embalmed shadows," "displaced likenesses," "fixed images," and "representations of our 'real' selves."[6] The scare quotes surrounding the word *real* as well as the x-ed out name of the novel's protagonist suggest that authentic knowledge of black subjectivity is not available from within a visual modality. Through an exuberantly kinetic narrative style modeled on rapping, Polite struggles to oppose and escape the world of commodity spectacle, in which black bodies are "rendered dead"—in other words, objectified into "quantitative piece[s] of merchandise" (73). But whether oral media can offer a reliable route out of spectacle ultimately remains uncertain: by the end of the novel, the sexual commodification of Sister X's body directly precipitates her violent death, which itself becomes a spectacle, a scene of voyeuristic curiosity.

Recent analyses by influential African-American cultural critics configure visual and aural media in remarkably similar terms but without Polite's steady attention to the capitalist infrastructure of both media. For example, in "Scene . . . Not Heard," Houston Baker considers the "consequences of the unheard scening of blackness in America," with specific reference to George Halliday's videotape of LAPD officers beating Rodney King, repeatedly replayed without sound on national television as well as by defense attorneys during the trial of the police officers.[7] Baker claims that visual stagings of blackness in America are always scenes of violence entailing "literal desubjectification and silencing" (42). If the visual media predominantly give us voiceless bodies that threaten urban order and thus require both visual surveillance and violent containment (42), Baker contends that the only possibilities of an alternate "interpretive hearing" (45) are found in rap accounts of "what precisely it sounds like to be violently scened in the United States."[8]

Whereas Baker believes that rap music "is likely to yield a hearing that forestalls further American urban disaster" (48), Paul Gilroy questions the capacity of contemporary hip-hop culture to serve as a vehicle of black political aspirations. In Gilroy's opinion, hip-hop culture has betrayed the black musical tradition, displacing its language of political freedom by a "racialised bio-politics" that sets out to "establish the limits of the authentic racial community exclusively through the visual representation of racial bodies."[9] Despite this disagreement on rap, however, Gilroy essentially concurs with Baker's argument that aurality rather than visuality is the more trustworthy medium of black cultural expression. If contemporary hip-hop culture no longer sustains the political spirit of black musical tradition, this is because of its fall from sound to image. The increasing subordination of audio to video in postmodern culture aids the "bio-politics" centered on sexuality rather than political freedom. Gilroy writes: "The growing dominance of specularity over aurality contributes a special force to representations of the exemplary racial body arrested in the gaze of desiring and identifying subjects. Misrecognised, objectified and verified, these images have become the storehouses of racial alterity now that the production of subjectivity operates through different sensory and technological mechanisms" (65). In Gilroy's essay, as in Baker's, a cultural sphere organized as a field of visual images is paralyzing for black politics; neither writer can view the increased visibility of black bodies in postmodern culture as an advance in political or even cultural representation.

Why precisely do cultural critics such as Gilroy or Baker regard visual representations of blackness in the postmodern era with such strong suspicion? In what Judith Butler terms "the racial schematization of the visible field,"[10] to be black is to be visually marked in peculiar ways—to be embodied as a primitive fetish object, irradiating danger and erotic power, that must be both contained and consumed.[11] In this respect, the apparently opposed facets of the black male body highlighted by Baker and Gilroy— the body as object of violent public control and the body saturated with sexual desire—can be understood as the doubled manifestation of a single, contradictory operation. Both Baker and Gilroy affirm aurality as a corrective to this kind of visual marking of black bodies, but neither clarifies exactly how aurality transcends the material conditions that govern visual media of cultural representation. In the absence of any explanation of why and how specific technologies of cultural representation serve different political uses, Baker's and Gilroy's essays encourage a technologistic understanding of aurality and visuality, suggesting that there is something intrinsic to these technologies that allows or inhibits their functioning as vehicles of authentic cultural expression.

Both visual and aural representations of black bodies in postmodern culture are embedded in the conditions of commodity consumption characteristic of the "society of the spectacle." Guy Debord's concept of spectacle offers a systematic understanding of how visual technologies best serve to naturalize a specific historical mode of social and economic organization. Debord defines "spectacle" not as a visual technology per se but as the representational order of an advanced capitalist economy in which all social relations and cultural products are subject to the laws of commodity fetishism. "The world of consumption is in reality the world of the mutual spectacularization of everyone," writes Debord;[12] in this world, visuality is elevated into the preeminent medium of cognition and representation. Obeying the logic of commodity fetishism, spectacle presents itself as an accurate reflection of a naturally given reality. But, Debord argues, spectacle is in fact a socially projected field of visibility characterized precisely by its distance from a putatively real world immediately available to the sense of sight.[13] In Debord's words, "The spectacle, as a tendency *to make one see* the world by means of various specialized mediations (it can no longer be grasped directly), naturally finds vision to be the privileged human sense . . . ; the most abstract, the most mystifiable sense corresponds to the generalized abstraction of present-day society."[14] The abstraction Debord refers to here is effected by "the becoming-world of the commodity, which is also the becoming-commodity of the world" (66)—a process of social and economic transformation based on the supersession of use value by exchange value.

All cultural production in the society of the spectacle is dictated by the laws of commodity exchange, but visuality most efficiently services a cultural order in which the spheres of commodity production and consumption have been extended through exploitation of the exchange value of signs.[15] Hal Foster argues that as commodity exchange becomes increasingly based on "sign exchange value," on the primacy of images, cultural consumption becomes scopic and voyeuristic.[16] Postmodern culture, even more so than its modern counterpart, inculcates an aestheticized observation of visual signs of racial and sexual difference in part because it pursues a logic of absorption rather than exclusion. If modern ideological systems gained their authority through marginalization of subcultural groups, postmodern spectacle incorporates previously invisible social groups by means of semiotic appropriation. In this system, as Foster notes, "the other is socially subjected as a sign and made commercially productive as a commodity. In this way the (subcultural) other is at once controlled in its recognition and dispersed in its commodification." All kinds of social differences, and especially racial and sexual differences, are "used productively" and indeed "often fabricated in the interests of social control as well as of commodity innovation."[17] Voyeuristic consumption of visual signs of difference operates as a compensatory mechanism within a system that has already leveled social particularities into the abstract equivalence of exchange value. A central contradiction of the society of the spectacle, then, is that it must continually embark on "an anxious search for lost difference, within a logic from which difference itself has been excluded."[18] Serving as it does to lubricate commodity capitalism, the hypervisibility of racial difference in postmodern culture cannot be construed as a clear-cut gain.

That the intensified consumption of blackness as cultural spectacle bears contradictory implications is nowhere more graphically evident than in postmodern discourses of urban development. Urban historians agree that the distinguishing feature of postmodern urban form is its "greater emphasis upon the spatial division of consumption relative to the spatial division of labor."[19] The redevelopment programs initiated during the 1960s as well as more recent trends of gentrification have been geared to transform city centers organized around declining industrial production into privatized spaces "explicitly produced for visual consumption."[20] Redevelopment projects designed to lure private investment into decaying urban downtowns have seductively deployed the age-old rhetoric of the city as a smorgasbord of social and cultural differences. As Malcolm Cross and Michael Keith have observed, in "Racism and the Postmodern City," recent ideologies of the "new urbanism" are "deeply racialized": the semiotic difference of racial minorities is aggressively commodified in the "exotic cultural pick-and-mix" of the revitalized postmodern city.[21] But this exuberant celebration of racial difference works fetishistically to mask the inequalities that are deepened as the postmodern city is reinvented into a "consumption artifact."[22] As discussed in chapter 2, redevelopment programs in various U.S. cities have "massively reproduced spatial apartheid."[23] The transformation of city centers into sites where cultural differences could be consumed as commodities required the expulsion of low-income and mostly racial minority residents, who were rendered homeless or relocated to segregated areas of public housing. Racial separation was thereby reinforced by the very same projects that exploited the cultural signifiers of racial difference in the interests of commodity consumption.

Celebratory accounts of the racial heterogeneity of postmodern culture are often supported by assertions of a decisive difference between the visual semiotics of modern and postmodern urban form. The spatial illegibility of the postmodern city is said to exemplify a new visual form distinct from its modern counterpart, typified by its accessibility to visual cognition.[24] Tracing key stages in the history of the American city, William Sharpe and Leonard Wallock, in their essay "From 'Great Town' to 'Nonplace Urban Realm': Reading the Modern City," offer a representative example of this sort of claim.[25] The modern industrial city of the early nineteenth century is characterized by concentrated settlement patterns and by a high degree of segregation between spaces of labor and residence as well as between residential spaces inhabited by different classes and ethnicities. In contrast, spatial form is not so readily mapped in the mid- to late-twentieth-century city, which Sharpe and Wallock describe as a decentered urban field rather than a clearly demarcated city. New electronic technologies of telecommunication and information processing, with their "time-eliminating and space-spanning" abilities (18), have transformed the city into "a nonspatial urban area" (21), engendering a correlative shift from "the visual vocabulary of the nineteenth century" to more abstract metaphors of urbanity (22). The increasing decentralization of U.S. cities has resulted in a "loss of semiotic apprehensibility": the "instantly legible and easily visible emblems of urban power and centrality [that characterized the modern city] . . . have almost systematically been obscured" (23).

Such accounts of postmodern cities as recalcitrant to visual cognition capture significant spatial shifts produced by the new information and telecommunications technologies. (The implications of these shifts for literary representations of urban reality and community form the focus of my fifth chapter.) However, as the novels by Octavia Butler, Sapphire, and John Edgar Wideman discussed in the previous chapter clarify, purely semiotic approaches to cities as visual texts miss an equally significant dimension of postmodern cities that may not be immediately apparent to the eye—the hardening of racial and economic hierarchies. To "read" the city solely at the level of visual form is to read it fetishistically, to become blind to the coordinates of power that are all the more insidious because they are concealed by the diffused visual appearance of postmodern cities.[26] Moreover, most accounts that highlight dramatic changes in urban visual form take Los Angeles as their paradigm of a postmodern city, but we must be careful not to generalize about postmodern urban form on the basis of Los Angeles, or to overstate the visual unreadability of even this archetypal postmodern city.[27]

Offering a valuable corrective to prevailing perceptions of the amorphous postmodern city,[28] Mike Davis, in his analysis of Los Angeles in *City of Quartz*, relentlessly lays bare the city's all-too-readable "totalitarian semiotics" of class and racial division.[29] Disputing the contention that electronic technologies have ushered in a sprawling urban space that resists visual mastery, Davis assembles a mass of details attesting to a "militarization of city life [that is] grimly visible at the street level" (223). If Sharpe and Wallock assert that "the familiar sign-posts that designate one's place and standing within the urban community are no longer adequate" in the postmodern urban context (39), Davis argues that contemporary urban spaces, even in Los Angeles, "are full of invisible signs warning off the underclass 'Other.' Although architectural critics are usually oblivious to how the built environment contributes to segregation, pariah groups . . . read the meaning immediately" (226). Davis's chapter "Fortress L.A." focuses on the visual semiotics of urban architecture as well as on emergent electronic technologies of urban surveillance. Even with its scrupulous attention to developments in architecture and policing specific to present-day cities, Davis's work contests the claim, common to both celebrants and detractors, that postmodern urbanism is sharply discontinuous from its modern variant, clarifying instead the lingering power of modern systems of visual surveillance and spatial containment.

A brief comparison of the disciplinary social functions performed by photographic and electronic technologies of observation in modern and postmodern cities should serve to illustrate this point. Michel Foucault has alerted us to the primacy of vision in modern urban technologies of social regulation.[30] In a Foucauldian account of the complicity between photography and policing in mid-nineteenth-century industrial cities, John Tagg argues that photographic technology drew its social authority as evidence from a "regime of truth" founded on the principle of revelatory vision: to expose individuals to the light of the camera was also to illuminate their social truth and to transform them into the objects of an emergent urban system of social control that equated vision with knowledge. Tagg argues, following Foucault, that what distinguished modern urban technologies of visual surveillance was that they individuated as they disciplined: their basic unit of observation was the individual, simultaneously objectified and subjectified, isolated and contained within the cell-like frame of the photograph. Emphasizing the exact match between visual images of deviant individuals and spatial units of containment, Tagg writes that the standardized police photograph "is a portrait of the product of the disciplinary method: the body made object; divided and studied; enclosed in a cellular structure of space whose architecture is the file-index; made docile and forced to yield up its truth; separated and individuated; subjected and made subject."[31]

Following this logic, we might expect that the shift from photographic to electronic technologies of visual observation would index a corresponding shift in the procedures of social regulation. This expectation is initially aroused but ultimately frustrated by Thomas Dumm's analysis of the transition from surveillance to monitoring technologies. Whereas modern surveillance methods depended on centralized, singular, panoptical vision, the electronic technology of the monitor relies on "the stereoscopic vision of more pluralistic techniques of observation."[32] The political significance of this technological shift is that unlike modern techniques of social control that aimed at correcting individuals, the more depersonalized electronic technologies are designed to exclude criminalized masses (such as the "underclass") that are seen to be unassimilable to social order. The shift from modern to postmodern techniques of visual observation, then, does not signify a less repressively policed urban order. If anything, as Dumm goes on to argue, decentralized technologies of electronic observation are increasingly deployed to protect an urban spatial order segregated around race and class lines; with the aid of electronic monitors, well-to-do communities of privatized consumption can more effectively seal their boundaries against the incursions of racial and class outsiders (188–91).

In his account of the normalizing social functions served by electronic visual technologies, Dumm draws on Mike Davis's analysis of the "new epistemology of policing" instituted by technologies of electronic surveillance.[33] Davis's discussion of these technologies refutes, even more forcefully than does Dumm's, assertions of a radical break between modern and postmodern regimes of visual observation. In fact, several of Davis's examples demonstrate the durable force of the "earlier modern connection of surveillance with the idea of a perfect visibility."[34] The "futuristic" technology of LAPD helicopters aspires to omniscient vision, with its thirty-million-candlepower spotlights that "can literally turn night into day" (252). Both public and private uses of monitoring technology have "apotheosize[d] the siege look" in urban architecture (223); libraries, shopping malls, downtown offices, and residential units are increasingly equipped with discreetly invisible but ubiquitous electronic eyes that track the flow of social traffic. Davis's example of the "panopticon mall" located near Watts, which "plagiarizes brazenly from Jeremy Bentham's renowned nineteenth-century design for the 'panopticon prison' with its economic central surveillance" (242–43), most dramatically captures the continuities between modern and postmodern techniques of visual observation.

It should be clear from Davis's examples that the dispersed and multiple perspectives that electronic surveillance technologies permit and even encourage at a formal level do not translate into a genuinely pluralistic urban space. These technologies instead help to maintain spatial divisions that reflect the increasingly polarized social and economic order of contemporary cities. The repressive aims and effects of postmodern regimes of visual observation and spatial control become most fully apparent when focused through the lens of race. Reinforcing a racialized social order, these regimes subject African-American urban populations in particularly overdetermined ways. Discourses about the "underclass" train the public eye to focus on the black poor as the agents of an unprecedented urban crisis. Underclass rhetoric systematically criminalizes the black urban poor and casts them as an intractable mass menacing to public order. Framing urban crisis as an issue of law and order, underclass rhetoric is symptomatic of a broad retreat from the integrationist and redistributive goals that briefly defined the national political agenda during the 1960s. By the 1970s, academic and mass media accounts of urban crisis began to demonize the African-American poor as the prime threat to urban security and national community. Reigning political paradigms of community over the last three decades have sought, in Margaret Weir's words, to "constitute an 'American people' in ways which excluded poor blacks. At times, more explicit use of blacks as 'others' has been employed to draw the lines of who is in and who is out of the new America."[35]

This kind of symbolic construction of black bodies as inimical to national order is repeatedly reinforced by contemporary visual media. In his essay "Dead Black Men and Other Fallout from the American Dream," John Wideman discusses the ways in which visual images of African-Americans serve to validate policies reinforcing racial segregation. "Dead Black Men," published in *Esquire* in 1992, is a journalistic account of Los Angeles in the wake of the not-guilty verdict in the trial of four police officers for their brutal beating of Rodney King. Commenting on television coverage of the violence that erupted in Los Angeles after the verdict, Wideman writes that the images of the rioters and looters resumed an enduring visual-media tradition of racializing urban disorder and of translating urban revolts against injustice (even when their agents are racially diverse) into a panic-stricken rhetoric of black barbarity (153). Representations of black bodies as "the very antithesis of ... social order"[36] are precisely what feed fetishistic desire for the sexualized black body. The same stigmatized body that requires violent control also epitomizes erotic potency. Postmodern visual culture revels in racial difference: in the commodity spectacle of the postmodern city, the black body is omnipresent as an emblem of sexual power. This pluralism at the level of cultural semiotics disguises the racial exclusions that make possible the creation of the postmodern city into an artifact of consumption.

Given that black bodies represent both the exotic fetish and the taboo object of postmodern urbanism, it becomes clear why so many African-American writers are questioning the political implications of contemporary visual technologies. The two novelists I examine in this chapter have both called critical attention to the contradictory terms of black presence in the national visual media. Toni Morrison has edited a collection of essays analyzing the media event that became a flashpoint for discussions of race, sexuality, and visuality—the televised confirmation hearings for Clarence Thomas's accession to the Supreme Court. In her introduction to this volume, Morrison writes that the hearings provided the public an "unprecedented opportunity to hover over and to cluck at, to meditate and ponder the limits and excesses of black bodies."[37] Identifying the ambivalent logic that drives visual representations of black bodies, Morrison argues that the "voyeuristic desire" aroused by televisual coverage of the hearings was "fueled by mythologies that render blacks publicly serviceable instruments of private dread and longing" (xvii–xviii). Even as black bodies are "voluptuously dwelled upon" by visual media, these same bodies also bear the negative charge of symbolizing "illicit sexuality and chaos" (xiv–xv). Wideman, in "Dead Black Men," similarly notes the contradiction attending visual representations of the black male body, which "is used to sell everything from breakfast cereal to automobiles.... Yet that same iconized, commodified black man's body is beaten, incarcerated, the nightmare thief, rapist, addict that Americans arm themselves against" (151).

Morrison's and Wideman's fiction recurrently replays this doubled appearance of the black body as an object of fear and desire, revealing that commodification and containment of this body form the interdependent dynamics of a single fetishistic operation. The sexual commodification of black bodies in these novels is always a violent process inseparably linked to public issues of urban order. Through such presentations, Morrison and Wideman implicitly discount utopian accounts of a pluralistic postmodern urbanism. *Reuben, Philadelphia Fire,* and *Jazz* all suggest that postmodern commodity spectacle continues to reproduce the epistemological principles as well as the instrumental functions of modern urban visuality. The repetitive cellular units that figure urban form in *Reuben,* the city divided into segregated and heavily policed zones in *Philadelphia Fire,* and the rigidly gridded structure of the city in *Jazz* all highlight the easy semiotic readability as well as the socially repressive effects of urban spatial form.

Moreover, through their critical treatment of the voyeuristic modes of knowing common to postmodern and modern techniques of urban observation, Morrison's and Wideman's novels disclose the enduring power of what Martin Jay terms the dominant "scopic regime of modernity."[38] Identified with Cartesian perspectivalism, this regime is generally associated with a fairly stable set of features: conflation of sight with knowledge; centering of vision around a singular, static, omniscient eye; assumption of a neutral, objective view from nowhere that conceals the historicity of vision; structuring of visual knowledge on division between subject and object; literal claims to representation, based on assumptions of direct correspondence between vision and world; and instrumentality to modern urban technologies of surveillance.[39]

Photography and Voyeurism in *Reuben*

In *Reuben,* Wideman explicitly takes on the modern scopic regime by means of his fictional depiction of Eadweard Muybridge, a seminal figure in the early history of photography and cinema. Muybridge is so critical to the novel's treatment of modern visuality that I shall introduce in some detail the epistemological issues raised by his work as well as their continuing resonance in our postmodern times before proceeding to an analysis of *Reuben*. Muybridge is best known for his mammoth book of photographs, *Animal Locomotion,* published in 1887, consisting of a series of sequential shots of animals and human beings performing a variety of physical movements. These photographs of animal and human locomotion sought to capture the scientific laws of motion invisible to the human eye unaided by camera technology. Although this volume approached motion analytically, disaggregating it into minute components intended to reveal its innermost secret, Muybridge also sought to synthesize the separate parts of motion by means of the zoopraxiscope, an early and crude prototype of the motion picture projector.

Contemporaneous responses to Muybridge's book of photographs as well as to his zoopraxiscope testified to the crisis in artistic representation sparked by photography. In one of his exhibitions, Muybridge projected moving pictures of a horse next to a painting meant to capture a horse in motion. If the comparison between photography and painting made "artists look absurd,"[40] this was precisely Muybridge's intention. Muybridge himself said that he wanted to show that artists had been guided by convention rather than fact in their depictions of motion and that the aim of his exhibition was to "reeducate their eyes."[41] A review of *Animal Locomotion* published in *The Nation* in 1888 voiced keen ambivalence about the educative effects of Muybridge's photography on art. The anonymous reviewer acclaimed Muybridge's photographs as landmark contributions to a scientific understanding of motion that also carried profound repercussions for art. The photographs themselves were not art but a revelation of "naked, absolute fact" that no artist could afford to neglect. But the reviewer went on to argue that because art is an "expression" rather than a "record" of reality, the artist should strive to capture the whole, not the discrete stages of motion exposed by Muybridge's camera. The reviewer advised artists to study the photographs in order to understand the mechanics of motion but to discard them before turning to their painting, a suggestion seconded by Muybridge himself, who cautioned that art literally modeled on photography will only succeed in creating "petrified" images rather than convincing illusions of motion.[42] What clearly emerges from contemporaneous responses to Muybridge's work is a firm distinction between the expressive illusion of art and the objective, truth-telling technology of photography.

The quintessential technology of modern vision, the camera was hailed in Muybridge's era as the "pencil of nature."[43] Assumptions about the literal truth-claims invested in the camera continue to shadow late-twentieth-century discussions of photography. Muybridge's conviction that his photographs transparently reflected an empirically given reality finds its most famous and eloquent recent echo in Roland Barthes's meditations on the precise nature of the reality captured in photographs. In *Camera Lucida,* Barthes asserts that the "evidential force" of the photograph de-rives from its literal rather than metaphorical relation to reality.[44] In con-trast to language, which is fictional and can never definitively authenticate itself, the photograph "is authentication itself" (87) because it seizes its referent in a manner distinct from all other systems of representation. A photograph is not simply "co-natural with its referent" (76); it is also "liter-ally an emanation of the referent" (80). Similarly stressing the "literalness" of photography's power, Susan Sontag agrees that a photograph can "usurp reality" because it is "a trace...directly stenciled off the real."[45] But Sontag is careful to clarify that despite their "presumption of veracity," all photographs are interpretations of the world (6–7), which are danger-ous precisely because of their seeming transparency of reference.

This point is extensively elaborated in Wideman's critique of televisual media in "Dead Black Men." Wideman writes that the apparent trans-parency of visual media prevents us from recognizing that what we are being shown is an interpretation rather than a neutral reflection of reality:

> The carpetbagging presence of press and TV is as dangerous and aggressive as the military occupation of black and Hispanic neigh-borhoods, perhaps more dangerous because we've been conditioned not to see the press, to treat it as an invisible fly on the wall even when its legions outnumber the troops.
>
> ...Television's power to create reality is literally incomprehensible because it infiltrates and usurps the space of comprehension, replaces our eyes and ears and feeds us the data we process into meaning. But the data aren't raw. Images, sound bites, are framed, organized not so much by one ideological stance or another, though that happens often enough, but by the nature of the beast, collecting, omitting, selecting sights and sounds. (154)

That the referential claims of modern visual technologies still widely com-pel belief, notwithstanding contentions that postmodern forms of visuality have altogether banished the question of the real,[46] was urgently brought to public attention by the event that stands at the center of Wideman's essay—the videotaped beating of Rodney King and the subsequent televi-sual replays of the "infamous video," which, according to Wideman, even-tually "etherized" public perceptions of the event (154). In a collection of essays, *Reading Rodney King/Reading Urban Uprising,* published a year after the Simi Valley verdict acquitting the police officers, several writers, in agreement with Wideman, felt the need to challenge commonsensical realist understandings of visual media and to emphasize that the visible field offered for consumption by these media is an episteme rather than a reality immediately given to the sense of sight.

This insistence appeared necessary in view of the disconcertingly successful use of George Halliday's videotape, by defense attorneys in the police trial, as visual proof that Rodney King's body was the catalyst rather than the victim of violence. In response, several contributors to *Reading Rodney King* reiterate that the texts produced by video technology possess no objective value as legal proof but that, instead, their truth value derives from the social contexts in which they are embedded. For example, Kimberle Crenshaw and Gary Peller analyze the "disaggregating" techniques used by defense attorneys in the trial—breaking down the videotape into discrete frame-by-frame stills without sound, so that no single frozen image in itself could be taken as proof of undue force. Crenshaw and Peller argue that by detaching images from their broader temporal and social context, this technique evacuates narrative and historical meaning from visual imagery. The insidious problem with disaggregated vision is that it presents itself as a truth free of ideological mediation, transparently made available by video technology.[47] Crenshaw and Peller, in common with Judith Butler, conclude that we cannot oppose racist readings that masquerade as literal seeing by invoking realist notions of vision, or, as Butler puts it, by "seek[ing] recourse to the visible as the sure ground of evidence."[48]

In "Dead Black Men," Wideman does not seem to share these writers' suspicion of the very idea of unmediated, objectively verifiable vision. At the end of the passage cited earlier, Wideman argues that ideologically processed televisual images can be criticized and corrected by making distinctions "between what the screen brings us and what we gather from the natural exercise of our eyes" (154). In this essay, Wideman does not explain how "natural" sight can escape social mediation and offer epistemological security for alternate visions critical of the "society of the spectacle." But this question forms a central concern of *Reuben*, which insists on the historicity—and, by implication, fallibility—of all vision, even though this means that the novel cannot defend its own oppositional vision on the grounds of epistemological accuracy.

In *Reuben*, Wideman discredits the camera's realist claims to representation by blurring the distinction between scientific truth and aesthetic illusion that helped authenticate Muybridge's photographs. If, according to Barthes, "It is the misfortune (but perhaps also the voluptuous pleasure) of language not to be able to authenticate itself" (85), *Reuben* suggests that photography is as fictional in its grasp of reality as is language. A passage in the opening chapter of the novel informs us that the truth displayed by Muybridge's photographs was an effect of illusion: his pictures of locomotion consisted of "a series of stills, succeeding one another fast enough to create the illusion of motion."[49] Muybridge himself appears in the novel to concede the insufficiency of his analytical method. Attempting to grasp motion, which occurs in time, by disaggregating it into a sequence of isolated, still frames, Muybridge's photographs miss altogether the temporal flow they seek to capture. The presumed objectivity of Muybridge's scientific method is vouchsafed by techniques of vision that conceal their own embeddedness in space and time. These techniques position the observing subject as a singular, stable, and disembodied eye. The novel aligns the lens of Muybridge's camera with the transcendent and omniscient eye of Cartesian perspective. "If we could see everything. If we bore God's eye in our forehead," wishes the fictional Muybridge as he lines up his "infinite banks of cameras" (127), unwittingly disclosing the contradiction implicit in Cartesian perspective—between its assumption of monocular vision (the singular "God's eye") and the "million *heres*" (126) potentially opened up by the very idea of perspective.

Reuben exploits this contradiction in modern perspective by means of the camera itself, which, although it is usually identified with the god-like spectator of Cartesian perspective, also radically "decentered" this perspective, clarifying its limitations of vision. As John Berger writes:

> The inherent contradiction in perspective was that it structured all images of reality to address a single spectator who, unlike God, could only be in one place at a time. After the invention of the camera this contradiction gradually became apparent. [With the camera], what you saw depended upon where you were when. What you saw was relative to your position in time and space. It was no longer possible to imagine everything converging on the human eye as on the vanishing point of infinity. . . . The camera . . . demonstrated that there was no centre.[50]

Reuben deflates the impossible ambition of modern techniques of vision by first associating the camera with the omniscient and singular eye of Cartesian perspective and then showing how the camera splinters perspective and throws the human eye into panic and confusion.

An outstanding example of this is the scene in chapter 7, when Reuben, walking through downtown Pittsburgh, imagines himself surveyed by an infinite series of cameras installed by the fictional Muybridge along the street and atop the buildings. But instead of yielding a composite image of the mobile Reuben, all that these cameras can reveal is a set of sundered, static, and partial perspectives (126–27). The novel's narrator undermines Muybridge's aspirations to scientific objectivity by scrupulously noting the temporal and spatial specificity of each photographic perspective, by

making visible the materiality of the medium of vision. We are made obtrusively aware that what we see is constrained by where we are, in the
penultimate chapter of the novel, which presents the killing of Waddell by
Toodles and Kwansa. The reader's view of Kwansa and Toodles is framed
by the lens of an imaginary movie camera. We first sight the two women
through a long-shot view and then zoom into a close-up identification
with Kwansa's perspective. As Waddell enters the bar behind Kwansa, we
are made uncomfortably aware of what we, restricted to Kwansa's eyes, cannot see. Waddell's murder is focalized through an anonymous bystander
who insistently punctuates his account with assurances about the authenticity of eyewitnessing: "I was there.... I saw everything" (212). Yet this is
the scene that most effectively renders (through its shifts between several
limited perspectives) the impossibility of seeing everything. The inadequacy
of an epistemology that identifies knowing with seeing is thoroughly exposed by the superficial eyewitness account that can tell us nothing that
we really want to know about the invisible emotions motivating the scene.

In modern epistemology, as Chris Jenks has argued, sight operates as a
sort of sensory highway transporting a world conceived as exterior into the
interiority of the mind, thereby instituting a dichotomous relation between
the subject and object of knowledge.[51] The camera, aggressively complicit
with this objectifying epistemology, similarly promotes a "chronic[ally]
voyeuristic relation to the world," reinforcing the self-other opposition
typical of modern approaches to knowledge.[52] In *Reuben*, the camera's
reifying mode of seeing is presented as the defining feature of urban vision. Through its pervasive use of doubles, a narrative device distinctive of
modern urban fiction, the novel conveys the difficulties of achieving reciprocal visual knowledge of others in the city. Most of the characters in the
novel, including Wally, Kwansa, and Reuben himself, unsuccessfully seek
mutuality of recognition in the various doubles they imagine are lurking
behind or beside them in the city. Wideman's novel also uses doubling as a
metaphor for the objectification of self into other entailed by urban social
intercourse, based as it is on a trading of visual impressions rather than
identities. Not surprisingly, it is through metaphors of photographic and
cinematic vision that Wideman describes the estrangement of characters
from themselves. The novel is rife with examples of characters passively
observing themselves as figures on a screen; in one such scene, in which
Wally treats what happens to him as "a film he watched on a screen," the
visual metaphor establishes a split between subject and object that dispos-
sesses him of himself: "if he could see himself that way, ... the only life he
knew was not his own" (111).

Photographic metaphors of doubling in *Reuben*, bearing out Roland
Barthes's remark that the photograph is "the advent of myself as other"

(11), powerfully render the disorienting fragmentation of identity in the city. As illustrated by Wally's experience of being a traveling man shuttling between various cities, the anonymity and mobility of urban life encourage an abstracted perception of the self. Once Wally accepts these conditions of urban identity, he becomes free to choose and exchange from a "merry-go-round circus of identities" (33). But with no certain grounds for selecting one identity over another, the circulation of interchangeable selves evokes the illusory freedom of an urban social system based on exchange values that mirror each other in an arbitrary process of substitution.

The doubling of character in urban fiction generally evokes a loss of authenticity, an apprehension of identity as a copy of an absent original. As Walter Benjamin has argued, this loss of authenticating presence was precipitated by the industrialization of photographic technology. Mechanical reproduction mobilized images, stripping them of their "aura," or their use value in a specific time and place, and putting them into circulation within an exchange system that levels all values into abstract equivalence.[53] *Reuben* employs photographic imagery to convey the homelessness, in Benjamin's sense, of urban value and identity. Uprooted from an original time and place, image-signs of the self are set loose by the same process, of industrial commodity production, that converts them into objects of new forms of scrutiny and consumption. In *Reuben,* the multiperspectivalism made possible by photography, even as it liberates and decenters vision, also underscores the camera's "profound, central applicability to industrial capitalism."[54] The "discrete, manageable units" of Muybridge's repetitive still frames of motion are bound up with what Benjamin has famously termed the "homogeneous, empty time" of industrial production,[55] a quantitative time instrumental to capitalist ideologies of progressive modernity. In the words of the fictional Muybridge, "we drive time upward and onward, worshiping duration, progress. We've debased time. It's no longer a playground we share with the gods; it's a commodity we buy and sell, get and spend, save and lose" (63).

The "discrete, manageable units" of Muybridge's photographs are also evocative of the spatial surveillance mechanisms of the modern industrial city. Muybridge's description of his photographs—"rows and rows of cells. Tiny, isolated cubicles with a pitiful little figure marooned in each one. Prisoners who couldn't touch, didn't even know the existence of the other" (63)—strikingly converges with John Tagg's account of the instrumental role played by photography in the early development of urban surveillance technologies. Tagg points out that these technologies find an apt metaphor in Muybridge's photography: "in the unobtrusive cells of the photographic frame; in its ever more minute division of time and motion; in its ever finer scrutiny of bodies in stringent laboratory conditions. [The industrial city] is a world for which the exhaustive catalogue of bodily movements in Muybridge's images stands as an ominous sign."[56]

Using Eadweard Muybridge as the nodal point for its investigation into several interrelated epistemological issues pertaining to the modern industrial city, *Reuben* contributes to broad critiques of the episteme of modern visuality. More importantly, the novel clarifies the continuing relevance of this critique to contemporary urban conditions, and specifically, to the ways in which the bodies of urban African-Americans are objectified by postmodern visual regimes of surveillance and representation. Media images of unruly black bodies help legitimize the spatial confinement of the black urban poor as well as the incarceration of unprecedented numbers of black men. The "liaisons between [urban] architecture and the American police state,"[57] to borrow Mike Davis's phrase, are evoked by Wideman's recurring metaphorical references to the city of Philadelphia as "a jail sentence" (114). According to Reuben, "All black men have a Philadelphia"; even if any particular black man manages to escape his Philadelphia, he always leaves behind his double, a "brother trapped there forever" (93).

As I argued earlier, the criminalized black body is inseparable from the fetishized black body in postmodern visual culture. *Reuben* clarifies this link between containment and commodification by employing the trope of the double to render both of these dimensions of black urban visibility and by suggesting that commodified sexual desire wreaks as much violence on black urban bodies as does public fear. Wideman's two conspicuous examples of commodified black male bodies are, predictably enough, of basketball players and musicians. Wally's job as a recruiter of promising high-school basketball players brings him into contact with coaches who appraise potential recruits as "prize stud[s]" (100). When Wally signs the deal and converts the recruits into "merchandise" (103), he becomes "the cutter of cords" (107), dislodging them from their small-town homes and inserting them into metropolitan circuits of exchange value. Their entry into the commodity exchange system violently splits and doubles their bodies, condemning them to perpetual mobility and homelessness: "Sever this boy and release a ghost that will spend its days floating back and forth between two places, two bodies, never able to call either one home" (107).

The second example of the commodified black body used to reap profit is that of Bimbo, a musician who acquires his reputation as a "superstud" when he stops singing romantic love songs and switches over to "humping music" (171). Because of the powerful association of black bodies with sexuality, it is only when he sexualizes his music to verge on obscenity that

Bimbo attains celebrity. The supreme irony of Bimbo's media status as a sexual icon is that his body is in fact crippled and paralyzed below the waist by an accident that literally "chopped him in half" (160). The image of "twin Bimbos," the actual one "pinned in the electric wheelchair" and the publicity image "cut loose, out in the street again setting world records for fucking" (172), graphically captures the contradictory uses served by the black male body—at once castrated and hypersexualized—in public imagination.

By showing that the commodification of the black male body into a token of sexual virility can safely occur only after this body is emasculated, *Reuben* suggests that racial "others," regardless of gender, must be feminized in order to serve as objects of voyeuristic desire. In this respect, the novel complicates the exclusively gendered accounts of the subject-object dichotomy inhering in modern techniques of vision.[58] The commodification of black male and female bodies proceeds along identical lines in *Reuben*, in both cases rendered through the imagery of doubling and homelessness, as well as through critical retakes of the most stereotypical images of the hypersexual black body. Associating its two main female characters, Kwansa and Flora, with prostitution, the novel recycles the image of the sexually promiscuous black woman, which, as so many black feminist critics have observed, still dominates visual media representations of black female bodies.[59] Wideman takes great risks in his characterization of Kwansa, who, in the words of a reviewer, "comes straight to us from the welfare system's blotter."[60] Jacquie Jones has remarked that postmodern visual media take an "accusatory stance" toward black women's bodies, casting them as too sexually available and/or as incapable of parenting.[61] Reprising these images, Wideman constructs in Kwansa the urban female type pervasively summoned—in "underclass" discourses on teenage pregnancy, out-of-wedlock births, and welfare mothers—to epitomize the pathologies of black urban poverty as well as the steep public costs of unregulated black female sexuality.

Kwansa is compelled to prostitute herself in order to supplement the meager welfare allowance she receives to support her son. Her commodification of her sexuality always occasions a violent splitting of her identity, with the disembodied subject observing the seemingly independent activity of a body she perceives as a detached object. For example, when Kwansa has sex with men from whom she accepts payment, she feels "her flesh slipping off" and "going on about its business" (8). As long as she can say "good-bye to her body," she can convince herself that "she was not a whore" (9). Similarly, Flora comes to terms with her prostitution by disengaging herself from her body: "This body's loaned to me and I rent it out. . . . I don't live in it anymore" (83). To give one last example, Felisha does a "disappearing act" each time she has sex: "She left her beautiful body behind for him to play with but nobody home" (104). In each of these instances, the process of commodification doubles and evacuates the body, converting its use value as "home" into the abstract exchange value of rent. Because visibility always involves the risk of objectification, disappearance into invisibility offers these women their only refuge from commodification.

As we saw at the beginning of this chapter, urban visuality is suspect in African-American literary and cultural studies for its reification of black bodies into commodity objects, whereas oral/aural modes of knowing are affirmed as the more authentic media for accessing black subjectivity and community. *Reuben* offers support for the first part of this position, demonstrating that seeing is caught up in the objectifying dynamics of commodity spectacle, but the novel does not propose that oral modes can somehow escape the logic of the spectacle and enable genuine communication among a community of subjects. *Spectacle* in this novel (as in Guy Debord's usage of the term) is not simply a visual technology but an entire social and economic system organized around the principles of commodity fetishism. In such a system, oral/aural technologies are as subject to the logic of the spectacle as are visual technologies.

Consequently, hearing cannot automatically establish a communal scene of mutually "subjectifying" communication. When characters such as Kwansa or Wally hear the voices of actual or imaginary others in their heads, these voices always diminish the listener's sense of self, as, for example, when Kwansa narrates her story to a group of imaginary auditors whose voices bombard her with the "same ole" accusatory images of her as an unfit welfare mother, a drug addict, and a prostitute (59). In one of the novel's most memorable passages, Reuben's memory is described through the metaphor of a radio talk show:

> Lately, his memory had become more like those all-night, call-in, radio talk shows, an unpredictable mix of voices coming from everywhere and nowhere, voices with nothing in common but an 800 number . . . voices unspeakably lonely, voices full of themselves or full of that profound emptiness apparent only when people come together in numbers to quell it. . . . Like the talk shows, if he paid attention night after night, his memories contained recurrent themes, characters who reappeared, suggesting continuity, narrative momentum, a haphazard semblance of plot. Yet no one was in charge. No host, no writer, no master of ceremonies. No shared notion of style or propriety among the callers. . . . Each voice was supreme, aggressive,

irreconcilable. Reuben's memory of his past was just this bizarre, urgent competition for air time, disembodied souls calling in from the four corners of the universe. (15)

As a striking metaphor for the novel itself and for urban writing in general, this babel of voices conveys the fragmentation of urban community as decisively as do the visual metaphors of knowing and communication presented in the novel. Far from activating the communal dynamics of call and response associated with vocal metaphors in African-American literary criticism,[62] this passage emphasizes the absence of a cultural community cemented by shared styles of communication. As I argue in the next chapter, the fractured community characteristic of urban spectacle is often countered in African-American fiction and literary criticism through oral tropes of folk community located in a pre-urban past. Such tropes project an elsewhere to the city that can be recaptured through memory. Wideman's metaphor of memory as a radio talk show refuses this kind of resolution to problems of urban literary representation, showing that memory and voice are themselves subject to the logic of the spectacle.

That oral tropes in *Reuben* cannot sponsor organic alternatives to the postmodern city does not, however, mean that Wideman presents urban spectacle as an all-determining system that precludes any possibility of critical vision. The novel does suggest such possibilities, which always emerge from within the terms of the urban system. The vehicle of alternate vision is a dialectical imagination that wrests opportunities of critical transformation from the very negativity of given social conditions. The device of the double offers a perfect illustration. The self-estrangement inherent in doubling can also mobilize identity in positive ways, enabling the imaginative creation of an "other, better self," as it does in the case of Kwansa (140). Alienation, an otherwise crippling feature of urban vision, here becomes a distancing mechanism necessary for reinventing identity. Doubling also works as a metaphor for affective identification with others that proceeds through and beyond visual recognition. Reuben suggests to Wally that even if the starting point of all social intercourse among urban strangers is sight, it is possible to "crack the glass" (171) and to imagine unseen linkages between oneself and others.

Reuben's statement that "Things the eye can't see are what makes [someone] your double" (170) implies that a recognition of affinity with others can only occur through extra-visual perception. But imagined connections with others in the novel are usually established by critically appropriating rather than escaping urban visuality. This is best exemplified by the miniature brass figure of a man that Reuben calls his "idol" (65) and "fetish" (66) as well as his double. At the more obvious level, this double, like a commodity fetish, compensates for the perceived inauthenticity of urban identity by embodying a lost plenitude—"a trace of what had once been, of a lost time when [Reuben] had been more, and the more was better" (65). Reuben's objectification of his "missing part" (66) represents a classic case of commodity fetishism, projecting human value onto inanimate objects. In this sense, Reuben's fetish-double masks the absence of reciprocal social relations in the city.

Unlike the commodity fetishist, however, Reuben acknowledges his own transference of social value onto the object when he names it a fetish. For Reuben the fetish works not as a literal substitute for the absence of social mutuality in the city but rather as a symbolic token reminding him of his self-imposed obligation to take responsibility for urban doubles as if they were his long-lost brothers. Identifying the fetish with a black man—any black man—"sealed" in a prison cell (66), Reuben wears it on a chain around his neck as a gesture of symbolic imprisonment. The fetish helps Reuben to "atone for so much forgetting" (68) and to withstand the amnesia that makes possible the city's promise of freedom—a promise Reuben can admit is illusory only as long as he can remember that Philadelphia feels like a jail sentence to vast numbers of black men. In this instance, the fetish, usually exemplary of the alienating dynamics of urban commodity spectacle, becomes the carrier of a compassionate social imagination.

The novel's resolution hinges on a similar affirmation of a symbolic, value-creating imagination that takes urban visuality and imprisonment as its points of departure. In the final chapter, Reuben imagines himself reuniting Kwansa with her lost son, a scene initially presented in decisively visual terms. The reader's perspective in the beginning of the scene is aligned with a camera that follows Reuben into a prison cell containing Kwansa's son. In common with other scenes in the novel that are presented in cinematic terms, this scene makes us conscious of the limitations of our visual perspective. Then, as our perspective narrows and becomes identified with Reuben's, a powerful beam of light appears and "fuses" the faces of Reuben and Kwansa's son: "We are momentarily blinded. We see nothing but a luminous, smoky shaft, as for an instant we are surrounded, drowned by light. The sides and backs of our skulls have dropped away" (215). We lose ourselves and our bodies, ride the waves of light long enough to hear Reuben tell Kwansa's son that he has come to take him home. It is clear from the images of blindness and disembodiment (our skulls dropping away) that the light illuminating this scene is the visionary light of imagination rather than the light of sensory vision. But the starting point of this imaginative vision is sight. That we enter this scene through the restricted perspective of camera vision suggests that we must proceed from within a visual modality and then exceed it by means of the imagination. Figuring the imagination through the metaphor of camera vision, the novel's conclusion seeks resolution within the framework of the spectacle.

This resolution also clarifies how the literary imagination might resist the commodity fetishism of urban spectacle—by disavowing the literal claims to representation advanced by photography and other visual media. The ambiguous concluding scene of the novel enacts Reuben's *imagined* release of Kwansa's son from his prison cell. And in fact, Reuben's most valuable function throughout the novel is to serve as an imaginary agent for the disempowered members of the Homewood community, to offer them the symbolic representation denied them by the media and the legal system, and to construct fictional resolutions to their problems. In all these respects, Reuben is a figure for the writer of fiction, whose claims to representation of urban community must always be metaphorical rather than literal. The power of Reuben's fictions is the potentially liberating power of illusion, which is liberating precisely because it acknowledges its fallibility, in contrast to the spectacle, which holds us captive by masquerading as an unmediated reflection of reality.[63] Reuben's assumption of responsibility for the Homewood community is tentatively affirmed as a release from not only the literalism but also the voyeurism of urban visuality. Reuben's dialectical revisioning of the fetish as a brother, and of light as a medium of fusion rather than of detached observation, proffers the possibility of achieving reciprocal forms of human recognition that overcome the subject-object dichotomy of modern urban vision.

Pornography and Voyeurism in *Philadelphia Fire*

Whereas in *Reuben,* voyeurism works mainly as a metaphor for the objectifying modes of knowing promoted by photography and other visual technologies, in *Philadelphia Fire* voyeurism is featured both literally and as a metaphor. The novel contains several extended scenes of sexual voyeurism that force attention to the gendered structure of the subject-object dichotomy intrinsic to modern techniques of vision. *Reuben,* as we saw previously, forecloses such attention by suggesting that racial "others," regardless of gender, are feminized as they are turned into objects of voyeuristic consumption. This foreclosure appears especially surprising because Eadweard Muybridge's central role in the novel would seem to offer a rich occasion for exploring the conjunction between sexual voyeurism and visual knowledge.

Muybridge's book *Animal Locomotion* contained several photographs of nude women performing the same types of movements as men but also some conventionally feminine "exercises of graceful movement," including "dropping handkerchiefs, flirting with fans, getting in and out of bed, in and out of hammocks, [and] opening parasols."[64] As Linda Williams points out, even when the women in the photographs are engaged in the same physical activities as men, these are accompanied by "superfluous detail" that differentiates their bodies from those of men, exemplifying the fetishism (the "more" that evokes plenitude) operative in visual representations of women. In this respect, according to Williams, Muybridge's photographs record "what John Berger has called the different 'social presence' of men and women—the fact, as Berger succinctly puts it, that '*men act* and *women appear*.'"[65]

Williams argues that Muybridge's work (both his still photographs and his protocinematic technology of the zoopraxiscope) straddles the genres of photography and pornography, clarifying the overlap between scientific will-to-truth and visual observation of feminine sexuality. In Muybridge's photography, driven by "the principle of maximum visibility," the will to knowledge "takes place through a voyeurism structured as a cognitive urge" (48). Elaborating on the complicity between photography and pornographic voyeurism, Annette Kuhn notes that both modes equate truth with visibility, and observation with objectification, rehearsing the subject-object division of positivist approaches to knowledge. Pornographic voyeurism makes conspicuously visible the gendered nature of this division, taking for granted the masculine position of the spectator and casting feminine sexuality as its riddling object of investigation.[66] Wideman's *Philadelphia Fire* fully exploits the opportunity, missed in *Reuben*, to explore this intersection of objectifying visual knowledge and masculine sexual voyeurism. In this novel's scenes of knowing, the object to be known is the nude female body and the subject of knowledge is always the masculine voyeur anxiously aware of the sexual curiosity driving his will to visual knowledge.

Cudjoe, the narrator of *Philadelphia Fire*, also a writer, is a literal voyeur who peeps at the bodies of naked women, himself perplexed by the question, "What was he looking for in women's bodies?"[67] Whatever it is, Cudjoe is unable to find it, and the persisting mystery of women's bodies justifies his compulsive desire for voyeuristic observation. The novel contains four extended scenes of voyeurism, in which Cudjoe veers between the conflicting emotions of guilt and pleasure. The female body appears as a fetish that incites pure pleasure in those scenes in which the woman appears actively to solicit the voyeur's gaze. In the first scene of voyeurism presented in the novel, the nameless woman in Clark Park is aware of Cudjoe watching her and, in fact, seems to arrange her body so as to display her genitals. The exhibitionist impulses that Cudjoe ascribes to this woman provide an illusion of reciprocity, overlaying his awareness that voyeuristic pleasure is by definition one-sided. This uncomfortable awareness erupts to the surface in the novel's final scene of voyeurism, where Cudjoe's guilt is compounded by the fact that he is watching, with sexual pleasure, the naked body of a prepubescent girl whom he feels bound to protect as a daughter. Cudjoe tries to mitigate his guilt by projecting his own thrill in watching onto the girl's body, so that it is she who enjoys being watched. But the illusion of mutuality fails in this scene, as Cudjoe ends up feeling "compromised by the sexuality of the moment" (124).

Cudjoe admits the invasiveness of his voyeuristic gaze in the scene in which he peeps through a window at eighteen-year-old Cassandra, the daughter of a friend, bathing naked in the moonlight. Even here, Cudjoe initially strains to believe that Cassandra, who is entirely unaware of being watched, "welcomes him, drinks him into every pore of her body" (63), but his pleasure in watching Cassandra is tainted by his knowledge that he is "spying," that it is "wrong to be stealing from her. Violating her privacy. Poaching" (64). Linda Williams has argued that what fetishism effectively displaces is reciprocal relations between self and other, pursuing instead a detached visual pleasure that seizes the other as an object (101). By this definition, most of the scenes of voyeurism in *Philadelphia Fire* are unsuccessful attempts at fetishism in that the lack at the core of the fetish—the lack of mutual relation with an other—forms the explicit subject of Cudjoe's anxious preoccupation. The subtext of fetishism often becomes the manifest text of Cudjoe's voyeurism, as his pleasure in watching is interrupted by his awareness that he cannot even desire tactile connection: "If a sturdy bridge connected his window to hers, he wouldn't cross it. She was close enough. Untouchable, unreachable, and that's what he liked" (54). The fact that the object of vision is "so near and yet so far" (56) forms an essential condition of all visual pleasure, which the situation of voyeurism brings into the foreground. The phrase "so near and yet so far" precisely captures the paradoxical logic of simultaneous presence and absence that characterizes the appearance of photographic objects: in Susan Sontag's words, "a photograph is both a pseudo-presence and a token of absence" (16). Just as photography offers a way of "certifying experience but also refusing it," so, too, does voyeurism.[68]

Sontag's phrase "both a pseudo-presence and a token of absence" can, of course, equally apply to the commodity fetish, which, too, elicits voyeuristic consumption. In *Critique of Commodity Aesthetics,* Wolfgang Fritz Haug analyzes the crucial ways in which sexuality services the voyeuristic logic of commodity fetishism. Haug argues that commodity exchange in advanced capitalist societies depends on a conflict between the interests of buyers and sellers: the buyer seeks out commodities for their specific use values, whereas the seller sees them as means of abstract valorization. The resolution to this conflict hinges on aesthetic illusion, which helps imbue the commodity with the appearance of use value and transforms commodity consumption into the consumption of image value rather than sensuous use value. In this process, aesthetic appreciation, sexual desire, and exchange value become so deeply interfused and removed from use value that sexual objects themselves are "rendered non-specific." Not only do sexual objects take on the form of the commodity, but all commodity objects begin to assume a sexual form: "by taking on sexuality as an assistant, exchange value transforms itself into sexuality." The general sexualization of all commodity objects abstracts and aestheticizes sexual desires, which are then best gratified by means of image consumption (or consumption of illusory use value). Haug concludes that this promise of "seemingly unhindered satisfaction" ultimately transforms the very structure of human sexuality: as the possibility of direct sensuous pleasure becomes increasingly remote, "a general voyeurism is reinforced, habituated, and determines the human instinctual structure."[69]

The voyeuristic desire activated by commodity fetishism is decisively gendered—a point unmarked by Haug but elaborated in Luce Irigaray's widely read essay "Women on the Market." Here, Irigaray amplifies Marxist accounts of commodity fetishism—such as Haug's—by identifying commodities with women. This move is justified not only by the fact that the capitalist institutions of private property and patriarchal family require the expropriation of women's reproductive use value but also by the rampant exploitation of women's iconized bodies to stoke commodity consumption. In other words, women's bodies are doubly commodified—as objects of exchange and also as symbolic signs that lend sexual appeal to all commodities. Irigaray writes that as the use value of women's bodies is converted into exchange value, these bodies are stripped of their particularity and sublimated into abstract bearers of value:

> When women are exchanged, woman's body must be treated as an abstraction. The exchange operation cannot take place in terms of some intrinsic, immanent value of the commodity.... It is thus not as "women" that they are exchanged, but as women reduced to some common feature.... On this basis, each one looks exactly like every other. They all have the same phantom-like reality.[70]

The transmutation of female bodies into "a standardized sign, an exchangeable signifier" (187) banishes their "concrete forms" as well as "all the possibilities of 'real' relations with them" (181).

The voyeuristic scenes in *Philadelphia Fire* enact an identical process of abstraction, making explicit the gendered logic of commodity fetishism. What Cudjoe most appreciates about the woman in the apartment window across from his is that she has "No name. No history. She was the body of woman. . . . All women. Any woman" (54). The woman in the window is like the woman in Clark Park, who is in turn like a woman Cudjoe knew but did not quite know in Greece. All these women must remain remote and interchangeable so that Cudjoe's voyeuristic pleasure is not threatened by the possibility of actual relations with any of them. When one of these women begins to remind Cudjoe of Caroline, his estranged wife, he quickly suppresses the memory. It is necessary that "she be other women too. All women" (54), because if she becomes a singular rather than generalized woman, she rekindles "the hurt" that has marred Cudjoe's "real" relations with women such as his wife (35). Unlike the invulnerable fetish, who is "a statue, a woman perfectly formed from marble" (27), women's real bodies are disturbing because they "fall apart" and become "contorted by grief" (56). The fact that Cudjoe will not be answerable for the pain he has caused his wife is what keeps him running throughout the novel, seeking through voyeurism an escape from reciprocal recognition: "That's what he couldn't face. The mirror in her eyes. The hurt. The truth. Run. Run. Never look back" (69–70).

In addition to the difficulties of human connection, the "truth," the "hurt" that the fetish bodies in *Philadelphia Fire* conceal is not, as we might expect, the hurt of castration but rather the hurt inflicted on human bodies by the workings of time, both natural and historical. The bodies that Cudjoe tries to fetishize are all seemingly exempt from the temporal processes that ravage real bodies. In this respect, too, these bodies resemble the commodity fetishes described by Irigaray—abstracted signifiers that suppress the materiality of particular female bodies. The woman in the window "possessed no insides. No periods. No illnesses, no female disorders. Wouldn't age or die" (56). Because of their reproductive capacity, women are typically associated with the gross materiality of nature and perceived as being more deeply immersed in the bodily cycles of birth, age, and death than are men. If this identification with biological process is what renders the actual bodies of women frightening and repellent, the fetish body is seductive because it promises an aestheticized sexual gratification along with a transcendence of messy corporeality. The two women, or rather girls, with whom Cudjoe fails to sustain the fetishistic illusion are Cassandra and Rebecca, who arouse anxiety precisely because he cannot abstract their bodies from the process of time. Cudjoe justifies spying on these girls with the rationale that "there's not much time, never enough time" (65), so he must learn their secrets and save them from the mortality that is already "clairvoyant" in their young bodies (123).

Like Muybridge, the voyeur, too, wants to stop time and to immortalize his objects of vision. A passage in *Philadelphia Fire* suggests that the photograph preserves time in a fetishistic manner strikingly similar to that of Cudjoe's voyeuristic approach. Musing over photographs of several generations of a family, the narrator writes that "in the face of time they are a record of its incomprehensibility but also its finitude, its peculiar, sensuous, visceral availability." Through its apparently indexical nature, its making present something that has existed in the past, the photograph offers "ocular proof" of the continuity of time and of the availability of the past in the present. But, of course, the belief that we can possess time by holding its visual image in our hands supplies an illusory solace against our actual loss of time: all we really own of time is "an emptiness as tangible as a photo" (119). What the fetish eliminates is the qualitative dimension, the use value of lived time, evoking instead the "homogeneous, empty time" of the commodity. As Debord writes, the absence of lived time entails a corollary absence of death; aging and dying are "strictly forbidden" in the world of the commodity spectacle (160). The visual fetish, whether female body or photograph, arrests time in a futile effort to compensate for the scarcity of lived time in advanced capitalist societies.

Appropriately enough, each of the novel's scenes of sexual voyeurism appears as a tableau that freezes the flow of the narrative.[71] But the dissociation of the voyeuristic scenes from the rest of the narrative is also puzzling. The ostensible subject of the novel, as suggested by its title, is the MOVE crisis that occurred in Philadelphia in 1985.[72] The protracted confrontation and deadlock between the city administration and MOVE, an African-American back-to-nature organization, culminated in a police bombing that set fire to MOVE's headquarters, resulting in eleven deaths and the destruction of sixty-one houses. The MOVE disaster, cited by Mike Davis as "the My Lai of the war against the underclass" (275), crystallizes Wideman's critique of the repressive violence directed at African-Americans in the name of urban law and order. Given this central concern, the novel's voyeuristic scenes appear curiously disconnected and incongruous, especially because the racial issues highlighted in the MOVE sections of the narrative are conspicuously missing from the sections on voyeurism. The race of the women observed by Cudjoe is never specified, an omission that fosters an exclusively gendered understanding of voyeurism. Gender and race thus seem to form the parallel but disjunct tracks of the novel's critique of postmodern urban visuality.

Although these tracks never directly meet, the voyeurism and MOVE sections of the novel are implicitly linked by their shared concern with the question of whether an innocent knowledge of the body is possible within the terms of urban commodity spectacle. As we have already seen, Cudjoe's voyeuristic observation of women's bodies is governed by the laws of exchange value. If, as Haug argues, in advanced capitalist societies "exchange value transforms itself into sexuality," then all looking within such societies becomes pornographic and voyeuristic. Disavowing this porno-graphic propensity, MOVE propagates an Edenic vision intended to restore the naked body to a primal condition of innocence. In the novel, MOVE pursues its naturalist agenda in direct opposition to the city, castigating urban order as the evil manifestation of a social system, driven by exces-sive consumption, that corrupts the state of nature. It is by repudiating commodity consumption and by opting out of the circuits of urban ex-change value that MOVE seeks to recover the natural use values of the body.

But MOVE is disciplined by the city administration because it threat-ens reigning ideologies of progressive urbanism. References to dreadlocks, funk, briar patches, and savagery clarify that racial panic motivates the city's violent containment of MOVE, replaying the familiar logic that primitivizes black bodies and forces them outside the limits of modern urban order. *Philadelphia Fire* strongly condemns the ideology of urban modernization that rationalizes the city's repressive action against MOVE, but, as dis-cussed in chapter 2, the novel does not fully endorse MOVE's organicist ideology. Cudjoe's narrative is strewn with images of a lost Eden, a place and time of innocent communion between self and other, man and woman, that predates the fall into the city. Although Cudjoe longs for an Edenic origin, he recognizes that such longings are as much symptoms of nostalgia for a purity that never existed as they are forms of utopian critique.

The scenes of sexual voyeurism in *Philadelphia Fire* underscore that knowledge of urban others is always guilty because it is compliant with the pornographic modality of commodity spectacle. The novel extends sexual voyeurism into a full-blown metaphor for urban modes of perception through persistent analogies between the knowable city and the naked female body. For example, Cassandra's skin is likened to the "thousand-eyed gate of a great city thrown open to receive" Cudjoe (63); in another scene, Cudjoe's perplexity at his wife obstructing his view of her genitals merges into his anger at her misreading of a road map. Hinging urban spatial security on visual knowledge of female sexuality, these images bear out Elizabeth Wilson's argument that the Sphinx (a word Cudjoe actually uses to describe one of his objects of voyeuristic vision [26]), or the enigma of female sexuality, is often at the heart of masculine discourses about urban disorder and crisis.[73] Similarly in *Reuben,* images of cross-dressing are used to render Wally's disorientation by the opaqueness and mobility of urban identities. Wally's fear that "You just never know" anything for sure in the city fixes on the possibility of women infiltrating masculine spaces (of business and finance in this case) disguised as men. It is only by stripping one such imaginary woman naked in front of a mirror that Wally feels he has restored an intelligible urban order (33).

Philadelphia Fire contains a single visionary image of the city's spatial order as a "miraculous design," a "prodigy that was comprehensible." Surveying the architecture of downtown Philadelphia, Cudjoe briefly overcomes voyeuristic vision through his modernist dream of the city as a visual terrain that can be cognitively mapped by the human imagination. The cityscape in this scene seamlessly sutures the observer into the position of the centered and god-like viewer of Cartesian perspective. The lines formed by the avenues and buildings all converge into the vanishing point of the spectator's eye, in fact requiring this eye to discover its visual form: "I belong to you, the city says. This is what I was meant to be. You can grasp the pattern. Make sense of me. Connect the dots. I was constructed for you" (44). But this illusion of perfect correspondence between spatial form and human imagination is superseded a few moments later by Cudjoe's disenchanted view of the segregated zones that actually comprise the order of downtown Philadelphia.

The novel's sole image of an urban space hospitable to the human imagination is dispelled by numerous counterimages of an atomized and militarized city that impedes reciprocal knowledge: "Sometimes I've thought of myself, of you, of ourselves, as walled cities, each of us a fortress, a citadel, pinpoints of something that is the inverse of light, all of us in our profusion spread like a map of stars, each of us fixed in our place on a canvas immense beyond knowing" (120). Like Mike Davis's description of "Fortress L.A.," this map of unknowing limns not a spatially illegible postmodern city but a city whose rigid spatial divisions and fractured communities mirror the blockage of human recognition. This is the world of the mutual unenlightenment of everyone: to quote Guy Debord, "the world of everyone's separation, estrangement, and nonparticipation."[74]

That voyeurism is an aggressive mode of invasion rather than of mutual illumination is horrifically elaborated in a scene in which Cudjoe portrays the omniscient narrator of fiction as a video camera that must surgically cut open a skull in order to gain access to the brain. Wanting to understand what goes on in the minds of his students, Cudjoe catches himself staring at "a small perfect skull, . . . the bone porous so when I trepanned away a side wall my entrance was silent, cunning, a perfect cross-section revealed . . . I sit, unobtrusive as a video camera at a keyhole and observe the goings on" (134). Restricted to the remote visual perspective of the camera spying through the keyhole, we learn little about the student's interior life. The equation of sight with knowledge is discredited in this scene, which raises a series of questions about Melissa (the student) that are unanswerable within the frame of our video camera perspective and which calls attention to all the invisible presences that we, "with all our privilege, cannot see" (137). The camera lens also fails to give us a narrative understanding of the scene it captures; all we've "stolen" from Melissa's life is a "long stunned moment between" (138), a moment with no before or after.

Like *Reuben, Philadelphia Fire* shows that modern and postmodern visual technologies alike promote a voyeuristic view of history by disaggregating durative time into commodified fragments. Cudjoe's troubled awareness of the scarcity of lived time in the society of the spectacle is powerfully conveyed in a scene in which the (unfetishizable) image of his wife's aging breast abruptly cuts to Cudjoe marveling at the speed and simultaneity of worldwide satellite transmission. If this juxtaposition implies that the instantaneity of electronic visual media intensifies our anxieties about our mortality and our alienation from biological time, the immediately preceding scene suggests that these media also estrange us from historical time. Cudjoe first learns of the MOVE disaster in Philadelphia as he is flipping through the twenty-nine cable channels that nourish the illusion of consumer choice. Cudjoe's desire for in-depth knowledge about what exactly happened in Philadelphia is thwarted as the news item cuts to "whatever, wherever with electronic speed" (101). Replaying the discontinuous movement of television programming, with the announcement of a catastrophic event bizarrely followed by commercials for Chiquita bananas and rowing machines, this scene recapitulates modernist critiques of visual media for shattering historical time into discrete and decontextualized images.

Cudjoe, the writer figure in Wideman's novel, seeks to counter the collective amnesia fostered by the society of the spectacle by writing a book about MOVE that will restore the "thick time" of narrative and historical understanding.[75] *Philadelphia Fire* attempts the same, with the narrator repeatedly affirming the essential interconnectedness of the events presented in the novel. For example, we are told that the exclusion of Jackie Robinson from a Philadelphia hotel was the real beginning of the MOVE event (108) and that the seemingly disjointed structure of the narrative really coheres around the topic of the MOVE fire (91). But such assertions notwithstanding, the novel's cutting and pasting of disconnected scenes and events too closely resembles the televisual mode. The narrator himself, appearing in the name of the author, John Edgar Wideman, admits that he feels his "narrative faculty weakening" (115). Narrativity, the mode of understanding that is so often affirmed as a corrective to the dehistoricizing effects of visual media,[76] is at once the most urgently sought and the most elusive value in *Philadelphia Fire*.

Narrative alternatives are difficult to sustain in *Philadelphia Fire* because writing itself has been invaded by the logic of the commodity spectacle. The historical book about MOVE that Cudjoe wants to write is mocked by a former member of the organization on the grounds that regardless of its content, the book remains an object that "people have to buy," and so it necessarily participates in the commodification of the MOVE story (19). Cudjoe himself worries that in writing the book, he is "stealing from the dead" (10), just as he steals from and poaches on the bodies of the women he subjects to his voyeuristic investigation. Even the writer's imaginative seizure of others' experiences is described through the metaphor of voyeurism. As Margaret Jones recounts her sexual encounters with the leader of MOVE, Cudjoe describes his effort of empathetic understanding as stripping, "sniffing," "nos[ing] under someone's clothes" (15–16). Similarly, at the memorial ceremony for the dead MOVE members that closes the novel, the writer is "a spy," just like Samuel Delany's Pryn in the city of Neveryóna. Aligning the writer's vision with the television cameras filming the event (194), *Philadelphia Fire* underscores the inability of writing to transcend the voyeuristic conditions of urban knowledge.

The scene cited earlier, in which the narrator's access to a student's mind is described through images of surgical penetration, ends—like Toni Morrison's *Jazz*—with a passage contrasting the distancing mode of visuality with the immediacy of oral communication. Here, the narrative self-reflexively calls attention to its own status as a book caught up in a silent, visual system of communication: "If I could, I would speak directly to her. Ask her questions.... But this fakery, viewer and viewed connected temporarily by a hole in a skull, does not allow real questions back and forth. Look, don't talk. Talk is touching, is disturbing the scene" (138). This passage seems to accredit the opposition between visual and oral tropes that prevails in African-American literary and cultural studies. *Philadelphia Fire* contains several moments when the narrator attempts to participate in various urban communities through hearing, as, for example, when he listens to adolescent voices speaking and singing in Clark Park or when he listens to the drums prophesying "the fire next time" at the memorial ceremony that closes the novel. Neither of these scenes realizes the immersion of writer with community that typifies the classic scene of hearing in the African-American literary tradition (or, to be more precise, in critical accounts of this tradition). In the first scene, the children's voices are as unintelligible to Cudjoe as are the visual signs he struggles to interpret throughout the novel; in the final scene, as we have already seen, the writer–community fusion is aborted by references to Cudjoe as a "spy," an outsider to the scene.

Philadelphia Fire also includes a rap lyric that appears to confirm Houston Baker's claim that rap music offers a unique "hearing" of urban violence in America. This rap song militates against historical amnesia, repetitively recounting the MOVE event, which has long since disappeared from the shallow memory bank of televisual media. The lyric also sounds a rare, prescient note that warns of violent discontentment seething beneath the surface of the city (161–62), and therefore, to paraphrase Baker, deserves a hearing that might forestall urban disaster. But in *Philadelphia Fire,* auditory signs are not the only or the most reliable indices of urban crisis: the graffiti on the city walls serves much the same purpose, of heralding imminent urban violence, as does the rap lyric. And in any case, both rap and graffiti are the expressive forms of an urban subcultural community that the professional writer, because of his age and class status, cannot really understand or join.

Like *Reuben, Philadelphia Fire* eschews oral resolutions to problems of urban representation. Both novels relentlessly expose the ways in which the literary imagination is co-opted by the visual dynamics of the society of the spectacle. Suspicion of the spectacle's power to simulate reality motivates Wideman's refusal of narrative realism in *Philadelphia Fire.*[77] In this novel, "realism" is cryptically defined as "the stolid arbitrariness of the paltry wares we set out each morning in the marketplace" (158). This definition posits an equivalence between literary realism and the commodity fetishism of the spectacle: the spectacle forms a marketplace in which an arbitrary (in the sense of socially projected) system of exchange value assumes the stolidity of a naturally given reality. In order to resist the "seenness" of the spectacle,[78] Wideman's novels disrupt and call into question their own truth-claims, forcing attention to the fragility of their fictional illusions. Emphasizing its own textuality—its status as a second-order system of linguistic representation that is necessarily inadequate to the real—*Philadelphia Fire,* in common with *Reuben,* disclaims the most seductive feature of spectacular vision, its advertisement of itself as a literal reproduction of reality.

Textuality and Voyeurism in *Jazz*

Toni Morrison agrees with Wideman that "spectacle" paralyzes critical intelligence by means of its ability to "monopolize appearance and social reality."[79] For both writers, it is the "already scripted" quality of spectacle that allows it smoothly to perform its task, which, in Morrison's words, is "the production of belief" (xvi). Governed by the laws of commodity exchange, the spectacle bestows visibility only on those versions of reality that can be profitably "sold and distributed as public truth" (xvii). In agreement with Debord, Morrison suggests that its visual modality is what makes spectacle "immune to correction." Spectacle can function efficiently as a complete and unfalsifiable system of representation because it "offers signs, symbols, and images that are more pervasive and persuasive than print" (xvi). But Morrison's novel *Jazz* does not sustain this distinction between spectacle and print. Here, the printed book is shown to be embroiled in the logic of urban commodity spectacle. A conspicuous difference between

Jazz and Wideman's novels is that Morrison's novel seeks an organic elsewhere to urban spectacle and seems ultimately to find it through oral and
tactile forms of communication. If voice and touch make possible a tangible connection to reality, this reality cannot be grasped except fleetingly
through the medium of the printed book, which, as a commodity, is caught
up in the abstract equivalences of exchange value. As an instance of urban
textuality, the book participates in an arbitrary system of visual signification that always "miss[es] the mark" (219)—in other words, always fails
to capture the real, which Morrison's novel identifies with a pre-urban,
pre-capitalist human nature situated in the rural South.

Appropriately enough, *Jazz* takes as its setting the 1920s era, which
witnessed the massive dislocation of African-Americans from the rural
South and their entry into an industrialized economy as well as into urban
commodity culture. Contemporaneous commentators regarded the urban
migrations as a "mass movement toward the larger and more democratic
chance."[80] But, as *Jazz* makes clear, this aspiration was widely viewed as a
threat to the stability of a racialized urban order. Violent hostility greeted
black soldiers returning from a war they had fought to establish their commitment to American democratic principles. During the Red Summer of
1919, race riots broke out in more than twenty cities, sparked in part
by the "new militancy" of returning black soldiers.[81] *Jazz* alludes to one
such riot that occurred in East St. Louis in 1917, during which nearly
two hundred African-Americans were killed and six thousand burnt out of
their houses. Dorcas, a character in Morrison's novel, is orphaned when
her mother is burnt and her father stomped to death during this riot.
An anonymous choric voice in *Jazz* suggests two possible explanations for
the 1917 riot—white consternation at the prospect of blacks attempting to
seize the democratic chance and black outrage at the systematic sabotaging
of this chance.

It was not only the new militant spirit of returning black soldiers but
also the arrival of thousands of black migrants into the cities that provoked
racial violence during this period. The urban migrations spawned fears
of economic competition and social conflict, even though the migrants
were tightly confined to the lowest-paying employment niches and segregated residential neighborhoods; to quote the choric voice from *Jazz*,
"how perfect was the control of the workers, none of whom (like crabs
in a barrel requiring no lid, no stick, not even a monitoring observation)
would get out of the barrel" (57). Notwithstanding this observation, the
novel depicts two notable efforts by African-Americans to claim access to
urban public space in the decade preceding the 1920s: the July 1917 silent
march down Fifth Avenue in New York City, protesting the East St. Louis
riot, and the February 1919 victory march, also down Fifth Avenue, of

the 369th Regiment returning from the war. Advertising black anger and pride, these marches made spectacularly visible the racial contestations over urban public space during this period.

If, through the triumphal march of the 369th Regiment, *Jazz* recalls the masculine racial militancy that aroused white panic, the novel also identifies another powerful source of urban panic during this period—the new public visibility of black female sexuality.[82] With the accelerated urbanization of black culture during the Jazz Age, black women's bodies came under national scrutiny as objects signifying the pleasures of illicit sexuality as well as the dread of social chaos. Moral panic about black female sexuality was fanned by the new jazz music, which was itself the prime signifier of racialized urban disorder. Characterized as primitive jungle music by opponents and enthusiasts alike, jazz was perceived to be so "harmful and degrading to civilized races" that it "may tear to pieces our whole social fabric."[83] Alarmist racial rhetorics about the atavistic threat posed by jazz music to modern urban order were appropriated by black middle-class urbanites, who sought to protect their own relatively privileged but precarious position within northern urban society by stressing their distance from the low-down, gutbucket jazz culture that was being imported into the cities by newly arriving migrants.[84] A significant source of the black middle class's distaste for jazz was its seeming complicity in primitivist conceptions of black sexuality. Contemporary associations of jazz with an excessive black sexuality menacing to urban order derived partly from the fact that jazz in the 1920s was usually performed in cabarets, saloons, and nightclubs located in segregated entertainment districts that overlapped with vice zones. The spatial proximity of jazz performances to illegal activities such as gambling, bootlegging, and especially prostitution fed its notorious reputation as "a whorehouse music," which, if left unchecked, would incite sexual anarchy.[85] The new urban music abetted the commodification of black female sexuality—apparent not only in the metonymic connection between jazz and prostitution but also in the sexually explicit lyrics of the classic women blues singers of the 1920s. These singers' exhibition of sexual desire was conditioned by their participation in the urban entertainment market, as recording industries shrewdly marketed black female sexuality as a profitable object of cultural consumption.[86]

In *Jazz*, black women's bodies form the very currency of urban commodity spectacle. Throughout the novel, the thrill of the city is rendered by means of fragmented visual images of black women's bodies—a high-heeled shoe dangling off a foot, silhouetted against an urban tableau of buildings—that stir erotic desire. Lingering on clothes, shoes, hats, purses, and make-up, the narrator constantly calls attention to the packaging of black women's bodies as signifiers of sexuality. *Jazz* explicitly links the two dynamics that run parallel in *Philadelphia Fire:* voyeuristic consumption of commodified female sexuality and violent containment of black bodies viewed as agents of urban crisis. Morrison's novel clarifies the doubled logic of racial primitivism whereby the primal sexuality invested in racial "others" is both fetishized as an object of commodity desire and feared as a threat to urban order. *Jazz* emphasizes this symbiotic connection between commodification and containment through its expert restaging of 1920s discourses about the epidemic of sexual anarchy unleashed by the new urban music.

Discourses of moral panic about jazz and black female sexuality are embodied in the character of Alice Manfred, who apprehensively regards the new urban music as "lowdown stuff that signaled Imminent Demise" (56). What Alice finds most disquieting about jazz is that it boldly brings black women's sexuality into public view, making it vulnerable to commercial exploitation. Alice is frightened of the city because "That was where whitemen leaned out of motor cars with folded dollar bills peeping from their palms. It was where salesmen touched her . . . as though she were part of the goods they had condescended to sell her" (54). In Alice's view, black urban women invite such gestures by flaunting their sexuality, by wearing "those ready-for-bed-in-the-street clothes" (55). Alice disapproves of jazz because it releases black female sexuality to float "like a public secret" in the city skies, underscoring her own failure to "privatize" her niece's body (67). In response, Alice spins a cautionary urban tale that represses her own sexuality as well as her "envy-streaked pleasure" in looking at the sexualized bodies of other women (55).

Like Wideman's *Reuben, Jazz* discloses the violent underside of the sexual desire that is projected onto commodified black bodies. In Morrison's novel, this violence is "laid bare" by the "bones of some broken woman" that appear each week in city newspapers (74). The same bodies that are commercially exploited by record companies as fetish objects exuding primitive sexuality are also the signifiers of a wanton sexual energy that must be suppressed in the interests of urban order. This violence against women's bodies is directly connected to their packaging as commodity objects: "where there was violence" there were also "Red dresses. Yellow shoes" (79). The brutal effects of commodification on black women's bodies take much the same form—of doubling and splitting—in *Jazz* as they do in *Reuben*. For example, in her desperate bid to resist commodity fetishism, Violet doubles herself into Violent, splitting her urban self (*this* Violet) off from "*that* [southern] Violet." At Dorcas's funeral, Violet becomes a passive spectator as Violent knifes the already dead Dorcas in an attempt to understand what made her the perfect object of her husband's desire. While the urban Violet feels deficient when measured against the fetish body of Dorcas, her southern persona has the resources to lash out against the commodity fetish. *That* Violet is the physically strong and sexually desirable southern woman who has the full hips her urban counterpart lacks and who is assured of being Joe's object of desire, unlike *this* Violet who walks about the city streets cold, incomplete, and unwanted. But in investing her southern double with the physical power and sexual plenitude that she believes she has lost since her move to the city, Violet reconstructs her rural southern origins in decidedly urban terms; the southern Violet is as much a phantasmatic product of urban fetishistic desire as an attempt to resist this desire.

Dorcas, whom Violet views as the very incarnation of the fetish, is no more immune to the violent bodily effects of commodification. Dorcas imagines that she is claiming sexual agency by dressing herself in provocative clothes, but her desire is in fact dictated by the publicity images that bombard her in the city. Dorcas learns well the message encoded in these images: everything is "like a picture show" to her (202), and she knows that "a badly dressed body is no body at all" (65). That Dorcas's sense of her sexuality is entirely mediated by visuality is clear from the fact that she leaves her devoted middle-aged lover for the younger Acton, who prods her to cultivate "a look" (190). In modeling her body on advertising icons, Dorcas becomes a voyeuristic spectator of her own body as well as the victim of a double murder, committed first by Joe Trace, who kills her in order to immortalize his own desire, and second by his wife Violet, who stabs Dorcas's corpse in an effort to discover the inner secret of her fetishistic appeal.

Although the bodies of black women form the more visible coin of urban commodity spectacle in *Jazz,* this spectacle also interpellates black men's bodies in parallel ways. It is true that in the novel it is women who mostly "appear," to use John Berger's word, as objects of voyeuristic desire. The novel's narrator is often identified with a masculine eye lusting over the details of women's bodies. But at times the indeterminate gender of the narrator serves to establish the parity and interchangeability of masculine and feminine positions of observation. Sliding easily between these positions, the narrator often describes the objectification of a male and a female body under another's gaze in exactly equivalent terms: "It is terrible when there is absolutely nothing to do or worth doing except to lie down and hope when you are naked she won't laugh at you. Or that he, holding your breasts, won't wish they were some other way" (63).

In a masculine example of the bodily lack produced by urban commodity spectacle, Joe Trace feels an "inside nothing" when he compares his middle-aged body to the bodies of young "roosters" on the street. These young men alone seem to be free and in control of the urban and musical tracks that symbolize the determinist logic of the spectacle. Because Joe is no longer young, he has to study and follow the track, which ultimately leads him to kill Dorcas for replacing him with one of these young "roosters" (132–33). Joe is a helpless victim of the spectacular logic of the city and its music, both of which arouse a hunger for "young loving" (120) that is best gratified by commodity consumption. As in *Philadelphia Fire,* the spectacle in *Jazz* rules out the natural bodily processes of aging. In the city, "there is no such thing as midlife"; if people get old, they have to resign themselves to being the mere voyeurs of urban life, to "sit around looking at goings-on as though it were a five-cent triple feature" (11).

Again, like *Philadelphia Fire, Jazz* presents historical memory as the most serious casualty of urban commodity culture. The city's most seductive lure is a forward-looking vision that demands an erasure of history: "Here comes the new. Look out. There goes the sad stuff. The bad stuff. The things nobody-could-help stuff. The way everybody was then and there. Forget that. History is over, you all, and everything's ahead at last" (7). Recent arrivals to the city can buy into its heady capitalist promise only through a willful amnesia about the rural South that they have left behind. This amnesia is reinforced by the commodification of black female sexuality in the city; it is desire for the clipping high-heeled shoe or the delicately dangling purse, details that "catch [the] eye," that makes the urbanite forget the natural delights of the rural South (34). The narrator's description of urban migration in the second chapter of the novel reads like a litany of losses. A lyrical rendering of all that the migrant forgets—"in no time at all he forgets little pebbly creeks and apple trees. . . . He forgets a sun that used to slide up like the yolk of a good country egg" (34)—sketches out a symbolic geography of the rural South as a natural origin from which city dwellers can sever themselves only by means of a thoroughgoing loss of memory.

Migrants to the city must forget the sensuous use values available in the rural South in order to participate in the exchange system of commodity consumption. Urban spectacle stimulates "homeless" desires that have been uprooted from their southern origins to flit restlessly from one object to another. Instances of this ceaseless displacement of urban desire along a chain of substitutions are so pervasive in the novel that I shall only mention a few examples. Joe's desire for Dorcas replaces his desire for the mother he never knew; this is illustrated in the scene preceding his shooting of Dorcas, which splices together Joe's two different searches, for his mother in the Virginia woods and for Dorcas in the streets of Harlem. Similarly, Joe fills Violet's sense of loss arising from her mother's suicide, and Dorcas associates the origin of her sexual desires with her memory of herself watching her mother burn to death. As Deborah McDowell points out, most objects of desire in the novel are surrogates for an absent mother;[87] the urban chain of exchange value can, in most cases, be tracked back to maternal origins lost in the rural South.

It is hardly surprising, then, that the only body in the novel that appears to exist outside the system of urban exchange value and to promise a primal connection to nature belongs to a character aptly named Wild, who lives in hiding deep within the Virginia woods. As a natural origin, Wild also symbolizes an innocent relation to the body that escapes the perverse logic of urban commodity spectacle. Wild's authenticity depends on her invisibility and on her resistance, when seen, to being fetishized: "Unseen because she knows better than to be seen. After all, who would see her . . . ? Who could, without fright? Of her looking eyes looking back?" (221). Wild's eyes looking back threaten the illusory control and safety of the voyeur's gaze; unlike the visual reassurance proffered by the fetish, Wild's appearance, like Medusa's, arouses fright in the viewer. The only occasion in the novel when readers are given a clear glimpse of Wild is through the eyes of the racially mixed Golden Gray, who struggles to identify himself as pure white. When he comes upon the naked and pregnant Wild lying on the roadside, Golden Gray decides that her "savage" body represents "everything he was not" and that "if it could just be contained, identified," it would offer him "proper protection" against the stain of blackness (149). For Golden Gray, Wild epitomizes the grotesque body of the racial other, which, identified and expelled, can help prop up his own (to him, racially neutral) identity. But overcome by fear of racial contagion, Golden Gray wishes Wild's body could be "stuffed into the ticking along with the bits of rag, stretched shut to hide her visible lumps and moving parts" (153). These lumps and parts, signifiers of an excessive corporeality, align Wild's character with a natural reality, the very obverse of the sublimated female bodies that circulate as signs within the system of exchange value. In frustrating fetishistic vision, Wild's body bears the novel's only hope of an organic elsewhere to urban commodity spectacle.

Until the final chapter of *Jazz*, this alternative is largely unavailable to the novel's characters and narrator because of their containment within the visual regime of urban knowledge. We are given occasional inklings of a way of knowing that lies beyond visuality, although these do not quite prepare us for the reversal that occurs in the last chapter of the novel. One of the few earlier passages to suggest that we can step outside the urban spectacle, or fall through its cracks into an elsewhere, appears in the first chapter of the novel. Here, Violet notices for the first time the "cracks" and "fissures" in the "globe light" that usually illuminates her consciousness of herself in the city. This globe light reveals "with perfect clarity a string of small, well-lit scenes" of herself occupied with various daily activities.

But in keeping with the novel's overall presentation of the self-alienating dynamics of urban spectacle, Violet does not see herself actively performing these tasks; instead, she "sees them being done." Violet assumes that the spectacle is a complete system with solid foundations in reality. However, "in truth, there is no foundation at all, but alleyways, crevices one steps across all the time. But the globe light is imperfect too. Closely examined, it shows seams, ill-glued cracks and weak places beyond which is anything. Anything at all" (22–23). In other words, if we could see past the spectacle's advertisement of itself as a total, inescapable system that is adequate to reality, and recognize its actually arbitrary and fractured nature, we might be able to stumble onto other truths that are excluded by this system, which is at once the system of urban spatial order (with its seemingly rational, calculated design that hides alleyways and crevices), of sight-based epistemology (the globe-light of knowledge), and of linguistic textuality. This last feature is made explicit when Violet stumbles into one of the cracks of the system and feels "the anything-at-all begin in her mouth. Words connected only to themselves pierced an otherwise normal moment" (23).

In keeping with the critical direction of this passage, the novel as a whole presents urban spectacle as a faulty and precarious social construct lacking any real foundation. For Morrison, an arbitrary relation between signs and reality is not a necessary limitation of all systems of representation but rather a specific historical outcome: the representational order of the spectacle is inauthentic because it is imbricated in the exchange dynamics of urban commodity capitalism. The novel's critique of urban commodity spectacle is brought sharply into focus in its treatment of urban writing as a compromised and inaccurate system of representation. As several critics have suggested, the narrator of *Jazz* is the book itself, the concrete physical object as well as the abstract commodity we hold in our hands as we read.[88] As such, the book is necessarily implicated in an arbitrary system of language, characterized by endless substitution of signs and deferral of value. Aligning print textuality with urban spectacle, the novel ironically thematizes its own seduction by urban modes of vision and, in a surprising twist at the end, tentatively affirms the book's power to imagine (although it cannot quite achieve) a firm contact with the real. The novel's critique as well as its projected transcendence of urban spectacular vision are concentrated in its last chapter, worth examining in close detail.

This chapter opens with the narrator's self-reflexive assessment of its own defective vision,[89] focused through the metaphor of urban writing as voyeurism. The narrator here casts itself as a voyeur who enjoys feeding on others' pain. Briefly considering and then dismissing the possibility of sharing rather than curiously observing the suffering of others, the narrator admits to "Feeling a bit false. What, I wonder, would I be without a few brilliant spots of blood to ponder? Without aching words that set, then miss, the mark?" (219). This failure of sympathetic vision, as well as of language, is causally related to the voyeurism of urban modes of perception. The narrator has been trying "to get in lives" by peeping through windows or holes cut into doors. The solipsism and one-sidedness of voyeuristic vision have misled the narrator into "thinking my space, my view, was the only one that mattered" (220). Voyeurism is explicitly presented as a uniquely urban mode of cognition, which mistakes sight for knowledge: "I was watching the streets, thrilled by the buildings pressing and pressed by stone; so glad to be looking out and in on heart-pockets closed to me" (220–21).

That voyeuristic vision is by definition nonreciprocal is made clear in this passage, which punctures the voyeur-narrator's illusion of invisibility and omniscience:

> I thought I knew them [the characters] and wasn't worried that they didn't really know about me. Now it's clear why they contradicted me at every turn: they knew me all along. Out of the corners of their eyes they watched me. And when I was feeling most invisible, . . . silent and unobservable, they were whispering about me to each other. . . . I thought I'd hidden myself so well as I watched them through windows and doors, took every opportunity I had to follow them, . . . and all the while they were watching me. . . . So I missed it altogether. (220)

This passage introduces a "moment of unease" into voyeuristic vision,[90] exposing the false mastery of perspective gained by positioning the self as the source of a unidirectional and invisible gaze. This perspective is relativized by the intrusion of the other's look, which transforms the voyeur from an omniscient, god-like subject into an object contingent on another's vision. The return of the voyeur's look in this scene does not initiate mutuality of vision but, to the contrary, arouses paranoia about the impotence of the self caught by the other's gaze: as this narrator confesses, "how shabbily my know-it-all self covered helplessness" (220).

Absorbed in voyeuristic observation of others, the narrator entirely misses the truth of what it sees, because it reduces the complex particularity of human interactions to the superficies of visual equivalence: "I saw the three of them, Felice, Joe and Violet, and they looked to me like a mirror image of Dorcas, Joe and Violet. I believed I saw everything important they did, and based on what I saw, I could imagine what I didn't" (221). The narrator is referring here to the novel's faulty method of emplotment, dictated by the repetitive grids of urban form. Joe, Violet, and

Dorcas form a melodramatic love triangle in the first part of the novel, which climaxes with Joe's murder of Dorcas. When the narrator sees Felice associating with Joe and Violet, it assumes that she is a mere substitute for Dorcas and predicts that this second threesome will exactly reproduce the first. In this respect, again, the narrator errs because of acceding to the abstract logic of equivalence that governs voyeuristic vision, which, as we saw in the discussion of *Philadelphia Fire,* must banish specificity and surprise in order to achieve security of vision.

Contrary to the narrator's expectations, the characters are ultimately able to escape the logic of urban spectacle and to achieve a genuine knowledge of themselves and others. This is illustrated most clearly in the case of Violet, who by the end of the novel has killed her object self and affirmed the "me" that remains (209). The narrator, too, in the closing pages of the novel, is able to correct its earlier errors of vision and to discern, through the characters, the possibility of an intimate human connection outside the terms of commodity fetishism. This new perception depends on a redefinition of the photographic metaphor associated with urban spectacle: "When I see them [the characters] now they are not sepia, still, losing their edges to the light of a future afternoon. Caught midway between was and must be" (226). In other words, the narrator refuses the deadening vision of the camera, which reifies subjects into "sepia" relics of the past. Instead, for the narrator, these subjects "are real"—a reality evoked through a shift from the frozen images of the camera's vision to the sound of the camera "clicking," the verb capturing the transitive process rather than the finished product of perception. The characters are "the sound of snapping fingers," which "attentive listeners" can hear even when the characters are beyond the range of visual perception (226). The switch from image to sound restores a dynamic temporality and introduces a "pulse" into the structure of vision, an erotic desire that moves its objects, in contrast to the reifying operation of voyeuristic vision.[91] The ability to hear "the snapping fingers, the clicking" rhythm of an extra-spectacular vision is facilitated by a dimming of the visual sense, by "the shade [that] stretches—just there—at the edge of the dream, or slips into the crevices" (227)—the same crevices, we might safely assume, that Violet stumbles into when she steps outside the globe light of the city spectacle. The association of the camera's click with a transformed temporality is extended in the immediately following metaphor of "a magician-made clock with hands the same size so you can't figure out what time it is, but you can hear the ticking, tap, snap" (227). This metaphor, like that of the clicking camera, offers a magical release from a quantitative urban time minutely measured through visual tracking into an alternate time whose qualitative value is experienced through the subtle differentiations ("tap, snap") of pulse and sound.

Whereas the metaphors of the clicking camera and the magical clock suggest possibilities of transformed experience that exist within the visual framework of the spectacle, the last two pages of the novel displace sight altogether in their affirmation of speech, hearing, and touch as the authentic sensory modes of knowledge and communication. In these final pages, the narrator describes Joe and Violet whispering under the bedcovers, enjoying a renewed love that takes "the body [as] its vehicle, not the point." Joe and Violet are under the covers "because they don't have to look at themselves anymore; there is no stud's eye, no chippie's glance to undo them. They are inward toward the other" (228). Because urban spectacle banishes reciprocity and reinforces voyeuristic habits of perception that objectify the body, escape from visuality is a prerequisite for love, which Joe and Violet are able to feel and express for the first time in their "undercover whispers" (228).

But if speaking and listening form the conditions of possibility for authentic communication, how can the novel, a mute commodity object that is visually consumed in silence, exceed the terms of urban spectacle? In the last two paragraphs of *Jazz*, the narrator, a figure for the book itself, longs for a reciprocal erotic relation with the reader couched in metaphors of orality. Expressing "envy" of Joe and Violet's newfound love, the narrator self-reflexively discloses the limitations of its own voyeuristic mode of communication:

> I myself have only known it [love] in secret and longed, aw longed to show it—to be able to say out loud what they have no need to say at all: *That I have loved only you, surrendered my whole self reckless to you and nobody else. That I want you to love me back and show it to me. That I love the way you hold me, how close you let me be to you. I like your fingers on and on, lifting, turning. I have watched your face for a long time now, and missed your eyes when you went away from me. Talking to you and hearing you answer—that's the kick.*
>
> But I can't say that aloud;...If I were able I'd say it. Say make me, remake me. You are free to do it and I am free to let you because look, look. Look where your hands are. Now. (229)

These concluding paragraphs of *Jazz* are remarkable for the intensity of their desire to draw sensuous use values from the conditions of commodity consumption that determine the act of reading. Visuality itself is transformed here, from the one-sidedness and detachment of voyeurism to the book's active solicitation of the reader's return gaze. Moreover, visuality is rendered less abstract and remote as the line of sight is directed toward the tactile image of the reader's hands caressing the book. Yet this desire for immediate sensuous contact is precisely what the book "can't say," because its visual format as well as its commodity status prohibit an un-mediated oral connection. That the book can (and does) *write* this desire, and that readers can "make" and "remake" the book's meaning with their various readings, offers little or no consolation, as is clear from the fact that it is the book's incapacity to speak that forms the focus of the novel's conclusion.[92]

The printed book is too closely implicated in the scopic regime of com-modity fetishism to be able to do anything more than to mourn its own inadequacies and limitations, to write what it "can't say." What's more, the book is deeply caught up in an arbitrary textual system of representa-tion that precludes immediate contact with the real. Whereas *Reuben* and *Philadelphia Fire,* rigorously following their critiques of urban spectacle to their logical conclusions, are compelled to disavow any claims of literal connection with an extratextual real, *Jazz* affirms the possibility of directly accessing this real, although not through the printed book or any visual media. In common with Morrison's other novels, *Jazz* identifies this real with a specific historical and geographical category—the black folk cul-ture of the rural South. This culture operates as an elsewhere to urban spectacle in several interrelated senses. As an oral rather than visual, folk rather than commodity culture, it still bears use value for a specifically black community, in contrast to the commercialized jazz, which, in Morrison's opinion, depreciates in racial value as it circulates within an urban (and indeed global) system of commodity exchange.[93] The rural South (espe-cially as depicted in *The Bluest Eye* and *Song of Solomon*) is also the site of an innocent natural relation to the body, free of the perversions bred by commodity fetishism. And finally, as I elaborate in the next chapter, the South supports the writer's claims to racial representation, eliminating the risks, errors, and mediations involved in constructing urban community.

Jazz is distinct from Morrison's other fiction in that it admits, albeit fleetingly, the possibility of forging black political community in urban con-ditions. Significantly, this possibility is glimpsed by the very same character, Alice Manfred, who otherwise regards black urban commodity culture with moral panic. In Alice's view, the commodification of black women's bod-ies into sexual objects is abetted by a commercialized urban jazz music. The novel's narrator endorses Alice's equation between urban commod-ity spectacle and mechanically reproduced jazz music through recurrent metaphorical comparisons between the grooves of phonograph records and the tracks of the city grid. Both images convey the determining power of the commodity spectacle, which fosters the illusion of consumer sovereignty even as it turns individuals into puppets lacking independent choice. But if jazz whets commodity "appetite" (59), this same music, in Alice's opinion, also "had something to do with the silent black women and men marching down Fifth Avenue to advertise their anger over two hundred dead in East St. Louis" (56–57). The march protesting the 1917 East St. Louis riot is accompanied by drums, beating the same rhythms as jazz music, that create a "gathering rope," a "secure and tight" cord of black political fellowship (58). Commodified sexual hunger and political anger are inextricably fused in this scene, which offers Morrison's most complex fictional treatment of urban commodity culture and qualifies her typical presentation of urbanization as a process that saps the communal use value of black culture.

Jazz is also unique among Morrison's novels for conceding the impossibility of realizing rural resolutions to the problems of urban commodity culture. The conditions of an exchange economy shape human (and sexual) relations even in the rural South presented in the novel. As Violet realizes while recalling her youthful days in Virginia when she and Joe first met and fell in love, "from the very beginning I was a substitute and so was he" (97); there is no pure, unmediated human relation, even in the rural South. But this insight—that urbanism forms our inescapable contemporary condition—is crossed by the novel's resolution and its ultimate affirmation of Wild as the original nature that predates the capitalist city. Toward the end of *Jazz,* the narrator is "touched" by Wild and "released" from its imprisonment in the urban spectacle (221). But the novel does not clarify how exactly we might touch Wild, recover our original nature, establish a reliable connection with reality from within the framework of the spectacle. For the most part, *Jazz* veers between a bleak view of literature's debilitation by the voyeuristic dynamics of the spectacle and a "wild" hope of redemption dependent on the displacement of writing by a folk oral modality. The limitations and contradictions of such imagined alternatives to postmodern urbanity form the subject of my next chapter, which focuses on the resolution to problems of urban literary representation offered by the southern folk aesthetic.

4.

Reading as Listening: The Southern Folk Aesthetic

The signs don't lie. At least not these signs.
—Gloria Naylor, *Mama Day*

In "The Politics of Fiction, Anthropology, and the Folk: Zora Neale Hurston," first published in 1991, Hazel Carby tries to account for the contemporary academic celebrity of Zora Neale Hurston. Carby argues that Hurston's work, which identifies authentic black culture with the rural South, evaded the cultural conflicts sparked by urbanization, and that the current academic reclamation of Hurston exemplifies a similar sort of evasion. Carby advises African-American literary critics "to acknowledge the complexity of [their] own discursive displacement of contemporary conflict and cultural transformation in the search for black cultural authenticity. The privileging of Hurston . . . at a moment of intense urban crisis and conflict is perhaps a sign of that displacement."[1] Carby's provocative argument can be extended beyond its specific reference to the canonization of Hurston and applied to the decisive turn toward southern folk culture under way in African-American literary studies. This literary turn south revives organic forms of racial community that are unavailable in contemporary urban conditions, and in this sense might be said to displace postmodern crises of literary representation.[2]

However, although the southern folk aesthetic does not frontally engage with present-day urban realities, the very fact of its escape may be greatly revealing of these realities. African-American literary texts that take the southern turn often explicitly posit the rural South of a bygone era as an imaginary elsewhere to postmodern urban existence. These texts are vulnerable to all sorts of critique, but we cannot censure them for being fictive, for shying away from direct confrontation with social reality. Samuel

Delany's novel *Neveryóna, or: The Tale of Signs and Cities,* which, as suggested by the two parts of its title, is set in a never-never-land that nevertheless obliquely reflects on the dilemmas of postmodern urban writing, preempts precisely such critique by opening with an epigraph taken from Susan Sontag's *Approaching Artaud.* The passage cited by Delany concerns literary quests for alternate forms of social order, driven by nostalgia for a past that never existed. Sontag argues that we cannot fault such quests for "refus[ing] to submit to the disillusionment of accurate historical knowledge" because they "never sought such knowledge" in the first place.[3]

Agreeing with Sontag, I examine in this chapter the ways in which the rural South works as a stimulant for the postmodern African-American literary imagination and the kinds of resolutions it yields to problems of urban literary representation. At first glance, the contemporary southern folk aesthetic seems puzzling because it reverses the geographical trajectory followed in African-American literature for well over a century. This tradition has been powerfully propelled by the promise of modernization, which has entailed literal and symbolic journeys out of the rural South into the urban North. At the beginning of the twentieth century, the hope of gaining access to modernity was couched in emphatically urban terms and required aesthetic distance from the "plantation traditions" of the rural South.[4] In the postmodern era, when integration of African-Americans into national public life remains incomplete and unevenly realized, disenchantment with the failed promise of modernity is impelling the reverse literary movement south. Refusing to "submit to the disillusionment of accurate historical knowledge," the southern folk aesthetic critically retreats from a century-long history of urbanization that has belied the hopes fueling the northern urban migrations. By returning to the rural South of the days of racial segregation, African-American writers can disavow the dream of full national integration and imaginatively recover the coherent black community that seems increasingly inaccessible in the postmodern urban present. But this kind of restoration of racial community—rooted in a lost past—can only occur at a fictive level, by means of "discursive displacement." Accordingly, although the southern folk aesthetic does not pursue accurate historical knowledge, it supplies such knowledge despite itself, as it were, by betraying the material impossibility of the literary escape it seeks.

Of the many recent novels that exemplify the southern folk aesthetic,[5] I focus on Toni Morrison's *Song of Solomon* and Gloria Naylor's *Mama Day,* because these two novels admit, often self-reflexively but sometimes inadvertently, the difficulties plaguing their own use of the rural South as a device of literary resolution to postmodern urban problems. These difficulties become manifest in Morrison's and Naylor's contradictory treatments of two interconnected systems of cultural value—magic and oral tradition—that are embedded in the rural South and presented as the distinguishing marks of an integral black community. *Song of Solomon* and *Mama Day* attempt to supplant reading by listening, as part of an endeavor to rehabilitate organic racial community. But this endeavor is thwarted because orality and magic in these novels are both mediated *by* metaphors of writing and mediated *to* a resistant urban reader, thereby restoring the problems of literary representation these novels set out to resolve. The difficulties of representation that dog these novels even in the imaginary domain of the rural South obliquely reveal the counterpressure of the postmodern urban real on their exorbitant efforts at literary transcendence. As a consequence, the very category of literature becomes fraught with ambivalence in both novels. If we read backward from this ambivalence toward literature, we can arrive at a refracted understanding of the postmodern urban conditions that these texts strive to transcend.

South to a Very Old Place

The publication of Alice Walker's "In Search of Our Mothers' Gardens" in 1974 initiated the turn toward southern folk culture in African-American women's literature and criticism.[6] The literary turn south has been manifested at several levels—in the reclamation of Zora Neale Hurston that began during the mid-1970s; in essays and fiction by Toni Morrison, Alice Walker, Gloria Naylor, Ntozake Shange, and others; in the criticism surrounding this fiction, which identifies the uniqueness of African-American women's literature with a folk tradition located in the rural South; and in a spate of autobiographies and memoirs about the rural South of a bygone era. That the southern folk aesthetic has become conventional in African-American literary studies is made clear from the fact that it has already been subjected to literary satire. Trey Ellis's novel *Platitudes* (1988) caricatures the literary tendency to feminize and locate authentic black culture in the rural South. The novel is made up of two competing texts: a southern folk text authored by a black woman whose very name, Isshee Ayam, stridently declares her claims to authenticity, and an urban, postmodernist text by a black male writer, Dewayne Wellington. The southern text is saturated with all the signs of racial authenticity—vernacular idioms, rootedness in nature, and a strong sense of place, family, cultural tradition, and community. In contrast, Wellington's text features an anomic urban male protagonist who moves easily among diverse sign systems meant to evoke the hybridity of postmodern urban culture. The two books within Ellis's book conduct an antagonistic dialogue throughout the novel, which ends in a trite and unconvincing rapprochement between the two authors: the sexual union of

Dewayne and Isshee heralds the synthesis of their opposing literary styles on the last page of the novel.

Although Ellis fails to develop the implications of the battle of the books presented in his novel, his very juxtaposition of an urban, postmodernist text with a southern folk text poses the question of why the southern folk aesthetic has gained momentum in the postmodern era. It is not only or primarily in the field of African-American literary studies that interest in southern cultural specificity has burgeoned. American historians, sociologists, and cultural commentators more broadly speaking have become obsessively preoccupied with the South, giving renewed life to the enduring question of what makes the region distinct from the rest of the nation. The southern folk aesthetic in African-American literary studies has much in common with broader movements to revive southern regionalism. The two returns south are distinct in some crucial respects, but both represent the South as a premodern or not quite fully modern space that can ground critiques of advanced capitalism.

One reason the South can function in this way is that, for most of its history, the region has remained more rural and less thoroughly industrialized than the rest of the nation. As William Havard argues, it is because the South was "arrested in a preindustrial state for the greater part of America's century of 'modern development'" that it has managed to preserve some unique traits that may prove greatly valuable to a nation hurtling into a "postindustrial" era. Havard identifies these regional traits as a strong sense of place and history, emphasis on family and local community, and preference for "face-to-face" over abstract and contractual social relations.[7] This nucleus of values appears repeatedly in *Why the South Matters,* a collection of essays by "Fifteen Southerners" (including Havard) published in 1981. Advertised as a reprise of the Agrarian manifesto *I'll Take My Stand,* published half a century earlier, this volume renews the Agrarian claim that the South has special lessons to teach a nation giddily chasing material progress. In most accounts of southern regional difference, localism and face-to-face communal orientation are highlighted as the main features that set the South apart from the rest of the nation. As one of the most passionate advocates of southern regionalism, John Shelton Reed, acknowledges, these southern values are typical of any "folk," "peasant," or "premodern" society with a "traditional value orientation" and are bound to be menaced by the processes of urbanization and industrial development.[8] It follows, then, that for the South to operate as an Archimedean lever for social critique, it must be discursively constructed as a rural zone of arrested development.

This sort of construction of the South—as a residual rural space—can only be maintained at a discursive level, for exactly contemporaneous with culturalist assertions of regional specificity is the dissipation of material distinctions between the South and the rest of the nation. Economic studies of the South concur that since the mid-1970s, virtually all economic indicators reveal a closing of the gap between the South and other regions of the country. Although the Second World War had boosted the southern economy, it was during the 1970s that southern industrial development really took off. This economic boom was aided by a number of interlocking factors, including industrial decline in the Northeast and the Midwest, which spurred relocation of manufacturing to the South. Capital was lured south by the promise of abundant natural resources, cheap labor, tax subsidies, and weak labor unions. As James Cobb shows, in his studies of southern industrialization, during the 1970s the "South found that its heritage of underdevelopment had suddenly become beneficial."[9] Precisely because of its status as an economic hinterland, the South, like many parts of the third world, became a profitable new site for industrial relocation and capital investment.

The southern economic boom of the 1970s hastened the convergence of the region with the rest of the nation, stoking all kinds of anxieties about "the Americanization of Dixie," to borrow from the title of John Egerton's well-known book.[10] Claims of southern cultural distinction, typically resting on rural grounds, could no longer be materially supported by the end of the 1970s, by which time patterns of urbanization in the South had fallen in line with the rest of the nation. By 1980, two-thirds of the southern population lived in metropolitan areas, which had been the prime beneficiaries of the industrial boom. Not only did the rapid urbanization of the area compromise its agrarian-based cultural identity but the very forms of urban development in the South since the mid-1970s began to replicate northern trends of suburban sprawl and inner-city decay, further diminishing the South's capacity to function as an elsewhere to postmodern urban existence.[11] In his lament for a disappearing southern culture, Egerton equates "Americanization" with urbanization, which in turn he associates with a "steady erosion of the sense of place, of community, of belonging."[12] Numerous other observers as well have noted the dramatic transformations of southern urban landscape, architecture, and culture during the 1970s, pointing to the increased presence of shopping malls, apartment complexes, and skyscrapers as disturbing evidence of the standardization of the South.[13]

Of course, it is no accident that a resurgent regionalism celebrating the distinct folk culture of the South has emerged precisely as the South is making its transition to a fully industrialized and urban region. Accelerated economic changes, of the modernizing kind that have occurred in the South since the 1970s, often spark reactive quests to conserve cultural values and traditions associated with an older way of life. As Immanuel Wallerstein has observed, the integration of new regions into the capitalist world system usually inspires a "reassertion of 'particularisms.'" Following this logic, the idea of a culturally distinct South was "created as a mental construct only a short time before it was historically eliminated as a material construct."[14] David Harvey takes a much harsher stance than does Wallerstein in his account of the regional cultural politics that have mushroomed in the postmodern era. Although Harvey is not concerned with the U.S. South in particular, he argues, like Wallerstein, that the global scale of capitalist reorganization since the 1970s has spawned cultural movements seeking to preserve the specificity of locale. The latest round of economic modernization has severely disrupted people's experience of place; because all places are being subsumed within a global economic order, no place can be understood intrinsically or in purely local terms. Reacting to this increasing abstraction of space, cultural politics in the postmodern era are marked by regional resistances, or movements to conserve values said to be rooted in particular places. Harvey is critical of this spatial turn in postmodern cultural politics because its quest for cultural conservation can all too easily veer over into political conservatism. Nostalgic celebrations of old ways of life being swept away by economic modernization often enshrine traditions that legitimized deeply inequitable social orders, while emphasis on localism can breed cultural insularity and ethnic chauvinism.[15]

Harvey's worries about the regional revivals of the postmodern era are well justified in the specific case of U.S. southern projects of cultural reclamation. The social and political conservatism implicit in most accounts of southern distinctiveness is made explicit in historian Eugene Genovese's recent brief for maintaining the cultural traditions of the Old South. Genovese's defense of the South follows the predictable track, pitting southern localism and community values against the increasing abstraction of social relations characteristic of the postmodern era. The postmodern period is distinguished by the "rise of a world market," which Genovese describes as "an impersonal arena in which human relations themselves are treated as commodities."[16] Genovese makes his case for localism with reference to this specific context of "worldwide economic integration that is taking place under the aegis of multinational corporate conglomerations" (98). This process of global economic integration was certainly transforming the U.S. South in particularly dramatic ways during the 1970s, by which time the region claimed at least half of all foreign capital investment in the United States.[17] A troubling consequence of this process is "cosmopolitanism," which Genovese fears is eradicating local communities and standards of cultural value (98). Among the factors that have contributed to the newfound cosmopolitanism of the South is the recent influx to southern cities of immigrants of color from Asia and Latin America, spurred by economic expansion. The increased presence of these racial minorities is precipitating dramatic changes in southern urban politics. Since the economic boom of the 1970s, southern cities have begun to switch over from the distinctively southern political model based on a rigid biracial caste system and protected by violence to a northern model of competitive multiethnic politics.[18] Once we specify the bases and effects of southern cosmopolitanism in the postmodern era, and grant, in Howard Preston's words, that the "one provincialism . . . most characteristic of the South is race,"[19] Genovese's argument for localism cannot but appear as a call for preserving the racial order of the Old South.

Genovese frankly admits that what he is defending is southern "conservatism," but he finesses the political ramifications of his argument in two ways. First, Genovese simply asserts that white racial supremacy is not inherent to southern conservatism (xi), leaving readers to conclude that it is merely by accident that the social order of the South has historically required the economic exploitation and political exclusion of its African-American population. Second, Genovese claims kinship between his and broadly leftist politics on the grounds that southern conservatism has always supported a powerful critique of advanced capitalism (31, 34). But the stories of racism and capitalism in the South are far more tangled than is suggested by Genovese's account. The dismantling of legalized racial segregation in the South was facilitated by advocates of economic development and in turn cleared the way for the economic modernization of the region. Business leaders in southern cities often functioned as "the advance agents of peaceful desegregation."[20] Modernizing economic elites sought to distance themselves from traditionalists on racial matters and to promote the image of a region eager to relinquish its conservative racial past in the interests of economic growth.

To recognize that racial desegregation and economic expansion occurred in tandem in the South is by no means to suggest that capitalist modernization inevitably produces social changes of a progressive sort and ushers in a more equitable racial order. Scholarship on the southern economic boom provides overwhelming evidence to the contrary, demonstrating that modernization in the South since the 1970s has followed a racialized logic of uneven development, bypassing the majority of African-Americans in the region. Many of the industrial firms relocating to the South during its boom period simply avoided "Black Belt" areas of concentrated African-American residence, and the expanding labor markets of the Sunbelt region were racially segmented, with African-Americans clustered in the lowest-wage occupations.[21] Capitalist modernization of the South has obviously not eliminated racial inequality, and the demise of de jure racial segregation was forced by a political movement for Civil Rights rather than occurring as a logical consequence of structural economic changes. Without subscribing to the view that capitalist development is inherently socially progressive, we should note that relatively liberal positions on racial desegregation became expedient for proponents of economic modernization in the South of the 1960s and 1970s.

The forces of economic and racial conservatism have been clearly aligned in the South, with traditionalists who oppose economic modernization explicitly defending a racist social order. Take as an example Fred Hobson's critique of the rapid economic development of Atlanta during the Civil Rights decade and those that immediately followed. Business boosters and the city administration strove to project an image of Atlanta as the "city too busy to hate," a city unwilling to allow racial conservatism to impede its quest for economic growth. Hobson condemns Atlanta for selling its soul to business, for giving up racism for "purely economic" and "utilitarian" rather than moral reasons, and he actually asserts that "For all its cruelty and inhumanity, racism possessed a certain integrity, a commitment, however distorted and twisted. It would never sell out."[22] Contrary to Genovese's unargued claims, racism emerges here as integral to U.S. southern tradition, with the "integrity" of this tradition hinging on the old racial order of the South.

In a deeply ambivalent meditation on the South, African-American short-story writer James Alan McPherson clarifies the links between urbanism, economic modernization, and racial cosmopolitanism that are obscured in Genovese's account. McPherson argues that the economically booming cities of the South, such as Atlanta, have begun to evolve into "cosmopolitan" areas allowing for "external coexistence between people from a variety of social and racial groups": "The impetus behind this evolutionary process is almost always economic. In the major economic centers such as Atlanta, an attempt has been made to establish a transcendent jurisprudence or a set of civic values over a broad range of ethnic groups. This jurisprudence makes for tolerance and cohesiveness and for an acceptance of diversity as a norm."[23] McPherson's emphasis on "transcendent jurisprudence" as a mechanism enabling racial tolerance, utopian as it may be, sharply counters the face-to-face and localist orientation of most accounts of southern folk tradition and in fact suggests how these distinctively southern values are implicated in the conservation of white racial privilege. Take, for example, Eugene Genovese's affirmation of southern antistatism or Havard's emphasis on face-to-face rather than abstract and "legal" social relations as uniquely defining of southern culture. Southerners have often contrasted the racial order of their region to the more abstract racism of the urban North and justified it precisely for its face-to-face quality, which presumably gave southern racism a more warm and intimate countenance than its northern counterpart. This nostalgic celebration of organic face-to-face communities carries conservative political ramifications in a general sense as well as in the specific instance of southern race relations. Social justice cannot always be immanently derived from concrete, face-to-face relations and often requires mediation by abstract political principles as well as extra-local adjudication: in the case of the South during the Civil Rights era, federal legal and military intervention was required to secure racial desegregation and black enfranchisement.

Crucial to the evaporation of the southern mystique in the post–Civil Rights era was the fact that racism could no longer be considered a solely southern problem. By the mid-1970s, for the first time in the history of the South, incoming African-Americans began to outnumber those departing the region. This reverse black migration was widely cited as proof of the fact that "racism no longer defines the Dixie difference."[24] The actual migration of African-Americans to the South was exactly concurrent with the black literary return south, as Farah Griffin notes in her study of African-American migration narratives.[25] However, the two returns seem to have been motivated by sharply contrary aims. The migration of African-Americans to the South from the mid-1970s onward was spurred primarily by economic decline in the Rustbelt and by the transformed economic, political, and racial conditions in the South resulting from the Civil Rights movement and the industrial boom. Scholarship on the migration documents that it was directed mainly toward metropolitan areas of the South, where expanded electoral and political power as well as enhanced employment opportunities could be more fully accessed by African-Americans than in the rural regions.[26]

But culturalist accounts of the reverse migration tell an entirely different story. For example, anthropologist Carol Stack flouts all available evidence that indicates it is changed social, political, and economic conditions that are fueling the black southern migration. According to Stack, African-Americans are returning to rural and largely segregated areas in the South that are federally characterized as counties of "persistent poverty."[27] Stack argues that cultural rather than economic factors are driving the migration, which she describes as an effort to "redeem a lost community" (xv). Polarizing the rural South against contemporary urban existence, Stack claims that the reverse migrants are fleeing a "postmodern world" typified by a pervasive experience of "rootlessness" (197). In their quest for "homeplaces," the migrants are returning to areas that are distant from big cities and Sunbelt industry, linked to traditional southern cash crops, with majority black populations, and with income levels far below national averages (19). As Stack puts it, "Twentieth-century life seemed to pass these places by.

Economic expansion in the rest of the country and the metropolitan sprawl that came to be identified with modern America might as well have been occurring on some other planet" (40). Like the southern regionalists, Stack can only sustain her image of the South as a refuge from modern and post-modern urban life by constructing it as a rural, racially segregated region mired in poverty.

The current reclamation of the South in African-American literary criticism overlaps with Stack's account in several key respects, not least in its portrayal of the South as the place where lost racial community can be redeemed. For example, Alice Walker declares, in her essay "The Black Writer and the Southern Experience," that "what the black writer inherits as a natural right is a sense of *community*. Something simple but surprisingly hard, especially these days, to come by."[28] If community is surprisingly hard to come by these days, especially in urban settings where community can only be imagined through strenuous acts of mediation, the rural South short-circuits this difficult work and furnishes community as the African-American writer's "natural right." The black southern community that Walker commemorates in this essay was cemented by the shared experience of poverty and racial injustice. Walker clarifies that she is not "nostalgic . . . for lost poverty" but rather for "the solidarity and sharing a modest experience can sometimes bring" (17). For Walker, the value of black southern heritage lies in its resistance to a racist system that daily threatened to diminish African-American humanity. Yet it is surely telling that Walker is unable to imagine racial community in conditions of political and economic advancement for African-Americans.

In common with the southern regionalists and Carol Stack's migrants, recent African-American literary-critical works are returning "South to a very old place"[29]—to a putatively premodern and racially segregated rural South predating the economic and political transformations of the 1960s and 1970s. This temporal setting is not accidental: the return to conditions of racial segregation and poverty is essential to the recovery of discrete black cultural traditions and communities. Toni Morrison has remarked that her first three novels are set in "closed, back worlds" (much like the homeplaces Stack describes as being left behind by twentieth-century life) and that even though *Song of Solomon* goes up to 1963, "it's sort of back there somewhere." Morrison explains that the novel's re-creation of a rural and racially segregated southern past supports its "quest for roots."[30] Hailing African-Americans as an essentially rural folk—"my people, we 'peasants'"[31]—Morrison equates "community values" with "village values" and curiously claims to write "village literature, fiction that is really for the village, for the tribe. Peasant literature for my people."[32] Aside from the fact that Morrison's novels circulate quite profitably within global

metropolitan markets, her desired literary constituency, whom she mis-
names a peasant people, was predominantly settled in metropolitan areas
even in the South by 1970.[33] If Morrison's literary project is impelled by
a "quest for roots," the old South is a logical destination for this quest.
Here, a distinct African-American folk culture developed in relative isolation from the mainstream largely as a result of legalized racial segregation
and would necessarily be put at risk by political moves toward integration.
Consequently, Morrison cannot take as her fictional setting the rapidly
urbanizing and industrializing South of the post–Civil Rights era.

Terms such as "village" or "peasant" literature shift the scene of African-
American writing away from its inescapably metropolitan conditions and,
in so doing, begin to clarify the work of displacement that Hazel Carby
claims is being performed by the southern folk aesthetic. The turn toward
a rural southern folk culture makes possible a fictional resolution of urban
authorial anxieties in several ways. The rural South of a bygone era provides access to a noncommodified, face-to-face mode of communication
that seems obsolete in modern and postmodern urban contexts. To writers
like Morrison, urbanization spelled the death of black oral tradition. In
the city, oral forms could no longer operate as culturally sustaining media
for African-Americans, for they were irredeemably compromised by the
processes of commodification and global dissemination. The acceleration
of these processes in the postmodern era—when all culture becomes incorporated into the system of commodity capitalism and when, as I argue
in chapter 3, black culture is used to lubricate this system—further motivates the literary turn south. As a means of disengaging from postmodern
commodity culture, the South is cast as a folk domain of racial and cultural
integrity.

This way of articulating the literary value of the rural South is by no
means unique to Toni Morrison. The links between black cultural community, poverty, and racial segregation are reiterated by most of the key
figures who are contributing to the southern folk aesthetic. In his study of
black women novelists, Houston Baker describes the "Old South" of the
era of racial segregation as the locus of an authentically black folk tradition. Deriding the "mulattoization" of black urban northern culture, Baker
envisions the rural South as "a field of 'particular' or vernacular imagery
unique to the Afro-American imagination."[34] Baker regards the figurative departure of some African-American women novelists to the urban
North as an act of racial betrayal, construing the urban migration as an
aesthetic compromise that follows from racial integration. Throughout his
study, Baker asserts an inverse relation between the value of black southern
culture on the one hand and economic and political power on the other.
African-American folk culture in the South operates at what Baker calls

a "meta" rather than "material" level: southern blacks developed a rich and resourceful cultural tradition as a direct consequence of their exclusion from political and economic power (38). By Baker's account, as by Morrison's or Alice Walker's, integral black cultural traditions and communities seem contingent on the foreclosure of material opportunities for African-Americans.

It comes as no surprise, then, that even one of the most prominent advocates of the self-avowedly politicized Black Aesthetic movement of the 1960s, Addison Gayle, has recently endorsed the literary move toward southern folk culture. In keeping with the urban emphasis of the Black Arts movements, Gayle had announced in 1970 that "the new Afro is to be found . . . in the Black ghettos of America."[35] In its commitment to a politically transformed future, Black Aesthetic ideology had spurned the cultural traditions associated with the oppressive racial history of the South. At the peak of the Black Arts movement, Gayle had asserted that in the interests of political change, black art "demands the allegiance of men who are capable of transcending the past and challenging the future."[36] But in a recent essay, Gayle exhorts African-American writers to "return to the intellectual past, to undertake the odyssey back into one's cultural heritage,"[37] and this odyssey entails a literary reassessment of the South.

In this essay, Gayle regrets that the Black Aesthetic movement distanced itself from the South, but he manages to fold the southern folk aesthetic back into nationalist aesthetics by representing the South as a black cultural domain starkly opposed to America and the West. For example, Gayle claims that the South supports "the genesis of a racial literature" (559) because it is here that African-Americans are closest to "the Africa of their ancestors" (558) and can therefore manage to live "wholly and fruitfully outside the ethical system of the West" (563). Although Gayle acknowledges "the fact that modernization, urbanization, and all the concomitant evils have come to the South" (563), he nevertheless identifies the South as the cultural terrain that can authenticate the contemporary African-American writer's literary project: the writer who taps into southern folklore can be "one with his community, and his works . . . legitimized by the community itself" (560).

The set of moves Gayle performs here is reprised in much recent African-American literary criticism on the South. In his introduction to the anthology *Black Southern Voices,* published in 1992, John Oliver Killens echoes Gayle in asserting that black southern literature projects a "system of values" that "is different from white America's." Like Gayle, Killens claims that the "people of the black South are much closer to their African roots." This imaginative affiliation with Africa is motivated by intense pessimism about the political prospects for African-Americans in modern America:

"The black Southern literary tradition gives the lie to the American profession of freedom and humaneness and democracy."[38] Seconding Killens, in his contribution to one of two special "Black South" issues of *African American Review*, Kiarri Cheatwood describes the U.S. South as one of the "authentic zones" of black cultural production because there, black people have always known that the term *American* had nothing to do with them.[39] The desire to withdraw from America, where putatively universal human rights have not been easily extended to African-Americans, impels the Africanization of the South, rendering the region a seedbed of black cultural specificity.

Disaffection with America is shared by both the black southern folk aesthetic and the broader southern regionalist movement, which too seeks to establish the difference of the South from the rest of the nation. But whereas the southern regionalists are reacting against the fact and idea of modernization per se, the southern turn in African-American literature represents a more historically specific response to the trajectory of modernization in the United States. Southern regionalism has cropped up periodically for more than a century and usually at those moments when the South is poised on the brink of industrialization, but for most of its history African-American literature has resolutely refused to entertain agrarian or pastoral retreats from modernity.[40] The atypical black literary return to a premodern rural South signals the exhaustion of the promise of modernity that galvanized the African-American literary tradition through the twentieth century. The southern folk aesthetic began to emerge as an identifiable literary movement at a juncture when disillusionment with the failed promise of urban modernization reached a peak, in the 1970s. The deindustrialization of northern and midwestern cities during this decade took a steep economic and symbolic toll on African-Americans. With the loss of manufacturing jobs, intensified racial segregation, and increased poverty, Rustbelt cities looked nothing like the land of opportunity that had lured black migrants in earlier decades. What's more, black urban culture was stigmatized—in widely circulating discourses on the "underclass"—as the main source of postmodern urban crisis. In this context, it is hardly surprising that imaginative restoration of black cultural community has seemed so urgent to African-American writers since the 1970s. The southern folk aesthetic contests widespread claims about the pathological culture of black city dwellers by affirming strong cultural traditions and communities. At the same time, by situating these communities in the rural South of a bygone era, this literary movement lends credence to pervasive beliefs that black urban communities are indeed in a state of crisis and that wholesome black communities cannot be imagined within late-twentieth-century urban conditions.

The geographical opposition between fractured urban life and redemptive southern community is often decidedly gendered in both literary-critical and social science scholarship. For example, historian Jacqueline Jones, whose work has done much to refute current "underclass" discourses that focus the sense of urban crisis on black populations exclusively, nonetheless ends up acceding to the terms of these discourses. Although Jones demonstrates certain continuities between southern plantations and northern urban ghettos, she also often ends up polarizing rural southern versus northern urban communities in customary ways. Jones identifies the unprecedented features of what she terms "postmodern" poverty with a masculine street culture of drugs, violence, and illicit consumption, which she argues is eroding black family and community life in northern cities. Describing northern city streets as "a harsh new world" and black masculine urban culture as a peculiarity of "postmodern America," Jones argues that this culture is undermining a "corporate ethos" nourished by black women and rooted in the South.[41]

This kind of gendering of postmodern urban crises as masculine is borne out in African-American literary criticism as well. Hazel Carby, when urging contemporary critics to acknowledge their discursive displacement of urban crisis, delineates this crisis as follows: "large parts of black America are under siege; the number of black males in jail in the 80s has doubled; the news media have recently confirmed what has been obvious to many of us for a while, that one in four young black males are in prison, on probation, on parole, or awaiting trial" (41). While urban crisis gets framed as a crisis of black masculinity, the sound communal values associated with the rural South are generally feminized. As Trey Ellis's caricature of the southern folk aesthetic suggests, this literary movement in itself has been identified with black women in various senses. Not only was the southern turn initiated and established in African-American *women's* fiction and criticism during the 1970s,[42] but even as it was subsequently extended by black male writers, the rural South remained a repository of cultural values that are traditionally identified with women—home, racial origin, maternal ancestry and familial stability, rootedness in place, and cultural continuity. Recall that for Houston Baker, the Old South is home to a racially pure cultural tradition that is "mulattoized" as it migrates to the urban North. In addition to employing a reproductive metaphor for racial purity, Baker explicitly feminizes the notion of a racially authentic culture, describing the rural South as the space of black mothers and the urban North as the white father's territory (36). Baker's polarized equations identify women as the guarantors of racial and cultural integrity. In this all-too-predictable move, surely disquieting to feminist readers, Baker casts women writers as cultural bulwarks that can stay the dislocating consequences of social change,[43] which is perceived to be occurring at accelerated rates in the postmodern era.

The Postmodern Romance of the Residual

The southern folk aesthetic is conservative in the literal sense in that it strives to conserve cultural traditions and forms of community felt to be at risk in the postmodern era and, further, in that it casts women as the best agents of this task of cultural conservation. The precise political implications of the southern folk aesthetic may be clarified through a close look at Toni Morrison's *Song of Solomon* and Gloria Naylor's *Mama Day,* which offer exemplary instances of a postmodern literary practice taking the folk turn in order to secure its claims to representing racial community. Both novels are structured around a set of contrasts between the city and a primitivized rural South—between an unnamed midwestern city and Shalimar, Virginia, in *Song of Solomon,* and in *Mama Day* between New York City and Willow Springs, an island off the southeastern coast of the United States. This geographical contrast is, moreover, a gendered opposition of the kind spoofed in Trey Ellis's *Platitudes.* In each novel, a male character (Milkman in *Song of Solomon* and George in *Mama Day*) personifies urban rootlessness and deracination, whereas rootedness in racial heritage is embodied in female characters with strong ties to the rural South. Pilate in *Song of Solomon* and Mama Day in Naylor's novel exemplify Toni Morrison's conception of the "ancestor." Identified with the oral storyteller, the ancestor figure serves as a custodian of cultural memory, transmitting to dislocated city dwellers the communal wisdom encoded in southern folk traditions.[44] In both novels, the disconnection of the city man from southern ancestral tradition is signaled by his affiliation with print literate rather than oral culture.

In its representation of black community, each novel obliquely registers the pressure exerted by discourses of urban crisis on postmodern African-American literature. In keeping with these discourses, which ascribe the alleged collapse of black urban community to sharpening class polarities, these novels premise racial community on absence of class stratification. The term *community* is applicable to Morrison's depiction of areas of black urban settlement during the 1940s and 1950s. These decades are generally identified as the golden age of the ghetto in contemporary discourses of urban crisis, an era when black urban ghettoes still supposedly functioned as tight-knit communities because of a high degree of intra-racial class solidarity. As Susan Willis and others have pointed out, Morrison's midwestern industrial cities are composed of neighborhoods, which attest to the survival and adaptation of southern "village" models of community in the city.[45] The Southside ghetto of *Song of Solomon* is such a neighborhood, where urban anonymity is mitigated by the prevalence of face-to-face interactions and where gossip and barbershop talk rather than newspapers or radio form the primary media for transmitting information.[46]

If, however, the neighborhood demonstrates the resilience of southern communal practices transplanted to the city, acquisition of educational privilege and professional class status splinters black urban community. Those few who manage to enter the middle class, such as Dr. Foster or Macon Dead in *Song of Solomon,* are estranged from the rest of the black urban community. This logic is illustrated through a wealth of incidents in *Song of Solomon,* including the Dead family's Sunday drives in the Packard that seals them off from the community, First Corinthians carrying a book on her subway ride home from her job as a domestic in the hope that her superior education will distinguish her from other maids, Milkman's exclusion from the masculine camaraderie of Feather's Pool Hall because of his father's status as property owner and landlord, and Guitar and Milkman's arguments about the gulf separating Southside from Honore Island, where Milkman's father owns a beach house.

Although *Song of Solomon* spans the period from the 1930s to the early 1960s whereas *Mama Day* is set during the 1990s, the similarity of their urban settings in these distinct time periods discredits progressive narratives of urban modernization. Both novels highlight the disappointment of the hopes of full participation in national life that fueled the northern urban migration. Racial segregation of public facilities is openly practiced in Morrison's northern city during the 1940s (we are told that in 1942 only two public toilets downtown admitted black people). The only difference in the New York of the 1990s is that segregation has "moved underground,"[47] prompting the novel's protagonist to long for the clarity of de jure rather than de facto segregation (19). In addition to the persistence of subtle forms of racial segregation, unequal access to employment opportunities further marks the distance between the actual northern city and the promised land that beckoned black migrants out of the rural South. Unemployed despite her degree in business management, Cocoa confronts a job market that appears to offer equal opportunity, but, she wonders, "an equal opportunity to be what, or earn what?" (19). Morrison's First Corinthians has an even more disheartening experience of the job market, as she discovers that the only work available to her is domestic service, notwithstanding her liberal arts degree from Bryn Mawr College.

This clear-sighted recognition of the bleak prospects for racial equality and economic opportunity in the urban North drives each novel's disenchanted retreat to the rural South. Moreover, given that the limited success of racial integration and economic advancement in the urban North is shown inevitably to fissure black communities, it makes perfect sense that the two novels situate their fully realized images of racial community in a segregated South. Taking segregation as a prerequisite for black community, both novels employ the trope of segregation-equals-congregation that recurs in recent historical studies of the Jim Crow South.[48] In an incisive discussion of this trope in "Romancing Jim Crow: Black Nostalgia for a Segregated Past," Adolph Reed explains why the "current nostalgia for the organic community black Americans supposedly lost with the success of the civil rights movement is so frighteningly shortsighted and dangerous."[49] Romancing Jim Crow entails the evocation of a "face-to-face community in which everyone has a role, status markers are clear, and convivial, automatic deference and noblesse oblige are the social organism's lifeblood, the substance of its mutual regard" (27).

Reed here might well be describing the black community of Willow Springs in Naylor's novel. In the city sections of *Mama Day,* as noted earlier, Cocoa misses the clarity of the olden days when "the want ads and housing listings—even up north—were clearly marked colored or white" (19). In the rural island of Willow Springs, we can recover this lost clarity, thanks to segregation and exclusion from national economy and politics. That Willow Springs is an island, connected to the mainland United States only by a flimsy bridge, is crucial to its functioning as a site of ideal community. This community is knit together by face-to-face contacts among its residents, all of whom know and trust each other so well that Mama Day can take a peach switch to discipline a neighbor's daughter. In Willow Springs, there is no sheriff, no courthouse, no politics or government because these are unnecessary in a community governed by "convivial, automatic deference and noblesse oblige." This mechanism of social order is illustrated on several occasions: when the bridge connecting the island to the mainland is destroyed by a storm, "it's understood everybody will get together and put it back up" (248); island inhabitants need not worry about importing medical supplies from the mainland because "we take care of our own" (256). When mainland real estate developers want to buy shoreline property on the island, "if Mama Day say no, everybody say no," because of a variant of noblesse oblige: the community consents to Mama Day's opinion because she is "a direct descendant" of the first black owner of the island (6).

One reason Reed faults such nostalgic images is that they banish the realities of class stratification within segregated black communities (28). In Naylor's Willow Springs, class distinctions are not entirely erased, but they are placed within a primitive agricultural order that neutralizes their divisive implications. Images of this type of social and economic order, to quote Reed again, are "propelled by a naïve trope of modernization that presumes our world to be constantly increasing in complexity and divisiveness, contrasting it to a comfortingly static past. This vision authenticates itself by dipping into a common reservoir of experience" (26). The unified social order of Willow Springs forms a "closed, back" world, as Morrison remarked of the temporal setting of her novel; in both cases, the rural South belongs to a "comfortingly static past" far removed from a conflict-ridden urban reality.[50] The folks in Willow Springs "know that even well-meaning progress and paradise don't go hand in hand" (185). Time stands still in Willow Springs; nothing much changes here but for the seasons. The few changes that do occur are easily absorbed into a communal fund of traditional experience, which guarantees the continuity of the island's cultural and social practices.

The tradition of Candle Walk, an annual gift-giving ritual, illustrates the stability and simplicity of southern social order. When the economy of Willow Springs was based solely on agriculture, "by the end of the year it was common knowledge who done turned a profit and who didn't," and Candle Walk was established as "a way of getting help without feeling obliged" (110). As this agricultural society becomes more diversified and stratified, with the younger generation working for wages on the mainland, the ritual threatens to deteriorate from a gift-giving practice to a competitive exchange of commodities. However, this potential disruption of communal solidarity and cultural tradition is easily dispelled, as Mama Day reassures the "older heads" (110) of the island that despite surface changes, the essence of the tradition—the balancing of economic disparities—will survive intact for generations to come. The capaciousness, flexibility, and durability of southern communal traditions are reaffirmed by the novel's closing image, of Mama Day herself distributing junk souvenirs bought in New York City on Candle Walk night.

Many of the same principles and tropes are at work in Morrison's representation of community in *Song of Solomon*. As in *Mama Day*, progress is suspect here because it entails unnecessary complications of social order and personal experience. Pilate's household, based as it is on a "residual image" of the agrarian South,[51] exudes comfort and rich experiential capital although (or, more precisely, because) it has no electricity, gas, or running water. The three women in this household live "pretty much as though progress was a word that meant walking a little farther on down the road."[52] As many readers of the novel have observed, Pilate's house constitutes a utopian space of gift-giving, unalienated labor freed from the rationalized ends of profit accumulation, and modest but satisfying consumption.[53]

If, as Susan Willis suggests, Pilate's house represents a selective, utopian re-creation of southern agrarian economy and thereby provides a lever for Morrison's critique of industrial capitalism,[54] the novel's "real" rural South, as represented by Shalimar, Virginia, presents a very different picture. Like Willow Springs, Shalimar is a "small world" in which a stranger walks into your house and turns out to be your cousin (293), and in which people are "connected, as though there was some cord or pulse or information they shared" (296). Just as the island of Willow Springs encompasses a community of insiders bound together by the ties of place, race, and shared cultural mythology, so does Shalimar. Both communities are suspicious of outsiders, especially those coming from cities. The Shalimar folk are even more insular than those of Willow Springs, so much so as to verge on the incestuous: all the women look alike, and the men look much like the women, and everyone in town claims kinship to the mythical ancestor, Solomon. Milkman concludes that "Visitors to Shalimar must be rare, and new blood that settled here nonexistent" (266).

As an urban visitor, Milkman discovers that his entry into the Shalimar community is blocked by his class status. The men at Solomon's store are affronted by "the city Negro who could buy a car as if it were a bottle of whiskey" (269); to them, Milkman embodies the powers of "big money up North" (270), of the conspicuous consumption they associate with city life. When these men look at Milkman, they see a black-skinned man with the heart of a white man (269). In a move that is replayed in many of Morrison's novels, class privilege mulattoizes racial identity, fragmenting a communal ethos cemented not only by racial segregation but also by economic disadvantage. Not surprisingly, then, the well-to-do Milkman has to divest himself of all the external markers of his class status before he is entitled to join the racial community of Shalimar. If, in the city, class irreparably fractures community, the rural South operates as a device of restoration; here, true community is achieved through the dissolution (rather than the resolution) of class conflicts.[55]

Although Shalimar and Willow Springs both gain racial cohesion through an erasure of class divisions, Morrison is careful not to gloss over the economic costs of black communal life in the segregated South. Crucial to Morrison's conception of southern racial community is her representation of Shalimar as a town in visible economic decay, a backwater excluded from national processes of production and consumption. The town is "so small [that] nothing financed by state funds or private enterprise reared a brick there" (262). The men in Shalimar (unlike the residents of Willow Springs) do not own farming land and must wait each morning to be trucked out to work on tobacco fields or mills owned by whites. Morrison's fictional southern town captures a persistently real feature of the rural South even in the boom era of the late twentieth century. The industrial development of the South since the 1970s has been skewed toward metropolitan areas and has largely bypassed rural areas of concentrated black residence. Poverty levels in these Black Belt areas are higher than anywhere else in the nation, prompting the increasing recurrence of the term *rural underclass*.[56] As Jacqueline Jones has remarked, rural poverty is assumed to be more wholesome and less degrading than its urban variants,[57] and perhaps this explains why the black "underclass" in the rural South is not at the crux of crisis-ridden national discourses of poverty. Perhaps for this reason, too, Morrison can set her image of sound black community in a poverty-stricken rural South, far removed from the allegedly pathological cultures of the urban poor. Morrison's treatment of Shalimar attests to the romance of the residual that typifies cultural politics in the postmodern era: the spaces that have been most conspicuously left behind by socioeconomic processes of modernization are widely construed as spaces of greatest cultural resistance to advanced capitalism.[58]

Obeying this logic of the residual, southern regionalist discourses tend to dissociate southern culture from urban commodity markets, notwithstanding the fact that a much-cited measure of the recent southern economic boom is the expansion and standardization of consumer markets.[59] The southern folk turn in African-American literature exploits a similar rhetorical polarity between rural southern and postmodern urban forms of consumption. For example, Kiarri Cheatwood contrasts the "handmade model" of southern culture to the "push-button, homogenized, fast-fooded, overdeveloped" consumption patterns of the urban North. Whereas authentic folk culture is still and only available in the "natural" environment of the South, northern cities offer meager cultural nourishment with their "denatured food—resulting in empty, fat-producing calories, as it were, for our minds and souls."[60] Gloria Naylor's novel pits northern and southern, urban and folk forms of consumption in strikingly similar terms. On the very first page of Cocoa's urban narrative, we are told that eating places in New York City are "designed for assembly-line nutrition" (3). The inauthenticity of urban consumption is illustrated by empty signifiers that bear little relation to substances, such as "when the stuff they poured into your cup certainly didn't qualify as coffee" (3). In the rural South, however, "you knew when you saw a catfish, you called it a catfish" (22). The southern sections of the novel contain extended passages that painstakingly describe women planting, picking, preparing, and preserving food, in keeping with a "handmade model" of folk consumption.

Willow Springs exemplifies an Arcadian social order that guarantees satisfaction through the fulfillment of modestly defined ("natural") consumer needs. Morrison's Shalimar is equally, though somewhat differently, contrasted to the postmodern city designed to function as a "consumption artifact."[61] The single detail that most vividly renders the town's economic stagnation is the image of Shalimar women holding absolutely nothing in their hands. This image is meant to impress upon readers not the bleakness of material deprivation but the wealth of spiritual value. We are clearly supposed to counterpose these poor rural women to the spoiled urban woman Hagar, whose arms can barely contain the packages overloaded with brand-name commodities that disastrously mediate her sense of personal value. Hagar lacks the silky copper-colored hair and the elegance of upper-crust Honore women, a lack she hopes to fill by means of commodity consumption. The intertwined class, caste, and color distinctions that trigger Hagar's crazed shopping spree are wished away in the rural South. In Shalimar, commodities are too scarce and the economic power to purchase them too limited to form a source of distinctions within the community. Added to this is the fact that everyone looks the same in Shalimar. The visual differences that signify class divisions in Morrison's unnamed city are dissolved in the rural South. It is telling that the only equitable intra-racial social order presented in *Song of Solomon* depends on a leveling of differences and that the optimum economic level for nurturing community is poverty.

Morrison's image of rural southern community blossoming in poverty betrays a certain anxiety on the part of the professional writer who feels her access to authentic racial representation blocked by class and educational privilege. Milkman's initiation into the Shalimar community reads as a fantasy of social reconciliation whereby class privilege can be divested as easily as Milkman sheds his expensive suit and gold watch. This fantasy of immersion in communal experience does not quite succeed in resolving the difficulties of mediation involved when writers aspire to speak for a "folk" from whom they feel irrevocably removed by class differences. Taken to its logical conclusion, the suggestion that poverty and segregation form the necessary preconditions for black community carries dangerous political implications. In an interview explaining why *Song of Solomon* evokes a "closed, back" world, Morrison says that black cultural tradition exists "in a kind of village lore" that is vigorously sustained over time because "an ethnic group that is culturally coherent and has not joined the larger mainstream keeps very much intact for survival. The consequences of the political thrust to share in the economy and power of the country were to disperse that."[62] *Song of Solomon* starkly delineates the ravaging effects of poverty and segregation, but the novel nonetheless maintains that these conditions breed the type of cultural community the writer wishes to salvage. The cultural and aesthetic values affirmed in Morrison's novel can only be preserved at the steep cost of stalling black aspirations toward full political and economic equality.

Among the charges that can be leveled against the trope of romancing Jim Crow is that it "falsifies the past,"[63] substituting a partial and idealized memory for historical truth. This objection can be applied to nonfictional texts such as the memoirs Adolph Reed criticizes in "Romancing Jim Crow," which lay claim to accurate reconstruction of an actual past.[64] Novels such as *Song of Solomon* and *Mama Day*, however, cannot be justly censured for misrepresenting a historical past that they do not claim to be recapturing in the first place. If these texts will not submit to "the disillusionment of historical knowledge" (to use Sontag's phrase), what kind of knowledge, or alternative to historical knowledge, do they seek? Both novels guard against a literal reading of their literary images of the rural South by emphasizing that they are reaching not for mimetic realism but for imaginative transcendence. That Shalimar does not exist on the Texaco map or that Willow Springs is "nowhere" (174), literally off the map of the United States, indicates that the rural South of these novels is not meant to be taken as a putatively real place that existed in the past but as a fictive terrain charted by the literary imagination. *Mama Day* in particular underscores, through an overload of pastoral allusions, that its South is a literary construct. This insistence on historical impossibility—and literary invention—deflects the type of political critique that can be persuasively leveled against recent nonfictional romancers of the Jim Crow South, including the southern regionalists discussed earlier in the chapter.

A significant distinction between the southern folk aesthetic as practiced by Naylor and Morrison and extra-literary southern regionalism is that the one calls for imaginary re-creations of the Old South, whereas the other seeks in fact to conserve the traditional social order of the region. After all, Naylor's and Morrison's novels are not recommending an actual return to segregation and political and economic exclusion. It is precisely because the material conditions of possibility for organic racial community are unavailable that these texts seek to recover such community at an imaginary level. An emphasis on literary modality allows for a unique resolution to the problem of racial community—to disembed cultural value from its historical conditions of possibility; to acknowledge the real horrors of the segregated South (and thus to support its destruction) but also to rescue from it a paradigm of community that is viable and sustaining only for literary culture.

This kind of resolution is, of course, contradictory in several respects. To maintain that segregation and poverty are terrible for those who must experience them but offer rich aesthetic resources for the writer, we must separate the interests of the writer of literature from those of the community she wants to represent. The southern folk aesthetic seeks to establish an exact identification between the writer and the "black folk"—in other words, to authenticate the writer's claims to addressing and speaking for a clearly recognizable black community. If the turn south is impelled by a desire for unmediated access to racial community, admitting the fictive status of this community necessarily restores the crisis of representation that these novels set out to resolve. The claims to representation implicit in the southern folk aesthetic rest on a gap between the literary ambitions of the writer, which are to resurrect a bygone black folk culture fertilized by racial oppression, and the interests of the "folk," which can only be rendered as inscrutable.

Unable to resolve crises of urban literary representation through their turns south, Morrison's and Naylor's novels vacillate between the claims of unmediated reflection and literary invention. Even as the two novels demand that we read their images of segregated southern community as literary creations, they simultaneously solicit literal readings of the two cultural value-systems—conjuring and oral tradition—that are embedded in the South. In other words, readers are urged to approach magic and orality not as literary metaphors but as the defining features of an actual black community that precedes the literary text and grounds its claims to racial representation. Magic and oral tradition in *Mama Day* and *Song of Solomon* are riddled with difficulties in reading that ultimately lead to interpretive impasse, betraying the contradictory workings of the southern folk aesthetic. Because magic and orality are so essential to the matrix of cultural values deemed unique to black southern community, I shall trace in some detail the idea of "conjuring," which synthesizes magic and orality, and which sustains the "counterculture of modernity" developed in a wide range of postmodern African-American fictional and critical texts.[65]

As I suggested earlier, literary discourses that locate black community in a segregated rural South usually posit an inverse relation between cultural value and material power. Houston Baker exemplifies this inverse logic in *Workings of the Spirit* as he argues that the "primacy of nonmaterial transactions in the African's initial negotiations of slavery and the slave trade led to a privileging of the roles and figures of medicine men, griots, conjurers, priests, and priestesses" (38). Throughout his book, Baker reiterates that spirit-work has served a compensatory function for "countless black generations who . . . were brutally denied . . . ownership or control of *material* means of production" (75). The same logic is at work in Ntozake Shange's *Sassafras, Cypress, and Indigo,* a novel central to Baker's analysis of conjure in African-American women's fiction. In Shange's novel, Uncle John explains to Indigo that "Them whites what owned slaves took everythin' was ourselves," leaving the slaves the sole recourse to cultural crafts that accredit the "reality of the unreal."[66] A century after the abolition of slavery, Indigo's magical talents, which show that "she's got too much South in her," also help supplement an impoverished material reality: "There wasn't much for Indigo in the world she'd been born to, so she made up what she needed. What she thought the black people needed."[67]

The image of Indigo conjuring up imaginary worlds that "the black people needed" confirms Baker's description of conjure as "a revered site of culturally specific interests and values" (99). Baker affirms the "definable African antecedents" of conjuring (79) in an effort to establish its racial specificity. In a parallel gesture, critics writing on *Mama Day* and *Song of Solomon* emphasize the African origins of conjuring. For example, Lindsey Tucker argues that Naylor's novel draws on African "magico-religious" views of the world, and Stelamaris Coser claims that *Song of Solomon* follows "a tradition of magical storytelling deeply rooted in Africa."[68] Gay Wilentz asserts that magic in Morrison's novel challenges Western scientific assumptions and attests to a distinctively African view of reality.[69] The use of magic in novels such as *Mama Day, Song of Solomon, Sassafras, Cypress, and Indigo,* and Toni Cade Bambara's *The Salt Eaters* is motivated by the desire to recover an "African" epistemology and to uncover "the probable realms of impossibility beyond the limits of scientific certainty."[70] As a form of "discredited knowledge," in Toni Morrison's phrase,[71] conjuring exposes the limitations of modern rationality and reinstates suprarational ways of knowing suppressed by the Enlightenment legacy.

Toni Morrison has said that in the black community she remembers from her childhood, magic supplied "an enormous resource for the solution of certain kinds of problems."[72] Morrison does not specify, and I am certainly putting her words to unintended uses in suggesting that magic provides an enormous resource for the solution of certain kinds of problems associated with urban literary representation. As I argued in chapter 3, Morrison's *Jazz* (along with other novels such as John Edgar Wideman's *Philadelphia Fire* and *Reuben* or Samuel Delany's *Neveryóna*) explores the difficulties of knowing others in the city. Voyeurism, the novel's metaphor for urban modes of knowing and writing, makes evident the distance separating the knower from the known, the text from the reader, and the writer from the community she seeks to know, address, and represent. Magic escapes the profanity of urban voyeurism and restores a sacralized world of intimately knowable community. Karla Holloway identifies magic as an epistemology unique to black women that closes the gap between subject and object.[73] The ancestor, rooted in the rural South, is central to this mode of perception that overcomes the division constitutive of modern knowledge: a figure of mediation, the ancestor occupies "the dissolved space that lies between the subject and its object of knowledge" (116). Mediation, however, involves a process quite distinct from the dissolution of subject-object boundaries that Holloway correctly aligns with magical modes. Construing mediation as an urban and writerly dynamic that spells alienation, the southern folk aesthetic calls on magic to conjure a face-to-face community characterized by transparency of intersubjective knowledge and communication. Social as well as literary mediation can then be eliminated, as is clear from Holloway's contention that the magical text "reflects its community" (1).

Charles Johnson's *Faith and the Good Thing* boldly outlines the literary values at stake in the magical resolution to problems of urban literary representation. Johnson's novel presents a folksy narrative of Faith's quest for "the good thing," which takes her from rural Georgia to Chicago and back to Georgia, ending, not surprisingly, in Faith's metamorphosis into a conjure woman. Faith's quest is catalyzed by her realization that "You could never know."[74] This fundamental unknowability of the modern world, arising from the gulf separating knower from known, makes objects of knowledge appear as "cold, inaccessible things *out there*" (16). According to the Swamp Hag, a conjure woman Faith visits as part of her quest for the truth, Faith's problem is that she was born in the "winter of the Age of Reason," an age committed to abstract and systematic theories of knowledge (192). Living in this desacralized world, Faith suffers from a "lack of intimacy with the world, [a] lack of unity" (192). The fall from communion with a mysterious nature into the age of science and reason begins when anthropoid apes learn the uses of their forearms, inaugurating the origin of culture, which entails the objectification of human desire and its mediation by tools and technology (66–67).

The novel ultimately resolves Faith's crisis of knowledge by suspending the question "Was it true?" and replacing it with the ethical and aesthetic questions "Was it good? Was it beautiful?" (30). This displacement is aided by magic, the mode not of knowledge but of "mythopoesis and love" (78). Magic helps restore a lost unity between subject and object of knowledge, and between humanity and the world. Faith's father, we are told, "lived in a world so full of magic that he could call pots and pans by proper names he'd given them" (16). As the Swamp Hag asks Faith, "who says you gotta understand the universe to love, to conjure it?" (194). Conjuring here works as a metaphor for a mystical fusion with the universe—a mode of apprehension that is guided by "love" and obviously counterposed to the voyeurism of urban modes of knowing.

Johnson's conception of conjuring in *Faith and the Good Thing* bears special repercussions for the writer of a certain type of literature: the good thing, we are ultimately told, exists only "in fabulous fictions and astral tales told in a mystery-freighted voice" (87). The connection between conjuring and nonmimetic writing is implied in the Swamp Hag's statement that after the mind wearies of rational systems of knowledge, it "grows blank and cool and clear and capable of conjuring" (193). The Swamp Hag's image of the blankness necessary for conjuring is materialized in the Doomsday Book gifted to Faith by a fellow questor for the good thing. This book, made up entirely of blank pages, offers the perfect solution to Faith's epistemological dilemma, permitting her to conjure into existence whatever realities she desires. The magical book, in order to figure forth the unconditional freedom of imaginative creation, must be blank, must elude the visual regime of the printed text. As Faith turns the empty pages of the book, she fills them with her own imaginative visions, simultaneously becoming both author and reader of the book.

Two intertwined elements of Johnson's treatment of magic in *Faith and the Good Thing* bear repeating: magic helps to displace epistemological crisis by way of "mythopoesis and love," and it suggests a model of literary communication that fuses the positions of reader and writer. The salience of these elements to the magical mode can be established by a quick glance at the critical discourse on conjuring. Houston Baker describes conjuring as a literary "space of mythomania" (99) that "decisively resolves issues of narrative authority" (93). Marjorie Pryse concurs that the conjuring metaphor bestows a folk-based authority on black women's novels that is distinct from the textual (Bible-based) authority of the patriarchal American literary tradition.[75] Given that folk claims to cultural authority usually privilege orality over textuality, it is not surprising that conjuring, assisted by oral tradition, installs a type of literary community that is explicitly set off from the readerly or the textual. Charles Johnson embodies the magical mode in the trope of a book, but this book is necessarily blank because the conjuring metaphor valorizes a resolutely antivisual epistemology. Vision, commonly considered the directing sense of modern urban apprehension, is also the sense most actively brought into play by print technology.[76] If the eye distanciates its objects, the turn to voice helps reinforce the magical mode aimed at achieving connection and immersion.

An opposition between seeing and hearing, vision and voice, forms a defining feature of fictional and critical treatments of conjuring. A passage from Toni Cade Bambara's *The Salt Eaters* (in which the magical healing process conducted by Minnie Ransom occurs through the medium of sound) highlights the embedding faculty of sound against the decontextualizing power of sight: "sound waves weren't all that self-sufficient, needed a material medium to transmit. But light waves need nothing to carry pictures in, to travel in, can go anywhere in the universe with their independent pictures."[77] Karla Holloway amplifies the significance of this distinction between sound and sight, arguing that the oral mode fuses storyteller and listener, and reorganizes the subjects and objects of knowledge into metaphorical community (31). With specific reference to *Mama Day,* Holloway claims that in "the relational world" of this text (217), the oralized narrative voice proves "able to bridge the subjective and objective worlds" (126). Marilyn Sanders Mobley, in a comparable reading of *Song of Solomon,* argues that the novel undermines seeing, which reifies the boundaries between self and other, and affirms instead an interconnected community made up of speaking and listening subjects.[78]

With no acknowledgment of dissonance, critics extend the oral/aural metaphor of intimate community to the situation of reading and writing, asserting, as does Holloway, that in the oralized magical text, the "reader's voice is invited to join its community of tellers" (126). A similar effort to mitigate the indeterminacy, mediation, and distanciation involved in the act of reading a book motivates Joyce Ann Joyce's definition of the conjurer critic. Pitted against a straw deconstructionist critic who reads the literary text against its grain in order to subvert its intended meanings, the conjurer-critic (also referred to as a "priestess") takes a collaborative approach, "mystically merg[ing]" author, critic, and community.[79] Jocelyn Donlon's model of oral storytelling serves much the same ends as Joyce's conjuring metaphor: whereas the print tradition encourages competing readings, members of oral communities tend to confirm rather than dispute what they hear, authenticating shared cultural modes of knowledge.[80] This brief critical survey should sufficiently clarify the manner in which conjuring and orality combine to produce an emphatically antimodern, anti-urban, and antitextual model of community. The tremendous appeal of this model lies in its elimination of the risks of mediation and its fictive recovery of a community of cultural insiders engaged in harmonious, crisis-free acts of knowing, speaking, and listening.

Reading as Listening

It is easy enough to see how *Song of Solomon* and *Mama Day* deploy the magical/oral mode to resolve the problems of writing for urban communities that can be apprehended only through difficult acts of mediation. In both novels, a male urban protagonist is subjected to a series of trials, including encounters with the supernatural, that involve the progressive unlearning of a rational, visual epistemology and an education in the skills of listening, which culminates in the protagonist's immersion into a folk cultural community. The gender of these protagonists is not accidental, nor is the equation of urban with male and folk with female. The seeing/listening distinction is often coded in gendered terms, as, for example, when Houston Baker claims that the conjuring text is "crafted not primarily for male viewing but for women's hearing" (203), or when Karla Holloway distinguishes between black men and women writers in terms of their differential privileging of vision and voice (6–13).[81] What *Song of*

Solomon and *Mama Day* dramatize, through the stories of Milkman and George, is the divestment of a masculine voyeuristic stance (associated with urbanity) and initiation into a folk women's community characterized by reciprocity and immediacy.

This aspect of the two novels has been subjected to extensive critical analysis, which I will only briefly summarize. Of the scene in *Song of Solomon* in which Macon Dead peeps into Pilate's house through a window, Kimberly Benston writes that Macon's voyeuristic observation of the women inside the house illustrates "the mastery of [a] reified perception." Whereas Macon's gaze is detached and disembodied, "the act of listening is trope and substance of renewal through sympathetic identification," of "immersion in the other's domain."[82] Joyce Irene Middleton focuses on the novel's effort to rejuvenate cultural community through "the African arts of listening and remembering."[83] Middleton traces the subordination of seeing to hearing at critical stages of Milkman's quest to recover cultural heritage. For example, the literate Milkman's attention to visual signs misleads him to overemphasize the differences in spelling between the names Solomon, Shalimar, and Charlemage; it is only when he learns to hear the similarities in sound that Milkman can begin piecing together the puzzle of his familial and cultural ancestry. This process of "learning through listening" (29) culminates in the hunt scene, where, in the darkness of the woods, "sound reigns over sight" (34). Listening closely to the sounds of nature, Milkman grasps an oral, preliterate language that eases his entry into black cultural community.

In a parallel analysis, Susan Meisenhelder shows that in *Mama Day,* visuality (in the form of charts, maps, books, photographs, and film) invariably alienates and yields misreadings of black culture, which the novel defines in predominantly oral/aural terms. Some prominent examples of the inaccuracy of sight-based knowledge that Meisenhelder cites are George's reductive understanding of women drawn from psychology books and diagrams of female anatomy; the real estate developers who view Willow Springs as a picture postcard; photographs that fail to capture the fullness of Cocoa's memories of George; and the misguided ethnographic text about the island's culture written by Reema's boy. Opposed to these instances of visual misperception (which are in most cases associated with masculine urban outsiders) is a folk mode of knowing that emphasizes communal integration.[84]

The readings I cite here are attentive to the strong oral drive of *Song of Solomon* and *Mama Day;* both novels perform the movement from visuality to orality as part of their effort to reinstate organic racial communities. But an obvious limitation of such readings is that they do not reckon with the print-literary medium through which oral communities are constructed in these novels. Attention to this medium disturbs the smooth passage from sight to hearing, giving rise to interpretive indeterminacy and finally thwarting the project of community building undertaken by Morrison and Naylor.

For example, the celebrated hunting scene in *Song of Solomon* appears so unequivocally to effect the transition from seeing to listening, from a textual to an aural mode of communication. The profound darkness of the scene wholly eclipses the possibility of reading. As Milkman listens to the dogs and men communicating "distinctive, complicated things" to each other (281), the narrator renders these sounds both literally through ono-matopoeia and figuratively through metaphorical analogies with various musical instruments. Then, for us who are reading rather than listening to this scene, comes the knot:

> It was all language. . . . No, it was not language; it was what was there before language. Before things were written down. Language in the time when men and animals did talk to one another, when a man could sit down with an ape and the two converse, when a tiger and a man could share the same tree, and each understand the other. (281)

As many critics have noted, this passage is obviously groping for a "nat-ural, preliterate language" that precedes symbolic, written discourse.[85] But this move toward a language of communion with nature is interrupted by the narrator's hesitation about the word *language*. The wordless sounds of the men and animals are language; no, they are not quite language but are prelinguistic sounds because language is identified with writing ("what there was before language" modified by "before things were written down"); but then again, this *is* language, now defined in oral terms as talk or speech. This paradoxically prelinguistic language is intended to express a harmonious understanding between men and nature that predates the fall into writing. In *Song of Solomon,* the recovery of this natural linguistic origin requires the removal of all technological interference, and especially the alienating technology of writing. But what stymies this passage is its dif-ficulty in reaching back to a language that precedes writing. Technological metaphors (the musical instruments needed to convey natural sounds) per-vade the passage, suggesting that there is no way of apprehending natural language without technological and literary mediation.

These contradictions are captured, with striking condensation, in an-other metaphor that immediately follows the passage quoted earlier. One of the hunters, Calvin, "whispered to the trees, whispered to the ground, touched them as a blind man caresses a page of Braille, pulling meaning through his fingers" (282). Throughout the hunt scene, the move toward authentic language has entailed a snuffing out of the visual sense that makes possible the acts of reading and writing. In keeping with this, the metaphor here evokes a *blind* man and begins by summoning other senses (of sound and touch) to replace vision. But this metaphor is nevertheless of a blind man *reading* a page of Braille, albeit through the fingers and not the eyes—an image that reinscribes, at a metaphorical level, the act of reading that it seeks to displace through the activation of senses other than sight. The reach for an oral linguistic origin is revealed here to be an inescapably written gesture. The technologies of reading and writing and the mediation of metaphor underwrite this gesture, conveying the impossibility of achieving a literal and immediate connection between language and nature.

A similar set of contradictions characterizes Naylor's approach to reading and listening in *Mama Day*. Knowledge gained through reading is explicitly devalued in the scene in which Miranda finds the slave owner Bascombe Wade's ledger, hidden in the attic by her father. There is "nothing to be read" in this book because its pages "are swollen and discolored" and the ink "all run together" (279)—visual images that underscore the unreliability of the written historical record. Miranda examines the bill of sale inserted into the book, hoping to learn from it the name of her "original" ancestor, who is also the founder of the island:

> *Tuesday, 3rd Day August,* then a 1 and half of what must be an 8, with the rest of the date faded away. *Sold to Mister Bascombe Wade of Willow Springs, one negress answering to the name Sa....* Water damage done removed the remainder of that line with the yellowish and blackened stains spreading down and taking out most of the others as well.... She's staring at the name and trying to guess. Sarah, Sabrina, Sally, Sadie, Sadonna—what? A loss she can't describe sweeps over her. (280)

Unable to reconstruct her ancestor's name, Miranda finds that reading compounds rather than fills the gaps in her knowledge. This scene forms the basis of Karla Holloway's argument that *Mama Day* discredits "scriptocentric" authority by showing that it is speaking and listening rather than reading that yield true historical knowledge for Miranda (127). Holloway's interpretation is supported by the fact that after Miranda gives up on deciphering her ancestor's name from the bill of sale, she falls asleep "murmuring the names of women. And in her dreams she finally meets Sapphira" (280). Although these lines suggest that genuine knowing occurs through the oral imagination, we must not forget that Sapphira's name is given only to the readers of the novel and not to any of its characters. Both Morrison's and Naylor's novels seek a cultural origin signified by the "real name" of the slave ancestor, which in *Song of Solomon* has been preserved through oral transmission. In *Mama Day* the ancestral name remains inaccessible to the community presented in the novel, for whom Sapphira Wade exists only in a prelinguistic dimension—she "don't live in the part of our memory we can use to form words" (4). But the readers of the novel are granted access to the real name, through the fully restored bill of sale and the family tree that form the prefatory texts for *Mama Day*.

What differentiates the reading situations of Miranda and the novel's readers, such that whereas one reading only drives home the unreliability of written evidence, the other implies that full knowledge can only be acquired through reading? The crucial difference lies not only in Naylor's redefinition of reading as listening but also in the kinds of written texts involved, one historical and the other fictional. Like many other postmodern novels that revisit the era of slavery, *Mama Day* evinces a deep distrust of historiography and of writing, more broadly speaking. As Sherley Anne Williams states, in the preface to her neo–slave narrative, *Dessa Rose*, African-Americans "remain at the mercy of literature and writing; often, these have betrayed us."[86] The washed-out bill of sale in Naylor's novel or the burnt evidence in Gayl Jones's *Corregidora* attests to the erasure of African-American experience from the official historical record, prompting both novelists to turn to oral tradition as a supplementary source of historical knowledge. Moreover, as instantiated by the historian Nehemiah's journal in *Dessa Rose* or by Schoolteacher's notebook in Toni Morrison's *Beloved,* with its listing of the slaves' animal and human traits, the modern print legacy was thoroughly implicated in slavery, shoring up its conception of humanity by disqualifying the slaves from written culture. Undermining the presumed objectivity of historical texts, these novels can press their claims for the unique truth-telling powers of fiction. It is only the oralized novel that can escape the compromised knowledge claims of historiography in particular as well as those of other genres of writing.

In *Mama Day*, fictional writing is set off not just from the slave master's ledger but also from the book written by the unnamed Reema's boy, who, corrupted by his mainland education, returns "determined to put Willow Springs on the map" (7). To Reema's boy, putting the island on the map involves writing an ethnographic text that will preserve the distinctive flavor of the folk culture of Willow Springs. Yet what this ethnographer ends up accomplishing is exactly the opposite. Instead of accounting for local lore and legends on their own terms, his book explains the island's culture with reference to mainland cultural norms. An instance of this is the vernacular phrase "18 and 23," which, referring to the year when Sapphira Wade acquired ownership of the island, carries a numinous power of suggestion that can only be understood within a magical register of interpretation. But Reema's boy concludes that the numbers were "really 81 and 32, which just so happened to be the lines of longitude and latitude marking off where Willow Springs sits on the map" (8). Perhaps misled by exposure to mainland academic vernacular theory, Reema's boy interprets the enigma of 18 and 23 as typical of the way in which marginalized groups assert cultural identity by "inverting hostile social and cultural parameters" (8). The omniscient narrator of this section of the novel overtly connects the ethnographic ambitions of Reema's boy to the rapacious, profit-making designs of the real estate developers who seek to transform Willow Springs into a picture postcard image of vacation paradise (8). Real estate development, tourism, and ethnography are all shown to participate in a suspect mode of knowledge production that the novel names "mapping." Readings (by tourists and ethnographers) that aim to put a unique locale or a culture "on the map" are complicit with real estate developers in the sense that they all transcode local cultural specificities into the abstract, homogeneous, quantifiable grids of capitalist commodity value.

Given the novel's critique of ethnographic texts for colluding in the capitalist production of value, what exempts the literary text from similar critique? How do novels, which are also commodity objects that circulate within a capitalist system of exchange value, supply less compromised forms of cultural knowledge? The answer, not surprisingly, is that they may do so by exchanging the distanced visual mastery of mapping for the sympathetic and collaborative position of the insider who listens. All Reema's boy needed to know about the culture of the island he "coulda heard" from its inhabitants had he only known "how to listen" (10). The novel's indictment of the ethnographic text authored by an urban outsider (even though Reema's boy was born on the island, his education on the mainland is shown to make him a cultural outsider) is meant to clarify the limits of cultural translation and to prepare the way for the novel's alternate production of cultural knowledge from the inside, as it were. The prologue dealing with the misguided reading and writing procedures of Reema's boy is immediately followed by a passage that sets out the ideal conditions for acquiring cultural knowledge. Unlike *Song of Solomon,* which tries unsuccessfully to displace reading by listening, *Mama Day* seeks to synthesize the two, to reconceptualize reading *as* listening. The authentic mode of knowing is defined here through metaphors of listening, but a listening that is not exactly compatible with an oral storytelling scene.

Real knowing is exemplified by "the way you been listening to us right now" (10), "you" being the reader and "us" the voice of the island's community. Although the collective pronoun *we* would seem to evoke an oral storytelling mode, the reception context established in this passage resembles that of book reading rather than listening: "Think about it: ain't nobody really talking to you. We're sitting here in Willow Springs, and you're God-knows-where. It's August 1999—ain't but a slim chance it's the same season where you are. Uh, huh, listen. Really listen this time: the only voice is your own" (10). Referencing the silence, solitude, and spatiotemporal distance that characterize the situation of book reading, this passage suggests that the production of an insider's knowledge of culture does not require the face-to-face conditions of oral community. If the only voice is our own and we are able to listen "without a single living soul really saying a word" (10), we are engaged in the act of animating and ventriloquizing the silent words of distant others—in other words, we are reading a book. What this passage strives to realize is a participatory model of communication based not on a literal but a figurative return to the oral storytelling situation: read this book *as if* you were an insider listening to the members of a closed community speaking among themselves. Without wishing away the inescapable conditions of its own reception, the novel tries to mitigate their alienating effects through the metaphor of reading as listening.

This becomes apparent at the end of the prologue, when the narrator, the voice of the community, informs us that "you done just heard about the legend.... You done heard it the way we know it, sitting on our porches and shelling June peas, quieting the midnight cough of a baby, taking apart the engine of a car—you done heard without a single living soul saying a word" (10). Here, the reader is so deeply immersed in the community that he or she requires no actual telling in order to listen and to know. The need for any mediation is eliminated in this image of cultural production and reception fully incorporated into the fabric of everyday life and labor—an image difficult to square with reading, which requires specialized, directed attention that precludes simultaneous engagement in other communal activities. Yet this *is* meant to be a description of an ideal reading situation, distinguished from commodity consumption and refigured as an inseparable part of an integrated vernacular culture. The conditions of book reading, as of all commodity consumption, necessarily involve some abstraction, unlike vernacular notions of cultural knowledge based on physical copresence. By embedding reading within a vernacular scene, the novel's prologue strives to reimagine its readership as a fully knowable community.

In addition to its prologue, *Mama Day* includes another instance of speaking and listening that more smoothly overrides the conditions of time and space distancing that attend book reading. The omniscient narrative voice of the Willow Springs community is supplemented by the alternating first-person narrations of George and Cocoa, each addressed to the other, forming a closed circuit of communication. What really distinguishes this narrative situation is that Cocoa is alive and George is dead. Perfectly befitting the magical mode, the narrative address here transcends all the constraints imposed by physical absence: removal in space and time is of no consequence, and even death does not suspend intimate dialogic communication. The two-way conversation between the dead George and the living Cocoa, in which the dead can hear and respond to the living, reverses the one-sided situation of novelistic reading, where the living voyeuristically spy on the dead. Or, in Walter Benjamin's eloquent expression, "What draws the reader to the novel is the hope of warming his shivering life with a death he reads about."[87] *Mama Day* deliberately denies us this voyeuristic pleasure that is inherent to novel reading. Refusing to zoom in on the character Bernice, who is grieving over the death of her son, the narrator disclaims the powers of omniscience in this scene: "Some things go beyond curiosity. Some things you just don't watch" (257). In novels, of course, nothing—not grief, not death—goes beyond curiosity. The George–Cocoa narration similarly suspends the voyeuristic conditions of novelistic knowledge through its reciprocal exchange between the living and the dead.

All the tropes of reading I have discussed so far—the displacement of reading by listening in the hunt scene in *Song of Solomon* and the attempted redefinition of reading as listening in the prologue as well as the George–Cocoa narration in *Mama Day*—share a desire to minimize the mediations involved in reading. Listening forms the preferred mode of knowing because it figuratively restores a reception context in which audiences as well as the circulation of meanings can be contained within a clearly bounded cultural locale. If urban novels such as Morrison's *Jazz,* John Edgar Wideman's *Philadelphia Fire,* and Samuel Delany's *Stars in My Pocket Like Grains of Sand* (discussed in the following chapter) show that original meanings get lost in the unforeseen displacements that characterize book reading, the southern aesthetic shifts the scene of reading to a folk locale in an effort to recover linguistic integrity.

As the hunting scene in *Song of Solomon* illustrates, the move south supports the quest for a natural language that achieves an exact fit between sign and referent. This language is unavailable to Milkman, the reader surrogate, in the city. Before he journeys south, all that Milkman knows are the recorded names, which in every instance (whether it is the Yankee officer's drunken scrawling of the name "Macon Dead" or the blind selection of family names from the Bible) reveal the arbitrariness of textual signs. During the early stages of his journey south, the city reader looks for all the wrong kind of signs—street signs mapping places onto textual grids of meaning. But there are no street signs in Danville, and only by unlearning textual and map-based skills of reading can Milkman approach his "original home" (273), where the "real names" (333) are hidden. Milkman initiates this process when he accidentally discovers the town of Shalimar, which he could not locate on the Texaco map.

Two significant shifts in Milkman's procedures of reading take place during his southern sojourn. The first is that all the magical ancestral tales that Milkman had heard but only partially understood and believed in the city now begin to feel real. Not only is Milkman able to reconstruct the "Song of Solomon" that contains in coded form his familial and cultural history, but he also finds that the stories about the South that seemed remote and "maybe not even true" in the city now "seem so real" because of his "being there in the place where it happened" (233). All the places where the story occurred still exist, as do many of the people with direct links to the story. If some of these people are dead, such as Circe, they are not really dead, for they are resurrected as ghosts who impart valuable information. If it is the tie between place and story that makes stories "real," and if they cannot feel real in the city, what exactly is the value of these stories of and from the South? Their value depends on a literal connection to the rural South, which, as I argued earlier, is presented in *Song of Solomon* as a construct of the literary imagination. But the fact of literary mediation is repressed when the reality effect of stories is embedded in an "original" place. The South once again appears, in contradictory fashion, as a metaphorical figure but also as a literally real place.

The second significant shift, which establishes the primacy of magi-cal over textual, literal over metaphorical readings, even more thoroughly abolishes the need for mediation. Just before Milkman finally decodes the "Song of Solomon," he detects a series of literal correspondences. The words of the children's song refer to places Milkman has seen, such as Solomon's Leap or Ryna's Gulch. Name, place, and song are all metonymi-cally identified with each other: the "Song of Solomon" is about a person named Solomon and is sung in a town named Solomon, and "Everyone in this town is named Solomon" (305). This closed circuit of reference forms an essential feature of southern folk language as presented in Morrison's and Naylor's novels. In Shalimar, a woman's "smile was just like her name, Sweet" (288).[88] In *Mama Day*'s divinatory reading of nature, "the signs don't lie. At least not these signs" (228). This closing of the gap between sign and referent, words and nature, is precisely what forms the appeal of the magical mode. If writing (firmly identified as an urban mode of sig-nification) is arbitrary, obscuring "the real names of people, places, and things," the magical reading procedures aligned with the South delve be-neath written signs and recorded names to afford access to the "names that [have] meaning," with meaning residing in an exact equivalence between language and reality.[89]

Both *Song of Solomon* and *Mama Day* evince what Marianne Hirsch calls a "nostalgia for the literal,"[90] which essentially amounts to nostalgia for crisis-free literary representation, for "a time when an artist could be

genuinely representative of the tribe and *in* it."[91] Magical modes of reading, which affirm literal connections between language and referent, story
and place, author and community, serve to establish stable grounds for the
writer's claims to racial representation. The push toward literal meanings
posits a closed circuit of community, characterized by sameness, cultural
coherence, and transparency of communication, and it allows the author
to claim a directly reflective relation to this community. The literal dimension of these novels requires an effacement of all kinds of mediation, and
especially of literary mediation, resulting in the book that strenuously denies its own textual modality. The contradictions of this project, which are
acknowledged only to be dispelled through tropes of reading as listening,
become fully apparent in the two novels' equivocal treatment of magic.

Toni Morrison claims that she did not have "any literary precedent
for what [she] was trying to do with the magic" in her novels. Although
Morrison dislikes the label "magic" because of its connotations of illiteracy
and ignorance,[92] she nonetheless retains the term because it attests to
the existence of a uniquely black epistemology. In an interview with Mel
Watkins, Morrison flatly asserts that "Black people believe in magic. Once
a woman asked me, 'Do you believe in ghosts?' I said, 'Yes. Do you believe
in germs?' It's part of our heritage."[93] Magic in Morrison's novels is meant
to reflect an already existing black cultural heritage and in this sense does
not require literary justification or precedent. If the writer can assume
communal belief in magic, readers would presumably be expected to read
magic as literally true rather than as a literary metaphor. This appears to be
the case in Morrison's and Naylor's novels, both of which urge literal rather
than metaphorical explanations of magic. For example, in *Song of Solomon*,
Milkman first takes recourse to the metaphorical explanation that he must
be dreaming when he encounters the ghost of Circe, but as the southern
section of the novel progresses, Milkman comes around to believing in the
literal truth of the magical tale of Solomon's flight.

In *Mama Day*, George, the reader surrogate, is urged to believe
Mama Day's magical explanation for his wife Cocoa's mysterious and life-
threatening illness. According to Mama Day and other residents of the
island, Cocoa's illness is caused by Ruby's conjuring, and George can save
her life only if he acts upon Mama Day's magical cure, which requires him
to go into her chicken coop and bring back what he finds there. When
Mama Day explains this to George, he replies that she is "talking in a lot
of metaphors," a response characteristic of a man who has been presented
throughout the novel as an avid reader of literature. But Mama Day discredits George's literary interpretation of magic: "Metaphors. Like what
they used in poetry and stuff. The stuff folks dreamed up when they was
making a fantasy, while what she was talking about was *real*" (294). This

insistence on the literal truth of magic functions in much the same way as does the magical tale of the flying ancestor in *Song of Solomon*, to index a belief system shared by a real community that preexists and authorizes the literary text.

But if the literary text is in fact mirroring an actually existing community of cultural insiders who believe in magic, why is the hypothetical reader of both novels cast as an outsider who has to be persuaded and compelled to believe? In both novels, belief in magic is posed as an issue, a question, a problem, rather than normalized as an epistemology shared by the text and its readers. Both novels take as their addressee a recalcitrant reader whose rational, realist expectations must be gradually revised and abandoned. When Milkman draws attention to the oddity of his situation—"Here he was walking around in the middle of the twentieth century trying to explain what a ghost had done" (298)—the reflective surface of the narrative is ruffled, forcing attention to the difficulties of interpretation attending magic in these texts.

The epistemological status of magic is even more uncertain in *Mama Day*. Even within the closed community of Willow Springs, magic is a contested belief system. Miss Pearl disapproves of it as an anti-Christian practice, and Dr. Buzzard, in Mama Day's opinion, debases it by reducing it to hocus-pocus. Mama Day herself seems to believe that magic should be understood in symbolic and psychological terms, such as when she remarks that "the only magic" contained in the seeds meant to cure Bernice's infertility is that "what she believes they are, they're gonna become" (96), or when she suggests that it is the intensity of Ruby's hatred rather than her conjuring that possesses the real power to harm Cocoa. But by the end of the novel Mama Day is insisting to George that magic is not metaphorical but "real." The truth-claims of conjuring perceptibly shift during the course of the novel, and this shift is instigated by the arrival of the city reader into the insular folk world of Willow Springs. Through George, who is aligned emphatically with print literature, the reader is also placed in the position of outsider to the Willow Springs community. George's charts and graphs, the trappings of his profession as an engineer, invoke the mapping procedures that both novels associate with modern urban modes of knowing. A technology aimed at scientific mastery of nature, engineering is overtly contrasted to magic, which works "under, around, and beside" but never "over nature" (262).

In keeping with his profession, George stubbornly seeks rational, scientific explanations for the strange phenomena he observes in Willow Springs, as, for example, when he argues that it is germs rather than magic that are responsible for Cocoa's illness. George's resistance to magic becomes a real dilemma by the end of the novel, as Cocoa's very life as well as the redemption of the Day women from the curse of their familial history begin to hang on the question of George's belief. We finally realize "how serious is this thing that [George] can't believe" (287) when his incredulity results in his death. If the earlier sections of the novel encourage a certain indeterminacy in our reading of magic, by showing that it is open to conflicting interpretations even within the Willow Springs community, the novel concludes by pressing the urgency of literal and unambiguous belief. Even the disagreement between Mama Day and Dr. Buzzard on the proper uses of conjuring is dissolved by the end, as a unified communal belief in magic is pitted against the fatal skepticism of the "city boy" (271).

These shifts in the novel's treatment of magic suggest that the true addressee of southern magical discourse is the urban outsider rather than the folk insider. It is for the benefit of this estranged reader that the communal system of belief must be purified of all inconsistency. If the real goal of magical discourse is not the transparent reflection of a coherent community of believers but the induction and conversion of a resistant urban reader, then how can magic possibly resolve problems of urban literary representation? By displacing these problems to a folk locale that can sustain knowable community, *Song of Solomon* and *Mama Day* seek escape from the mediations involved in urban reading. But the intrusion of the urban reader on the southern scene shatters the integrity of the folk community that the magical and oral modes strive to institute as a pretextual "real." When this community must be translated and justified to a disbelieving urban reader, the basic premise underlying these texts' use of magic and orality is cast into doubt, and, as a result, the folk community is revealed to be a product of literary mediation rather than literal reflection. Even as the southern folk aesthetic appears to be resolving the difficulties of constituting knowable community in postmodern times, this resolution cannot work because it remains irresolute about whether the southern folk community is imaginary or real, literary fabrication or literal reflection.

The contradictory ambitions that are staked in the southern folk aesthetic of *Mama Day* and *Song of Solomon* become clearer by comparison with Charles Johnson's *Faith and the Good Thing*. The magical resolution works in Johnson's novel because here conjuring is clearly defined as a metaphor for a nonmimetic literary imagination. In *Faith and the Good Thing,* we can let go of the referent; we can bracket the question "Is it true?" and unambiguously affirm the inventive powers of the literary imagination. The blank book offers a perfect trope for Johnson's resolution to questions of literary value in that this book makes visible the pure emptiness of the real, thereby enhancing and freeing the powers of a literary faculty that can conjure beauty, belief, and value out of nothing. Johnson's novel can do away with referential demands from literature because it stakes no particular claims to racial representation. In *Faith and the Good Thing,* conjuring symbolizes the literary imagination in general and does not purport to reflect an actually existing, racially specific cultural practice. Moreover, Johnson's novel makes no claims about the political value of art, claims that would require a very different reply to the question "Is it true?" If anything, *Faith and the Good Thing* celebrates a literary value that must be dissociated from political concerns in order to exert its special powers, which inhere in its aesthetic transcendence of the real.

Because of their political ambitions to speak for and to an actual black community, Morrison and Naylor cannot assent to the radical rupture between literary sign and referent that is effected through Johnson's figure of the blank book. *Song of Solomon* and *Mama Day* strain toward a literal definition of conjuring in an effort to verify their claims to racial representation. Taken literally, conjuring furnishes ready-made community, community as the writer's "natural right,"[94] thereby banishing the mediations involved in literary representation. But the move toward literal readings of southern folk community in Morrison's and Naylor's novels is blocked by a counter-emphasis on the cultural translation needed to make these communities credible to the urban reader. The magical resolution takes more complex forms in *Song of Solomon* and *Mama Day* than it does in *Faith and the Good Thing* because Morrison's and Naylor's novels can neither decide nor suspend the question "Is it true?" This vacillation between the claims of reflecting and inventing black cultural community signals a keen distrust of the category of literature. In essays and interviews, Morrison persistently states that the original sources of her fictional images are "not the traditional novelistic or readerly ones" but are instead drawn from black oral culture.[95] Morrison disavows literary credentials because these are inappropriate to the type of fiction she wishes to write—a fiction that is "not . . . merely literary" but that takes as its ideal audience "an illiterate or preliterate reader" (387). That Morrison must be aware of the impossibility of addressing such a reader is clear from her phrasing: she "*want*[*s*]" the reader of her novels "to respond on the same plane as an illiterate or preliterate reader *would*" (387, emphasis added), rather than claiming that her literature is actually directed at a preliterate or illiterate audience.

A literary frame of reference feels discomforting to Morrison partly because literary readership forms a cultural province that is at once highly specialized and geographically scattered—a province that is certainly not coextensive with the "tribe" or the "village" or the organic community. As John Brenkman observes, the "reading public to which novelistic discourse is addressed differs from the community that produces, from and of itself, the vernacular culture" conjured through magic in Morrison's novels. The "communicative space" of literary, as distinct from vernacular, culture is the space of "the socially complex, multicultural public."[96] In *Song of Solomon*, Morrison's attempt to displace reading by listening is motivated by the impulse to protect black vernacular culture from being assimilated into a not quite multicultural public domain. Morrison's suspicion of literature is rooted in her sense that "the word 'public'... itself" is bankrupt in the postmodern era as well as in her awareness of the asymmetrical terms of African-American integration into national culture.[97] Morrison famously declares that "It is clear to the most reductionist intellect... that the time for undiscriminating racial unity has passed" (xxx). But she does not wholeheartedly welcome the passing of this era because the contact between the supposedly multicultural public and African-American vernacular culture follows the unequal dynamics of appropriation rather than mutual exchange: "being rescued into an adversarial culture can carry a huge debt" (xxvii), namely, the loss or surrender of "the language of one's own culture" (xxviii).

The idioms of the "original culture" (xxix) can be preserved only at the cost of exclusion from economic and political power. Both *Song of Solomon* and *Mama Day* admit the dangers of maintaining cultural community at such cost, and for this reason neither novel unequivocally promotes literal readings of folk communities situated in a segregated rural South. Yet the two novels do not wholeheartedly seize the category of literature to supersede black folk community. When *Song of Solomon* and *Mama Day* seek to minimize their status as print texts and to refigure reading as listening, they betray an acute unease about the diminishing credibility of literary claims to representing a discrete black cultural community. These claims appear at once tenuous and urgent in a contemporary scene in which alarmist discourses proclaim an unprecedented urban crisis measured by the collapse of black community. Read in this light, Morrison's and Naylor's ambivalence about literary value returns us full circle to the postmodern urban crises the southern folk aesthetic is designed to displace.

The critical value of the southern folk aesthetic as exemplified by Morrison's and Naylor's novels becomes clearer when compared with other contemporaneous literary movements that purport to confront more squarely the realities of postmodern urban life. The New Black Aesthetic, as elaborated in Trey Ellis's manifesto for the movement as well as in a host of fictional, essayistic, and autobiographical texts,[98] pointedly defines itself as a reaction against literary paradigms of black authenticity. Greg Tate describes this movement as a postmodern phenomenon in that it is driven by a ludic impulse to "[open] up the entire text of blackness to fun and games."[99] If the rural South supports Morrison's ambition to "write literature that [is] irrevocably, indisputably Black,"[100] New Black Aesthetic writer Reginald McKnight confesses to having "assiduously searched for the essence of blackness and again and again returned...empty-handed."[101] Parodying a key trope of the southern folk aesthetic, Darryl Pinckney's novel *High Cotton* sends its protagonist to the "Old Country" of the South in a quest for racial essence. This quest for a "quick immersion" into black culture fails because, in contrast to Milkman's discovery of oral ancestral tradition, Pinckney's antihero experiences the South largely through a television set in the home of a snobbish aunt who disdains contact with less privileged members of the local black community.[102] Failing to deliver on the southern promise of its title, *High Cotton* depicts a South that is as culturally standardized and class stratified as any other region in the nation.

Perhaps the most refreshing aspect of New Black Aesthetic literature is its unabashed affirmation of the expanded opportunities accruing from middle-class status and its reluctance to romanticize poverty as the basis for authentic black community.[103] Highlighting the class differences that cut across any unitary model of racial community, Trey Ellis's manifesto frankly admits that the New Black Aesthetic movement is "a little elitist, avant-garde thing" (240) that cannot possibly lay claim to broad-based racial representation. The "critical mass" of mostly urban professionals who comprise the New Black Aesthetic movement (237) is clearly a product of the limited success of racial integration and affirmative action programs. As "victims/beneficiaries of the Civil Rights movement,"[104] these artists both lament and affirm their distance from what Toni Morrison calls an earlier time of "undiscriminating racial unity." Identifying themselves as "cultural mulattoes,"[105] Reginald McKnight and Trey Ellis embrace the racial cross-fertilization that is widely presumed to distinguish postmodern U.S. culture. The New Black Aesthetic writer can acknowledge both Toni and Jim Morrison as cultural ancestors, as does Ellis (234), and find no incongruity between blackness and Bach (as in the case of the protagonist of Rita Dove's novel about racial integration, *Through the Ivory Gate*).

But New Black Aesthetic texts often propagate a facile model of cultural pluralism, suggesting that multiculturalism is a free-for-all affair that occurs in a political-economic vacuum. Ellis's unapologetic description of his cohort as a "minority's minority" is disarmingly honest (234), yet in his brief for cultural mulattoism, Ellis takes the class privilege of this elite for granted and maintains a certain blindness toward the unequal terms of racial integration.[106] This myopic vision is clearly apparent in *Platitudes,* where stylistic hybridity parades as an accurate rendition of postmodern urban culture. In contrast to the oral emphasis of the southern folk aesthetic, *Platitudes* plays with word-processing functions (such as ParaShifter) to emphasize the textuality and technological contingency of all culture in the age of electronic reproduction. Postmodern culture in this novel is represented by a promiscuous mix of texts (PSAT tests, porn magazines, science fiction stories), specialized languages (teenspeak, sports commentary, advertising lingo, computer jargon), and media (printed books, electronic texts, television programs). But these heterogeneous texts are linked by nothing other than spatial contiguity. The novel's nomadic style offers no interpretive handle on its textual mixture, encouraging by default a random sampling of cultural differences. Although Ellis demonstrates through the career anxieties of his two author figures that the literary sphere is shaped by market forces, his representation of postmodern urban culture as a free smorgasbord of styles yields little understanding of the uneven distribution of cultural capital among different social groups.

The southern folk aesthetic provides a corrective to precisely this sort of affirmation of the hybridity of postmodern urban culture. As I argued in chapter 3, discourses of postmodern urbanism flaunt their semiotic inclusion of racial differences even as the material form of U.S. postmodern cities attests to the reality of reinforced racial segregation. Despite its many limitations, the southern folk aesthetic is valuable for its critical exposure of the hollowness of postmodern discourses of cultural pluralism. Incredulity toward these discourses motivates Naylor's and Morrison's fictional retreat into a rural South. The insularity of this segregated setting as well as its putative distance from urban commodity markets guard against commercial cannibalization of black culture. Fortunately, however, withdrawal into organic racial community on the one hand and glib embrace of multicultural rhetoric on the other are not the only available literary responses to postmodern urban conditions. A third approach—committed to a postmodern and decisively urban cultural politics, while remaining sharply alert to the materialist dimensions of culture—is elaborated in Samuel Delany's novel *Stars in My Pocket Like Grains of Sand,* which forms the focus of my final chapter.

5.

Reading as Mediation: Urbanity in the Age of Information

In the way that an urban complex soon becomes a kind of intensified sampling of the products and produce of the geosector around it, so a free-data transfer point becomes a kind of partial city against the night, an image of a city without a city's substance, gaining what solidity it possesses from endlessly cross-filled data webs.
—Samuel R. Delany, *Stars in My Pocket Like Grains of Sand*

As the epigraph for this chapter suggests, electronic technologies of information are profoundly transforming perceptions of urban form in the late twentieth century. Many of the terms used to describe postmodern cities—such as *netropolis, teletopia,* or *cyburbia*[1]—are inspired by these new technologies, suggesting that cities are being reimagined less as visible territorial structures than as virtual circuits of information. Terms such as *web* and *network* are widely used to refer to the structure not only of information systems and cities but also of the electronic textual forms (such as hypertext) that are said to be displacing the artifact of the printed book. Current discourses on urban form and textuality are deeply interlinked, as is clear from the seepage of common metaphors among these discourses. Just as the postmodern city as a matrix of information appears to supplant the physical city, so, too, do digital technologies of text production and transmission threaten to dissolve the solid materiality of the printed book, abstracting text into an invisible realm of information bits. If, according to the prophets of electronic hypertextuality, the clearly apprehensible spatial structure of the modern industrial city is mirrored by book culture, with its uniform visual patterns of print and its hierarchical relation between authoritative writers and passive readers, digital texts and postmodern cities are commonly celebrated as dynamic networks that defy totalized order.

What is most striking about these overlapping discourses on cities and texts is the heavy political work performed by their technological metaphors. Both sides of current debates on print and electronic textuality are conjoined by technological fetishism.[2] Proponents of print culture, who decry the new electronic technologies as catalysts of social fragmentation, also construe the printed book as a technological embodiment of the stable and universal values of modern culture. Similarly, those who espouse varieties of electronic "liberation technology" take the network-like structure of hypertext as evidence of the democratic and open-ended forms of postmodern society.[3] In the absence of careful analyses of the economic, political, and social conditions of technological development, tropes of books and networks become self-evident carriers of political meanings.

The epigraph for this chapter is taken from a work of science fiction—a genre that perhaps more than any other has vigorously grappled with the social, cultural, and political implications of the new information technologies and with the dramatic restructuring of urban form sponsored by these technologies. It seems appropriate to close this book on books and cities with a chapter on Samuel Delany's novel *Stars in My Pocket Like Grains of Sand* (1984),[4] because science fiction at its best can point a way out of technological determinism by prompting historical understandings of technology. I do not mean to suggest here that science fiction offers some kind of literal purchase on social reality, in contrast to the overblown metaphors used in current discourses on electronic technologies. This would seem to be a counterintuitive suggestion, given that science fiction is generally assumed to construct blatantly imaginary scenarios of future societies. I take up further in this chapter Samuel Delany's influential account of the dialogue that science fiction conducts with social reality. Here, by way of introduction, I shall briefly mention two of Delany's propositions: first, that science fiction presents a "significant distortion of the present" rather than a plausible depiction of future societies, and, second, that in science fiction texts, "technology often allegorizes rhetoricity."[5]

The latter proposition highlights the manner in which science fiction compels attention to the technological "contouring" of its fictional worlds (*SI*, 170), heightening awareness of the metaphors through which readers apprehend their lived worlds. In this sense, science fiction forces us to take technological metaphors for social reality seriously, often by literalizing them, and thereby paradoxically clarifying their workings *as* rhetorical devices. When technology allegorizes rhetoricity, readers are alerted to the fuzzy political work often performed by technological metaphors. As a world-making enterprise, science fiction hones our consciousness of the processes by which we rhetorically constitute our material and textual worlds. In this sense, works of science fiction produce a "significant distortion" of the present.

In keeping with the first of Delany's propositions about science fiction, in this chapter I read *Stars in My Pocket* in conjunction with contemporaneous debates on urbanity and textuality but not with the assumption that the novel's rendition of an information-saturated universe reflects a real informational society. Rather, I show that Delany's novel takes up certain problems of representation specific to postmodern cities conceived as webs of information, and entertains a range of possible solutions to these problems by materializing them in multiple imaginary contexts. *Stars in My Pocket* refuses the technological reductions of both utopian and dystopian accounts of postmodern urbanism, instead reminding readers that our present social and technological order is not the "end-product of history."[6] Science fiction mediates social change in unique ways, sometimes by helping to accommodate the imagination to change,[7] and often, as in Delany's case, by tempering perceptions of change as crisis. This posture is especially valuable in an era when change is widely perceived as thoroughgoing social rupture, as, for example, in prevalent accounts of the spatial city eclipsed by the cybercity or of the printed book rendered obsolete by electronic textuality. In keeping with this spirit of discontinuity, the new is posed as a radical threat to the old rather than as a possible extension of it. One problem with this way of perceiving transformation is that it encourages nostalgic fixation on the past, abets polarized responses to the present and the future, and gives fuel to rhetorics of social crisis.

The categories that are widely felt to be in crisis in discourses on postmodern urbanism are material reality and social stability; utopian and dystopian accounts of the contemporary city alike depend on placing these categories in crisis. In this chapter, I first sketch out the common terms in which these crises are articulated, paying special attention to the technological metaphors used to vivify the sense of urban crisis. This selective survey pinpoints two problems of representation specific to cities conceived as virtual networks of information: How do we ground political claims in an era in which the referent seems to be vanishing? And, what ethical modes of apprehending racial difference are possible within the technological conditions of postmodern cities? Samuel Delany's fictional extensions and resolutions of these problems form the focus of the rest of the chapter.

Real Places and Cyberspaces

A hallmark of discourses on postmodern urbanism is the currency of semiotic metaphors for cities,[8] which betray the difficulty of grasping an urban

reality that seems increasingly immaterial, spatially dispersed, and technologically mediated. The spatial city itself seems to be the prime casualty of
the postmodern era, if we take as our model the physical form of the modern city, with its concentrated and clearly demarcated structure. This is the
argument advanced by Melvin Webber, one of the most influential early
analysts of the postmodern city as a "nonplace urban realm."[9] According to
Webber, urbanity is now a general phenomenon rather than the exclusive
trait of the city dweller. We can no longer speak of urbanity as a bounded
territorial area or as a function of spatial propinquity because electronic
technologies of information and telecommunications are blurring earlier
distinctions between city and country or city and suburb. Webber contends
that the essence of urbanity no longer resides in visible form but, instead,
in the concentration and variety of information received. Much like Samuel
Delany's analogy between urban complexes and data-transfer points,
Webber figures the postmodern city "as a communications system, as a
vastly complex switchboard through which messages and goods of various
sorts are routed."[10]

Following Webber, several observers have emphasized spatial sprawl as
the outstanding feature of postmodern urban geography; terms such as
edge city or *exopolis* capture the amorphous and diffused quality of urban
complexes organized as flows of information.[11] Manuel Castells has argued that in "the informational city," the meaning of local places is being
overlaid by a global "space of flows"—in other words, by a virtual, international network of information.[12] Most critics of the informational city
tend to overstate the dematerializing effects of information technologies,
with some, like Christine Boyer, going so far as to state that cities themselves have become the "sacrificial sites of cyberspace."[13] The attenuation
of a sense of place is inversely signaled by the proliferation of place-based
metaphors in postmodern cultural and social theory.[14] Straining to accommodate the imagination to the abstract space of flows, various forms of
postmodern culture represent place as an object of intense investment.
Two obvious examples are the imaging of cyberspace as a visible urban
landscape in science fiction films and the emphasis on local contexts in
postmodern theories. At the level of urban geography, architects and city
planners strive to re-create a distinctive aura of place, as is evident from
recent reterritorializing trends in urban architecture, such as critical regionalism, contextualism, and projects to restore local color and vernacular
specificity.[15] As Christine Boyer has shown, "city tableaux" and historically
preserved sites proliferated in U.S. cities during the late 1970s and 1980s
as part of an effort to arrest the postmodern "sense of nonplace."[16] But
these sites failed to restore an authentic spirit of place because they recycled
past urban styles in the ludic, nonreferential mode of pastiche and because

they staged cityscapes as simulacra, provoking Michael Sorkin's analogy between postmodern cities and theme parks.[17]

A sense of tangible reality seems to be on the wane not only because the concentrated exchange functions that form the essence of urbanity have shifted to an invisible, nonspatial domain but also because the urban places that we *can* see no longer hold out the reassurance that "seeing is believing." The postmodern city overworks the visual sense as much as the modern city, but the ontological status of what we see becomes more uncertain with the shift from mechanical to digital technologies of visual reproduction. As we saw in chapter 3, the mechanical means of reproduction associated with the modern city—primarily photography—were touted as exact reflections of empirical reality. The camera's literal claims to representation were staked on the grounds that photographs bear visual traces of an original material presence and so constitute referential tokens of objects that were once really there.

Before going on to clarify the manner in which digital technologies of reproduction posit a different relation between copy and original, image and referent, I should stress once again my argument in the third chapter as well as the cautionary note with which I began this chapter: the postmodern city does not mark a clean and total break from the modern city, and new technologies seldom simply abolish old ones. Just as, in one of the worlds of *Stars in My Pocket,* brooms survive long after the invention of sonic cleaning devices, so, too, do indexical and simulatory technologies of reproduction still jostle each other in postmodern culture. If anything, as I argue in chapter 3, the camera's eye-witnessing claims to truth still widely compel belief, and realism remains the commonsense epistemology of our times. In this chapter, I highlight what is new about electronic technology, but with the caveat that this is an emergent technology with uncertain and variable social consequences.

A passage from Delany's novel offers a compelling point of entry into a discussion of the novel aspects of information technologies. In Velm, one of the worlds presented in the novel, most spatial environments (including interior decor, "natural" landscape, and even climate) are simulated by means of holographic projections. The passage I wish to highlight appears immediately after an off-world guest invades the narrator's room and switches off the projection lenses that had made the bare room appear to be furnished and surrounded by a view of hills and streams. Once the illusion is restored, the narrator meditates:

> I know how much of my world—its streets, its hills, its runs, its rains, the halls, the heat, the sky, the stars, the stream itself—is and is not illusion. But for a moment, as I sat by my desk, still lost in

the disruption from George's invasion, I felt foreign as a creature from one of those primitive geosectors on some world where all reproductive media are safely contained in clearly visible frames, who, for the first time, confronts a modern society where all is what we once called... "spectacle." (336)

This passage seems perfectly to illustrate the peculiar temporality of science fiction, as described by Fredric Jameson: science fiction stimulates critical insight by estranging the present and configuring it as the past of a future world.[18] We might assume that this passage is depicting a possible future when technologies of simulation have become the dominant modes of perception (as compared to the present, when they still remain emergent). But the passage can be read just as persuasively to be describing a moment of technological transition that is very similar to our present moment. What looks like an alien future could very well be the present conjured up with some "significant distortion"; the shock of recognition induced by this passage is akin to the shock with which we realize, while reading Octavia Butler's *Parable of the Sower*, that the dystopian future depicted in that novel uncannily re-creates aspects of the present.

The word *spectacle* is such a buzzword of our times that we easily recognize that the perceptual world described in the passage is not that distant from our present "society of the spectacle."[19] And the past of this world might also be our past, when reproductive media (such as photography) were contained in safely visible frames. And indeed, with digital technologies, visual images become entirely mediated projections of a content that only exists inside computer databases as an invisible field of information. A digitized image is made up of pixels, or discrete bits of programmed information carrying exact numerical values for color, location, and other visual components. As Margot Lovejoy notes, digital images cannot accurately be considered reproductive media because they do not really copy anything. These images are virtual in the sense that they are not optical traces of preexisting material objects (as are photographs) but are instead mathematical models of reality. Digitization thus marks a significant shift in representation from copying to modeling.[20] With this technology, the referent recedes even as the reality-effect of visual images becomes more credible than ever before.

Returning to the passage from Delany's novel, the frames of earlier reproductive media were clearly visible in the sense that reproductions were framed *as* reproductions and thereby marked off from the real. A distance between reality and reproduction was still implicitly at play when a medium like photography staked a claim to accurate imitation of reality. It is this distinction between copy and original that is blurred with simulation media, calling into question the very notion of representation, which necessarily involves distance and mediation. The images produced by the new media are so thoroughly mediated that their real origin is immaterial bits of data rather than tangible objects, yet these images model reality so convincingly that the technology that makes them perceptible becomes invisible.

With the shift from reproduction to simulation, reality is simultaneously enhanced and attenuated, provoking ecstatic or dire proclamations about the "disappearance of the real." Edward Soja speculates that in the "scam-scapes" of the postmodern city, "stubbornly Modernist modes of resistance and demystification will probably not be enough," because the "illusion of the new geographies" carries "historically unexpected power."[21] Although (or maybe because) he overstates the disintegration of reality under the pressure of information technology, Soja pinpoints a problem that plagues postmodern theorists—of how to provide epistemological legitimation for political projects in a world in which reality cannot easily be distinguished from illusion. Both categories must remain intact for modernist modes of critique to work. The paradigm for these is the Marxist demystification of commodity fetishism, a critical procedure that reveals the real social relations of production masked by the illusory allure of the commodity. According to the implicit logic of Soja's argument, this critical paradigm is now defunct because the postmodern commodity has become a perfect simulacrum, disabling the distinction between appearance and reality. We cannot unmask the secrets of the simulacrum because, in Soja's words, "the terrain has shifted too much, the landmarks that anchored our old political maps have mostly disappeared."[22] Soja's spatial metaphors suggest that epistemological doubt has been stretched to an extreme where it veers over into an ontological assertion.

Yet despite Soja's exhortation that we try to invent postmodern modes of political criticism that do not require us to resuscitate the real, it seems that some notion of the real is a necessary fulcrum for oppositional political visions. Most accounts of the hyperreal city invoke various versions of corporeal reality to ground their projects of political and ethical critique. Michael Heim and Richard Kearney, for example, have argued that the technological environment of postmodern cities confounds any decidable distinction between sign and reality, virtual and actual worlds. Unchecked irrealism incapacitates the human imagination and degrades the "sense of community" to the point of "unprecedented barbarism."[23] Both Heim and Kearney suggest that the way out of the labyrinths of the simulacral city lies in face-to-face contacts with others. For Heim, "The living, non-representable face is the primal source of responsibility, the direct, warm link between private bodies. Without directly meeting others physically, our ethics languishes" (102). And Kearney similarly claims that only the "naked face" of the other can restore a firm sense of reality: "the images of all signifying systems...remain ultimately answerable to the concrete ethical exigency of the *face to face relation.*"[24]

This desire for a mystical encounter with the "nonrepresentable" or "naked" face of the other is the inverse side of claims about the decline of reality in postmodern times; both exemplify reactive responses to an environment so thoroughly mediated that the technological frames themselves have become invisible. Advocates of face-to-face relations as the foundation of postmodern ethics partake in what Jacques Derrida has called the "metaphysics of presence" in that they yearn for a corporeal authenticity that can only be imagined outside the terms of all technologies of representation.[25] An ethics founded on the "naked" or "nonrepresentable" face is impossible to realize within contemporary technological conditions and perhaps not even desirable as an ideal. Because we have no choice but to live in an urbanized, technologically contoured world, basing our ethics on face-to-face relations can only amount to nostalgia for a past that never existed. As Iris Young has argued, it is futile to discount all mediation as evil, and incorrect to assume that face-to-face relations are unmediated.[26] Bare apprehension of the other is not possible even outside the contexts of modern and postmodern media of reproduction; no human face can appear to us entirely shorn of prior representations, even if these are "only" mental.

Heim claims that without "the primal interface..., ethical awareness shrinks" (102). But neither Kearney nor Heim explains why the naked face should elicit a more sound ethical response than a face mediated by mental representations of concepts such as justice and civility. The only way of knowing the unmediated reality of the other is by altogether erasing the boundary between self and other, by achieving a total merger with the other. Does it follow, then, that we must extend civility only to those whom we can know completely? As I show further, Delany's novel aspires to an alternate ideal of civility understood as a relation of tolerance among strangers, demanding difficult acts of mediation and incomplete comprehension. This is, of course, an urban ideal: as Delany reminds us, the root meaning of politeness is "the proper way to act in a city" (*SI*, 268).

In common with Heim and Kearney, Christine Boyer mourns the decline of material reality, shared community, and "face-to-face communication" in the postmodern city,[27] but she locates the reality that cries out for ethical recognition within an urban rather than organic setting. The immaterial network of cyber-reality hides "the lag-time spaces of the city" (38), "areas of forced delay put on hold in the process of postmodernization" (20). These places (frequently identified with inner cities in Boyer's account) are the touchstones of a material reality that is repressed by cyber metaphors for cities. Boyer resorts to metaphors of embodiment to render the disquieting reality of these lag-time spaces: "Reality is increasingly immaterial.... Meanwhile, the contemporary city stands with all of its gaping wounds as crime escalates, megacities erupt, blood continues to spill, disease accelerates, and unemployment and undereducation continue" (11). It is hardly surprising that these real spaces turn out to be inhabited by women and racial minorities. Boyer argues that "as issues of race and gender begin to emerge in the lag-time spaces of the city, we can transcend these anxieties and therein refuse their corporeal demands thanks to the hypermaterialistic synthetic connections of computer networks in which the body, technology, and community are reduced to the hallucinatory metaphors of cyberspace" (38).

Boyer is trying here to expose the work of political containment performed by metaphors of cities as cyberspaces. These hallucinatory metaphors (Boyer is probably alluding to William Gibson's description of cyberspace as "a consensual hallucination")[28] efface the raw material realities experienced by the poor, women, and racial minorities—those who are either excluded from or relegated to the lower rungs of the information economy. These groups presumably inhabit a more real domain because they experience the material conditions of their lives as immediate constraints. Food, shelter, health, and other basic physical needs remain unmet for many residents of postmodern cities, and this distressing reality is obscured in metaphors of cities as cyber-nets. By implication, Boyer's corporeal metaphors of the wounded, bleeding city more accurately capture the real conditions of contemporary urban life than do "the hallucinatory metaphors of cyberspace."

It is not surprising that Boyer should use corporeal metaphors to restore the repressed real text of the postmodern city, for the body is often considered the prime casualty of information technologies. As Paul Virilio observes, these technologies effect a virtual urbanization of the body: plugged into various prosthetic devices, the body becomes the node of a circuit of information and communication, and, in this sense, becomes the "ultimate urban territory." But this body, umbilically attached to computer terminals, is also immobilized and deterritorialized. In Virilio's vivid metaphor, the virtually mobile citizen of cyberspace is modeled on the "motorized handicapped."[29] It is this image of a disabled body that Boyer accentuates rather than a human sensorium that might be technologically augmented. The cyborg body in itself operates as a metaphor for social alienation and political apathy in Boyer's account, so it seems almost inevitable when Boyer vests political awareness and responsibility in metaphors of a more real corporeality.[30]

Boyer's gesture is not so different, after all, from Heim's and Kearney's appeals to the naked face, which provides a firm ethical foothold in material reality. In each case, "others" have to be embodied in very specific ways before we can heed their ethical and political demands. These polarities between the hyperreal and the wounded city, the technologically mediated and the organic community, the benumbed prosthetic body of the terminal citizen and the brute "corporeal demands" of marginalized others, break down under close inspection, because the body is not only the "sacrificial site" but also the supreme fetish of postmodern urbanism. As I argue in chapter 3, it is certain kinds of bodies—those belonging to African-Americans and women—that are imbued with presence.[31] An insistence on the heightened embodiment of these groups can easily slide over into fetishism, symbolically compensating for their economic and political marginalization. African-Americans and women are seen to exist at a more material level because they do not largely occupy decision-making positions in the "space of flows," where financial power invisibly circulates. Investing these groups with intensified corporeal presence is not likely to stir political awareness in the right ways because, in doing so, we risk disguising a structural position of relative powerlessness into a desirable ontological condition (of increased presence).

In search of Archimedean levers for political change, critics of postmodern urbanity end up pitting their conceptions of reality against the inauthenticity of the cybercity, either pushing the real utterly outside contemporary urban conditions (as in Heim's and Kearney's primal scene of face-to-face interaction) or locating it in urban areas that represent zones of radical otherness within the cybercity (as in Boyer's lag-time spaces). These accounts bear out David Harvey's complaint that in contemporary cultural theory, possibilities of transformation are often identified with "residual" or "surplus" areas that inexplicably evade the dominant logic of the rest of the social process or system.[32] When alternatives are so starkly juxtaposed against dominant conditions, it becomes hard to imagine the mediation between domains that would be a prerequisite for social change. Such notions of alternate reality, even as they present themselves in absolute opposition to contemporary social conditions, actually take their bearings from these conditions, which generate all-or-nothing ways of thinking about reality.

Webs and Networks: The Postmodern Politics of Difference

It is true that with simulation technologies the real itself seems to become undecidable, but it is nevertheless important to remember the common-sensical fact that technologies trading in immaterial elements (such as information bits) have material supports not only in physical infrastructure but also in economic and political institutions,[33] which likewise bear upon the seemingly more real facts of poverty or unemployment. Technocrats of cyberspace are no more or less real than unskilled labor; to grasp the reality of postmodern cities, we would have to regard both as equally significant and interconnected social facts of our times. We would have to resist the impulse to valorize either corporeal or hallucinatory space as the truly real space of the postmodern city and instead view them as mutually constitutive and yet conflicting spaces. The truth of the postmodern city might then emerge from the structural tension between disparate realities.

As several urban scholars have shown, the development of information technologies has at once enabled and been conditioned by processes of global capitalist restructuring in response to the economic crises of the 1970s. By facilitating the automation of jobs, the subcontracting of production and distribution, and the reorganization of corporations toward networks rather than conglomerates, information technologies have played an instrumental role in fostering the more flexible modes of production that are widely regarded as the distinguishing feature of global capitalism. Advanced technologies of information processing have opened up a new sector of highly skilled and well-paid technical and professional jobs. By enhancing productivity, these technologies are also reducing lower-skilled jobs in factories and offices, thus creating a surplus labor pool that is partially absorbed into an expanding service sector. As white men predominantly constitute the technocracy and women, racial minorities, and immigrants are concentrated in low-paid service jobs, the employment structure of the information economy is bisected along the lines of race and gender.[34]

This bipolar employment structure is visually manifest in the spatial order of the large cities that form crucial nodes of the information economy. The central business districts of these cities constitute the core areas where most of the new high-skilled technical jobs are clustered. These areas are often adjacent to the old core areas inhabited by a labor pool (made up largely of racial minorities) that has been made obsolete by the disappearance of manufacturing jobs from central cities and by its lack of the technical skills required for the new jobs. This combination of factors gives rise to the dual city, where "a large sector of professional and managerial middle-class [coexists] with a growing urban underclass."[35] As Manuel Castells argues, a conspicuous aspect of this contradictory development is the varying experience of place and space for different social strata, depending on the manner and degree of their incorporation into the information economy. Managerial and professional elites, connected to cosmopolitan circuits of communication and information, are more easily able to overreach the limits of place in their daily work and leisure activities, whereas those who occupy the lower tiers of the information economy (disproportionately women and racial minorities in the United States) remain segregated within the spatial confines of their "information ghettoes."[36]

With the visible splintering of social structure and spatial form brought about under the impact of the new information technologies, it becomes increasingly difficult to ascertain what, if anything, holds it all together. Metaphors of cities as webs or networks or spaces of flows capture the instability and open-endedness of this process of social and spatial transformation. Caught up in the swirl of change, it is easy to overstate the indeterminacies of the process and to overlook the sticking points where the process congeals into a structure.[37] But the flexibility and decentralization of power suggested by the network as a unit of organization have proved highly amenable to the goals of capitalist restructuring. Moreover, a nodal urban form has not been entirely dissolved by the space-spanning capacities of the new information and communications technologies. As Saskia Sassen has shown, the spatial dispersal brought about by the new technologies has in fact necessitated greater agglomeration, with large cities serving as nuclei of information flow and corporate financial power. Cities such as New York remain nodal because of the density of their links to the international economy and to advanced communication and information circuits.[38] As Castells points out, in 1984 there were more personal computers in Manhattan than in all of Europe put together.[39]

Although multinodal forms are the more blatant features of postmodern urban geography, countertendencies are equally apparent in the rapidly multiplying gated communities and segregated zones that map out clear class and racial divisions. The network metaphor captures a significant truth about current changes in social and spatial organization, but the webs and flows of postmodern cities are not exactly random or undetermined. Political and public policy decisions are shaping in crucial ways the evolution of postmodern urban form, which is not an automatic outcome of structural economic or technological processes. As Sassen argues, far from losing significance, nation-states have actively facilitated international capital mobility through the "production of new forms of legality."[40] In the specific instance of the United States, urban space has been re-formed by the political realignment of the Reagan years, characterized by deregulation of capital, regressive taxation policies, drastic shrinkages in social welfare programs, and the weakening of labor claims.[41]

If these systematic features lend relative stability to the postmodern city, allowing us to grasp it as a structure, this is nevertheless a precarious and provisional structure containing nodes of internal contradiction. One of these points of tension in the informational city may be the sharp polarizations it produces at different levels: in the segmentation of jobs and wages and the concomitant thinning of the middle, or in the stark discontinuities between urban spaces (such as renovated downtown areas of consumption adjoining the areas Boyer terms lag-time spaces). Polarization of categories and values is also rampant in postmodern culture: between tangible places and invisible spaces of flow, between "tribalization of local communities" and cosmopolitanism,[42] between organic and cyborg corporealities, between face-to-face and virtual communities, and between mystical quests for an absolutely verifiable reality and bleak pronouncements about the complete extinction of reality. These dichotomies form the potentially explosive stress points of the informational city. We could not perceive them as such without some working concept of structured totality, but as stress points they also indicate the internal conflicts that prevent the informational city from achieving complete coherence, closure, and permanence.

Accounts of the postmodern city often fall prey to polarizing habits of thought precisely because of a strong and politically motivated aversion to structural modes of thinking. By the logic of much postmodern urban theory, structure automatically amounts to hierarchy, and totalities inevitably spell totalitarianism. The web or the network then logically becomes the metaphor for a heterotopic urban fabric that eludes rigid systematization. For example, in Melvin Webber's famous description, the "nonplace urban realm" is not "a unitary place" but a lateral form that contains "no Euclidean divisions—only continuous variation, spatial discontinuity, persisting disparity, complex pluralism, and dynamic ambiguity."[43] The postmodern city imaged as a matrix, kaleidoscope, collage, or bricolage not only repels cognitive and theoretical mastery but also often prefigures a utopian space of free play between heterogeneous social elements.[44] In an eloquent critique of the vaguely defined political values that infuse network and web metaphors of the city, Christine Boyer warns that as we "war against totalities, afraid of their prescriptions and over-determinations" (38), we err in taking the opposite direction to an extreme, presuming that "open-ended networks" automatically "revers[e] hierarchical order and closed representations" (32). In other words, we assume that certain spatial or technological forms in themselves carry necessary political consequences and that transformations at the level of discourse will automatically ensure material changes. By replacing the language of totality with the rhetoric of indeterminacy, we believe we have "reinstated freedom of choice and enabled the voice of alterity to rise" (28).

But aversion to the idea of totality actually disables an apprehension of genuine alterity. Differences can only be perceived as such with reference to some principle of relation, but the only relation proposed between the diverse elements of the postmodern city is that of sheer adjacency. Without some concept of a structured totality, differences become irreducible and incommunicable to each other. And, in fact, even as differences multiply at a discursive level, spatial segregation, social containment, and economic polarization are the hallmarks of postmodern cities, graphically depicted in novels such as John Edgar Wideman's *Philadelphia Fire* or Octavia Butler's *Parable of the Sower.* The principle of juxtaposition does not suffice to explain how and why different urban spaces—such as glittering urban downtowns and public housing projects—come to be at once adjacent, rigidly demarcated, and structurally interdependent.

To image postmodern cities as random interplays between differences at a time when social divisions are becoming polarized may be a gesture of concealment, containment, and compensation.[45] Information, commodities, and labor move within the worldwide web of a thoroughly internationalized economy, and advanced technologies of telecommunications and information processing make different times and places instantaneously copresent, provoking both delirium and anxiety about the types of new community that are thereby made possible. Within the national context of the United States, postmodernism as an ensemble of intellectual and cultural trends emerges in tandem with movements demanding economic, political, and social equality for African-Americans and women. In the even more specific context of U.S. urban history, metaphors of the city as a bricolage gain currency at the very moment when violent urban uprisings in various cities are interpreted (by the Kerner Commission) as proof and explosive consequence of the racial polarization of the nation. The postmodern politics of difference can be easily dismissed as a weak response to the racial conflicts of this era, chiefly for its failure to translate a discursive critique of the unitary subject of modern politics into a project of social transformation. Assertions about the heterogeneity of postmodern culture can be rhetorical ruses: incorporating others at a discursive level substitutes for the more difficult task of confronting the material conditions that proscribe the equitable coexistence of diverse social constituencies. But as an ideal, the "politics of difference" renews an age-old vision of urban life as a scene of vibrant encounter among various social groups.[46] This urban ideal seems difficult to grasp in contemporary times, when social differences jostle together, but only through advanced forms of technological mediation. The postmodern city is neither a scene of face-to-face interaction, in which self and other are fully present to each other, nor a setting where cross-cultural communication is subject to clear spatial and temporal constraints. Given these neither/nor (or both/and) conditions of postmodern urbanity, it is not surprising that the question of how to apprehend otherness and difference becomes an insistent epistemological and political concern.

A perfect genre for exploring this question is science fiction, with its close encounters with alien times and places, especially as these are made available by various forms of technology. Samuel Delany is often counted among the generation of writers who postmodernized science fiction.[47] In

Fred Pfeil's dissenting account, science fiction takes its postmodern turn during the 1980s, as it begins to shift its exploration of social otherness beyond the binary framework of modernism toward a "complex rhizomatics of affiliation and difference," which forms the basis of an anti-essentialist politics. Pfeil associates Delany with the metafictional and modernist science fiction of the 1970s, characterized by its preoccupation with problems of aesthetic experimentation more than with problems in social thought.[48] But this distinction unravels in Delany's work, where self-reflexive attention to the rhetorical modes through which science fiction fabricates its worlds prompts readers to historicize and reassess contemporaneous ways of modeling social reality.

Samuel Delany has tried to develop an emphatically urban politics commensurate with the technological and social conditions of postmodern life. The terminology of webs and networks, omnipresent in postmodern discourses on the informational city and on electronic textuality, is also scattered throughout *Stars in My Pocket Like Grains of Sand*. The novel features a political organization called the Sygn, as well as an information-processing system called the Web, which governs the flow of data across the various worlds comprising the novel's interstellar universe. Delany has noted that this terminology spilled over into the novel from his reading of poststructuralist theory, adding that in his seduction by the vocabulary of signs and webs, "what [he] was balking at was essentialism" (*SI*, 249). But with all his meticulous efforts to render the undecidability of meaning and the decentered nature of the subject, Delany has no grandiose delusions about the political consequences of a poststructuralist project such as deconstruction, which actually cautions, to the contrary, that essentialism cannot be escaped at the discursive level. The rules of deconstruction "remind us that it is not intellectual constructs that free us from metaphysics—other than as a fleeting, interim effect of a certain critique" (*SI*, 14). "Critique is not resistance," insists Delany (*SI*, 209); "rather, it is material changes alone that shift metaphysical grounds" (*SI*, 14).

Delany's work has both furthered and been driven by a politics of difference, organized around the multiple axes of race, gender, and sexuality. But Delany argues that some of these political movements—specifically the gay rights and women's movements—"found themselves backsliding into far more reactionary positions" as they began drifting away from "the civil rights movement as a model" (*SI*, 217). To Delany, this model epitomizes a thoroughgoing movement toward a "materially realized society":

> What the civil rights model privileges is, of course, a constant review of power, money, violence, education, freedom, shelter, health, and food.

You have to know the state of all of those—and have some sense of the history of them all—practically day by day, if you're going to stabilize any sort of theoretical progress, in any radical liberation program. (*SI,* 218)

With this reservation, Delany advocates a politics of difference because it exposes as delusory the coherence of modern notions of the subject. In an afterword to the 1990 edition of *Stars in My Pocket,* Delany challenges Fredric Jameson's contention that the centered subject that existed during the modern era of classical capitalism has now dissolved: "I think that any time when there was such a notion of a centered subject, especially when related to the white, western, patriarchal nuclear family, not only was it an ideological mirage, it was a mirage that necessarily grew up to mask the psychological, economic, and material oppression of an 'other.'"[49] If the modern subject achieves the mirage of centrality by means of its oppression of others, the postmodern politics of difference posits a notion of the "subject-in-history" that can, in principle, "be denied to *no* one" (*SI,* 204). This subject disavows all claims to transcendent knowledge because it is embedded in a spatial and temporal world that it can know only through its own linguistic and material operations upon this world. In this sense, the knowledge claims of the postmodern subject are profoundly historical and, by implication, revisable. According to Delany, this view of the subject may be descried in a range of "postmodern marginal enterprises," including "some black fiction, certain feminist fiction, . . . much science fiction, some gay fiction" (*SI,* 199), and it figures centrally in *Stars in My Pocket,* to which I now turn.

The Splendor and Misery of Bodies, of Cities

Before entering into an intensive discussion of the novel, a summary-description may be in order, for *Stars in My Pocket* is currently out of print and is not likely to be familiar to most of my readers. It is impossible to convey, in a bare-bones plot summary, the dazzling richness of this novel, which inheres in finely tuned descriptions of the vagaries of cross-cultural communication and of the complexities of sense perception generated by information technologies. The first of the novel's three sections is set in a world named Rhyonon, which is revealed to the reader largely through the impoverished perspective of Rat Korga, an underprivileged, illiterate, and troubled human male who is regarded as a "burden to . . . [his] city" (3). In the first scene of the novel, Korga undergoes a synapse-jamming procedure, also known as Radical Anxiety Termination, that converts him into a more functional citizen of his world. Rhyonon is a severely repressive and inequitable world in a state of political turbulence and on the brink of economic collapse. Its government has resisted connecting with General Information (or GI), a system used by most of the worlds in the novel's universe, which allows for almost instantaneous neural access to all the transworld data collected in the system. GI is administered by a shadowy, behind-the-scenes organization named the Web, which was established to manage "the information glut that [is] ... the hallmark" of the novel's universe (159). An invisible entity, the Web overarches two political organizations, the Family and the Sygn, which are vying for supremacy over the more than six thousand planets that make up the Federation of Habitable Worlds. Most worlds are aligned with one or other of these political systems, but not Rhyonon, which is undecided but leaning toward the Family. The first section of the novel ends when Rhyonon is destroyed by an unexplained explosion, which, we later learn, may have been engineered by the Xlv, a truly alien species that has remained incommunicable. The sole survivor of Rhyonon is Rat Korga, spared because he is inside an underground refrigerated storage vault at the time of the explosion.

From the hierarchical world of Rhyonon, polarized into "bitches" and "dogs," rats and human beings, homosexuals and heterosexuals, we are jolted into Velm, a world that seems to be a utopian counterpoint to the dystopia of Rhyonon. In the southern regions of Velm, human beings mate, verbally communicate, and live in harmony with the evelmi, an intelligent trisaurian species that possesses language and can also neurally access GI. The coexistence of evelmi and human beings over a long period of time has produced cultural fusions as well as transformations in the sensorium of each species. The "urban complex" of Morgre in southern Velm is the primary setting for the "Monologues" that comprise the bulky middle of the novel. These are narrated by Marq Dyeth, a homosexual human male, like Korga, but whereas Korga is "a hugely informatively deprived individual from a generally informatively deprived world" (162), Marq is an Industrial Diplomat employed by the Web, who supervises the import and export of information among worlds. The plot of the novel is really set in motion when a Web official informs Marq that Korga has been rescued from the rubble of Rhyonon by the Web and fitted with prosthetic eyes and legs, and, most importantly, a prosthetic neural device that, in compensation for the damage done by the RAT synapse-jamming procedure, permits Korga to be hooked into General Information, connecting him with worlds and species other than his own now-destroyed human world.

All this information about Korga's rescue and reincarnation as a cyborg is imparted to Marq because the Web has determined that Korga very nearly approximates Marq's perfect object of sexual desire and should therefore be sent to live on Morgre. Much of the rest of the novel describes in intricate detail the events of Korga's one-day visit to the city, including the social rituals of interspecies meals, trips to the runs (or demarcated areas of free and anonymous sexual activity), and a dragon hunt followed by a song of celebration. Not much happens in this section of the novel, but it portrays with astonishing nuance the precarious ballet of understanding and error that makes up social encounters between different worlds.

Korga's visit is abruptly terminated because his alien presence incites such terrified fascination that masses of Morgre inhabitants surround Marq's familial home in hopes of glimpsing the stranger who is sole survivor of a destroyed world. In a plot twist that is insufficiently motivated, the disorder latent in the gathering crowds, compounded by the hovering presence of Xlv spaceships above Morgre, raises fears about the impending possibility of Cultural Fugue (or world destruction) on Velm, prompting the Web to remove Korga to another unspecified world. In the brief epilogue to the novel, Marq, seeking to convey the anguish he feels the morning after his loss of Korga, actually writes around this loss in a tightly compressed discourse on the transworld semiotics of the metaphor of morning.

Stars in My Pocket might well have been titled *The Splendor and Misery of Bodies, of Cities,* the projected title of its still-awaited sequel, for it explores the utopian and dystopian propensities of the technologies that are transforming bodies and cities. The novel captures the dematerializing effects of information technologies through its cyborg bodies and its cities that are essentially "allegor[ies] of ... informative complexities" (77). But as science fiction rather than a realist representation of the informational city, *Stars in My Pocket* extends these technologies in unpredictable directions that readers may initially find difficult to imagine, locked as we can be into a sense of inevitability about the modes of technological development on our world. As Delany has argued, readers make sense of the worlds projected in science fiction texts only through continual mediation between the fictional world and the reader's real world.[50] This process of reading and world making prods us to notice more keenly the historical specificities of our own world, but it also disembeds us from the seeming givenness of this world, freeing us to imagine other possible trajectories.

In *Stars in My Pocket*, technological development is shown to be historically variable and socially malleable. If dystopian accounts of postmodern urbanism suggest that the new technologies are eradicating tangible places and realities, the novel imagines scenarios in which this is not a necessary effect of information technologies—scenarios in which technologies of simulation can enhance sensuous apprehension of the world. The universe presented in the novel is easily recognizable as an extrapolated variant of the cybercity or teletopia. The monologues constituting the middle section of the novel are collected under the title "Visible and Invisible Persons Distributed in Space," which alludes to Marq's encounters with actual and virtual bodies in the course of his professional travels. In this universe, business conferences are conducted telematically through hyperwave projections, and artificial milieus and climates are projected by means of "mobile environmental simulation units" (173), fulfilling contemporary prophecies that technologies of virtual reality will eventually bring us "weather theater."[51]

What makes it most difficult for this-worldly readers to apprehend the sense environment of *Stars in My Pocket* is that metaphors of perception in the world of Velm have shifted from sight to taste as a result of decades of genetic and cultural interchange between human beings and the many-tongued evelmi. Here, the word *spectacle,* which "in one ancient human language or another referred to vision," has "shifted to denote taste" (336). The sculptures in this world, or at least in those parts of the world where the two species coexist harmoniously, are for tasting as well as viewing, and colloquial language is strewn with taste-based metaphors for experience, such as "I taste your meaning" (256). This shift in perception and language, once we become accustomed to it, transports us to a wondrously augmented world, where reality is at once overlaid by technologies of simulation and available literally to be licked in all its sensuous immediacy. In the urban complex of Morgre, a marvel of technological construction, we can seldom be sure if bodies are really there or only virtually so, yet corporeal pleasures are intensified rather than depleted by the advanced technologies. Sensuous delight and technological illusion reach a unique utopian synthesis in Morgre as a result of its progressive political history of interspecies cultural exchange. Our future may never take this particular form, but we are led to imagine the political conditions under which current technologies could take utopian directions, contexts both resembling and radically other than our own, where the body and its delights do not have to be the "sacrificial sites" of technology.

If *Stars in My Pocket* projects certain conditions under which technologies of simulation do not necessarily threaten bodily experience, it also suggests some beneficial political uses of illusion. As we saw earlier, Edward Soja's call for a new politics adequate to postmodern urban contexts of simulation remains largely unanswered; most proposed visions of political responsibility hark back to mystical scenes of face-to-face encounter and corporeal presence. Delany's novel offers an alternate vision of how strangers might live together in cities, conjoined by mutual love of illusion. In northern Velm, human beings and evelmi slaughter each other on the grounds of inherent biological differences between the species, whereas in the south, the two species coexist in peace. Seeking to explain this difference between the two regions, which can only be a political difference, an evelmi scholar says, echoing Karl Marx:[52]

> The real affinity between us [humans and evelmi] is that all our myriad cultures, and all yours, are founded on love of illusion.... It is not that we both build home-caves, construct travel-guiders that stretch for thousands of kilometers over the land, lay out social grounds, or put together musical compositions and complex combinations of food and flavored stone, but that we both build, construct, lay out, and put together these things according to plans, visions, imaginative schemes that, until we have realized them, have no real existence. (226–27)

The power of illusion is the power to create "meaning without referent" (227) and can be politically potent insofar as it allows us to aspire toward ideals—such as peace or justice—that bear no necessary correspondence with materially given realities. In northern Velm, insistence on meanings that claim exactly to match real referents (such as cultural conflict between species taken as a reflection of innate distinctions) carries politically disastrous consequences. In a world such as ours, where political appeals to putatively natural referents such as race, gender, or sexuality rationalize social inequality, counterappeals to the unmediated reality of corporeal presence may not offer the best political alternatives. Instead, Delany's novel suggests, ethical accountability might be heightened by an awareness that political values never simply inhere in embodied presences or natural realities but are achieved through the abstracting and mediating activities of the imagination.

To affirm the politically transformative capacity of illusion is not, however, to imply that politics can float free of the world of material reality. Like most postmodern ecotopias,[53] *Stars in My Pocket* associates the "misery of bodies, of cities" with modern models of development that are imported and imposed without concern for regional differences. The city of Morgre in southern Velm works as a technological artifact because its construction and maintenance are founded on ecologically sound principles, and its architectural forms preserve and update local histories of land use wherever feasible. At the same time, much of the milieu of this city is a marvel of technological fabrication; the inconveniences of climate and geography have been mitigated by means of advanced environmental simulation. The novel does not, then, suggest that given natural conditions should curb technological development. Rather, Morgre exemplifies a precariously fine balance between natural contingencies and the technological and political imagination.

The postmodern investment in local contexts is meant to counter not just the abstract and functional logic of modern architecture and urban planning but also the seeming disintegration of local specificities under the impact of information technologies. Digital technologies reduce all data into a common binary code, making it possible to standardize information and to reproduce it in a variety of contexts. This decontextualizing facility sparks reactive movements to preserve indigenous values and vernacular traditions.[54] In Delany's novel, the formation of a universal database arouses intense political and cultural anxiety. The novel's universe is webbed by a standardized system, GI, that provides instant access to information about any part of the universe on mere mental request. The "brilliant translation devices" of this system have enabled communication among thousands of species (93) but have nonetheless left unresolved the problems of intercultural knowledge and interpretation. Because the narrator, Marq Dyeth, is a diplomat by profession, these problems are always at the forefront of the novel. Marq defines diplomacy as a system "by which you decide whether other people possess a context for understanding what you want to say or not, and, if not, for adding appropriate contextual material to your communication" (167). The information system managed by the Web is intended to function as a "diplomatic" transmitter of cultural data, always aiming to provide context-specific information, but, as illustrated by the many instances in which interworld communication devolves into a comedy of errors, no universal system of information exchange can impart a full sense of local history or effectively capture all the subtleties of semiotic codes specific to different contexts.

Stars in My Pocket elaborates the postmodern commitment to local contextualism with exceptional rigor, resisting the tendency to hypostasize local contexts and thereby to lose sight of the structured linkages among various locales. The very fact that the narrator of the novel is a diplomat engaged in the import and export of information emphasizes the lines of connection and communication among different worlds. Even in a universe spanned by a system of general information, regional variations continue to matter—not as irreducible differences but as effects of an uneven integration of information technologies into diverse political contexts. The contrast between the information policies of Rhyonon and Velm starkly clarifies how political vectors shape the logic of uneven development. Velm follows a liberal policy, with General Information freely available to all citizens. This, combined with the fact that its form of government is "bureaucratic anarchy" (apparently a variant of socialism in that it has "no concept for uneven-distribution-of-exchange-power" [107]), makes Velm an instance of utopian possibility. In the dystopian case of Rhyonon, conservative and insular policies toward information (GI is banned on Rhyonon) protect a socioeconomic order stratified into a technocracy of "men" and an "information underclass" made up of rats and slaves.

The cases of Rhyonon and Velm indicate that even when information is, in principle, universally available, there is no such thing as a pure logic of technological development free of political mediation. A popular contemporary slogan, "Information wants to be free," expresses the widespread assumption that information technologies are intrinsically libertarian and, if allowed to develop without political interference, will automatically bring about a pluralist society. This sort of presumption is belied in *Stars in My Pocket* by the simple fact that General Information is a system controlled by the Web rather than a free-floating field of data. The Web itself is not a neutral and transparent medium for the processing and exchange of information. Theoretically, the Web is supposed to provide free access to data, but in practice the flow of information is subject to politically motivated gaps and repressions that are misrepresented as technical malfunctions. When Marq hears rumors about the destruction of Rhyonon, he requests information from GI, only to be stalled by the "run-around circuit" set up by the Web (94). In politically volatile situations, the Web either erases all the pertinent references from the GI database, screening this erasure with the announcement that the requested information is "undergoing extensive revision" (94), or it provides an overload of irrelevant data that nullifies the question. This sophisticated style of censorship suggests that webs and networks, far from heralding the very shape of freedom, can be made up of "all sorts of restraining strands" (86) and can embody political systems within which power operates in insidious and undetectable ways. Delany's Web also continues to deploy more traditionally repressive (and allegedly outmoded) means of power, such as when Marq is warned that further curiosity on his part will damage his professional status.

Along with Marq, the readers of *Stars in My Pocket* never do learn whether the Xlv were responsible for the destruction of Rhyonon or why the Web obliterated all information about an entire world. Throughout the novel, the Web operates behind the scenes, not only administering the flow of information but also discouraging interworld travel and interstellar imports, and even dictating the plot of the novel by instigating and abruptly terminating the love affair of Marq and Korga. Although we see some of the effects orchestrated by the Web, its political motivations remain inscrutable. Some readers have cited this as a chief defect of the novel and wished for more precise delineations of the Web's mode of governing the data complex that makes up the novel's universe.[55] But perhaps the shadowy and unrepresentable status of the Web is precisely the point. As Fredric Jameson has remarked, the nebulous conspiracy theories and paranoid plots that are ubiquitous in postmodern fiction may reflect a novel feature of the postmodern condition—the difficulty of grasping the world-space of multinational capitalism in its totality.[56] Delany's Web may be interpreted in this light as an attempt to evoke the totality of a global (or, more precisely, interplanetary) system that no one can directly apprehend or represent. But the totality constituted by the Web is never immediately knowable as such and is shown—by the pervasive threat of world destruction that it cannot contain—to be a precariously unstable system. Made up of "restraining strands" as well as linkages, of nodes where data flow is concentrated as well as the gaps represented by information ghettoes, Delany's Web evokes an internally contradictory totality.

One form of heterogeneity that exists within the Web is the conflict between two political ideologies, the Sygn and the Family, which pursue exactly contrary approaches to the problems of cultural value that arise in an age of information. As most parts of the world become incorporated into a global web of information and communication, cultural values are uprooted and mobilized within a variety of unpredictable contexts, and questions about how to delimit cultural traditions become deeply fraught. These issues are of urgent concern in contemporary debates on postmodern urbanism. As David Harvey and Manuel Castells, among others, have argued, the accelerated transformations of space under the latest phase of capitalist global restructuring, facilitated by information technologies, are fueling the contradictory trends of postmodern culture. On the one hand, we find affirmations of cultural fluidity, dynamism, innovation, indeterminacy, and heterogeneity, expressed through metaphors of deterritorialized urban networks and virtual spaces of flows. On the other hand, we find reterritorializing movements in quest of roots, ethnic purity, and stable cultural traditions.[57] As I suggest in chapter 4, the recent revival of U.S. southern regionalism can be seen as a version of reterritorializing cultural politics. The Family model in Delany's novel overlaps in key respects with southern regionalism; both seek to root a system of cultural values in "original" locales (the Old South in one case and Old Earth in the other) that are imagined in sharply anti-urban terms. The Sygn, in contrast, represents an urban model of culture in that it attempts to accommodate the processes of dissemination that can waylay cultural meanings in the city.

The Family pursues cultural stability through its "dream of a classic past as pictured on a world that may never even have existed" (86). Taking "Old Eyrth" as a fixed point of origin, the Family posits an essential human nature that has remained intact despite the historical and geographical transformations wrought by centuries of interplanetary travel. The worlds subscribing to Family ideology display slogans that enjoin human beings not to forget their origins, such as "Do not profane your origins on Eld Eyrth," "Lest I forget thee, Oh Urth," "Fail not the eternal presence of Eurd," and "Forget not your debts and beginnings on Earth" (116–17). These variant spellings reveal the transmutation of the point of origin as it is remembered and reconstructed in different locales, but for the Family, these are superficially dissimilar manifestations of a deeper, eternal truth. The Sygn also cherishes historical memory, but differently defined. An ideology that takes a textual rather than organic approach to culture, the Sygn is "committed to the living interaction and difference" between species and worlds (86).

The history of the Retreat of the Arvin, a temple converted to a library in Morgre, clarifies the points of disagreement between the Family and the Sygn. The retreat was built by human Family adherents on a site that once housed an ancient evelmi temple for a local moon deity named Arvin. Violently erasing the history of the site, the Family's retreat enshrines iconic objects imported from another world that is commemorated as a point of origin. These objects—including a gold inch, a quartz crystal measuring out the standard time of Old Eyrth, and a plastic molecular model of human DNA—are emblems of human value as created on one specific world but reified by the Family into relics of transcendent human value. When the Sygn becomes the official dogma of Morgre, the Family retreat is renamed the Retreat of the Arvin in an effort to restore the effaced history of the "original site," and the "imported holy objects" are replaced by a library. Obviously, the divergence between the Family and the Sygn is not absolute, for both are committed to preserving history, but with the difference that the Family preaches a modern version of History with a capital H, whereas the Sygn is "concerned with preserving the local history of local spaces" (103). According to the Family's imperialist ideology, history unfolds as a unitary and continuous development, fulfilling the teleology immanent in the point of origin, whereas the Sygn defines history as an alienation from putative origins: "Violence to the known turns home into history" (102). Whereas the Family conceives origins in essentialist and universally applicable terms, for the Sygn origins are retrospective constructs forged from the experience of temporal and geographical displacement.

The very definition of humanity is at stake in the schism between the Family and the Sygn. Not surprisingly, in an age in which mangled human bodies and brains are resurrected as cyborgs, and in which the human sensorium has been drastically modified by prosthetic devices as well as by centuries of interbreeding with other species, human "nature" becomes a subject of hot contestation. The rationale for labeling an ideology of cultural stability the "Family" is fairly obvious, given that families function as key sites of mediation between nature and culture, often serving to normalize contingent social structures as timeless natural verities. Familial stability is at the crux of contemporary discourses on urban crisis; as we saw in chapter 2, John Wideman's *Philadelphia Fire,* Sapphire's *PUSH,* and Octavia Butler's *Parable of the Sower* clarify the dangerous ways in which certain familial forms, parading as organic norms, are used to pathologize the urban poor. In consonance with these novels, *Stars in My Pocket* also lays bare the not-so-hidden political work performed by familial metaphors and models. The Family propounds a nuclear model of the family that, once it is generalized into a norm, begins inevitably to delegitimize the many other arrangements of actually existing families and to reify a historical structure into an eternal truth about humanity.

The Sygn's alternate model of reproductive community, the "nurture stream," valorizes internal differentiation over organic essence. Direct genetic reproduction is seldom practiced in southern Velm because, based on unbroken perpetuation of a biologically given essence, it ideologically subtends the violent conflicts between human beings and evelmi in the north. In southern Velm, which is aligned with the Sygn and peacefully cohabited by humans and evelmi, "direct egg-and-sperm relations" have been largely superseded by other forms of reproductive community. The term "nurture stream" bespeaks the Sygn's aversion to naturalist definitions of species integrity. "Stream" is an evelmi term used to refer to "their educational paths, their universities." With the melding of human and evelmi cultures, "the appropriation of the educational sign to the nurturing situation" results in the hybrid concept of the "nurture stream" (126), attesting to the Sygn's privileging of cultural history over natural destiny and of compound rather than singular definitions of species identity.

Given its commitment to interplay between diverse cultures and species, Sygn ideology does not impose any absolute limits on species transformation or legislate constraints on sexual behavior. In the city of Morgre, the only Sygn-affiliated society sketched in the novel, all varieties of sexual intercourse are permitted and practiced, including interspecies sex and homosexuality. Biological distinctions among species are not regarded as immutable social boundaries. When Marq suggests that biological differences between humans and evelmi inhibit mutual understanding, his evelmi friend remarks, "Ah, yours is a political statement if I ever heard one," and reminds him that such statements are at the root of the interspecies tensions in northern Velm (109). Nowhere in the novel are biological distinctions minimized; if anything, Delany's painstaking descriptions of the specificities of evelmi corporeal experience are what make the novel initially so difficult to read. But, as we allow our imaginations to become receptive to the otherness of the evelmi, we begin to admit the expansion of human experience that can accrue from interplay between species (and races).

What the Sygn takes to be an enriching history of "cultural exchange" appears, from the vantage point of the Family, as a devolutionary process of "cultural contamination" (254). Efforts to stabilize cultural identity require continual policing of boundaries between races and species. As a site of biological reproduction, sexuality becomes an obvious area of control and regulation, a means of either preserving or corrupting racial integrity. This imbricated logic of racial and sexual purity, which is only too familiar to Delany's U.S. readership, is invoked by the Thants in the novel's climactic banquet scene. After their conversion from the Sygn to the Family and their decision to serve as a model family on the unstable planet of Nepiy, the Thants appeal to nature to establish their own prohibitive sexual and cultural practices as "older, purer, human" (320). Their defense of human essence requires firm distinctions between animal and human species, between genders, and between civilized and barbaric sexual practices, all normalized by the concept of family:

> Are they human? Yes, but they've been reduced to beasts . . . , reduced to animals who copulate with animals, call animals their sisters and mothers. . . . Not only the males with the females, the females do it with females, within the race, across the races . . . as if they had not even reached the elementary stage of culture . . . where a family takes its appropriate course. (320–21)

To distill the implications of this particular passage and of the Family/Sygn opposition in general, let us recall Samuel Delany's comment, cited earlier, that the modern subject has been nourished by the structure of the patriarchal nuclear family. This centered subject is a mirage that inhabits a "dream outside of historical time," as is evident from the Family's postulation of a human essence immune to spatial and temporal ruptures. Balking at this kind of essentialism, Delany appropriates textual metaphors (of Web and Sygn) from poststructuralist theory to elaborate a notion of "the subject-in-history" that can be "denied to no one."

Modern Books and Postmodern Texts

Poststructuralist conceptions of textuality are said to be literally instantiated by electronic technologies of text production, transmission, and reception—and by hypertext in particular. George Landow, the guru of hypertextuality, defines it as "an information technology consisting of individual blocks of text, or lexias, and the electronic links that join them" and asserts that electronic textuality and poststructuralist theory "both grow out of dissatisfaction with the related phenomena of the printed book and hierarchical thought."[58] The electronic assault on print coincides with postmodern critiques of modern culture, for the printed book is conceived as "modernity's mental space"[59] as well as the carrier of the "modern literary system."[60] Current debates on books and electronic texts tend to fall into dichotomized utopian and dystopian stances, but with both camps conjoined by technological fetishism as well as by the assumption that electronic technology is entirely sweeping away the modern cultural values inhering in the printed book.

In our "late age of print,"[61] we have gained enough distance from the book to be able to perceive it as a technological and ideological artifact rather than as a transparent medium of cultural expression. The postmodern era is widely regarded as an age in transition from a modern industrial society to a society of information. The industrial system of Fordist or standardized mass production finds its perfect emblem in the commodity object of the printed book, whereas electronic text is a commodity typical of a system of flexible and customized production. From this follows the contention that the ideal reader of printed books is reduced to the lowest common denominator, whereas electronic text assumes a sophisticated and quirky reader. Print supposedly orders the reader–author relation into a hierarchical division of labor, privileging the author as the producer of textual meaning and relegating the reader to the role of passive consumer. But electronic textuality promotes the reader to the position of collaborator in the production of textual meaning.[62]

These different conceptions of authors and readers are often derived from the distinct technological forms of print and electronic texts. The book is a thing, a "capsule of suspended time," in Patrick Bazin's phrase.[63] Stability, integrity, and closure are among the attributes emanating from the physical nature of the book. To many postmodern observers, everything associated with the book, from chapter divisions and indices to the architecture of the library, reveals its proclivity toward rigid, hierarchically ordered forms.[64] Print technology allegedly incarcerates the word by means of standardized typographic conventions as well as the binding of text within pages and covers.[65] Text, as Delany has remarked, "is process rather than thing" (*SI*, 56), and if print technology imprisons text within the material object of the book, electronic technologies liberate text from book primarily by abstracting it into the immaterial realm of digitized information. As George Landow has emphasized, digital text exists as "codes and not as physical marks on a physical surface; it is always virtual, always a simulacrum for which no physical instantiation exists."[66] When placed within an electronic system of linkages, digital text becomes a network of interconnected textual units, seeming to exemplify Roland Barthes's statement that "the Text's metaphor is that of the network."[67]

There is remarkable consensus about the ideological consequences that presumably follow from these material distinctions between printed books and electronic texts. As a discrete object that physically sets verbal matter

into a pattern fixed for all time, the book supports several interrelated ideologies and conventions characteristic of the "modern literary system": the
work defined by conceptual originality, coherence, and unity; the cult of
the individual author, possessor of copyright, owner of property, and orig-
inator of textual meaning; and the institution of a canon of great, durable
works of art meant to elicit a solemn, reverential awe from readers.[68] In
contrast, as John Slatin points out, the work of art becomes mutable in
an age of electronic reproduction.[69] Advanced hypertextual systems are
made up of linkages among numerous texts of varying genres, allowing
for multiple trajectories of reading. Readers select their own itineraries
through the network, subverting textual boundaries and hierarchies. In
this sense, hypertext constitutes a "differential network" without centers
or margins, main texts or supplements.[70] As mere clicks on the part of
readers can turn primary texts into subsidiary ones (and vice versa) and can
visually instantiate the web of connections among various texts, textual
integrity dissolves and the concepts of intertextuality and dissemination
take on literal form. If the centering operations of print technology bolster
the modern conventions of supreme authors and eternal canons of art, the
centrifugal structure of hypertext empowers all sorts of readers and ushers
in an era of postmodern populism.

It should be obvious from this schematic summary that momentous political claims are staked on either technology. On one side are the prophets
of doom, including Neil Postman and Sven Birkerts (and more cautious
prognosticators such as Myron Tuman), who regard electronic technology as the nemesis of the worthy modern tradition of individual reflection,
hermeneutic depth, and critical distance from the polluting spheres of mass
culture and the marketplace, with all these qualities taken as intrinsic effects of print technology.[71] On the other side are the gurus of "liberation
technology," notably Richard Lanham and George Landow, who rejoice
that the exclusionary modern culture encoded in the printed book is being
overthrown by a fluid and dynamic technology that captures in its very
form the essence of postmodern pluralism. Although the two sides differ
on what kind of politics is more desirable, they agree over the distinct political implications that inhere in each technology, with both sides allowing
technology to "substitute for politics."[72]

Samuel Delany formulates the distinction between modern and postmodern culture in much the same terms as I've just outlined. In an interview published two years after *Stars in My Pocket,* Delany distances science
fiction from a modernist conception of "Serious Art" that demands a "re-
spectful, silent, attentive, pseudo-religious attitude" from its readers (*SI,*
194). Delany claims that science fiction "anticipated postmodernism" in
its critique of the modernist notions of sacral art, authoritative creators,

and reverential readers. Within the reading protocols of science fiction, the artwork is "not venerated in the mode of a religious object—ever! The SF writer is *not* an author—that is, an authority figure: a source of interpretive constraints" (*SI*, 194). To dissociate his work from such conceptions of literary art, Delany deliberately identifies himself as a writer rather than an author.[73]

According to Delany, what allowed science fiction to develop in an oppositional relation to modernist aesthetics was its unique institutional and publishing history. Whereas the cult of "Serious Art" was nurtured by the academic discipline of literary studies, the paraliterary genre of science fiction was boosted by the paperback revolution of the late 1950s and early 1960s, which "establishment critics" feared would augur "the end of Literature with a capital L" (*SI*, 38–39).[74] Delany claims that science fiction writers and readers enjoyed an intimate and reciprocal relation because critical appreciation of science fiction developed within the popular and informal forum of fanzines rather than within a disciplinary framework. Delany frequently polarizes science fiction against literature, suggesting that an overstated opposition between the two categories is a necessary critical gesture: "Literature has an established critical tradition and condition. Its continuities have been so inculcated, so sedimented, so ossified. . . . To disrupt that ossification we *have* to stress discontinuities" (*SI*, 195).[75]

Delany's critique of modernist aesthetics in *Stars in My Pocket* seems consonant with contemporary accounts of print versus electronic textuality to the extent that the epitome of the modernist artwork in the novel is also the only textual object in the novel's universe that is termed a "book." This "clumsy, beautiful" book (135) is an obsolete artifact in a world in which tiny "text-crystals" contain material that is made visible through "portable reader[s]" (134). The only extant book in Delany's novel bears the aura of a fetish because its leather binding lends it a rich, sensuous tangibility, in contrast to the "denatured physicality" of text-crystals.[76] But this "book," far from being an object that Delany's contemporaries would recognize as a book, is a mongrel "technotype" (119) that confounds hard-and-fast distinctions between print and electronic textuality. A distinguishing feature of electronic technology is that it separates text from reading apparatus, requiring different forms of projection technology to make text, which consists of digitized information, visible to readers.[77] This distinction is blurred in Delany's novel, where the text is a highly compacted object that is at once book, screen, and projection device. The leather binding of this book turns over to a glass screen; finger-tab switches on the back of the book activate a projection mechanism that makes letters and pictures appear as holographic images above the screen. To some characters in the novel, this artifact is more plausibly termed a sculpture or a theatrical stage than a book (120), and others liken its holographic projections to statues and performances (136). All these images call attention to the ambiguous modality of the book-screen technotype: as sculpture, the text evinces the stasis and fixity associated with printed books, but as a theatrical stage, the screen evokes the kinetic and performative propensities of electronic textuality.

With this peculiar technotype, what late-twentieth-century readers might regard as a shift from book to screen has already occurred in the distant past of the novel's universe, but the resultant object is still "what they used to call a book" (119). The distinctive temporality of science fiction enables Delany to scramble the deterministic assumptions governing contemporary accounts of print and electronic textuality. *Stars in My Pocket* ostensibly depicts the future world projected by advocates of electronic textuality, in which books as we know them have become extinct. In this world, even the electronic textual forms that represent emergent technologies in the actual world of Delany's readers have become archaic fetish objects. If we focus solely on the issue of technological development, the novel seems to be rendering our future as the remote past of another world, but if we attend to questions of cultural and political change, we can discern, in the "future" world of the novel, a rendering of our present with some "significant distortion."

This science fiction device compels readers to view the present as an open-ended moment of conflict and transition. In the world of Delany's novel, technological changes in the forms of text production and transmission have not followed a trajectory of wholesale rupture, as is clear from the fact that the textual artifacts of the "future" exhibit a compound of book and screen components. Moreover, in Delany's novel, books and electronic texts do not exemplify neat distinctions between modern and postmodern aesthetics and cultural politics. Contrary to Richard Lanham's claim that the shift from book to screen is rightly alarming to humanists,[78] *Stars in My Pocket* shows that the dominance of electronic textual technologies will not in itself displace the ideologies of art, authorship, and reading implicit in the modern literary system. The contents of this book-screen include volumes of verse, letters, journals, and critical and biographical studies by and about Vondramach Okk, the most famous individual in the novel's universe. Although this book resembles a hypertext in that it contains diverse generic materials and several contributing writers, it nevertheless coheres around the authorial personality of Okk.

The only contents of the book-screen that are described in detail are lyrics and epic poems in a language invented by Okk, which employs "both a phonetic and an ideographic writing system as well as a whole series of shiftrunes." Marq describes shiftrunes as letters that are "pronounced one way on their first occurrence in a text, another on their second, another on their third, and so on in a fixed sequence" (121), allowing for an interplay between visual and phonetic alliteration. Investing visual signs with variable sonic dimensions, Okk's writing system chafes against the silence and fixity of printed signs and aspires to the performative condition of electronic textuality, which, as Walter Ong and Marshall McLuhan have observed, infuses writing with orality.[79] The shifting pronunciation of the runes also suggests the mutability of "scripted speech," a term that has been used to describe electronic writing.[80] Okk's shiftrune poems are designed to be participatory in the sense that the writer provides partial lines and initial letters to be completed differently by various readers.

But despite its interactive, malleable, and performative properties, Okk's text continues to signify within the ideological mode of literary modernism. Marq wonders, "how could anyone who didn't know Vondramach Okk's private tongue appreciate the participatory works?" (128). Although Okk's poetry technically incorporates readers as coproducers, it does not effectively restructure hierarchical relations between writers and readers because its obscure language is communicable only to a specialized circle of initiates. The dynamic form of Okk's poems does little to democratize her discourse or to displace the modernist cult of the author as creator of a private and original style. As Okk's case demonstrates, innovation at the formal and technological levels can be equally compatible with modernist and postmodernist aesthetics, and in neither case can it guarantee politically subversive effects.

What Delany wishes to destabilize is the modern notion of the centered subject, which literary modernism has helped reproduce through its cultic approach to artworks as expressions of unique authorial sensibility. In a broader sense as well, as Delany reiterates, the reading codes of literary texts "have been organized, tyrannized even, by ... 'the priority of the subject'" (*SI*, 31). Delany's fiction seeks to disrupt these reading codes because the modern subject enshrined in literature achieves its mirage of centrality by excluding the West's others. It comes as no surprise that the modernist author Vondramach Okk is an imperialist conqueror of worlds as well as a notable advocate of Family ideology, which defends the integrity of cultural origins from corrupting interchange with others. In the spirit of this purist and insular ideology, Okk declares that "Poetry is what is avoided as it is surrounded by translation" (128). But *Stars in My Pocket* is centrally a novel about translation, which is crucial to establishing lines of communication among the myriad species comprising the novel's universe. According to Okk's definition of poetry, hinging as it does on notions of linguistic purity and originality, translation amounts to violation. And given that Okk writes in an idiosyncratic language of her own invention, her poetry is authentic to the extent that it remains unreadable to all but a restricted audience of initiates. Militating against this modernist notion of literary language, *Stars in My Pocket* presents a universe in which translation is unavoidable and, as a consequence, poetry, as defined by Okk, becomes a necessary casualty. The novel promotes alternate modes of reading that are best instantiated within the paraliterary genre of science fiction.

Reading Ancestors, Dragons, and Morning

As is clear from recent public anxiety about the "death of literature," print-based notions of literacy in the United States are being dramatically redefined with the shift to electronic culture.[81] With this presumed crisis in literacy, the legacy of modern Western humanism, encapsulated in the literary canon of Great Books, is felt to be at risk. Within the discipline of literary studies, reading is essentially understood as "an agency of self-making," a means of extending the reader's consciousness through deep engagement with the author's special subjectivity.[82] The literary canon is being displaced from its position of cultural centrality by the greater accessibility of mixed media made possible by electronic technology. As everything becomes a text in postmodern culture, the authority as well as the specificity of literary works and reading procedures begin to dissolve. Proponents of electronic technology hail this textualization of all objects as a progressive trend that will democratize the theories and practices of literacy and open the sacrosanct domain of aesthetics to hitherto excluded social constituencies.[83] Pluralized conceptions of multimedia literacy applicable to high and popular, canonical and minority cultures are crucial to the claim that electronic culture is more finely attuned to social diversity than its modern print precursor. The emergent postmodern literacy is often defined as a process of mediation among heterogeneous social groups rather than as a tool for enriching individual consciousness.[84]

Contributing to this redefinition of literacy, *Stars in My Pocket* espouses reading procedures that are explicitly anti-literary and that take their bearings from technologies of information processing, simulation, and virtual reality. The term *reading* in Delany's novel is expanded to refer to the very process of knowing the world and others. In the novel's world, perception is so thoroughly mediated by technology that all knowledge amounts to an interpretation of complex codes of information. Echoing advocates of electronic literacy, Delany has said that his reasons "for wanting to broaden the meaning of reading . . . are finally political" (*SI*, 278). These reasons may be best clarified through comparison with the tropes of reading and writing examined earlier in this study. The tropes of "writing as voyeurism" and "reading as listening" commonly present writing as an inauthentic mode of apprehending the other. In the novels by Toni Morrison and John Wideman discussed in chapter 3, writing is shown to be an invasive urban technology that fails to yield authentic intersubjective knowledge. Novels associated with the southern folk aesthetic refigure reading as listening in an effort to recapture face-to-face conditions in which self and other can be fully present to each other without any technological interference. The tendency to perceive all technological mediation as distortion and to locate communal authenticity in scenes of face-to-face contact is not unique to these novels. As the discussion of postmodern ethics earlier in this chapter should make clear, the epistemological crises generated by the new information technologies are often resolved by appeal to face-to-face modes of knowing as necessary bases for ethical responsibility.

In Delany's novel, technological mediation forms an inescapable condition of all knowledge. When much of the world is constituted by technologies of simulation and virtual reality (as is the case in the novel's universe), no object of knowledge can be transparently available. All reality in *Stars in My Pocket* is "written" in the sense that it is given to human comprehension only as a coded network of signs, and all knowing is "reading" in that it entails mediation of signs rather than immediate perception of referents. In common with Morrison's and Wideman's tropes of writing as voyeurism or surgical invasion, *Stars in My Pocket* presents reading as violation: "I do not see," writes Delany, "how reading can be other than a violent process."[85] But instead of recoiling from such conditions of reading and writing into the primal communion putatively offered by tropes of voice and hearing, Delany seeks responsible modes of knowing the other that are available within advanced technological conditions.

One particular scene of reading in *Stars in My Pocket*—in which Marq struggles to decipher a simulation of his ancestor, Gylda Dyeth—offers an antithesis to the trope of reading as listening. Vocal signs in Morrison's *Song of Solomon* and Gloria Naylor's *Mama Day* can override the "testamentary essence" of writing, to borrow Derrida's phrase,[86] as is clear from their various characters' conversations with dead ancestors. *Stars in My Pocket* also features a dialogue with a dead ancestor, but with the signal difference that Marq converses with a "mechanical reproduction" rather than with the spirit of his ancestor (114). Vocal signs can presumably recapture the full presence of the referent: in the face-to-face community portrayed in Naylor's novel, "The signs don't lie."[87] In contrast, the simulated projection of Marq's ancestor is "not the real thing at all" (114) but is instead "a book, . . . a text, . . . a set of signs" (340). Marq's great grandmother appears in the form of a "simulated synapse-casting" (114), or a sculptural projection of light. When activated, the reproduction speaks and responds to Marq as she might have were she still alive. Although this ancestor is available for hearing as well as seeing, either sense restores only the illusory likeness and not the real essence of Gylda Dyeth. Vocal signs must be read and interpreted just like visual signs; neither type of sign offers direct access to the real. Turning the ancestor into an unbearable "hermeneutic enterprise" (340), *Stars in My Pocket* aims to interrupt the metaphysics of voice that supports notions of innocent human origins, from which writing is then construed as a fall into historicity. If the reading procedures of literature enshrine a universal and transcendent human consciousness, the metaphysics of voice fattens this consciousness by conferring on it the illusion of unmediated self-presence. Redefining listening as reading, the scene of Marq's encounter with his simulated ancestor refuses the solace of pure origins, organic essences, and transhistorical human values.

Another scene of reading in *Stars in My Pocket* illustrates even more superbly the anti-literary reading codes that Delany deems peculiar to science fiction—codes that dislocate the reading subject as it penetrates and processes a radically "other" object. This is the scene in which Marq Dyeth and Rat Korga go dragon hunting. The hunter aims a radar bow that hooks onto a cerebral mapping of the dragon and, "after a lot of translation," plays it back on the hunter's cerebral surface (263). The technology in this scene most closely approximates that of virtual reality, although it entails mechanisms of direct neural access that are not currently available. Michael Heim has claimed that technologies of virtual reality offer an unprecedented opportunity to "shift" the metaphysics of presence, in large part because these technologies make present the "informational equivalent of things" rather than the things themselves in all their naked splendor (132–33). Hunting the dragon is equivalent to processing a neural transmission of information about the dragon and is therefore an exercise in perception highly mediated by technology. Yet the scene also reveals the potential of this technology to extend the imagination and sensorium: hunting the dragon is a deeply immersive, sensuous experience.[88]

The most splendid moment of this scene occurs when Korga, exhilarated by his experience of dragon hunting, exclaims, "It's like reading!" (264). Here, reading is becoming-other in a flash of imaginative identification that is also an act of violent penetration. Reading is catching a quarry by means of a simultaneously invasive and augmenting technology. The trope of reading as dragon hunting yields a mode of knowing the other that is anything but face to face, and that is, in fact, thoroughly caught in the "horizon of intersubjective violence" that defines reading and writing.[89] The "originary violence of writing" stems from the fact that it suspends the "vocative absolute" and situates meaning within a system of differences. All signification is implicated in this violence; there is no innocent prehistory of writing, and the self-presence that writing appears to disrupt was never given in the first place.[90]

Whereas vocal signs reach for a direct grasp of reality, the trope of reading as virtually becoming-dragon enacts a complex interplay between reality and simulation, presence and absence, immediacy and distance. Virtual reality is "real in effect but not in fact"; to be virtually present somewhere is to be "present remotely."[91] Virtual reality offers sensory fusion, but, as the dragon-hunting scene dramatizes, this fusion involves "a lot of translation." Most importantly, the experience of virtual reality actually doubles the subject. The figure that is present in virtual space is a "stand-in self," which, as Heim remarks, "can never fully represent" the human subject (101). As Marq's radar bow connects with the dragon's brain, he is "doubled in one sense, skewed in four others" (261). He must "double all syntax" and resort to "we/they" to convey his experience of "knowing the dragon from the inside" (263).

This splitting of the reading subject is not restricted to the virtual context of dragon hunting. Even in an earlier scene of Korga's acquisition of literacy on Rhyonon, reading engenders a "doubled voice," a "stutter in the mind" (34). Although Korga's first experience of reading is largely described through metaphors of voice, his internally spoken words are "*all* attached to a bevy of written signs" (33). The most striking consequence of Korga's literacy is that it dissociates him from himself, introducing "another voice, which felt and sounded and settled in his mind as if it were his own (but *had* to have come from somewhere else)" (31). The scene of Korga's first reading undoubtedly carries traces of the modern humanist notion of literacy as a tool that expands critical awareness. Korga's acquisition of literacy gives him a "world" as well as the power to make "contestatory statement[s]" about this world (48). But the outstanding effect of literacy is not to extend Korga's interiority or to institute him as the self-present subject of modern humanism. Instead, the process of reading is an encounter with otherness ("another voice") that decenters and exteriorizes Korga's subjectivity. In this scene, metaphors of voice are ultimately supplanted by textual metaphors of identity: the "new condition" produced by literacy "was not so much an alternate voice . . . as it was a web, a text weaving endlessly about him, erupting into and falling from consciousness" (36). This scene, like many others in the novel, elaborates Delany's commitment to an antihumanist notion of the subject as constituted within a differential "play of signs" (37).

Delany has said that what attracted him to poststructuralism was the idea that meaning is always "extrinsic" to the sign and resides in the "relation between signifiers" (*SI*, 248). The most important lesson to be drawn from poststructuralist theories of language and subjectivity is that "you can never escape mediation" (*SI*, 221). The idea of mediation insistently recurs in Delany's numerous pronouncements on textuality and reading, such as, for example, "textuality is mediation *per se*" (*SI*, 221), or "reading is that which is mediation itself."[92] In emphasizing mediation as formative of meaning and identity, Delany seeks to displace the subject of modern humanism, whose delusory mastery of the universe is predicated on a perfect fit between language and reality. Delany's movement away from the "subject-dominated precincts of literature" is aided by both his choice of genre and his predilection for poststructuralist theories of textuality.[93] If these theories teach us that the desire for presence is "born from the abyss (the indefinite multiplication) of representation,"[94] Delany's science fiction reinforces this lesson by disseminating an "antimodernist" subject that takes shape within the textual web of the new technologies (*SI*, 200). In electronic texts, signs refer only to other signs, and meanings are to be found in the ramifying structure of connections rather than within the sign.[95] In this sense, as Myron Tuman observes, electronic technologies are sponsoring the "wider contemporary movement away from a serious, introspective, relentlessly psychological [and] hermeneutic tradition of interpretation—one often associated with modernism . . . —and toward a decidedly more ludic . . . postmodern concern with defining reading, and cultural criticism generally, as the play of signs."[96] Taking the new technologies as the material bases for his metaphors of reading, Delany's novel carefully explores the political implications of this shift from modern to postmodern technologies of reading.

The epilogue to *Stars in My Pocket* reads as a lesson in poststructuralist semiotics. A bereft Marq struggles to come to terms with his loss of Korga through a rambling discourse on the meanings of "morning" on various worlds. The real subject of this discourse—the morning after Marq's loss of Korga—is present only in its absence. Marq can only approach the meaning of *the* morning by writing around it, writing about other mornings. Metaphors of reading are strewn all over the epilogue, to emphasize that all knowledge is mediation of signs and that no sign yields a firm hold on reality. In interviews, Delany often expounds the semiotic view that "what we called 'the real world' seems to be nothing *but* codes" and it is only by "cross-comparing" various codes that we can know reality (*SI*, 23). The epilogue to *Stars in My Pocket* relentlessly drives home the point that "morning" is a historically and geographically variable sign and that this sign is arbitrary in the sense that it bears no natural relation to reality. On the numerous planets that Marq visits, he encounters varying phenomena, most, but not all, of which involve some change in light. Marq can "read" these phenomena as signs of morning only because of his familiarity with the signs of evening and night on this world as well as with signs of morning on other worlds. As Marq moves from one matutinal scene to another, the meaning of morning emerges from the differential relation between various signifiers. The point of this semiotics lesson is not to multiply the meanings of a sign and thereby relativize it beyond recognition but rather to reveal the decentering of the subject in the process of signification.

The most spectacular moment of Delany's semiotics lesson on morning is Marq's sighting of the giant red sun of the Aurigae system as it appears through the viewing canopy of a spaceship run by the Family. The announcements preceding the event inform Marq and the other passengers that the viewing canopy will "deopaque" or "transpare" so that they can "look directly on" the great sun (350). More than once in the epilogue, Delany uses the obsolete word *transpare,* defined in a seventeenth-century dictionary as "to appear through, to be evident, or clear." Delany is obviously using this word to ironic effect in this scene, where, despite the reference to transparent vision, the Aurigae is hardly perceptible as a brute fact of the natural universe. It is technology that transpares the viewing canopy in the first place, creating the illusion of naked sight. But the passengers' sighting of the Aurigae is technologically modulated in other senses as well, for the gigantic sun appears to rise and set as a result of a simulated rotation of the spaceship, and this "dawn" is accompanied by stagy aubadinal music. Even the information about the Aurigae supplied to the passengers is ideologically filtered. Not surprisingly, given that this is a Family spaceship, facts about the Aurigae are packaged in "solarcentric" terms (353): in other words, information about the Aurigae is given by way of analogy with Sol, the star around which the earth (origin of the human "Family") revolves.

As an adherent of the Sygn, which one critic has termed a "poststructuralist religion,"[97] Marq counters the solarcentrism of Family ideology by highlighting the manner in which signs for dawn undergo violent transformation as he moves from one planet to another. Travel is vital to Delany's conception of reading as mediation, because to travel is to become aware of "the shifts, the displacements, the uncertainties that, together, make up what we call meanings" (360). Marq's primary function as a transworld semiotician is to track the volatile trajectory of meaning across a range of contexts. Travel, which is both movement along a textual chain of signifiers and cross-referencing between different codic systems, exposes the mirage on which centric notions of identity depend. To travel is to experience "the problematics of that identity at its most intense: to see that identity shatter, fragment, and to realize that its solidity was always an illusion" (358). The Family's centric ideology of human identity rests on a myth of origins that is fed by literary uses of morning as a metaphor for birth or beginning. Tracing the history of these uses, Marq discerns no clear referent that might help fix the meaning of matutinal metaphors. Marq thus distills the main lesson to be drawn from the trope of reading as traveling: "in the light of the suns of six-thousand-plus worlds, 'dawn' becomes (another) fuzzy-edged phenomenon. Add to this the extreme locality of the use of morning/dawn as a metaphor for commencement/birth, and the whole notion crumbles" (359).

Having relied on poststructuralist semiotics to "crumble" the subject as well as the object of modern knowledge, Delany also recognizes that the semiotic view of language and reality runs the risk of "solipsism" (*SI*, 24). His most critical qualification of the semiotic view is to posit a world prior to language and to maintain that the world can be known through language, with the admission that this knowledge can never be comprehensive or infallible. In keeping with this materialist understanding of language, Delany discredits idealist and "meta" claims that "since language . . . *can't* be trusted to be rigorous about the world," it must form a closed circuit that can only refer to itself (*SI*, 54). According to Delany's alternate conception of the relation between words and world, there is no such thing as language "without a world to inform it, without a world in which it has been and will be developing, a world which is constantly changing it, and to which, changing or stable, it is always a response." Not only is language subsumed by the world, but it also reflects the world in a rather complicated sense:

> The reason that language is codic is because everything else in the world is too . . . ; and language is in the world and of it. Language and world . . . is another perfectly useful distinction, . . . but . . . the distinction is only useful *if* we acknowledge their hierarchical relation. . . .
> The world absorbs language. Language does not encase the world—although the world displays language-like (that is, codic) properties at every turn. (*SI*, 54)

Because language partakes in the codic systems of the universe, its laws and properties are not entirely inherent but are modeled on the universe. The proposition that language is overdetermined by the world allows for a concept of referentiality that is, in fact, vital to Delany's political claims about the reading procedures unique to science fiction.

These claims rest on a set of overlapping distinctions between science fiction and literature, some of which have already been introduced earlier in this discussion. If the reading protocols of literature are organized around a psychological understanding of the human subject, science fiction is committed to the idea that the "physical and social" world is explicable and "negotiable" (*SI*, 251). If literature apotheosizes a transcendent being suspended in a "dream outside of historical time," science fiction "takes more cognizance of history than literature" (*SI*, 185) and has long leaned "toward a materialist explanation of history" (*SI*, 72). Science fiction is materialist in the sense that it always reflects on current ways of knowing the world of objects, and it is historical because its invented worlds can only be grasped through dialogue with contemporaneous conceptions of social reality. Through its oblique "dialogue . . . with the real world,"[98] science fiction consummates a special form of referentiality.

Delany has argued that science fiction's "mimetic relation to the real world" is different from that of all literary genres, including even fantasy (*SI*, 35). Delany's sense of the unique referentiality of science fiction hinges on his distinction between metaphorical and literal uses of language. Statements such as "Then her world exploded" or "Gregor Samsa . . . realized he'd transformed into a huge beetle" signify very differently in science fiction and literature.[99] When encountered in a literary text, such statements would be read figuratively and chiefly for what they could illuminate about subjective psychological states. In a science fiction text, however, such statements carry literal meanings, and Delany asserts that it is primarily through its "literalization of the language" that science fiction conducts "its dialogue . . . with the real world."[100] In other words, when reading a science fiction text, we would have to specify what social and technological features of the real world must have changed in order for the sentence "The door dilated" to make sense and be literally true.[101] Whereas such a sentence would work as an "emotionally muzzy metaphor" in a literary work, the same sentence would signify literal truths about the material world given in a work of science fiction.[102]

This distinction between metaphorical and literal uses of language helps support Delany's claim that science fiction remains committed to a materialist view of language that has been all but abandoned in literary genres. In Delany's opinion, modern (and presumably postmodern) literature is cramped by the "metafictive fallacy of transparent reading." This fallacy entails the assumption that in some bygone, premodern era, language and writing could authentically represent reality but have now fallen prey to the evils of mediation. As a result, modern writing disavows any effort to reflect on reality and becomes a "meta" discourse about itself. What Delany proposes instead is that we relinquish the illusion that reading and writing once innocently reflected reality. If we begin with the premise that language is "mediation itself" and has never been otherwise, we may then grasp language as an imperfect and self-revising tool for producing historical knowledge about the world.[103] Through this formulation, Delany is able to avoid the false dichotomies that have mired recent encounters between poststructuralism and historical materialism. An acknowledgment of the ineluctability and fallibility of linguistic mediation humbles and historicizes all claims to mastery over the real, but it need not cripple any effort to know, understand, and act upon the world.

Stars in My Pocket instantiates the materialist conception of language that Delany has spelled out in essays and interviews through its keen attention to the interplay between language and world. If a strictly semiotic approach runs the risk of idealism by bracketing questions about the historicity of language, countless examples in Delany's novel build up to a historical view of language as a system that "often changed and changed quickly under the pressures of a new environment" (73). The reciprocal yet in the final analysis hierarchical relation between language and world is rendered by means of several observations on metaphorical and literal uses of language. Metaphors in Delany's fictional universe usually point to a drift of language away from the referent and are mostly reserved for literary usage. For example, the word *day* on the planet Nepiy has become obsolete as a colloquial term on account of geographical and ecological changes. Because of a permanent overlying cloud layer, *day* bears no literal meaning but thrives as a "literary word" (68). Or, *dawn* signifies violence and chaos on the planet Klyvos as a result of a combination of geographical, ecological, and political factors. Such examples of the overdetermination of word by world abound in the novel. By insistently nudging the reader's attention to the (often obscured) literal bases of literary metaphors, the novel seeks to clarify the ways in which language responds to the material world.

This emphasis on the literal dimensions of language should not, however, be read as an attempt to stabilize the representational claims of language on solid referential grounds. Teresa de Lauretis misreads Delany's distinction between literary and science fictional uses of language in this way, arguing that science fiction restores use value to language by literalizing it. The "concrete, sensible specificity" of signs in science fiction protects it from the entropy afflicting postmodern literary texts that highlight the exchange value (or the metaphorical currency) of signs.[104] De Lauretis draws heavily on Delany's own utterances on the distinctions between literature and science fiction, which are often so overstated as to invite this type of misreading.[105] But the notion of referentiality that Delany wants to retain for science fiction is highly mediated, requiring the reader to juggle continually between the use and exchange values of signs, between the literal referents and metaphorical slippages of language.

The process by which Marq "reads" signs of morning on alien worlds in the epilogue illustrates the ways in which meanings are simultaneously unstable and overdetermined, subject to both displacement and redundancy. Marq is able to recognize varying and unfamiliar phenomena as "morning" by transcoding them into a semiotic system with which he is familiar. To know dawn on a new world is "to read the whole roster of signs you are used to for morning over the expanse of what you see, and at the same time see those meanings start to transpare as one begins to see the possibilities—a world of possibilities—clear behind them" (356). This is one of those rare passages in the novel where meaning is said to "transpare" and where language is figured as a window through which we can clearly perceive a natural world that lies behind it. Yet even here, the literal referent of the sign "morning" is perceptible only through an act of reading, and the meaning of morning accrues from a "whole roster of signs" brought from other worlds. In other words, the use value of the sign becomes apprehensible only through its exchange value within a system of signs. This codic system is characterized by redundancy, or overdetermina- tion, in that it partakes of a universe that is itself coded. It is in this mediated sense that language refers to the world and yields meanings that are coher- ent and stable. The imagery of "transparing" in the passage quoted above gives way, a couple of pages later, to the observation that the "referential shards" of language contain "infinite spaces" between them, spaces that are "opaque to direct human comprehension" (358).

Delany's semiotics lesson on morning demands agile micro-movement between centrifugal and centripetal, disseminating and stabilizing, entropic and referential tendencies of language on a virtually page-by-page and of- ten sentence-by-sentence basis. More effectively even than his theorizing on language, this rigorous and self-revising process of reading conveys the complexity of the dialogue that science fiction conducts with the real world.[106] At a macrolevel as well, the reading protocols of science fic- tion require constant movement back and forth between metaphor and mimesis, figurative and literal uses of language. The worlds created in sci- ence fiction are blatant inventions that obviously do not refer to reality in any direct or literal way. As Damien Broderick has argued, science fic- tion deploys metaphorical strategies insofar as it constructs its worlds "not from the schemata of the commonplace but out of endlessly inventive and open-ended analogies, catachreses, paradigm-elisions, puns, conceits; out of dream echoes or deformations and satirical distortions of the quotid- ian, and scientific or pseudoscientific diagrams of the inaccessible." Yet, as Broderick further argues (quoting David Hartwell), science fiction, un- like literary fantasy, demands that we read its novel signifiers as if they were mimetic, and as if the text were "a literal report of something that, by a thin thread of possibility, could be true, given a specified set of circumstances, at some other time, in some other place."[107]

Delany's account of the reading protocols of science fiction supports a similar conception of its special referentiality, which involves continual shuttling between the metaphorical and literal dimensions of language as well as between its fabricated worlds and the reader's real world. But Delany often singles out the literal elements of science fiction texts when he wishes to outline their difference from literary texts. This overemphasis on the literal is not intended to bring back the referent in any simple sense but rather to distance science fiction as far as possible from the "subject-dominated precincts of literature" by redirecting attention to the object and the real world. In both his theory and practice of science fiction, Delany invokes the literal to support a set of materialist, but not foundational or straightforwardly referential, claims to representation.

The Proper Way to Act in a City

All the writers examined in this study variously grapple with the problem of how to ground claims to representation in a world where the referent seems to elude the grip of language. For these writers, as well as for many theorists of postmodernism, the problem of linguistic representation is twinned with the question of political value: some notion of a reality that can be grasped through language seems essential to making political claims about writing. Delany, too, sees the two problems—of linguistic and political representation—as intimately linked: "The relation between language and politics is subsumed in the old philosophical problem of the relation between language and truth—the problem of representation" (*SI*, 51). As we have seen in earlier chapters, writers often tackle this problem by urging literal readings of their texts. An appeal to literal meanings is meant to enhance the ability of writing to be truthful about contemporaneous social reality (as in the case of Octavia Butler or Sapphire) or to reflect the interests of African-American community (as in Toni Morrison's and Gloria Naylor's novels). Caught in a parallel dilemma of representation, Delany emphasizes the literal dimensions of the language of science fiction in order to establish its special purchase on the real world.

This is a crucial move for Delany because, in common with the other writers discussed here, he "believe[s] the real is synonymous with the political." But he takes care to add that "no, I don't believe in any transcendent or metaphysically grounded real that is somehow present, either perceptually or mystically" (*SI*, 283). Delany's gesture, of positing a "real" that is not "metaphysically grounded," offers a way out of the all-or-nothing, either/or modes of much postmodern cultural theory, which flees from an exaggeratedly irreal world into the mysticism of face-to-face presence. Delany takes the textual turn in order to resist this kind of nostalgic withdrawal and to make ethical claims that take advanced technological mediation as their condition of possibility. But the textual turn in Delany's work never devolves into a formalism that disables political and historical analyses, as tends to be true of semiotic approaches to postmodern cities. One of Delany's "prime concerns" as a writer of science fiction is to succeed at "presenting real problems and entertaining real solutions."[108] Contemporary discussions of postmodern cities and texts often treat technology as surrogate politics and thereby occlude the possibility of arriving at real solutions to the social problems of the information age.

One such problem is how to imagine communities befitting contemporary social conditions—a problem exacerbated by the promiscuous global intercourse among signs of social difference made possible by the new technologies. As a novel that features a cyborg alien and a diplomat, *Stars in My Pocket* extensively and intensively addresses the problem of cross-cultural communication. In the epilogue, Marq views the Aurigae in the company of several passengers who are not members of the human species. One such creature cannot see, taste, or smell, although she possesses twelve other sensory faculties unfamiliar to human beings. Whereas Marq's binocular vision can register the "stupendous curvature" of the Aurigae, the alien cannot see it at all. Yet she perceives something that both she and Marq can call morning: she hears the simulated dawn through an "aural rendition that requires the light to be translated into ultrasound waves" (354). And although she cannot speak, she converses with Marq about the Aurigae through a "human-speech translation device" (352). The "vagaries of translation" (354) become comically obvious when the alien woman recognizes her provincialism in mistakenly assuming that, because Marq is human, he must have been to Earth, his "racial origin planet." Upon discovering her mistake, she wants to "chuckle" with amusement, but she cannot because of a malfunction in the "laughter switches" of her translation mechanism (353).

Although this scene does not minimize in any way the alterity of each species to the other or gloss over the innate and culturally acquired dissimilarities (as well as the technological glitches) that impede communication across species, what is really notable about the encounter between Marq and the alien is that they *can* converse quite efficiently. With all the vagaries of translation, they can still share a joke, agree on what counts as provincialism in their interstellar universe, and even understand verbal renderings of sense perceptions that they do not have in common. Marq communicates his own impression of the Aurigae morning through the variegated "shadings and subtleties" of taste, smell, and sight, the very sense faculties that lie beyond his addressee's experiential reach. Then follows a passage too marvelous to be subjected to the vagaries of paraphrase:

"Precisely," said that steel translator's voice for this creature who possibly possessed none of her own.... "That is precisely the way it sounds to me. I could not have put it any better," leaving me

to wonder what, precisely, precision was on the other side of that
steel disk. That she and I had both found something matutinal to
contemplate, for whatever our vastly different reasons, in that huge
fire, seemed the most stupendous of cosmic accidents and was, finally,
where all real wonder lay. (354)

Of course, there is nothing accidental about the fact that the massive form
of the Aurigae can signify "morning" to both Marq and the alien and that
they can communicate to each other, however imperfectly, what morning
means to each. According to Delany's conception of language, "Where
there is communication, there's redundancy, which is what allows words
to call up similar meanings for both of us" (*SI*, 25). Although Delany's
fiction is very finely calibrated to the semantic permutations of signs in
different locales, it also reveals the relative stability of the codic system,
where meaning congeals into recognizable forms. Perhaps the most difficult achievement of *Stars in My Pocket* is that it is able to sustain, over some
350 pages, an equally steady focus on the vagaries and the sticking points
of cross-cultural communication.

This double focus bears significant implications for the postmodern politics of difference that has fueled Delany's work and that his work, in turn,
can help refine. Because overdetermination is a hallmark of the universe
sketched in Delany's theoretical and fictional writings, and because "stability is a function of overdetermination" (*SI*, 32), his writing urges attention
to the structural relations within which differences acquire their meanings. His emphasis on overdetermination also allows Delany to resist the
all-too-common move of reifying differences into incommunicable otherness. What is ultimately at stake in Delany's work is the very possibility
of sustaining ideals of urban sociality in postmodern conditions. Delany's
commitment to urbanity is a far cry from facile affirmations of the semiotic heterogeneity of postmodern cities, precisely because his writing poses
questions about the material differences among differences that are suppressed by the semiotic approach. *Stars in My Pocket* is a scrupulously urban
novel in that it insists on the necessity of communicating across differences
but without finessing the difficulties of this process. The novel's trope of
reading as the only means of knowing the other offers a model of social
intercourse that does not hark back to mythically innocent origins and
lost organic communities. Because urban social intercourse is mediated by
technology (and disorientingly so in the case of postmodern urbanism), we
can never imbibe the full presence of the other, even when we are standing
face to face with this other.

African-American writers have special stakes in questioning the construct of the face-to-face community, innocent of technological mediation
and of the "originary violence of writing." Jacques Derrida, for one, has

systematically exposed the ethnocentrism that insidiously attends uses of this construct in modern Western anthropology.[109] Samuel Delany, too, has observed that notions of premodern communities uncontaminated by technology typically primitivize the others of the modern West as "a people ... *without* history" (*SI*, 204) and underwrite material as well as symbolic violence against these "others": "the notion of a pure culture (the presumed object of anthropology) becomes one with an imperialistic ideology that justifies abuses toward a society because that society 'has no history'" (*SI*, 205). The interdependence of historicity and writing in this ideology has, of course, borne uniquely abusive implications for peoples of African origin, rationalizing their colonization and enslavement. Even in postmodern America, with all its avowed sensitivity to different language games, appreciation of the distinctive culture of African-Americans tends to focus on oral and performance modes, primitivizing them as the others of Western modernity and almost justifying (or, at the very least, compensating for) their systematic exclusion from progressive narratives of modernity. Delany's insistence on the *writtenness* of all cultures and his extension of reading to cover all acts of knowing everywhere become ways of investing all peoples with historicity, albeit within a discontinuous trajectory of uneven development.

Cities are pivotal to Delany's postmodern politics because they are scenes of imbrication in social difference, and in this sense, *Stars in My Pocket* both upholds an ideal of urbanity and helps measure the failure of actually existing cities to realize this ideal. For despite the rhetorical invocation of differences rampant in postmodern culture, U.S. urban life is increasingly tending toward racial and class insularity, whether through retribalizing cultural movements or material strategies of social and spatial containment. Without succumbing to elation or despair about the prospects for U.S. urban life, Delany presses the simple (but so often discounted) point that urbanism forms the inescapable horizon of any ethical vision of contemporary social life.

In an interview with Susan Grossman, Delany talks about the "real changes in people's worldviews" sparked by the information explosion. To illustrate, he recounts conversations he had in the early 1960s with "various white people who had come from various places away from the large urban centers of the country," who would claim that they could not possibly be racially prejudiced because they had never even seen a black person until they came to the city. Yet in the course of the conversation, they would talk about their fear and unease in the presence of black people. The real change brought about by the information explosion, according to Delany, is that this kind of disclaimer of prejudice is no longer possible: "Today, ... even if there aren't many blacks in Mohucket, Idaho, television and movies at least allow people there to see that blacks exist" (*SI*, 265). In other words, information technologies have brought about the virtual urbanization of the entire nation, lending greater visibility to racial differences and forcing the question of how to accommodate those who are perceived as others.

Missing the point of Delany's story, Susan Grossman responds that you cannot be a racist if racial difference is outside your context, that "any sort of 'ism' requires a frame of attitudes to be inside of." Delany counters that racism "can just as easily be a frame of attitudes to be *outside* as well." The people from Mohucket, Idaho, are "*outside* a frame of egalitarian ideals. What brings you inside such a frame of ideals is having to deal with social difference on a daily basis. But the people who do not have the necessary problems to solve by egalitarian means—which are, in the city, the most efficient means—tend to be simply and brutally controlled by fear of what's strange" (*SI*, 265). In principle, the city constitutes a "frame of egalitarian ideals" because encounters with strangers and potentially violent conflicts are expected features of urban life, and trust or tradition cannot be relied on to resolve social conflicts, as is presumed to be the case for organic communities. Identifying egalitarianism, or "the notion of equality before the law" (*SI*, 265), as the guiding principle of urbanity, Delany's work suggests a valuable alternative to current ways of addressing racial difference.

Delany's emphasis on "egalitarian ideals" and on "the notion of equality before the law" makes him an unusual advocate of the postmodern politics of difference. Other prominent defenders of this politics, such as Iris Young, want, like Delany, a democratic society modeled on the principle of urbanity rather than community. Whereas the term *community* implies social homogeneity, urban "contact," as Delany conceives it, is remarkable for the fact that it occurs among members of different social classes and races.[110] Similarly, Young discredits the ideal of community because, in promoting "a model of face-to-face relations . . . , it devalues and denies difference." Instead, Young proposes a norm of social life based on urbanity, which she defines as a "'being-together' of strangers" in an environment marked by "temporal and spatial distancing and differentiation."[111] But urbanity to Young does not represent a "frame of egalitarian ideals" as it does to Delany; in fact, her commitment to difference leads her to shun modern liberal notions of social justice, which take as their fundamental unit a citizen stripped of specificity. Young's critique of modern law is made in sympathy with women and African-Americans, whose embodied particularity furnishes the otherness against which modern reason is defined.[112] In his version of "postmodern ethics," Zygmunt Bauman is similarly leery of modern law for presupposing as its subject a universalizable entity rather than a member of a localized community.[113] Like Young, Bauman wants to develop a politics or ethics of difference that is commensurate with the conditions of contemporary urban life—in other words, one that takes into account the reality of spatiotemporal distanciation (14, 43). Neither Young nor Bauman believes that social justice can be derived immanently from within specific locales or communities, and each seeks some principle of mediation, but this becomes impossible to theorize given their shared suspicion of comprehensive and uniform legal codes. Some degree of abstraction, though, is necessary to any politics designed for social units larger than face-to-face communities.

Bauman writes approvingly of the antistatism of postmodern ethics (138, 183)—a gesture, let us remember, that reverberates powerfully in contemporary discourses of southern regional difference. Let us also recall that in response to the implicit racialism of these discourses, James Alan McPherson calls for mechanisms of "transcendent jurisprudence" as the best means of enforcing racial tolerance.[114] Writers like McPherson and Delany are not unwary of modern claims to transcendence or unconscious of the racial abuses of humanism, but for neither writer does a critique of the racial blind spots of humanism amount to wholesale abandonment of modern political principles. Perhaps the most important distinction between Delany and others partial to the postmodern politics of difference is that his politics of difference is actually a politics rather than a cultural or epistemological standpoint of difference. The question insistently posed by Delany's writing, whether fiction, theory, or urban history, is: What would it take to bring about a society in which differences are not used as alibis for material oppression? Even in his novel *Stars in My Pocket,* Delany is as minutely concerned with the infrastructure as with the superstructure of social difference. The point here is not whether we should model our society on the city of Morgre in southern Velm but that Delany chooses to frame the question of difference in these terms.

Any imaginable project seeking "a materially realized society" for the free play of differences will entail a critical extension of modern political principles such as egalitarianism. Accordingly, in his book on urban development, *Times Square Red, Times Square Blue,* Delany argues that a diverse society requires architectural planning, and public policies mandating class and racial intermingling—this even as he opposes the colossal bent of modern urban planning (166–67). Culture plays a vital role in Delany's urban utopia: as he remarks in *Times Square Red,* "the 'freedom' to 'be' 'black' [would be meaningless] in a world where black music, literature, culture, language, foods, and churches and all the social practices that have been generated through the process of historical exclusion were suddenly suppressed" (194). But the historical materialism of Delany's writing, along with its poststructuralism, saves it from the culturalism and racial romanticism of most versions of the politics of difference. Rather than offering baptismal immersion into racial otherness, Delany's writing anatomizes the material as well as cultural conditions that proscribe the equal coexistence of different social constituencies. In this way, Delany's work aspires to the more modest yet difficult goal of civility—or, "the proper way to act in a city."

Afterword

The tenor of literary criticism on cities and communities in African-American literature has been set by two influential essays by Toni Morrison published in the early 1980s, "City Limits, Village Values" and "Rootedness: The Ancestor as Foundation." In the first of these, Morrison argues that the anti-urbanism of black writers stems from the fact that African-Americans have had no part "in founding or shaping the city."[1] When a rare black writer does express affection for urban life, this is always for the "village" within the city. Morrison is careful initially not to dichotomize the "village" against the city, for example, describing Harlem as a village and suggesting that the values of "clannish" community and ancestral continuity are not restricted to any particular geographical locale. But as the essay progresses, these values get linked with terms, such as "tribal," that are difficult to square with late-twentieth-century urban life in the United States. The end of the essay bluntly expresses Morrison's own anti-urbanism, generalized into a descriptive observation about African-American literature. "Community values (I call them village values)," writes Morrison, without explaining why these categories should be so equated. The ancestor, who is the repository of communal values for Morrison, "cannot thrive in the dungeon of the city" (43). The essay closes with the statement that "among black writers, the city has huge limits and the village profound values" (43).

"Rootedness," published three years later, directly takes on the crisis of racial representation confronting African-American writers who, by the late twentieth century, cannot imagine their audience as an organic community. "There must have been a time when an artist could be genuinely representative *of* the tribe and *in* it," muses Morrison, identifying this possibility with the "peasant cultures" of the rural South.[2] These cultures did not "need" the genre of the novel because they possessed assured and settled values that were encoded in their oral traditions. But as the "peasant class" was thrown "into disarray" by urbanization, which disrupted oral traditions, "the novel [became] needed by African-Americans now in a way that it was not needed before" (340). The task of the novel is to supply "new information" and counsel to city dwellers who have been recently dislocated from southern oral tradition. In this narrative, the rise of the novel is consequent on urbanization and modernization, measuring the distance black culture has traveled away from oral tradition and folk community. Curiously, then, at the very end of the essay, Morrison asserts: "If anything I do, in the way of writing novels . . . isn't about the village or the community or about you, then it is not about anything . . . —which is to say, yes, the work must be political" (344). Here, the novel is political to the extent that it can address an audience—"you"—that is equivalent to the village or the community. But by the logic of Morrison's own argument, the emergence of the novel is contingent on the disappearance of exactly this sort of community.

The incoherence of Morrison's argument in "City Limits" and "Rootedness" betrays the extreme difficulty of sustaining folk claims to racial representation in the medium of print literature. Any assertion about the political value of fiction has to address the question of who reads novels and what effects novels have on their readerships. This is, of course, a very difficult question to answer definitively, because print readerships cannot be clearly foreseen and the links between literature and political change never precisely calculated. All that we can say with certainty is that the readership of African-American fiction is culturally and geographically wide-ranging—far from the tribe or village community. In "Rootedness," Morrison gets around this problem of audience by displacing it to the level of genre: "I try to incorporate, into that traditional genre the novel, unorthodox novelistic characteristics—so that it is, in my view, Black" (342). Her fiction presumably maintains a vital connection to black cultural community insofar as it formally appropriates the distinctive features of the lost black oral tradition. Some such features that Morrison specifies are auditory quality, ancestral presence, participatory relationship between author and reader, a choric voice that stands in for community, and a blending of supernatural and mundane registers that Morrison deems "indicative" of black "cosmology" (342).

One of my intentions in writing *Signs and Cities,* as I mention in the introduction, was to understand why a writer like Toni Morrison, who is something of a literary institution in herself, wants to address her work to a "preliterate or illiterate reader." Identifying her ideal audience in this paradoxical way, Morrison can assert an intimate relation between her writing and a wider African-American population whose primary frame of cultural reference is not literary fiction. Morrison's theory of the novel, with all its contradictions, has been immensely productive for her own literary practice. The death of oral tradition is necessary to the emergence of the novel, yet the novel gains racial authenticity to the extent that it formally incorporates the oral tradition it supersedes.[3] Morrison's essays are most appropriately approached as aesthetic manifestoes defending a particular set of literary choices, which, in Morrison's case, have yielded stunning innovations in the genre of the novel. But because of Morrison's towering presence as both a novelist and a literary critic, her pronouncements are generally applied without any critical qualifications to African-American literature as a whole. The qualities Morrison cites as distinctive of black fiction circulate widely in literary criticism on this fiction, serving to guarantee the racial difference of certain kinds of novels, mainly those that present themselves as extensions of southern oral tradition.

Morrison is an exceptionally rich and formally experimental writer, and this goes a long way toward explaining why her works, both fictional and critical, are canonized; her writing, thick with layered meanings, amply rewards the special disciplinary skills of literary critics. But obviously this is not the entire story, for novelists such as Toni Cade Bambara or Leon Forrest also work with a densely textured linguistic canvas and have published essays of cultural criticism, but no theories of African-American literature derive from their work. The reason for this may be that even when Bambara and Forrest take on issues of ancestry, conjuring, oral tradition, or the South and the city—the familiar coin of literary criticism on African-American writers—they do not offer readers the fix of tribal values or aestheticized racial difference.

Aesthetic tribalism represents one powerful strain in postmodern culture, and in African-American literature, this strain develops out of political pessimism about the prospect of achieving racial integration on equal terms. As I have argued throughout this book, African-American writers have good reasons to be suspicious of the ways in which black racial difference signifies in the postmodern period, at once fodder for commodity capitalism and a basis for material inequality. In this context, aesthetic tribalism provides some critical leverage on the facile multiracialism of postmodern commodity culture, but understandable as it may be, tribalism is not the only response available to African-American writers. Novels such as Bambara's *The Salt Eaters* and Forrest's *Divine Days,* or the more recent *Mosquito* by Gayl Jones and Carolivia Herron's *Thereafter Johnnie,* just to mention a few, challenge prevailing ways of thinking about race, culture, and urbanity, avoiding the organicist temptation but never losing sight of material burden of race in postmodern U.S. life. In *Signs and Cities* we tried to bring into view less familiar strains of African-American fiction, not only to reflect critically on predominant texts and trends (such as Morrison's fiction or the southern folk aesthetic) and thereby extend our understanding of black literary production but also to make us think differently about the workings of race and the political stakes of black literary culture in the postmodern era.

Very many postmodern African-American novelists are stirred by a "polemical passion" against the present that is "forward-looking, not nostalgic."[4] In the particular historical context of my study, this involves a commitment to urbanity as the horizon of social and cultural life and a refusal to legitimize political claims about literature by appeal to lost organic communities. Although polemics driven by nostalgia may serve critical and creative uses, this is not likely to be the case at present. As I argue in my first chapter, nostalgic notions of segregated southern community or the golden days of the ghetto are doing really dangerous kinds of political work, being used as sticks with which to beat the black urban poor. Literary and cultural representations of urbanity and community are not passively reflecting this state of affairs but are actively shaping public responses to the perceived crisis of postmodern cities. In public discourses on U.S. urban life, African-Americans rarely appear as anything other than "patients, victims, wards, and pathologies," as Toni Morrison notes in "City Limits" (37). But anti-urbanism is not the most effective reaction to influential discourses pathologizing contemporary black urban life. Some African-American writers are refusing to surrender ideals of urbanity even as they remain sharply critical of the racial order of actually existing cities.

To end where I began, Colson Whitehead's *The Intuitionist* takes a unique approach to the questions of race, urbanity, and modernity that also concern Toni Morrison in "Rootedness" and "City Limits." Like Morrison (and all the other novelists discussed here), Whitehead participates in a postmodern interrogation of the grand narrative of urban modernization, showing that this narrative gains coherence through racial exclusion. But instead of altogether disavowing urban life, Whitehead's novel undertakes a critical excavation, revealing African-Americans to be the hidden architects of modern cities. At once recursive and progressive, this project of corrective reading resumes and revises the emancipatory narratives of print literacy and urban migration that propelled African-American literature for over a century. The protagonist of Whitehead's novel, Lila Mae Watson, follows the trajectory of social advancement through acquisition of literacy, leaving her southern home to assume a position as the first black woman elevator inspector in New York city. But the truly progressive moment in Lila Mae's story occurs when, discovering that James Fulton was African-American, she develops a "new literacy" toward a defining document of urban modernity.[5] Whitehead, like Octavia Butler in *Parable of the Sower* or Sapphire in *PUSH,* loops back to the beginnings of the African-American literary tradition to press his case for the continuing importance of print literacy for working-class African-Americans. Once Lila Mae becomes aware of Fulton's racial secret, she teaches herself "how to read, like a slave does, one forbidden word at a time" (230). (The scene of Rat Korga's acquisition of literacy in Delany's *Stars in My Pocket,* although set on an extraterrestrial planet, also echoes the classic slave-narrative scenario in which learning to read is an illicit act of discovery.)

The immediate result of Lila Mae's critical literacy is to make her question the universalist pretensions of modern humanism. She now wonders whether Fulton's use of the terms "we" and "the race," generally presumed to refer to the human species, does not in fact carry racially particular significance. Fulton came to renounce the Empiricist tradition of elevator knowledge that he had helped to codify because he began to chafe against its sight-based epistemology. The Empiricists, wrote Fulton, "were slaves to what they could see." Mindful of Fulton's racial identity, Lila Mae now interprets his rejection of Empiricism as an indictment of an Enlightenment epistemology that builds a system of racial differences on pseudoscientific visual evidence: "They looked at the skin of things. . . . White people's reality is built on what things appear to be—that's the business of Empiricism" (239).

Fulton's invention of Intuitionism also begins to signify rather differently to Lila Mae in light of her awareness of Fulton's race. Intuitionist philosophy is meant to instruct "the dull and plodding citizens of modernity that there is a power beyond rationality" (231), and this makes perfect sense to Lila Mae once she understands the complicity between racism and modern reason. Through his Intuitionist approach to elevators, Fulton yearns to reenchant the world of objects and to transcend the subject-object dichotomy of modern knowledge. As Fulton's most devoted disciple, Lila Mae performs her job of elevator inspection by closing her eyes and communicating with the various genies of the elevator, which speak to her "in her mind's own tongue" (226). Lila Mae's intuitive inspection puts her in the company of Ishmael Reed's Papa LaBas, who practices detection as spirit work, Charles Johnson's Faith, who longs to know the world through mythopoesis, and Naylor's conjure-woman, Mama Day, all of whom practice what Paul Gilroy has called a black "counterculture of modernity."[6]

In some strands of postmodern African-American fiction and literary criticism (notably those associated with the southern folk aesthetic), supra-rational modes of knowing are identified as unique to people of African descent, establishing their radical otherness to Western modernity as well as their privileged access to reality. Whitehead's novel takes this route some of the way, with intuition supplying a mystical and absolute epistemological guarantee for visions critical of modernity. Just as "the signs don't lie" to Mama Day,[7] Lila Mae boasts a hundred percent accuracy for her elevator inspection: "She is never wrong. It's her intuition" (255). But Whitehead vacillates on the question of whether intuition is a specifically African-American faculty, flirting with but not entirely endorsing romantic racial-ism. To be sure, there is a racial logic to the development of Intuitionism. At times Lila Mae doubts whether Fulton was in fact African-American, but a rereading of his volumes of Intuitionist philosophy confirms his race: "Fulton was colored. In his books, the hatred of the corrupt order of this world, the keen longing for the next one" (232). Here, Intuitionism is presented as an epistemological standpoint likely to be most appealing to those who suffer most from the racial order of modern cities. But in the world of the novel, African-Americans do not have a monopoly on intu-ition. Intuitionism is all the rage, with elevator manufacturing companies avidly chasing the financial profits bound to flow from Fulton's invention of the black box, or the perfect elevator. Intuitionism is also one of two political camps within the guild of elevator inspectors, with Lila Mae as its only African-American member.

What is most unusual about Whitehead's novel is that it presents in-tuition as a medium of futurity, a way of extending rather than recoiling from the project of urban modernity. And Lila Mae is shown to have a vested interest in this project, as a working-class black woman who has labored to sustain the infrastructure of the modern city even as she has been written out of progressive narratives of urban modernity. Far from enabling a return to simpler, primitive forms of community, intuition in this novel offers a way of doing modernity differently, of getting it right the next time around. Fulton's black box is expected to make possible the "second elevation" (198), which will require a total overhaul of existing cities in order to make room for the more pliable cities of the future. All the imagery of elevation, uplift, verticality, and transcendence that surrounds the black box testifies to its modern lineage.

The novel closes with the scene of Lila Mae busy writing up the tech-nological blueprint for the cities of the future. The substance and details of this utopian text are not specified; in the novel's present, the black box exists as sheer latency. Like the Book of Thoth in Ishmael Reed's *Mumbo Jumbo*, Fulton's (and later Lila Mae's) manuscript is written in hieroglyphic code, circulates in the form of scattered notes and torn-out pages, and is numinous with mystery. Like many of the novelists discussed here—those, like Butler, Delany, Sapphire, or Wideman, who remain committed to imagining African-Americans as full "citizen[s] of the city to come"[8]—Whitehead implies that the book, the modern print tradition, will have to be refashioned before it can redeem its utopian promise.

Notes

Introduction

1. Colson Whitehead, *The Intuitionist* (New York: Anchor, 1999), 82, 158; hereafter cited parenthetically.

2. See the opening section of chapter 1 for a clarification of my usage of the term *postmodern*.

3. *Signs and Cities* is not meant to offer an exhaustive or definitive account of the distinguishing form or content of postmodern African-American fiction. Many novels that would certainly be identified as postmodern, such as Darryl Pinckney's *High Cotton*, Reginald McKnight's *I Get on the Bus*, Toni Morrison's *Beloved*, Randall Keenan's *A Visitation of Spirits*, or Gayl Jones's *Mosquito*, are not centrally concerned with books or cities. Some novels, such as Toni Cade Bambara's *Those Bones Are Not My Child*, Sarah Phillips's *Andrea Lee*, Xam Wilson-Cartier's *Muse-Echo Blues*, or John Edgar Wideman's *Two Cities*, focus on urban issues but do not directly consider problems of literary representation. Others, such as David Bradley's *The Chaneysville Incident* or Ernest Gaines's *A Lesson before Dying*, explicitly test the print literate tradition through tropes of reading and writing but do not engage questions of urbanity. I have deliberately narrowed the scope of this book to include only those novels that deploy tropes of the book to revaluate the double legacy of print literacy and urban modernity.

4. Michel Foucault, "Truth and Power," in *Power/Knowledge* (New York: Pantheon, 1980), 127; Andreas Huyssen, *After the Great Divide: Modernism, Mass Culture, Postmodernism* (Bloomington: Indiana University Press, 1986), 216.

5. Community grasped as a "concrete abstraction" entails "concrete representations" of local experience that are fully explicable only by recourse to "abstract and non-observable" structural processes. See David Harvey, *The Urban Experience* (Baltimore: Johns Hopkins University Press, 1989), 9.

6. Benedict Anderson, *Imagined Communities* (New York: Verso, 1983), 6, 36.

7. The phrase is from Jay David Bolter, *Writing Space: The Computer, Hypertext, and the History of Writing* (Hillsdale, N.J.: Lawrence Erlbaum, 1991), 2.

8. Ben Agger, *Fast Capitalism: A Critical Theory of Significance* (Urbana and Chicago: University of Illinois Press, 1989), 56, 18.

9. This is the title of a book by Alvin Kernan, which argues that electronic technology is killing off print literature. Kernan, *The Death of Literature* (New Haven: Yale University Press, 1990).

10. Henry Louis Gates Jr., "Introduction: The Language of Slavery," in *The Slave's Narrative*, ed. Charles T. Davis and Henry Louis Gates Jr. (New York: Oxford University Press, 1985), v, xxix.

11. I am referring to the Dick and Jane textbook in Morrison's novel, which emblematizes the entry of African-Americans into urban commodity culture as well as their drive toward racial integration.

12. Alain Locke, "The New Negro," in *The New Negro,* ed. Alain Locke (1925; reprint, New York: Macmillan, 1992), 6.

13. Richard Wright, "Introduction," in *Black Metropolis,* by St. Clair Drake and Horace Cayton (1945; reprint, Chicago: University of Chicago Press, 1993), xxi, xxv.

14. Richard Wright, *12 Million Black Voices* (New York: Thunder's Mouth Press, 1941), 64, 147.

15. Toni Morrison, "Memory, Creation, and Writing," *Thought* 59 (1984): 387.

16. The term is from Carla Hesse, "Books in Time," in *The Future of the Book,* ed. Geoffrey Nunberg (Berkeley and Los Angeles: University of California Press, 1996), 22.

17. I take the term *technotype* from Samuel R. Delany, *Stars in My Pocket Like Grains of Sand* (New York: Bantam, 1984), 119.

18. Scott Lash and John Urry, *Economies of Signs and Space* (London: Sage, 1994), 64, 143.

19. Affirmative readings of the politically resistant proclivity of hip-hop music, presumed to be equivalent to the culture of the black urban poor, abound. For instance, see Houston A. Baker Jr., *Black Studies, Rap, and the Academy* (Chicago: University of Chicago Press, 1993); Stephen Nathan Haymes, *Race, Culture, and the City* (Albany: SUNY Press, 1995); and Russell Potter, *Spectacular Vernaculars: Hip-Hop and the Politics of Postmodernism* (Albany: SUNY Press, 1995). A rare exception, which offers a densely textured analysis of hip-hop culture grounded in the political economy of U.S. cities, is Carl Nightingale, "The Global Inner City," in *W. E. B. Du Bois, Race, and the City,* ed. Michael B. Katz and Thomas Sugrue (Philadelphia: University of Pennsylvania Press, 1998), 217–58.

20. I quote Cornel West, from Anders Stephanson, "Interview with Cornel West," in *Universal Abandon: The Politics of Postmodernism,* ed. Andrew Ross (Minneapolis: University of Minnesota Press, 1988), 277.

21. Cornel West, "Black Strivings in a Twilight Civilization," in Cornel West and Henry Louis Gates Jr., *The Future of the Race* (New York: Vintage, 1996), 81.

22. Stephanson, "Interview with Cornel West," 276, 280.

23. Ibid., 277.

24. W. Lawrence Hogue, *Race, Modernity, Postmodernity* (Albany: SUNY Press, 1996), 45, 68–70.

25. Brian McHale, *Postmodernist Fiction* (New York: Routledge, 1987), 180–96.

26. My title is inspired by Samuel R. Delany's novel *Neveryóna, or: The Tale of Signs and Cities* (Hanover, N.H.: Wesleyan University Press, 1993).

27. Samuel R. Delany, *Silent Interviews* (Hanover, N.H.: Wesleyan University Press, 1994), 135.

28. Samuel R. Delany, *Times Square Red, Times Square Blue* (New York: New York University Press, 1999), 161–63.

29. I quote Fredric Jameson, *Postmodernism, or, The Cultural Logic of Late Capitalism* (Durham, N.C.: Duke University Press, 1991), 48.

30. Examples of such approaches include John A. Agnew, John Mercer, and David E. Sohper, eds., *The City in Cultural Context* (Boston: Allen and Unwin, 1984); Robert Bocock and Kenneth Thompson, eds., *Social and Cultural Forms of Modernity* (Cambridge, Mass.: Polity Press, 1992), esp. James Donald, "Metropolis: The City as Text," 417–61; Ruth Fincher and Jane M. Jacobs, eds., *Cities of Difference* (New York and London: Guilford Press, 1998); M. Gottdiener and Alexandros P. Lagopoulos, eds., *The City and the Sign: An Introduction to Urban Semiotics* (New York: Columbia University Press, 1986); Jane M. Jacobs, "The City Unbound: Qualitative Approaches to the City," *Urban Studies* 30, no. 4/5 (May 1993): 827–48; Gerry Kearns and Chris Philo, eds., *Selling Places: The City as Cultural Capital* (New York: Pergamon Press, 1993); and Anthony D. King, ed., *Re-Presenting the City: Ethnicity, Capital and Culture in the Twenty-First Century Metropolis* (New York: New York

University Press, 1996). For a critique of such semiotic approaches, see Janet Wolff, "The Real City, the Discursive City, the Disappearing City: Postmodernism and Urban Sociology," *Theory and Society* 21 (1992): 553–60.

31. Agger, *Fast Capitalism*, 74.

32. Ibid., 82.

33. On the enhanced pictorial dimensions of electronic media, see Bolter, *Writing Space,* 79. On the "secondary orality" of electronic culture, see Walter J. Ong, *Orality and Literacy: The Technologizing of the Word* (New York: Methuen, 1982), 136; and Marshall McLuhan, *The Gutenberg Galaxy: The Making of Typographic Man* (Toronto: University of Toronto Press, 1962), 72.

Chapter One

1. On the postindustrial thesis, see Daniel Bell, *The Coming of Post-Industrial Society* (New York: Basic Books, 1973); and Jean-François Lyotard, *The Postmodern Condition: A Report on Knowledge,* trans. Geoff Bennington and Brian Massumi (Minneapolis: University of Minnesota Press, 1984). The theory of postmodernism as the cultural dominant of multinational capitalism is that of Fredric Jameson, *Postmodernism, or, the Cultural Logic of Late Capitalism* (Durham, N.C.: Duke University Press, 1991). The case for a qualitatively new phase of "disorganized capitalism" as the material underpinning of postmodernism is made by Scott Lash and John Urry, *Economies of Signs and Space* (London: Sage, 1994). For a concise genealogy of periodizing concepts of postmodernism, see Perry Anderson, *The Origins of Postmodernity* (London and New York: Verso, 1998).

2. For example, see Alex Callinicos, *Against Postmodernism: A Marxist Critique* (Cambridge, Mass.: Polity Press, 1989), chap. 1.

3. David Harvey, *The Condition of Postmodernity* (Cambridge, Mass.: Blackwell, 1990), 145; hereafter cited parenthetically.

4. To the literary authors I examine in this study, the terms *modern, modernity,* and *modernism* have varying referents, and I modulate my own use of these terms according to context.

5. For example, see Callinicos, *Against Postmodernism*, 131.

6. Lyotard, *Postmodern Condition*, xxiii–xxiv; hereafter cited parenthetically. Jonathan Arac, *Critical Genealogies: Historical Situations for Postmodern Literary Studies* (New York: Columbia University Press, 1987), 286.

7. Doreen Massey, *Space, Place, and Gender* (Minneapolis: University of Minnesota Press, 1994), 6–11, 136–42.

8. In an attempt to move beyond the rigid polarities that stultify much recent debate on modern and postmodern politics, Robin D. G. Kelley provides numerous lesser-known instances of political movements that find no necessary discrepancy between struggling on particular grounds and seeking to extend humanist ideals. See Kelley, *Yo Mama's Disfunktional: Fighting the Culture Wars in Urban America* (Boston: Beacon Press, 1997), 109–12.

9. Massey, *Space, Place, and Gender*, 122–23.

10. Paul Gilroy, "Living Memory: A Meeting with Toni Morrison," in *Small Acts: Thoughts on the Politics of Black Cultures* (London: Serpent's Tail, 1993), 178.

11. Wahneema Lubiano, "Shuckin' Off the African-American Native Other: What's 'Po-Mo' Got to Do with It?" *Cultural Critique* (spring 1991): 154, 160; Lubiano, "The Postmodernist Rag: Political Identity and the Vernacular in *Song of Solomon,*" in *New Essays on Song of Solomon,* ed. Valerie Smith (Cambridge: Cambridge University Press, 1995), 94–95.

12. Phillip Brian Harper, *Framing the Margins: The Social Logic of Postmodern Culture* (New York: Oxford University Press, 1994), 3–4.

13. David Harvey, *Justice, Nature and the Geography of Difference* (Oxford: Blackwell, 1996), 96–104.

14. For Raymond Williams's discussion of periodicity in terms of dominant, residual, and emergent strains, see Williams, *Marxism and Literature* (Oxford: Oxford University Press, 1977), 121–27.

15. Jameson, *Postmodernism,* 309; also see 366.

16. Anders Stephanson, "Regarding Postmodernism: A Conversation with Fredric Jameson," in *Universal Abandon: The Politics of Postmodernism,* ed. Andrew Ross (Minneapolis: University of Minnesota Press, 1988), 16.

17. bell hooks, "Choosing the Margins as a Space of Radical Openness," in *Yearning: Race, Gender, and Cultural Politics* (Boston: South End Press, 1990), 148; hereafter cited parenthetically.

18. Edward W. Soja, *Thirdspace: Journeys to Los Angeles and Other Real-and-Imagined Places* (Oxford: Blackwell, 1996), 10; hereafter cited parenthetically.

19. Neil Smith, *Uneven Development: Nature, Capital, and the Production of Space* (New York: Blackwell, 1984).

20. Fredric Jameson, *The Cultural Turn: Selected Writings on the Postmodern, 1983–1998* (New York: Verso, 1998), 43.

21. Mike Featherstone, "In Pursuit of the Postmodern: An Introduction," *Theory, Culture, and Society* 5 (1988): 199–200; Zygmunt Bauman, "The Fall of the Legislator," in *Postmodernism: A Reader,* ed. Thomas Docherty (New York: Columbia University Press, 1993), 137.

22. On the racial and class polarizations produced by processes of deindustrialization, see Barry Bluestone and Bennett Harrison, *The Deindustrialization of America* (New York: Basic Books, 1982), 54, 87, 95; Robin M. Law and Jennifer R. Wolch, "Social Reproduction in the City: Restructuring in Time and Space," in *The Restless Urban Landscape,* ed. Paul L. Knox (Englewood Cliffs, N.J.: Prentice-Hall, 1993), 165–206; and Clarence Lusane, *Race in the Global Era* (Boston: South End Press, 1997), 9–12.

23. John D. Kasarda, "Urban Change and Minority Opportunities," in *The New Urban Reality,* ed. Paul E. Peterson (Washington, D.C.: Brookings Institution, 1985), 33.

24. William Julius Wilson, *The Truly Disadvantaged: The Inner City, the Underclass, and Public Policy* (Chicago: University of Chicago, 1987), 41–42; and Wilson, *When Work Disappears: The World of the New Urban Poor* (New York: Vintage, 1996), 25–42.

25. See David Bartelt, "Housing the 'Underclass,'" in *The "Underclass" Debate: Views from History,* ed. Michael B. Katz (Princeton: Princeton University Press, 1993), 118–57; Douglas Massey and Nancy Denton, *American Apartheid: Segregation and the Making of the Underclass* (Cambridge: Harvard University Press, 1993).

26. William Julius Wilson, *The Declining Significance of Race* (Chicago: University of Chicago Press, 1980), 88–121.

27. Bluestone and Harrison, *Deindustrialization of America,* 180–88.

28. See Michael B. Katz, "Reframing the 'Underclass' Debate," in Katz, *"Underclass" Debate,* 458–66.

29. Michael B. Katz, *The Undeserving Poor: From the War on Poverty to the War on Welfare* (New York: Pantheon, 1989), 196. On the use of underclass rhetoric to justify a political retreat from redistributive political goals, also see Stephen Steinberg, *Turning Back: The Retreat from Racial Justice in American Thought and Policy* (Boston: Beacon Press, 1995), 97–155.

30. Margaret Weir, "From Equal Opportunity to 'The New Social Contract': Race and the Politics of the American 'Underclass,'" in *Racism, the City, and the State,* ed. Malcolm Cross and Michael Keith (New York: Routledge, 1993), 98.

31. "The American Underclass," *Time,* August 29, 1977, 14.

32. Nicholas Lemann, "The Origins of the Underclass," pt. 1, *Atlantic Monthly,* June 1986, 35; Ken Auletta, *The Underclass* (New York: Random House, 1982).

33. Wilson, *Truly Disadvantaged,* 21–29; hereafter cited parenthetically.

34. Elijah Anderson's widely read ethnographic study, *Streetwise: Race, Class, and Change in an Urban Community* (Chicago: University of Chicago Press, 1990), corroborated Wilson's picture of a past era of class-integrated black ghetto neighborhoods, contrasted to the social breakdown of present-day ghetto communities.

35. On the historical "myopia" of the underclass debate, see Thomas Sugrue, "The Structures of Urban Poverty," in Katz, *"Underclass" Debate,* 86, 114.

36. For example, see Joe William Trotter Jr., "Blacks in the Urban North: The 'Underclass Question' in Historical Perspective," in Katz, "*Underclass*" *Debate*, 66–67. For other forceful critiques of Wilson's middle-class exodus thesis, see Reynolds Farley, "Residential Segregation of Social and Economic Groups among Blacks, 1970–80," in *The Urban Underclass,* ed. Christopher Jencks and Paul E. Peterson (Washington D.C.: Brookings Institution, 1991), 274–98; Bill E. Lawson, "Uplifting the Race: Middle-Class Blacks and the Truly Disadvantaged," in *The Underclass Question,* ed. Bill E. Lawson (Philadelphia: Temple University Press, 1992), 90–113; Kevin Gaines, *Uplifting the Race: Black Leadership, Politics, and Culture in the Twentieth Century* (Chapel Hill: University of North Carolina Press, 1996), 88–90.

37. See Gaines, *Uplifting the Race,* 176.

38. Antonio McDaniel, "The 'Philadelphia Negro' Then and Now," in *W. E. B. Du Bois, Race, and the City,* ed. Michael B. Katz and Thomas Sugrue (Philadelphia: University of Pennsylvania Press, 1998), 187–88.

39. Raymond Williams, *The Country and the City* (London: Oxford University Press, 1973), 12.

40. Richard Lacayo, "Between Two Worlds," *Time,* March 13, 1989, 67. Also see Isabel Wilkerson, "Middle-Class Blacks Try to Grip a Ladder While Lending a Hand," *New York Times,* November 26, 1990, sec. A, 1.

41. For example, see Kenneth Maurice Jones, "The Buppies," *The Crisis* 93, no. 4 (April 1986): 17–18, 20, 22–24, 63–64; Nathan Hare and Regina Jollivette Frazier, "Is the Middle Class Blowing It?" *Ebony,* August 1987, 85–86, 89–90; Alvin F. Poussaint, "The Price of Success," *Ebony,* August 1987, 76, 78, 80; and Bebe Moore Campbell, "Staying in the Community," *Essence,* December 1989, 96–98, 100, 112.

42. Bart Landry, *The New Black Middle Class* (Berkeley and Los Angeles: University of California Press, 1987), 2–3. For other academic studies of the black middle class in the post–Civil Rights era, see Charles T. Banner-Haley, *The Fruits of Integration: Black Middle-Class Ideology and Culture, 1960–1990* (Jackson: University Press of Mississippi, 1994); Thomas J. Durant and Joyce S. Louden, "The Black Middle Class in America: Historical and Contemporary Perspectives," *Phylon* 47, no. 4 (1986): 253–63; Alphonso Pinkney, *The Myth of Black Progress* (New York: Cambridge University Press, 1984), 99–114; and Joseph R. Washington Jr., ed., *Dilemmas of the New Black Middle Class* (Joseph R. Washington Jr., 1980).

43. Toni Morrison, "Home," in *The House That Race Built* (New York: Vintage, 1998), 11. Morrison also noted the "wariness" and "intense resentment" felt by "off-campus communities" at being "spoken for" by intellectuals (12). James McPherson, "Junior and John Doe," in *Lure and Loathing: Essays on Race, Identity, and the Ambivalence of Assimilation,* ed. Gerald Early (New York: Penguin, 1993), 187; Ishmael Reed, *Airing Dirty Laundry* (New York and Reading, Mass.: Addison-Wesley Publishing, 1993), 236; Toni Cade Bambara, "Deep Sight and Rescue Missions," in Early, *Lure and Loathing,* 292; and Campbell, "Staying in the Community."

44. Reed, *Airing Dirty Laundry,* 3.

45. Orlando Patterson, "The Black Community: Is There a Future?" in *The Third Century: America as a Post-Industrial Society,* ed. Seymour Lipset (Stanford: Hoover Institution Press, 1979), 273–74; Henry Louis Gates Jr., "Two Nations . . . Both Black," *Forbes,* September 14, 1992, 138.

46. Cornel West, "Nihilism in Black America," in *Race Matters* (Boston: Beacon Press, 1993), 12–13.

47. Cornel West, "Philosophy and the Urban Underclass," in Lawson, *Underclass Question,* 195–96.

48. Cornel West, "Black Strivings in a Twilight Civilization," in Henry Louis Gates Jr. and Cornel West, *The Future of the Race* (New York: Vintage, 1996), 110; Gates, "Two Nations . . . Both Black," 138; Glenn Loury, "The Moral Quandary of the Black Community," *Public Interest* 79 (spring 1985): 9–10.

49. The quoted phrase is from Michael Dawson, "A Black Counterpublic? Economic Earthquakes, Racial Agenda(s), and Black Politics," in *The Black Public Sphere,* ed. Black Public Sphere Collective (Chicago: University of Chicago Press, 1995), 199. Also see Martin

Kilson, "The New Black Political Class," in Washington, *Dilemmas of the New Black Middle Class,* 96–97; Manning Marable, "Race, Identity, and Political Culture," in *Black Popular Culture,* ed. Gina Dent (Seattle: Bay Press, 1992), 296; and Adolph Reed Jr., *Stirrings in the Jug: Black Politics in the Post-Segregation Era* (Minneapolis: University of Minnesota Press, 1999), 15–16.

50. Reed, *Stirrings in the Jug,* 20, 36.

51. Harold Cruse, *The Crisis of the Negro Intellectual* (New York: Quill, 1984), 560.

52. Reed, *Stirrings in the Jug,* 88. For critical analyses of the ways in which such urban regimes have served black middle-class political interests, also see Johanna Fernandez, "The Fire This Time: Harlem and Its Discontents at the Turn of the Century," in *Dispatches from the Ebony Tower,* ed. Manning Marable (New York: Columbia University Press, 2000), 108–20; and Steven Gregory, "Race, Identity, and Political Activism: The Shifting Contours of the African American Public Sphere," in Black Public Sphere Collective, *Black Public Sphere,* 151–68.

53. Reed, *Stirrings in the Jug,* 88.

54. On this, see Howard Winant, "Postmodern Racial Politics in the United States: Difference and Inequality," *Socialist Review* 20 (1990): 124.

55. Toni Morrison, "Introduction: Friday on the Potomac," in *Race-ing Justice, Engender-ing Power: Essays on Anita Hill, Clarence Thomas and the Construction of Social Reality,* ed. Toni Morrison (New York: Pantheon Books, 1992), xxx.

56. Michael Berube, "Public Academy," *New Yorker,* January 9, 1995, 75. Robert S. Boynton, "The New Intellectuals," *Atlantic Monthly,* March 1995, 6, similarly notes the new intellectuals' rejection of the identity politics of black nationalism.

57. Russell Jacoby, *The Last Intellectuals: American Culture in the Age of Academe* (New York: Basic Books, 1987), 5–8.

58. Boynton, "New Intellectuals," 65; Berube, "Public Academy," 75, 78.

59. Edward Soja and Barbara Hooper, "The Spaces That Difference Makes: Some Notes on the Geographical Margins of the New Cultural Politics," in *Place and the Politics of Identity,* ed. Michael Keith and Steve Pile (London: Routledge, 1993), 186; hereafter cited parenthetically.

60. Cornel West, "The New Cultural Politics of Difference," in *Out There: Marginalization and Contemporary Cultures,* ed. Russell Ferguson, Martha Gever, Trinh T. Minh-ha, and Cornel West (Cambridge: MIT Press, 1990), 35.

61. Greg Tate, "Cult-Nats Meet Freaky-Deke: The Return of the Black Aesthetic" (1986), reprinted in *Flyboy in the Buttermilk* (New York: Simon and Schuster, 1992), 206.

62. Trey Ellis, "The New Black Aesthetic," *Callaloo* 12, no. 1 (winter 1989): 236.

63. W. Lawrence Hogue, *Race, Modernity, Postmodernity* (Albany: SUNY Press, 1996), 6. Lubiano, "Shuckin' Off the African-American Native Other," likewise argues that black literary postmodernism enables a new politics of difference that continues to valorize African-American cultural practices while challenging the essentialist notions of identity and the monolithic models of community associated with nationalism.

64. hooks, "Postmodern Blackness," in *Yearning,* 25.

65. John Oliver Killens, "The Black Writer vis-à-vis His Country," in *The Black Aesthetic,* ed. Addison Gayle Jr. (New York: Doubleday, 1971), 359.

66. James A. Emmanuel, "Blackness Can: A Quest for Aesthetics," in Gayle, *Black Aesthetic,* 195; Killens, "Black Writer vis-à-vis His Country," 367.

67. Adam David Miller, "Some Observations on a Black Aesthetic," in Gayle, *Black Aesthetic,* 378.

68. bell hooks, "The Chitlin Circuit: On Black Community," in *Yearning,* 36; hereafter cited parenthetically.

69. Anders Stephanson, "Interview with Cornel West," in Ross, *Universal Abandon,* 276; hereafter cited parenthetically.

70. W. E. B. Du Bois, "The Talented Tenth" (1903), reprinted in Gates and West, *Future of the Race,* 157, 139.

71. West, "Black Strivings," 58–59, 64–65. *Future of the Race* centrally examines the question of whether Du Bois's model is still applicable to late-twentieth-century conditions. In their jointly authored preface, Gates and West refer to present-day black intellectuals as "heirs to the Talented Tenth" and ask how this elite can "assume a renewed leadership role" within the black community (xv). Both authors are pessimistic about the prospect, although Gates in particular betrays a lingering attachment to the Talented Tenth model. In his contribution to the book, "Parable of the Talents," Gates writes that the widening gulf between poor and prosperous African-Americans makes it difficult to invoke Du Bois's "salvific conception of the Talented Tenth without bitterness"; the dire conditions of black underclass existence are a "reproach to those of us who once dreamed of collective uplift" (25). West's essay in this book is hereafter cited parenthetically.

72. Ishmael Reed, introduction to *MultiAmerica: Essays on Cultural Wars and Cultural Peace,* ed. Ishmael Reed (New York: Viking Penguin, 1997), xvi; Reed, "Black Pleasure: An Oxymoron," in *Soul: Black Power, Politics, and Pleasure,* ed. Monique Guillory and Richard C. Green (New York: New York University Press, 1998), 170–71; and Reed, in a roundtable titled "Ain't We Got Soul?" in Guillory and Green, *Soul,* 280.

73. Andreas Huyssen, *After the Great Divide: Modernism, Mass Culture, Postmodernism* (Bloomington: Indiana University Press, 1986), 194.

74. bell hooks and Cornel West, *Breaking Bread: Insurgent Black Intellectual Life* (Boston: South End Press, 1991), 14–15. In her forceful critique of "the postmodern talented tenth" (including Cornel West and bell hooks), Joy James argues that it is precisely collective accountability that is erased from contemporary versions of uplift ideology. See Joy James, "The Future of Black Studies: Political Communities and the 'Talented Tenth,'" in Marable, *Dispatches from the Ebony Tower,* 153–57; and James, *Transcending the Talented Tenth* (New York: Routledge, 1997), 29–30, 134, 160. Also see Kevin Gaines's argument that racial uplift ideology has become the "orthodoxy" of the post–Civil Rights era (*Uplifting the Race,* 259).

75. Gates, "Two Nations . . . Both Black," 134.

76. West, "Philosophy and the Urban Underclass," 194.

77. Cornel West, "The Dilemma of the Black Intellectual," in hooks and West, *Breaking Bread,* 132. Jerry G. Watts, "Dilemmas of Black Intellectuals," *Dissent* (fall 1989), similarly argues that education for African-Americans "has historically been premised on a utilitarian ethos, centered around the quest for economic security and upward mobility." Watts points out that although "this is quite understandable," it nevertheless "hinders the development of a black intellectual community" (503).

78. West, "Nihilism in Black Culture," 16–17.

79. Connie Goddard, "Blacks and the Book World: Aiming for the Mainstream," *Publishers Weekly,* January 20, 1992, 29, 32. On the expansion of a black middle-class readership during the 1980s and 1990s, also see Calvin Reid, "Blacks and the Book World: Building a Readership," *Publishers Weekly,* January 20, 1992, 36–38; and Carolyn M. Brown, "Writing a New Chapter in Book Publishing," *Black Enterprise,* February 1995, 108–18.

80. Elizabeth Maguire, "University Presses and the Black Reader," in Black Public Sphere Collective, *Black Public Sphere,* 324.

81. LeRoi Jones, "The Last Days of the American Empire," in *Home: Social Essays* (New York: William Morrow, 1966), 197.

82. hooks and West, *Breaking Bread,* 45, 162.

83. Ibid., 136.

84. West, "Black Strivings," 81.

85. LeRoi Jones, "The Myth of a Negro Literature," in *Home,* 106.

86. Larry Neal, "And Shine Swam On," in *Visions of a Liberated Future* (New York: Thunder's Mouth Press, 1989), 20–21.

87. Jones, "Myth of a Negro Literature," 106, 108–9; Neal, "And Shine Swam On," 21–22.

88. Kelley, *Yo Mama's Disfunktional,* 16, 3.

89. I am drawing here on Bauman's argument ("Fall of the Legislator," 139) that in the postmodern era, the modern notion of intellectuals as cultural legislators is replaced by the notion of intellectuals as cultural interpreters.

90. Reed, *Stirrings in the Jug,* 16–17.

91. James, *Transcending the Talented Tenth,* 136; Kobena Mercer, "Black Art and the Burden of Representation," in *Welcome to the Jungle: New Positions in Black Cultural Studies* (New York: Routledge, 1994), 240, 249.

92. Henry Louis Gates Jr., *The Signifying Monkey: A Theory of African-American Literary Criticism* (New York: Oxford University Press, 1988), 165; hereafter cited parenthetically. As far as I am aware, the term "Talking Book" was first used by Ishmael Reed to describe his own fiction, in *Shrovetide in New Orleans* (New York: Doubleday, 1978), 160.

93. Robert Stepto, *From Behind the Veil: A Study of Afro-American Narrative* (1979; reprint, Urbana and Chicago: University of Illinois Press, 1991); hereafter cited parenthetically. On the links between print literacy and political freedom in African-American literature, also see William Andrews, *To Tell a Free Story: The First Century of Afro-American Autobiography* (Urbana and Chicago: University of Illinois Press, 1986); and Carla Peterson, *"Doers of the Word": African-American Women Speakers and Writers in the North (1830–1880)* (New York: Oxford University Press, 1995).

94. For example, see Houston A. Baker Jr., "Autobiographical Acts and the Voice of the Southern Slave," in *The Slave's Narrative,* ed. Charles T. Davis and Henry Louis Gates Jr. (New York: Oxford University Press, 1985), 253.

95. Frederick Douglass, *Narrative of the Life of Frederick Douglass, An American Slave* (1845; reprint, New York: Penguin, 1982), 121.

96. Robert Stepto, "Distrust of the Reader in Afro-American Narrative" (1986), reprinted in *From Behind the Veil,* 196; hereafter cited parenthetically.

97. For example, see Susan Willis, *Specifying: Black Women Writing the American Experience* (Madison: University of Wisconsin Press, 1987); and Marjorie Pryse and Hortense Spillers, eds., *Conjuring: Black Women, Fiction, and Literary Tradition* (Bloomington: Indiana University Press, 1985). On call and response in African-American fiction, see Michael Awkward, *Inspiriting Influences: Tradition, Revision, and Afro-American Women's Novels* (New York: Columbia University Press, 1989); and John Callahan, *In the African-American Grain: The Pursuit of Voice in Twentieth-Century Black Fiction* (Urbana and Chicago: University of Illinois Press, 1988). Along with Callahan, others who argue that the antiphonal structure of black music yields a powerful metaphor for democracy include Paul Gilroy, *The Black Atlantic* (Cambridge: Harvard University Press, 1993), 200; and Craig Hansen Werner, *Playing the Changes: From Afro-Modernism to the Jazz Impulse* (Urbana and Chicago: University of Illinois Press, 1994), xviii.

98. This applies not only to the work of Gates and Stepto but also to Houston Baker's explicitly synchronic rather than diachronic vernacular paradigm of black literature based on the blues, in *Blues, Ideology, and Afro-American Literature: A Vernacular Theory* (Chicago: University of Chicago Press, 1987).

99. John Guillory, *Cultural Capital: The Problem of Literary Canon Formation* (Chicago: University of Chicago Press, 1993), 18, 16.

100. Ibid., xii. On the ascendance of this professional-managerial class and the concomitant marginalization of modern humanist intellectuals in the postmodern era, see Bell, *Coming of Post-Industrial Society,* 214; and Bauman, "Fall of the Legislator," 137.

101. Banner-Haley, *Fruits of Integration,* 113.

102. James, *Transcending the Talented Tenth,* 135, 137.

103. West, "Nihilism in Black America," 19.

104. Cornel West, "Black Culture and Postmodernism," in *Remaking History,* ed. Barbara Kruger and Phil Mariani (Seattle: Bay Press, 1989), 96. Similarly, bell hooks, who wrote her Ph.D. thesis on Toni Morrison, confesses that she chooses not to publish literary criticism

because its inability to reach across class barriers restricts it to a "narrow audien and West, *Breaking Bread,* 71).

105. Walter Mosley, "Black to the Future," *New York Times Magazine,* N 1998, 34.

106. Ibid.

107. Greg Tate, "Ghetto in the Sky: Samuel Delany's Black Whole," in *Flyboy in the Buttermilk,* 160, 165–66. In a similar move, although in a literary-critical rather than popular response to Delany's fiction, Robert Elliott Fox often stretches Delany's writing beyond recognition in order to show that it illuminates aspects of "the black experience." See Elliott Fox, *Conscientious Sorcerers: The Black Postmodernist Fiction of LeRoi Jones/Amiri Baraka, Ishmael Reed, and Samuel R. Delany* (New York: Greenwood Press, 1987), esp. 118–19.

108. Mercer, "Black Art and the Burden of Representation," 240.

109. Tate, "Ghetto in the Sky," 165.

110. Ross Posnock, *Color and Culture: Black Writers and the Making of the Modern Intellectual* (Cambridge: Harvard University Press, 1998), 262; hereafter cited parenthetically.

111. Samuel R. Delany, afterword to *Stars in My Pocket Like Grains of Sand* (1984; reprint, New York: Bantam, 1990), 384.

112. Samuel R. Delany, *Silent Interviews* (Hanover, N.H.: Wesleyan University Press, 1994), 199; hereafter cited parenthetically.

113. Gates, *Signifying Monkey,* 217–34.

114. David Mikics, "Postmodernism, Ethnicity, and Underground Revisionism in Ishmael Reed," in *Essays in Postmodern Culture,* ed. Eyal Amiram and John Unsworth (New York: Oxford University Press, 1993), 297, 301.

115. "Addison Gayle Interviewed by Saundra Towns," *Black Position* 2 (1972): 17.

116. Patrick McGee, *Ishmael Reed and the Ends of Race* (New York: St. Martin's Press, 1997), 16.

117. Ishmael Reed, cited in Reginald Martin, *Ishmael Reed and the New Black Aesthetic Critics* (New York: St. Martin's Press, 1997), 63.

118. Stephanson, "Interview with Cornel West," 277–78.

119. Delany, *Silent Interviews,* 38–39.

120. Ishmael Reed, *Mumbo Jumbo* (New York: Simon and Schuster, 1972), 6; hereafter cited parenthetically.

121. Huyssen, *After the Great Divide,* 168.

122. Patrick Boylan, *Thoth, the Hermes of Egypt* (London: Oxford University Press, 1922), 59. My discussion of the various facets and functions of the mythical Thoth are drawn from Boylan's book as well as from Rudolph Anthes, "Mythology in Ancient Egypt," in *Mythologies of the Ancient World,* ed. Samuel Noah Kramer (New York: Doubleday, 1961), 15–92; and Carleton T. Hodge, "Thoth and Oral Tradition," in *General and American Ethnolinguistics,* ed. Mary Ritchie Key and Henry M. Hoenigsweld (Berlin: Mouton de Gruyter, 1989), 407–16.

123. John Edgar Wideman, *Reuben* (New York: Penguin, 1987), 67.

Chapter Two

1. Sapphire, *PUSH* (New York: Vintage, 1996), 124; hereafter cited parenthetically.

2. Octavia Butler, *Parable of the Sower* (New York: Warner Books, 1993), 5; hereafter cited parenthetically.

3. Stephen Potts, "'We Keep Playing the Same Record': A Conversation with Octavia E. Butler," *Science-Fiction Studies* 23, no. 3 (November 1996): 336.

4. Ibid.

5. John Edgar Wideman, "Dead Black Men and Other Fallout from the American Dream," *Esquire,* September 1992, 152, 156. Mike Davis, *City of Quartz* (New York: Vintage, 1990), chap. 4.

6. David Harvey, *The Urban Experience* (Baltimore: Johns Hopkins University Press, 1989), 43. Also see Sharon Zukin, *Landscapes of Power* (Berkeley: University of California Press, 1991); and Margaret Crawford, "The World in a Shopping Mall," in *Variations on a Theme Park: The New American City and the End of Public Space,* ed. Michael Sorkin (New York: Hill and Wang, 1992), 3–30.

My account of the increased privatization of urban development in the last three decades is drawn from the following sources: Norman I. Fainstein and Susan S. Fainstein, "Restructuring the American City: A Comparative Perspective," in *Urban Policy under Capitalism,* ed. Norman I. Fainstein and Susan S. Fainstein (Beverly Hills, Calif.: Sage, 1982), 161–89; Ray Forest, "The Privatization of Collective Consumption," in *Urban Life in Transition,* ed. M. Gottdiener and Chris G. Pickvance (Newbury Park, Calif.: Sage, 1991), 169–95; Paul L. Knox, "Capital, Material Culture and Socio-Spatial Differentiation," in *The Restless Urban Landscape,* ed. Paul L. Knox (Englewood Cliffs, N.J.: Prentice-Hall, 1993), 1–34; Gregory D. Squires, "Partnership and the Pursuit of the Private City," in Gottdiener and Pickvance, *Urban Life in Transition,* 196–221; Gregory D. Squires, ed., *Unequal Partnerships: The Political Economy of Urban Redevelopment in Postwar America* (New Brunswick, N.J.: Rutgers University Press, 1989); William K. Tabb, "The Failures of National Urban Policy," in *Marxism and the Metropolis: New Perspectives on Urban Political Economy,* ed. William K. Tabb and Larry Sawers (New York: Oxford University Press, 1984), 255–69; Donald Tomaskovic-Devey and S. M. Miller, "Recapitalization: The Basic U.S. Urban Policy of the 1980s," in Fainstein and Fainstein, *Urban Policy under Capitalism,* 23–42.

7. For critiques of the growth ideology that has sponsored recent urban development, see Rosalyn Deutsche, "Uneven Development: Public Art in New York City," *October* 47 (winter 1998): 3–52; Gregory D. Squires, "Public–Private Partnerships: Who Gets What and Why," in Squires, *Unequal Partnerships,* 1–11; and Tomaskovic-Devey and Miller, "Recapitalization," 25.

8. John Edgar Wideman, *Philadelphia Fire* (New York: Vintage, 1990), 46; hereafter cited parenthetically.

9. On urban redevelopment in Philadelphia, see David W. Bartelt, "Renewing Center City Philadelphia: Whose City? Which Public's Interests?" in Squires, *Unequal Partnerships,* 80–102; Robert A. Beauregard, "The Turbulence of Housing Markets: Investment, Disinvestment and Reinvestment in Philadelphia, 1963–86," in Knox, *Restless Urban Landscape,* 55–82; Robert A. Beauregard, "The Spatial Transformation of Postwar Philadelphia," in *Atop the Urban Hierarchy,* ed. Robert A. Beauregard (Totowa, N.J.: Rowman and Littlefield, 1989), 195–23; Nancy Kleniewski, "From Industrial to Corporate City: The Role of Urban Renewal," in Tabb and Sawers, *Marxism and the Metropolis,* 205–22; James F. Richardson, "The Evolving Dynamics of American Urban Development," in *Cities in the 21st Century,* ed. Gary Gappert and Richard V. Knight (Beverly Hills, Calif.: Sage, 1982), 37–46; and Neil Smith, *The New Urban Frontier: Gentrification and the Revanchist City* (London and New York: Routledge, 1996), chap. 6.

For accounts of how national patterns of urban development have displaced poor and racial minority groups, exacerbated racial segregation, and heightened class and racial polarization, see David Bartelt, "Housing the Underclass," in *The "Underclass" Debate: Views from History,* ed. Michael B. Katz (Princeton: Princeton University Press, 1993), 118–57; Robert D. Bullard and Joe R. Feagin, "Racism and the City," in Gottdiener and Pickvance, *Urban Life in Transition,* 55–76; Norman I. Fainstein, "Black Ghettoization and Social Mobility," in *The Bubbling Cauldron: Race, Ethnicity, and the Urban Crisis,* ed. Michael Peter Smith and Joe R. Feagin (Minneapolis: Minnesota University Press, 1995), 123–41; Fainstein and Fainstein, "Restructuring the American City," 161–89; Dennis R. Judd, "Symbolic Politics and Urban Policies: Why African Americans Got So Little from the Democrats," in *Without Justice for All,* ed. Adolph Reed Jr. (Boulder: Westview Press, 1999), 123–50; John R. Logan and Harvey L. Molotch, *Urban Fortunes: The Political Economy of Place* (Berkeley: University of California Press, 1987), chap. 4; Andrew Mair, "The Homeless and the Post-Industrial City," *Political*

Geography Quarterly 5, no. 4 (October 1986): 351–68; Douglas Massey and Nancy Denton, *American Apartheid: Segregation and the Making of the Underclass* (Cambridge: Harvard University Press, 1993), 56–57; Gregory D. Squires, *Capital and Communities in Black and White* (Albany: SUNY Press, 1994), chap. 5; Gregory R. Weiher, *The Fractured Metropolis: Political Fragmentation and Metropolitan Segregation* (Albany: SUNY Press, 1991); and Peter Williams and Neil Smith, "From 'Renaissance' to Restructuring: The Dynamics of Contemporary Urban Development," in *Gentrification of the City*, ed. Neil Smith and Peter Williams (Boston: Allen and Unwin, 1986), 204–24.

10. On uneven urban development in Manhattan, see M. Christine Boyer, "The City of Illusion: New York's Public Places," in Knox, *Restless Urban Landscape*, 111–26; Deutsche, "Uneven Development"; Norman I. Fainstein and Susan S. Fainstein, "New York City: The Manhattan Business District, 1945–88," in Squires, *Unequal Partnerships*, 59–79; and Peter Marcuse, "Abandonment, Gentrification, and Displacement: The Linkages in New York City," in Smith and Williams, *Gentrification of the City*, 153–77.

11. The quoted phrase is from an official of the Downtown–Lower Manhattan Association, sponsored by David Rockefeller (cited in Fainstein and Fainstein, "Manhattan Business District," 65).

12. Smith, *New Urban Frontier*, 143. The gentrification of Harlem is well under way at the beginning of the twenty-first century.

13. Peter Langer, "Four Images of Organized Diversity: Bazaar, Jungle, Organism, and Machine," in *Cities of the Mind*, ed. Lloyd Rodwin and Robert M. Hollister (New York: Plenum, 1984), states that the marketplace metaphor imagines the city "as a place of astonishing richness of activity and diversity unparalleled in rural areas . . . , a place of almost infinite exploration and opportunity, a center of exchange" (100). Also on market images of the city, see Michael A. Hindery and Thomas A. Reiner, "City Planning: Images of the Ideal and the Existing City," in Rodwin and Hollister, *Cities of the Mind*, 138.

14. John Edgar Wideman, "The Divisible Man," *Life*, May 1988, 116. In a 1986 address to his alma mater, the University of Pennsylvania, Wideman, after stating, "I don't think progress is a valid notion," went on to repudiate common equations of urbanism with progress. Cited in Chip Brown, "Blood Circle," *Esquire*, August 1989, 132.

15. On the restaurant renaissance of Center City Philadelphia during the 1980s, see Beauregard, "Spatial Transformation of Postwar Philadelphia," 225.

16. On this, see Stuart Ewen, *All-Consuming Images: The Politics of Style in Contemporary Culture* (New York: Basic Books, 1988), 241.

17. Wideman, "Dead Black Men," 156.

18. Harvey, *Urban Experience*, 9, 250.

19. For example, see Boyer, "City of Illusion"; and Deutsche, "Uneven Development."

20. M. Christine Boyer, *CyberCities: Visual Perception in the Age of Electronic Communication* (Princeton: Princeton Architectural Press, 1996), describes those sections of the city that are inhabited by the poor and racial minorities and are regarded as having been left behind by processes of development as "lag-time spaces" (38).

21. Boyer, "City of Illusion," 113; Deusche, "Uneven Development," 4.

22. The phrase is from Harvey, *Urban Experience*, 9.

23. Deutsche, "Uneven Development," 5.

24. Davis, *City of Quartz*, 226.

25. Michael B. Katz, *The Undeserving Poor: From the War on Poverty to the War on Welfare* (New York: Pantheon Books, 1989), 8.

26. Ibid., 216. Charles Murray, *Losing Ground: American Social Policy, 1950–1980* (New York: Basic Books, 1984), fueled such assumptions, arguing that the poverty as well as the allegedly deviant reproductive practices of African-American women were actually being perpetuated by federal aid.

27. Christopher Jencks, "Is the American Underclass Growing?" in *The Urban Underclass*, ed. Christopher Jencks and Paul E. Peterson (Washington, D.C.: Brookings Institution,

1991), 83–93, discusses the term *reproductive underclass.* For critical accounts of the racial and gender implications of recent welfare debates, see Michael K. Brown, "Race in the American Welfare State: The Ambiguities of 'Universalistic' Social Policy since the New Deal," and Mimi Abramovitz and Ann Withorn, "Playing by the Rules: Welfare Reform and the New Authoritarian State," both in Reed, *Without Justice for All,* 93–122 and 151–74, respectively.

28. Brett Williams, "The Great Family Fraud of Postwar America," in Reed, *Without Justice for All,* 65–89. Also see Stephen Steinberg, *Turning Back: The Retreat from Racial Justice in American Thought and Policy* (Boston: Beacon Press, 1995), 130–32.

29. Robin D. G. Kelley describes the "golden age of the ghetto" as a "dominant trope in the popular social-science literature on the so-called underclass." Kelley writes that this trope asserts "the existence (until recently) of a tight-knit, harmonious black community–an age when any elder could beat a misbehaving child, when the black middle class mingled with the poor and offered themselves as 'role models,' when black professionals cared more about their downtrodden race than about their bank accounts." See Kelley, "'We Are Not What We Seem': Rethinking Black Working-Class Opposition in the Jim Crow South," in *The New African-American Urban History,* ed. Kenneth W. Goings and Raymond A. Mohl (Thousand Oaks, Calif.: Sage, 1996), 193.

30. Raymond Williams, *The Country and the City* (London: Oxford University Press, 1973), 54.

31. Ibid., 12, 83.

32. Toni Morrison, "Rootedness: The Ancestor as Foundation," in *Black Women Writers (1950–1980),* ed. Mari Evans (New York: Doubleday, 1984), 339–45; Toni Morrison, "City Limits, Village Values," in *Literature and the Urban Experience,* ed. Michael C. Jaye and Ann Chalmers Watts (New Brunswick, N.J.: Rutgers University Press, 1981), 35–43. See chapter 4 of this volume for a fuller discussion of ancestry and southern tradition.

33. By "village" models of community, I refer not only to the kind of community, based in an imagined and preindustrial rural south, that Toni Morrison evokes in the essays cited in the previous note, but also to Hindery and Reiner's discussion of the village ideal of community, which, "with its connotations of stability, integration and solidarity, self-sufficiency, [and] maintenance of traditional ways," represents "a challenging reaction . . . to the excesses of the industrial city" ("City Planning," 136).

34. Potts, "'We Keep Playing the Same Record,'" 333. For an example of such a critique, see Dorothy Allison, "The Future of Female: Octavia Butler's Mother Lode," in *Reading Black, Reading Feminist,* ed. Henry Louis Gates Jr. (New York: Meridian, 1990), 471–80.

35. bell hooks, *Yearning: Race, Gender, and Cultural Politics* (Boston: South End Press, 1990), 42.

36. In "Dead Black Men," John Wideman explicitly critiques the ways in which notions of home circulate within the underclass debate: referring to "the problem of our cities," Wideman writes that "the very American address to this problem has been to ignore it or label it with words like *underclass* or *homeless.* . . . The very notion of 'home,' containing as it does visions of white picket fences, Dick, Jane, and Spot, Mom and Daddy, trivializes and sentimentalizes the plight of huge segments of the population for whom such homes never have and never will exist. The problem is not that people don't have homes, they have no country, no government willing to claim them, assist them" (156).

37. If many urban community movements over the last few decades have struggled to preserve local stability, it is important to remember, conversely, that the life of the rural poor is often characterized by enforced mobility. See the discussion of the movement and migration of poor black agricultural laborers in the South, as dictated by employment conditions, in Jacqueline Jones, "Southern Diaspora," in Katz, *"Underclass" Debate,* 39–46.

38. Logan and Molotch, *Urban Fortunes,* 35. I am also drawing here on Harvey, *Urban Experience,* 250–55; J. Nicholas Entrikin, *The Betweenness of Place: Towards a Geography of Modernity* (Baltimore: Johns Hopkins University Press, 1991), 31, 41, 57–58, 77–80; Zukin, *Landscapes of Power,* 12–14; and Manuel Castells, *The City and the Grassroots* (Berkeley: University of California Press, 1983), 308.

39. Diane McKinney-Whetstone, *Tumbling* (New York: Simon and Schuster, 1996), 340. I thank Sandra Richards for bringing this novel to my attention.

40. In each of these respects, the Earthseed community resembles the "ecotopias" that Krishan Kumar discusses in *Utopia and Anti-Utopia in Modern Times* (New York: Blackwell, 1987). Kumar writes that the literary ecotopias that burgeoned during and after the 1960s present small, self-governing, cooperative communities that, out of their ecological concern for diminishing natural resources, advocate modest levels of economic growth and consumption (406–9).

41. I am drawing here on Ruth Levitas's discussion of Arcadian resolutions to the problem of human needs: in Arcadian images of ideal society, "wants do not outstrip satisfactions, not because satisfactions are limitless, but because wants are reduced to a 'natural' level. Arcadia implicitly involves a distinction between true and false needs and abolishes the scarcity gap by limiting true needs to believable available satisfactions." Levitas, *The Concept of Utopia* (Syracuse: Syracuse University Press, 1990), 162. The Earthseed community in Butler's novel refuses to predetermine true and false needs, in keeping with its dynamic conception of human nature as fundamentally unstable and changeable.

42. I am echoing Fredric Jameson here: "It is . . . the limits, the systemic restrictions and repressions, or empty places, in the Utopian blueprint that are the most interesting, for these alone testify to the ways a culture or system marks the most visionary mind and contains its movement toward transcendence." Jameson, *Postmodernism, or, The Cultural Logic of Late Capitalism* (Durham, N.C.: Duke University Press, 1991), 208.

43. Castells, *City and the Grassroots,* 331.

44. Williams, *Country and the City,* 12.

45. Leo Marx, *The Machine in the Garden* (New York: Oxford University Press, 1964), 23.

46. Hizkias Assefa and Paul Wahrhaftig, *The MOVE Crisis in Philadelphia* (Pittsburgh: University of Pittsburgh Press, 1990), 10–11.

47. Ibid., 11.

48. Marx, *Machine in the Garden,* 65.

49. It is telling and entirely unsurprising that an article on MOVE (by Jim Quinn) in *Philadelphia Magazine* was titled "The Heart of Darkness" (as cited in Assefa and Wahrhaftig, *MOVE Crisis in Philadelphia,* 18).

50. In a 1982 interview, Wideman said, with reference to his Homewood trilogy, that "Family is the metaphor that describes the whole community of Homewood. . . . It goes back to traditional African notions of community." Cited in James W. Coleman, "Going Back Home: The Literary Development of John Edgar Wideman," *CLA Journal* 28, no. 3 (March 1985): 328. Several critics writing on the Homewood trilogy construe family as Wideman's sustaining myth, enabling him to counter the "atomization of individuals caused by the pressures of contemporary urban Afro-American life." Matthew Wilson, "The Circles of History in John Edgar Wideman's *The Homewood Trilogy,*" *CLA Journal* 33, no. 3 (March 1990): 259. However, *Philadelphia Fire* does not share the earlier fiction's portrayal of the family as a bulwark against urban collapse or as a viable metaphor for urban community.

51. MOVE was commonly referred to in the media as an Afrocentric organization, perhaps because all MOVE members adopted the last name "Africa."

52. Marshall McLuhan, *The Gutenberg Galaxy: The Making of Typographic Man* (Toronto: University of Toronto Press, 1962); and Walter J. Ong, *Orality and Literacy: The Technologizing of the Word* (New York: Methuen, 1982).

53. Randall Kenan, "An Interview with Octavia Butler," *Callaloo* 14, no. 2 (spring 1991): 495. Potts, "'We Keep Playing the Same Record,'" 336.

54. John Anderson and Hilary Hevenor, *Burning Down the House: MOVE and the Tragedy of Philadelphia* (New York: Norton, 1987), 4.

55. Michel de Certeau, *The Practice of Everyday Life* (Berkeley: University of California Press, 1984), 167, 169, 174.

56. See Massey and Denton, *American Apartheid,* 59. In "Dead Black Men," Wideman wonders whether the commodity riots in Los Angeles after the Rodney King verdict heralded "the beginning of the end of capitalism" (152).

57. For an extensive discussion of these debates about (postmodern) electronic and (modern) print technologies, see chapter 5.

58. See, for example, Richard Lanham, *The Electronic Word: Democracy, Technology, and the Arts* (Chicago: University of Chicago Press, 1993), 10.

59. On the self-making agency of print literacy, see Sven Birkerts, *The Gutenberg Elegies: The Fate of Reading in an Electronic Age* (New York: Fawcett-Columbine, 1994), 74–92.

60. On the assumption in modern thought that "literacy and progress are identical," see Robert Disch, introduction to *The Future of Literacy,* ed. Robert Disch (Englewood Cliffs, N.J.: Prentice-Hall, 1973), 3.

61. For example, Travis's story of how his mother, a domestic servant, taught him to read and write despite her employer's prohibition of literacy ends with an explicit allusion to slave narratives (196).

62. Jack Goody and Ian Watt, "Literate Culture: Some General Considerations," in Disch, *Future of Literacy,* 52.

63. John Edgar Wideman, *Brothers and Keepers* (New York: Penguin, 1984), 27.

64. Charles Rowell, "An Interview with John Edgar Wideman," *Callaloo* 13, no. 1 (1990): 51, 52.

65. The quoted phrase is from R. Z. Sheppard, review of *Philadelphia Fire, Time,* October 1, 1990, 90.

66. Charles Scruggs, *Sweet Home: Invisible Cities in the Afro-American Novel* (Baltimore: Johns Hopkins University Press, 1993), 26–31.

67. See Rene Wellek, "The Attack on Literature," in Disch, *Future of Literacy,* 127–39.

68. Louis Kampf, "The Humanities and Inhumanities," in Disch, *Future of Literacy,* 121.

69. Antonin Artaud, "No More Masterpieces" (1958), reprinted in Disch, *Future of Literacy,* 110.

70. Disch, introduction to *Future of Literacy,* 7.

71. I quote Wideman, preface to *The Homewood Trilogy* (New York: Avon, 1985), vii.

72. Carla Hesse, "Books in Time," in *The Future of the Book,* ed. Geoffrey Nunberg (Berkeley: University of California Press, 1996), 32.

73. Lanham, *Electronic Word,* 38.

74. This activist academic ideal is articulated in the essays collected in John Blassingame, ed., *New Perspectives on Black Studies* (Urbana: University of Illinois Press, 1971), and reaffirmed in Houston Baker Jr.'s retrospective account of early black studies programs: "Both formally and informally Black Studies forged a connection between everyday black urban life and traditionally disinterested academic provinces." Baker, *Black Studies, Rap, and the Academy* (Chicago: University of Chicago Press, 1993), 23.

75. Rowell, "Interview with John Edgar Wideman," 53, 57, 54.

76. Ibid., 54.

77. Jack Kroll, review of *Philadelphia Fire, Time,* October 1, 1990, 67; Darryl Pinckney, review of *Philadelphia Fire, Times Literary Supplement,* August 23, 1991, 19.

78. Jan Clausen, "Native Fathers," *Kenyon Review* 14, no. 2 (spring 1992): 50.

79. The quote is from Darryl Pinckney's review of *Philadelphia Fire,* 19.

80. H. Jerome Jackson, "Sci-Fi Tales from Octavia Butler," *Crisis,* April 1994, 4.

81. Disch, introduction to *Future of Literacy,* 3.

82. Ong, *Orality and Literacy,* 2, 135. Modernist anxieties about the erosion of print culture in the electronic era are voiced in Birkerts, *Gutenberg Elegies.*

Chapter Three

1. Samuel R. Delany, *Neveryóna, or: The Tale of Signs and Cities* (Hanover, N.H.: Wesleyan University Press, 1993), 38, 280.

2. Throughout this chapter I use the term *spectacle* in Guy Debord's sense, as shorthand for the system of visuality, governed by the principles of commodity fetishism, characteristic of advanced capitalist societies. Debord, *The Society of the Spectacle* (Detroit: Black and Red, 1983).

3. The quotation is from Jean-Louis Comolli, "Machines of the Visible," in *The Cinematic Apparatus,* ed. Teresa de Lauretis and Stephen Heath (New York: St. Martin's Press, 1980).

4. Toni Morrison, *Jazz* (New York: Knopf, 1992), 3; hereafter cited parenthetically.

5. Michele Wallace, "Modernism, Postmodernism, and the Problem of the Visual in Afro-American Culture," in *Aesthetics in Feminist Perspective,* ed. Hilde Hein and Carolyn Korsmeyer (Bloomington: Indiana University Press, 1993), 207, 210–11.

6. Carlene Polite, *Sister X and the Victims of Foul Play* (New York: Farrar, Straus and Giroux, 1975), 72, 77; hereafter cited parenthetically. Debord's work is explicitly invoked in the novel, through statements such as "It is evident historically that this is [a] . . . 'merchandise and spectacle' society" (73).

7. Houston A. Baker Jr., "Scene . . . Not Heard," in *Reading Rodney King/Reading Urban Uprising,* ed. Robert Gooding-Williams (New York: Routledge, 1993), 44; hereafter cited parenthetically.

8. On this issue, also see Elizabeth Alexander, "'Can You Be Black and Look at This?': Reading the Rodney King Video," in *The Black Public Sphere,* ed. Black Public Sphere Collective (Chicago: University of Chicago Press, 1995), 81–98. Like Baker, Alexander suggests that by restoring hearing to the act of witnessing, we can supplement the visual evidence contained in the Halliday videotape. But Alexander treats visual media more complexly than does Baker. Even if viewing the "all-too-visible texts at hand of spectacular . . . violence" (85) is "unbearable," it is nevertheless necessary, in "the absence of first-person witnessing," to view these texts as sources of knowledge about the forces threatening African-American bodies (89). Alexander also provides an important qualification to the common argument that visual media necessarily disable community when she writes that "while black men are contained when these [violent] images are made public, black viewers are taking in evidence that provides ground for collective identification" (94).

9. Paul Gilroy, "'After the Love Has Gone': Bio-Politics and Etho-Poetics in the Black Public Sphere," in Black Public Sphere Collective, *Black Public Sphere,* 59; hereafter cited parenthetically.

10. Judith Butler, "Endangered/Endangering: Schematic Racism and White Paranoia," in Gooding-Williams, *Reading Rodney King,* 16.

11. On this peculiar marking of the black body in visual regimes of racial representation, see Isaac Julien and Kobena Mercer, "Introduction: De Margin and De Centre," *Screen* 29, no. 4 (1988): 32; Richard Dyer, "White," *Screen* 29, no. 4 (1988): 20; and Victor Burgin, "Paranoiac Space," in *Visualizing Theory,* ed. Lucien Taylor (New York: Routledge, 1994), 237.

12. Guy Debord, cited in Chris Jenks, "Watching Your Step: The History and Practice of the Flaneur," in *Visual Culture,* ed. Chris Jenks (New York: Routledge, 1995), 155.

13. I also draw here on Hal Foster's distinction between "vision" (which connotes the physical operation of sight) and "visuality" (which refers to sight as a social fact). Foster, preface to *Vision and Visuality,* ed. Hal Foster (Seattle: Bay Press, 1988), ix.

14. Debord, *Society of the Spectacle,* 18; hereafter cited parenthetically.

15. On the increasing significance of sign exchange value to capitalist commodity consumption, see Manuel Castells, afterword to *The Urban Question* (Cambridge: MIT Press, 1989); Stuart Ewen, *All Consuming Images* (New York: Harper Collins, 1988); Wolfgang Fritz Haug, *Critique of Commodity Aesthetics,* trans. Robert Bock (Minneapolis: University of Minnesota Press, 1986); and Martyn J. Lee, *Consumer Culture Reborn* (New York: Routledge, 1993).

16. Hal Foster, *Recodings: Art, Spectacle, Cultural Politics* (Seattle: Bay Press, 1985), 92.

17. Ibid., 167.

18. Jacques Attali, cited ibid., 171.

19. David Harvey, *The Urban Experience* (Baltimore: Johns Hopkins University Press, 1989), 40. Also see Castells, afterword to *Urban Question.*

20. Sharon Zukin, *Landscapes of Power* (Berkeley: University of California Press, 1991), 219.

21. Michael Keith and Malcolm Cross, "Racism and the Postmodern City," in *Racism, the City and the State,* ed. Malcolm Cross and Michael Keith (New York: Routledge, 1993), 8–9.

22. Harvey, *Urban Experience,* 43.

23. Mike Davis, *City of Quartz* (New York: Vintage, 1992), 230.

24. The essays collected in David B. Downing and Susan Bazargan, eds.,*Image and Ideology in Modern/Postmodern Discourse* (Albany: SUNY Press, 1991), interrogate this kind of polarization between modern and postmodern regimes of visuality. Although urban form is not a central concern of this volume, it resonates with my argument here, questioning the claim that postmodern visuality achieves a "fracturing, dispersal, and dissemination" of a rigid modern order (14).

25. William Sharpe and Leonard Wallock, "From 'Great Town' to 'Nonplace Urban Realm': Reading the Modern City," in *Visions of the Modern City,* ed. William Sharpe and Leonard Wallock (New York: Proceedings of the Heyman Center for the Humanities, Columbia University, 1983), 7–46; hereafter cited parenthetically.

26. On this, see Michael Sorkin, "Introduction: Variations on a Theme Park," and Trevor Boddy, "Underground and Overhead: Building the Analogous City," both included in *Variations on a Theme Park: The New American City and the End of Public Space,* ed. Michael Sorkin (New York: Hill and Wang, 1992), xi–xv, and 123–53, respectively.

27. Edward Soja's analysis of the "postmodern geography" of Los Angeles is a valuable exception to this tendency. After arguing that the diffused and decentralized geography of the city is postmodern in that it obscures visible nodes of power and resists totalized apprehension, Soja goes on to qualify this account: "Yet the centres hold. Even as some things fall apart, dissipate, new nodalities form and old ones are reinforced. The specifying centrifuge is always spinning but the centripetal force of nodality never disappears. And it is the persistent residual of political power which continues to precipitate, specify, and contextualize the urban, making it all stick together." Soja, *Postmodern Geographies: The Reassertion of Space in Critical Social Theory* (New York: Verso, 1989), 234.

28. The most influential of such accounts is Fredric Jameson, *Postmodernism, or, The Cultural Logic of Late Capitalism* (Durham, N.C.: Duke University Press. 1991), chap. 1.

29. Davis, *City of Quartz,* 231; hereafter cited parenthetically.

30. Michel Foucault, *Discipline and Punish: The Birth of the Prison,* trans. Alan Sheridan (New York: Random House, 1979).

31. John Tagg, *The Burden of Representation: Essays on Photographies and Histories* (Minneapolis: University of Minnesota Press, 1988), 76.

32. Thomas Dumm, "The New Enclosures: Racism in the Normalized Community," in Gooding-Williams, *Reading Rodney King,* 186; hereafter cited parenthetically.

33. Davis,*City of Quartz,* 251.

34. The quoted phrase is from Dumm, "New Enclosures," 182.

35. Margaret Weir, "From Equal Opportunity to 'The New Social Contract': Race and the Politics of the American 'Underclass,'" in Cross and Keith, *Racism, the City and the State,* 105. Weir's account is reinforced by Mike Davis's discussion of the repressive intents and consequences of contemporary political discourses on urban poverty. Like Weir, Davis highlights the moral panic aroused by the 1960s urban revolts, in fact describing the hardening visual semiotics and spatial divisions of contemporary U.S. cities as features of "a design backlash against the urban insurrections of the 1960s" (*City of Quartz,* 238). In the specific case of Los Angeles, Davis writes that "In the wake of the Watts rebellion, and perceived Black threat to crucial nodes of white power (spelled out in lurid detail in the McCone Commission Report), resegregated spatial security became the paramount concern" (230).

36. Robert Gooding-Williams, "Look, A Negro!" in Gooding-Williams, *Reading Rodney King*, 167.

37. Toni Morrison, "Introduction: Friday on the Potomac," in *Race-ing Justice, Engendering Power*, ed. Toni Morrison (New York: Pantheon, 1992), xvii; hereafter cited parenthetically.

38. Martin Jay, "Scopic Regimes of Modernity," in Foster, *Vision and Visuality*, 3–23.

39. This summary critique of the modern scopic regime is distilled from the following sources: Jay, "Scopic Regimes of Modernity"; Rosalind Krauss, "The Im/Pulse to See," in Foster, *Vision and Visuality*, 51–75; Chris Jenks, "The Centrality of the Eye in Western Culture," and Don Slater, "Photography and Modern Vision," both included in Jenks, *Visual Culture*, 1–25 and 218–37, respectively. For discussions of the instrumentality of modern ideologies and technologies of vision to urban surveillance and discipline, see Foucault, *Discipline and Punish*; Tagg, *Burden of Representation*; James Donald, "The City, the Cinema: Modern Spaces," in Jenks, *Visual Culture*, 77–95; Nancy Armstrong, "City Things: Photography and the Urbanization Process," in *Human, All Too Human*, ed. Diana Fuss (New York: Routledge, 1996), 93–130; and Paul Virilio, *The Vision Machine*, trans. Julie Rose (Bloomington: Indiana University Press, 1994). To speak of a singular "scopic regime of modernity" is, of course, a reduction useful for polemical purposes. For complex accounts of contradictions, internal ruptures, and divergent currents within the generalized category of "modern vision," see Jay, "Scopic Regimes of Modernity" (an essay that traces three competing modern visual regimes—Cartesian perspectivalism, the Dutch art of describing, and baroque vision); and Jonathan Crary, "Modernizing Vision," in Foster, *Vision and Visuality*, 29–44, which unsettles common notions of a continuous and coherent modern Western visual tradition by arguing for a shift, in the early nineteenth century, from a paradigm of vision based on the principles of the camera obscura—the paradigm of Cartesian perspectivalism—to a more subjective and embedded notion of vision based on new optical-nerve theories.

40. Kevin MacDonnell, *Eadweard Muybridge: The Man Who Invented the Moving Picture* (Boston: Little, Brown, 1972), 25.

41. Robert Bartlett Haas, *Muybridge: Man in Motion* (Berkeley: University of California Press, 1976), 116.

42. Muybridge and the anonymous reviewer in *The Nation* are both cited ibid., 156–57.

43. Slater, "Photography and Modern Vision," citing Fox Talbot's title for the first book of photography, *The Pencil of Nature*, states that "photography is the epitome of positivist representation, of the correspondence of sign to referent, because *nature represents itself*. . . . Photography is thus modern vision in every sense, but above all in its alliance to the modern epistemology of vision through its realism" (223).

44. Roland Barthes, *Camera Lucida*, trans. Richard Howard (New York: Hill and Wang, 1981), 89; hereafter cited parenthetically.

45. Susan Sontag, *On Photography* (New York: Doubleday, 1977), 158, 154; hereafter cited parenthetically.

46. For the best-known articulation of this position, see Jean Baudrillard, *Simulations*, trans. Paul Foss, Paul Patton, and Philip Bertchman (New York: Semiotexte, 1983).

47. Kimberle Crenshaw and Gary Peller, "Reel Time/Real Justice," in Gooding-Williams, *Reading Rodney King*, 56–70.

48. Butler, "Endangered/Endangering," 40.

49. John Edgar Wideman, *Reuben* (New York: Penguin, 1987), 16; hereafter cited parenthetically.

50. John Berger, *Ways of Seeing* (New York: Penguin, 1972), 16–18. In "Machines of the Visible," Comolli makes the similar point that "The photograph stands as at once the triumph and the grave of the eye. There is a violent decentering of the place of mastery in which since the Renaissance the look had come to reign"; as the mechanical eye of the camera sees more as well as more surely, "the human eye finds itself affected with a series of limits and doubts" (123).

51. Jenks, "Centrality of the Eye in Western Culture," 3–4.

52. Sontag, *On Photography*, 11, 119.

53. Walter Benjamin, "A Small History of Photography," in *One-Way Street and Other Writings*, trans. Edmund Jephcott and Kingsley Shorter (London: Verso, 1979), 250; and Benjamin, "The Work of Art in the Age of Mechanical Reproduction," in *Illuminations*, trans. Harry Zohn (New York: Schocken Books, 1968), 217–51.

54. John Berger, *About Looking* (New York: Vintage, 1980), 52.

55. I quote Walter Benjamin, from "Theses on the Philosophy of History," in *Illuminations*, 261.

56. Tagg, *Burden of Representation*, 87.

57. Davis, *City of Quartz*, 228.

58. In Berger's famous summary of the gendered structure of the subject-object dichotomy of modern vision, "Men look at women. Women watch themselves being looked at. This determines not only most relations between men and women but also the relation of women to themselves. The surveyor of woman in herself is male: the surveyed female. Thus she turns herself into an object—and most particularly an object of vision: a sight" (*Ways of Seeing*, 47).

59. For example, see bell hooks, *Black Looks: Race and Representation* (Boston: South End Press, 1992), 62–65; Michele Wallace, "Afterword: 'Why Are There No Great Black Artists': The Problem of Visuality in African-American Culture," in *Black Popular Culture*, ed. Gina Dent (Seattle: Bay Press, 1992), 342; and Jacquie Jones, "The Accusatory Space," in Dent, *Black Popular Culture*, 97.

60. Madison Smartt Bell, review of *Reuben*, *North American Review*, June 1988, 60.

61. Jones, "Accusatory Space," 97.

62. For example, see Michael Awkward, *Inspiriting Influences: Tradition, Revision, and Afro-American Women's Novels* (New York: Columbia University Press, 1989); Keith Byerman, *Fingering the Jagged Grain* (Athens: University of Georgia Press, 1985); and John Callahan, *In the African-American Grain: The Pursuit of Voice* (Urbana: University of Illinois Press, 1988).

63. Klaus Schmidt persuasively argues that in *Reuben*, Wideman obtrusively makes use of techniques derived from photography and cinema in order to "dis-illusion" readers and to stress the artificiality and constructedness of the narrative reality as well as of the fictional community presented in the novel. See Schmidt, "Reading Black Postmodernism: John Edgar Wideman's *Reuben*," in *Flip Sides: New Critical Essays on American Literature*, ed. Klaus Schmidt (Frankfurt: Peter Lang, 1995), 91–94.

64. Haas, *Muybridge*, 148.

65. Linda Williams, *Hard Core: Power, Pleasure, and the "Frenzy of the Visible"* (Berkeley: University of California Press, 1989), 40; hereafter cited parenthetically.

66. Annette Kuhn, *The Power of the Image: Essays on Representation and Sexuality* (London: Routledge, 1985), 33–34, 40.

67. John Edgar Wideman, *Philadelphia Fire* (New York: Vintage, 1990), 27; hereafter cited parenthetically.

68. Sontag, *On Photography*, 9. Also see Kuhn, *Power of the Image*, 30–31.

69. Haug, *Critique of Commodity Aesthetics*, 55–56.

70. Luce Irigaray, "Women on the Market," in *This Sex Which Is Not One*, trans. Catherine Porter (Ithaca, N.Y.: Cornell University Press, 1985), 175; hereafter cited parenthetically.

71. I am drawing on Laura Mulvey's argument in "Visual Pleasure and Narrative Cinema" (1975), reprinted in Mulvey, *Visual and Other Pleasures* (Bloomington: Indiana University Press, 1989), that fetishistic scopophilia retards narrative. But I do not subscribe to Mulvey's argument that voyeurism, in contrast to fetishism, necessarily incites narrative, or to her stark distinction between voyeurism and fetishism (21–22). As *Philadelphia Fire* illustrates, voyeuristic observation can be fetishistic and can stall the linear flow of the narrative.

72. For a fuller discussion of the novel's treatment of the MOVE crisis, see chapter 2.

73. Elizabeth Wilson, *The Sphinx in the City: Urban Life, the Control of Disorder, and Women* (Berkeley: University of California Press, 1991), 6–7.

74. Guy Debord, cited in Jenks, "Watching Your Step," 155.

75. Jan Clausen, "Native Fathers," *Kenyon Review* 14, no. 2 (1992): 44–55, writes that the temporal medium of *Philadelphia Fire* is "*thick*" time, palpable time, not the slippery cinematic present" (49). Robert Morace, too, argues that the narrative style and structure of *Philadelphia Fire* resist the visual media's "politics of forgetting" and instead make us see the MOVE event as "a node in a network, as part of a web of relations." See Morace, "The Facts in Black and White: Cheever's *The Falconer* and Wideman's *Philadelphia Fire*," in *Powerless Fictions? Ethics, Cultural Critique, and American Fiction in the Age of Postmodernism*, ed. Ricardo Miguel Alfonso (Atlanta: Rodopi, 1996), 106–7. But *Philadelphia Fire* is structured by what Neil Postman describes as the "this . . . now this" mode of the electronic visual media; Postman, *Amusing Ourselves to Death* (New York: Penguin, 1985), chap. 7. Morace is correct in arguing that the novel's slow and difficult pace works to counter the speed and instantaneity of visual electronic media. However, through its choppy and discontinuous structure and its failure to achieve a synthetic, totalized historical vision, the novel underscores the extent to which contemporary urban writing has been invaded by visual media.

76. For example, see Berger, *About Looking*, 65; Sontag, *On Photography*, 23; Postman, *Amusing Ourselves to Death*, chap. 7; and Sven Birkerts, *The Gutenberg Elegies* (New York: Fawcett Columbine, 1994), 137–38.

77. In a review of *Reuben* in the *Times Literary Supplement* (August 5, 1988), Richard Gibson criticized the novel for its lack of social realism: "Although Wideman writes about a black ghetto, he is not a social realist. Precise description is missing from his work. . . . Wideman may be criticized for telling us little that is new about the black urban scene" (857). A passage in *Philadelphia Fire* appears to ironize, through indirect citation, precisely such demands for social realism, which, Gibson implies, is the most suitable form for black urban fiction: "What we need is realism, the naturalistic panorama of a cityscape unfolding. Demographics, statistics, objectivity. Perhaps a view of the city from on high, the fish-eye lens catching everything within its distortion, skyscraper heads together, rising like sucked up through a straw" (157). The image of the fish-eye lens here, in keeping with Wideman's overall critique of the "realist" claims of visual representational media, suggests that even the most seemingly transparent media are not free of distortion.

78. Jenks, in "Watching Your Step," writes: "The spectacle is that which constitutes the visual convention and fixity of contemporary imagery. It is a reactionary force in that it resists interpretation. It is a prior appropriation of the visual into the acceptably viewable, and this 'acceptability' befits the going order. The spectacle indicates rules of what to see and how to see it, it is the 'seenness,' the (re)presentational aspect of phenomena that are promoted, not the politics or aesthetics of their being 'see-worthy'" (155).

79. Toni Morrison, "The Official Story: Dead Man Golfing," in *Birth of a Nation'hood: Gaze, Script, and Spectacle in the O. J. Simpson Case*, ed. Toni Morrison and Claudia Brodsky Lacour (New York: Pantheon, 1977), xvii; hereafter cited parenthetically.

80. Alain Locke, "The New Negro," in *The New Negro*, ed. Alain Locke (1925; reprint, New York: Atheneum, 1992), 6.

81. Cary D. Wintz, *Black Culture and the Harlem Renaissance* (Houston: Rice University Press, 1988), 13. Also see David Levering Lewis, *When Harlem Was in Vogue* (New York: Oxford University Press, 1981), chap. 1.

82. Hazel Carby, "Policing the Black Woman's Body in an Urban Context," *Critical Inquiry* 18 (summer 1992): 739, discusses the "moral panic" characterizing public discourses about urban black female sexuality that emerged during the 1920s.

83. Neil Leonard, *Jazz and the White Americans* (Chicago: University of Chicago Press, 1962), 43.

84. For discussions of the intra-racial class conflicts surrounding the urban reception of jazz during the 1920s, see Kathy Ogren, *The Jazz Revolution* (New York: Oxford University

Press, 1989), 114–38; and Burton Peretti, *The Creation of Jazz: Music, Race, and Culture in Urban America* (Urbana: University of Illinois Press, 1992), 58–63.

85. Quoted in Leroy Ostransky, *Jazz City: The Impact of Our Cities on the Development of Jazz* (Englewood Cliffs, N.J.: Prentice-Hall, 1978), 34.

86. See William Barlow's discussion of the effects of commercialization and recording on the sexual content of 1920s blues lyrics, *Looking Up at Down: The Emergence of Blues Culture* (Philadelphia: Temple University Press, 1989), 142. Also see Ann Du Cille's discussion of the commodification of sexuality in classic women's blues, *The Coupling Convention: Sex, Text, and Tradition in Black Women's Fiction* (New York: Oxford University Press, 1993), 66–74.

87. Deborah McDowell, "Harlem Nocturne," *Women's Review of Books* 9, no. 9 (June 1992): 3.

88. On this, see especially John Leonard, review of *Jazz* (1992), reprinted in *Toni Morrison: Critical Perspectives Past and Present,* ed. Henry Louis Gates Jr. and K. A. Appiah (New York: Amistad, 1993), 49.

89. The gender of the novel's narrator is nowhere clearly indicated—and so, my somewhat awkward use of the pronoun *it.*

90. I draw here on Jacqueline Rose's discussion of the precarious mastery assumed in voyeuristic vision. In *Sexuality in the Field of Vision* (New York: Verso, 1982), Rose writes that "The *voyeur* is not ... in a position of pure manipulation of an object, albeit distant, but is always threatened by the potential exteriorisation of his own function" (194).

91. If the modern scopic regime typically assumes a dematerialized field of vision and effaces the observer's embeddedness in a particular time and place, alternatives to modern vision often introduce a "pulse" or "throb" or "beat" into the act of seeing, in an attempt to restore temporality, corporeality, and erotic desire into the visual field. See Krauss, "The Im/Pulse to See," 51–75; and Martin Jay, "The Disenchantment of the Eye: Surrealism and the Crisis of Ocularcentrism," in Taylor, *Visualizing Theory,* 188.

92. Despite the distance this passage establishes between the novelized narrator and the oral storyteller, readers who have become accustomed to the oralized narrators typical of Morrison's fiction are tempted to invest the narrator of *Jazz* with the properties of oral modes of communication such as music and storytelling. For example, Marilyn Sanders Mobley writes that "like the music for which the novel is named," *Jazz* "connects the reader with the narrator, the text with the reader, the call with the response"; Mobley, "The Mellow Moods and Difficult Truths of Toni Morrison," *Southern Review* 29, no. 3 (1993), 623. Also see Dorothea Drummond Mbalia, "Women Who Run with Wild: The Need for Sisterhoods in *Jazz,*" *Modern Fiction Studies* 39, nos. 3/4 (1993): 624; and Eusebio L. Rodrigues, "Experiencing *Jazz,*" *Modern Fiction Studies* 39, nos. 3/4 (1993): 745. Some sections of *Jazz* do bear the distinctive marks of oralized narration that are now so familiar to Morrison's readers, but these are overwritten by the final chapter of the novel, which laments the narrator's inability to activate the communal call-and-response dynamic of black oral forms.

93. Toni Morrison, "Rootedness: The Ancestor as Foundation," in *Black Women Writers (1950–1980),* ed. Mari Evans (New York: Doubleday, 1984), 339–45, explains why, in her opinion, black urban music lost its use value for the community: "For a long time, the art form that was healing for Black people was music. That music is no longer *exclusively* ours; we don't have exclusive rights to it. Other people sing it and play it; it is the mode of contemporary music everywhere" (340). Although this passage refers to the widespread appropriation of "contemporary" black music and does not specify the historical moment at which black music lost its status as an exclusively black cultural form, Morrison's broader purpose in this essay—to sketch the changes in oral tradition and fiction caused by the Great Migration—identifies the early twentieth century as the moment of crisis when black music lost its communal use value and cultural particularity in the process of urbanization and commercialization. In an interview with Angels Carabi published three years after *Jazz,* Morrison specifically mentions the 1920s as a watershed in black cultural history and spells out some of the troubling effects of commercialization of black music in this period: "On one hand, art that is disseminated is good, that's what it's for. But on the other hand is the constant discrediting of the musicians

and their impact: commercially, they made no money.... The white musicians in the States were feeding off of [jazz], claiming it as their own, but the original musicians were unable to get aesthetic and critical acclaim there. I believe the 20's began to be the moment when black culture, rather than American culture, began to alter the whole country and eventually the western world.... So that's why I used the term jazz [in the novel], because it sums all this up." Angels Carabi, "Toni Morrison," *Belles Lettres: A Review of Books by Women* 10, no. 2 (spring 1995): 40.

Chapter Four

1. Hazel Carby, "The Politics of Fiction, Anthropology, and the Folk: Zora Neale Hurston," in *History and Memory in African-American Culture,* ed. Genevieve Fabre and Robert O'Meally (New York: Oxford University Press, 1991), 41.

2. Exactly contrary to Carby, Susan Willis evaluates the southern folk aesthetic in African-American women's fiction as a complex literary device for coming to grips with the social and cultural conflicts wrought by urbanization. In novels by Toni Morrison, Alice Walker, and others, the South functions not as "a purely nostalgic image of the past" but as "a metaphoric memory" that focuses a critique of industrial capitalism. See Willis, "Eruptions of Funk: Historicizing Toni Morrison," *Black Literature and Literary Theory,* ed. Henry Louis Gates Jr. (New York: Methuen, 1984), 264; and Willis, *Specifying: Black Women Writing the American Experience* (Madison: University of Wisconsin Press, 1987), 10.

3. From the epigraph to Samuel R. Delany, *Neveryóna, or: The Tale of Signs and Cities* (Hanover, N.H.: Wesleyan University Press, 1993).

4. For example, see James Weldon Johnson, preface to *The Book of American Negro Poetry,* ed. James Weldon Johnson (1921; reprint, New York: Harcourt Brace Jovanovich, 1969), 41–42.

5. Examples include Toni Cade Bambara's *The Salt Eaters,* Ntozake Shange's *Sassafras, Cypress, and Indigo,* and Alice Walker's *Meridian* and *The Color Purple.*

6. Over the next decade, numerous other works elaborated the turn south in black feminist literary criticism. See Alice Walker, "In Search of Our Mothers' Gardens" (1974), reprinted in Alice Walker, *In Search of Our Mothers' Gardens* (New York: Harcourt, 1984), 231–43; Toni Morrison, "City Limits, Village Values: Concepts of the Neighborhood in Black Fiction," in *Literature and the Urban Experience,* ed. Michael C. Jaye and Ann Chalmers Watts (New Brunswick, N.J.: Rutgers University Press, 1981), 35–43; Toni Morrison, "Rootedness: The Ancestor as Foundation," in *Black Women Writers (1950–1980),* ed. Mari Evans (New York: Doubleday, 1984), 339–45; Barbara Christian, *Black Feminist Criticism* (New York: Pergamon, 1985); and Marjorie Pryse, "Zora Neale Hurston, Alice Walker and the 'Ancient Power' of Black Women," in *Conjuring: Black Women, Fiction, and Literary Tradition,* ed. Marjorie Pryse and Hortense Spillers (Bloomington: Indiana University Press, 1985), 1–24.

7. William C. Havard, "The Distinctive South: Fading or Reviving?" in *Why the South Will Survive,* by Fifteen Southerners (Athens: University of Georgia Press, 1981), 39, 41. African-American journalist Paul Delaney similarly characterizes the southern "heritage of person-to-person relationships" and "aversion to abstractions"; Delaney, "A New South for Blacks?" in *Dixie Dateline: A Journalistic Portrait of the Contemporary South,* ed. John B. Boles (Houston: Rice University Press, 1983), 46.

8. John Shelton Reed, "The Same Old Stand?" in Fifteen Southerners, *Why the South Will Survive,* 21. Also see John Shelton Reed, "New South or No South? Regional Culture in 2036," in *The South Moves into Its Future,* ed. Joseph S. Himes (Tuscaloosa: University of Alabama Press, 1991), 228–31.

9. James C. Cobb, *Industrialization and Southern Society, 1877–1984* (Lexington: University Press of Kentucky, 1984), 67. On industrial development in the South during the 1970s, see James C. Cobb, *The Selling of the South: The Southern Crusade for Industrial Development* (Baton Rouge: Louisiana State University Press, 1982); John D. Kasarda, Holly L. Hughes, and Michael D. Irwin, "Demographic and Economic Restructuring in the South,"

in Himes, *The South Moves into Its Future*, 32–68; and Bernard L. Weinstein and Robert E. Firestine, *Regional Growth and Decline in the United States: The Rise of the Sunbelt and the Decline of the Northeast* (New York: Praeger, 1978).

10. John Egerton, *The Americanization of Dixie: The Southernization of America* (New York: Harper and Row, 1974).

11. On patterns of urbanization in the South since the 1970s, see John B. Boles, *The South through Time: A History of an American Region* (Upper Saddle River, N.J.: Prentice-Hall, 1995), 2:547–49; Robert D. Bullard, "Introduction: Lure of the New South," and "Conclusion: Problems and Prospects," in *In Search of the New South: The Black Urban Experience in the 1970s and 1980s,* ed. Robert D. Bullard (Tuscaloosa: University of Alabama Press, 1989), 1–15 and 161–67; David R. Goldfield, "The City as Southern History: The Past and the Promise of Tomorrow," in *The Future South: A Historical Perspective for the Twenty-First Century,* ed. Joe P. Dunn and Howard L. Preston (Urbana and Chicago: University of Illinois Press, 1991), 31–40; Dewey W. Grantham, *The South in Modern America* (New York: Harper Collins, 1994); Lawrence H. Larsen, *The Urban South: A History* (Lexington: University Press of Kentucky, 1990), 140–59; Randall M. Miller, "The Development of the Modern Urban South: An Historical Overview," in *Shades of the Sunbelt: Essays on Ethnicity, Race, and the Urban South,* ed. Randall M. Miller and George E. Pozzetta (New York and Westport, Conn.: Greenwood Press, 1988), 1–20; and Neal R. Peirce, "The Southern City Today," in Boles, *Dixie Dateline,* 100–101.

12. Egerton, *Americanization of Dixie,* 73, xx, xxi, 109.

13. For example, see Grantham, *South in Modern America,* 262; and Fred Hobson, "A South Too Busy to Hate?" in Fifteen Southerners, *Why the South Will Survive,* 46.

14. Immanuel Wallerstein, "What Can One Mean by Southern Culture?" in *The Evolution of Southern Culture,* ed. Numan V. Bartley (Athens: University of Georgia Press, 1988), 12, 11. On the strengthening of claims to southern cultural distinctiveness just as the South statistically converged with the rest of the nation, also see Boles, *South through Time,* 587; Cobb, *Industrialization and Southern Society,* 143; and Grantham, *South in Modern America,* 194–95.

15. David Harvey, *The Condition of Postmodernity* (Cambridge, Mass.: Blackwell, 1990), esp. pt. 3.

16. Eugene D. Genovese, *The Southern Tradition* (Cambridge: Harvard University Press, 1994), 15; hereafter cited parenthetically.

17. See Cobb, *Selling of the South,* 188.

18. On the multiracial populations of Sunbelt cities that are increasingly tied to a global economic system, see Kasarda, Hughes, and Irwin, "Demographic and Economic Restructuring in the South," 62–67. On the shift in southern political models, see Ronald H. Bayor, "Race, Ethnicity, and Political Change in the Urban Sunbelt South," in Miller and Pozetta, *Shades of the Sunbelt,* 127–42.

19. Howard L. Preston, "Will Dixie Disappear?" in Dunn and Preston, *Future South,* 189.

20. Cobb, *Industrialization and Southern Society,* 112. Also see Cobb, *Selling of the South,* 122–31; and Paul Luebke, "Southern Conservatism and Liberalism: Past and Future," in Himes, *The South Moves into Its Future,* 236–53.

21. On the racialized pattern of uneven development in the South since the 1970s, see Bullard, "Introduction: Lure of the New South," 2, 7–15; Cobb, *Industrialization and Southern Society,* 85–86, 136–40; Thomas A. Lyson, *Two Sides to the Sunbelt* (New York: Praeger, 1989); and Weinstein and Firestine, *Regional Growth and Decline in the United States,* 148–50.

22. Hobson, "A South Too Busy to Hate?" 49.

23. James Alan McPherson, "A Region Not Home: The View from Exile," in *The Prevailing South: Life and Politics in a Changing Region,* ed. Dudley Clendinen (Atlanta: Longstreet Press, 1988), 202.

24. Boles, *South through Time,* 584.

25. Farah Jasmine Griffin, *"Who Set You Flowin'?": The African-American Migration Narrative* (New York: Oxford University Press, 1995), 146. Griffin draws an important distinction between the romanticization of the South in American popular culture and the return to the South in African-American literature. Whereas the first seeks to shore up an old South against the social changes wrought by the Civil Rights movement, the second is made possible by the Civil Rights movement in a different sense. It is only after the transformation of race relations after the Civil Rights period that African-American writers could begin imaginatively redeeming the South. Before this era, Griffin argues, the South is represented in African-American literature primarily as the scene of racial horror, and the migration narrative that predominates is the journey out of the South into the urban North (142–46).

26. See Bullard, "Conclusion: Problems and Prospects," 162; David R. Goldfield, *Black, White, and Southern: Race Relations and Southern Culture 1940 to the Present* (Baton Rouge: Louisiana State University Press, 1990), 221, 244–45; and Preston, "Will Dixie Disappear?" 190.

27. Carol Stack, *Call to Home: African Americans Reclaim the Rural South* (New York: Harper Collins, 1996), xv; hereafter cited parenthetically.

28. Alice Walker, "The Black Writer and the Southern Experience," in *In Search of Our Mothers' Gardens,* 17; hereafter cited parenthetically.

29. I borrow this phrase from the title of Albert Murray's book *South to a Very Old Place* (New York: Vintage, 1971).

30. Toni Morrison, quoted in Charles Ruas, "Toni Morrison" (1981), reprinted in *Conversations with Toni Morrison,* ed. Danille Taylor-Guthrie (Jackson: University of Mississippi Press, 1994), 110.

31. Thomas LeClair, "'The Language Must Not Sweat': A Conversation with Toni Morrison," in *Toni Morrison: Critical Perspectives Past and Present,* ed. Henry Louis Gates Jr. and K. A. Appiah (New York: Amistad, 1993), 370–71.

32. Morrison, "City Limits, Village Values," 38; LeClair, "The Language Must Not Sweat," 370.

33. By 1970, nearly 70 percent of the South's black population resided in cities, compared with 35 percent in 1940 (Goldfield, *Black, White, and Southern,* 203).

34. Houston Baker Jr., *Workings of the Spirit: The Poetics of Afro-American Women's Writing* (Chicago: University of Chicago Press, 1991), 35, 61, 30; hereafter cited parenthetically.

35. Addison Gayle Jr., *The Black Situation* (New York: Horizon Press, 1970), 61.

36. Ibid., 79.

37. Addison Gayle Jr., "Reclaiming the Southern Experience: The Black Aesthetic 10 Years Later," in *Black Southern Voices,* ed. John Oliver Killens and Jerry W. Ward Jr. (New York: Meridian, 1992), 559; hereafter cited parenthetically.

38. John Oliver Killens, introduction to Killens and Ward, *Black Southern Voices,* 3, 4.

39. Kiarri T.-H. Cheatwood, "Fire-Casting an Eternal De-Fascination with Death," *African American Review* (Black South issue, pt. 2) 27, no. 3 (summer 1993): 308, 301.

40. On this, see Yoshinubo Hakutani and Robert Butler, introduction to *The City in African-American Literature,* ed. Yoshinubo Hakutani and Robert Butler (Cranbury, N.J.: Associated University Presses, 1995), 9–11; and Melvin Dixon, *Ride Out the Wilderness: Geography and Identity in Afro-American Literature* (Urbana: University of Illinois Press, 1987), 17.

41. Jacqueline Jones, *The Dispossessed: America's Underclasses from the Civil War to the Present* (New York: Harper Collins, 1992), 278–84.

42. It is important to note here that black women novelists and critics initially took the southern folk turn in order to distance themselves from dominant paradigms of black literary production that privileged the urban North over the rural South. Examples of such paradigms include the Harlem Renaissance, the naturalist era dominated by Richard Wright (who famously derided Zora Neale Hurston's southern folk aesthetic), and the Black Arts movements of the 1960s. Because these paradigms valorized decisively masculine models of

urban culture, black women writers turned South in an attempt to open up a uniquely female cultural space and to establish distinct principles for black women's literary production.

43. Notions of southern cultural distinction that rest on folk traditions entail conservative definitions of women's social roles. Numan Bartley points out that the women's movement in the South wreaked havoc on traditional notions of folk culture and community, which required women to devote themselves to home and family. As increasing numbers of southern women began to abandon these traditional roles and to enter the labor market, they were seen to threaten the folk culture taken to be distinctive of the region. Bartley, *The New South, 1945–1980* (Baton Rouge: Louisiana State University Press, 1995), 468.

44. On the ancestor, see Morrison, "Rootedness" and "City Limits, Village Values." Morrison's conception of the ancestor is extended by Joanne Braxton, "Ancestral Presence: The Outraged Mother Figure in Contemporary Afra-American Writing," in *Wild Women in the Whirlwind: Afra-American Culture and the Contemporary Literary Renaissance,* ed. Joanne Braxton and Andree Nicola McLaughlin (New Brunswick, N.J.: Rutgers University Press, 1990), 299–315; Griffin, *"Who Set You Flowin'?"* 5–6; and Karla Holloway, *Moorings and Metaphors: Figures of Culture and Gender in Black Women's Fiction* (New Brunswick, N.J.: Rutgers University Press, 1992), 116.

45. Willis, "Eruptions of Funk," 271. Charles Scruggs assumes that the city represented in *Song of Solomon* is Detroit and that Morrison does not mention it by name because she "believes that neighborhoods are more real to black people than cities." Scruggs, "The Nature of Desire in Toni Morrison's *Song of Solomon,*" *Arizona Quarterly* 38, no. 4 (1982): 319.

46. Freddie's gossip is the primary source through which members of the Southside community gain information about the personal lives of others; public information (such as news of Emmett Till's murder) is transmitted by word of mouth in Tommy's barbershop.

47. Gloria Naylor, *Mama Day* (New York: Vintage, 1989), 18; hereafter cited parenthetically.

48. A prominent work that invokes this trope and argues that racial segregation in the South enabled the creation and maintenance of black political and cultural communities is Earl Lewis, *In Their Own Interests: Race, Class, and Power in Twentieth-Century Norfolk, Virginia* (Berkeley: University of California Press, 1991).

49. Adolph Reed Jr., "Romancing Jim Crow: Black Nostalgia for a Segregated Past," *Village Voice,* April 16, 1996, 24; hereafter cited parenthetically.

50. In this respect, both novels bear out Mary Mebane's contention that writing about southern blacks is often afflicted with the "problem of stasis." Mebane, "Black Folk of the American South: Two Portraits," in *The American South: Portrait of a Culture,* ed. Louis D. Rubin Jr. (Baton Rouge: Louisiana State University Press, 1980), 87.

51. The quoted phrase is from Willis, *Specifying,* 9.

52. Toni Morrison, *Song of Solomon* (New York: New American Library, 1977), 27; hereafter cited parenthetically.

53. See Willis, *Specifying,* 12–13; and Kimberly W. Benston, "Re-Weaving the 'Ulysses Scene': Enchantment, Post-Oedipal Identity, and the Buried Text of Blackness in Toni Morrison's *Song of Solomon,*" in *Comparative American Identities,* ed. Hortense Spillers (New York: Routledge, 1991), 89.

54. Willis, *Specifying,* 12.

55. A South where this sort of racial community, free of divisive class distinctions, can be recovered must of necessity be a fictional construct. In the South contemporaneous with the writing of Morrison's novel, middle-class blacks made huge gains as they found niches in the growing economy. The rapid expansion of the black middle class is widening the gap between prosperous and poor blacks in the South, and heightening intra-racial class divisions in the South are spawning discourses about the splintering of black community here as in other parts of the nation. See Boles, *South through Time,* 549; Goldfield, *Black, White, and Southern,* 205, 220–21, 254.

56. On the persistence of black rural poverty in the economically resurgent South, see Lyson, *Two Sides to the Sunbelt,* 11, 78, 102; and Jones, *Dispossessed,* 286–88. If, for Morrison,

African-American exclusion from political power is a necessary condition for the cultivation of a unique black cultural tradition, rural areas of the South offer an apt setting for her fiction in this respect as well. As a result of economic dependency and white intimidation, African-Americans in poor areas of the rural South have often been unable to exercise political rights even in the post–Civil Rights era. See Orville Vernon Burton, "Race Relations in the Rural South since 1945," and Wayne Parent and Peter A. Petrakis, "Populism Left and Right: Politics of the Rural South," both in *The Rural South since World War II,* ed. R. Douglas Hurt (Baton Rouge: Louisiana State University Press, 1998), 28–55 and 149–67, respectively. The term *underclass* is used to describe black rural southern populations in Bullard, "Introduction: Lure of the New South," 15; Goldfield, *Black, White, and Southern,* 251–52; Kasarda, Hughes, and Irwin, "Demographic and Economic Restructuring in the South," 62; Lyson, *Two Sides to the Sunbelt,* 4. Kasarda, Hughes, and Irwin observe that although poverty levels in the South have been converging with national levels since the 1970s, "the geographic distribution of poverty in the South remains distinct," concentrated largely in rural areas (60).

57. Jones, *Dispossessed,* 270.

58. For a critical account of the tendency, in postmodern cultural politics, to romanticize residual spaces, see David Harvey, *Justice, Nature, and the Geography of Difference* (Cambridge, Mass.: Blackwell, 1996), 96.

59. On the expansion of consumer industries and markets in the South since the 1970s, see Grantham, *South in Modern America,* 195; and Larsen, *Urban South,* 140–41. Laments about a fast-disappearing, distinctively southern culture often focus on the standardization of consumption patterns. For example, see Hobson on the "malling" of the South ("A South Too Busy to Hate?" 46), or Egerton, for whom a conspicuous sign of the cultural homogenization of the South is that here, as in other parts of the nation, "Consumption is what it's all about" (*Americanization of Dixie,* 214).

60. Cheatwood, "Fire-Casting an Eternal De-Fascination with Death," 312, 309.

61. The phrase is David Harvey's, from *The Urban Experience* (Baltimore: Johns Hopkins University Press, 1985), 43.

62. Ruas, "Toni Morrison," 112.

63. Reed, "Romancing Jim Crow," 24.

64. Some memoirs that commemorate a segregated South are Raymond Andrews, *The Last Radio Baby: A Memoir* (Atlanta: Peachtree, 1990); Henry Louis Gates Jr., *Colored People* (New York: Knopf, 1994); Dorothy Spruill Redford, *Somerset Homecoming: Recovering a Lost Heritage* (New York: Doubleday, 1988); and Clifton L. Taulbert, *Once upon a Time When We Were Colored* (Tulsa, Okla.: Council Oak, 1989). Memoirs revisiting the post–Civil Rights South are Eddy L. Harris, *South of Haunted Dreams* (New York: Simon and Schuster, 1993); and Murray, *South to a Very Old Place.*

65. The quoted phrase is from Paul Gilroy, *The Black Atlantic: Modernity and Double Consciousness* (Cambridge: Harvard University Press, 1993), 36. Also see Wahneema Lubiano, "The Postmodernist Rag: Political Identity and the Vernacular in *Song of Solomon,*" in *New Essays on "Song of Solomon,"* ed. Valerie Smith (New York: Cambridge University Press, 1995), 93–116, for a discussion of how African-American postmodernist fiction, through vernacular modes of apprehending reality, offers an epistemological standpoint for exposing the omissions and limitations of Enlightenment modernism.

66. Ntozake Shange, *Sassafras, Cypress, and Indigo* (New York: St. Martin's Press, 1982), 27, 26.

67. Ibid., 4.

68. Lindsey Tucker, "Recovering the Conjure Woman: Texts and Contexts in Gloria Naylor's *Mama Day," African American Review* 28, no. 2 (1994): 73; Stelamaris Coser, *Bridging the Americas: The Literature of Toni Morrison, Paule Marshall, and Gayl Jones* (Philadelphia: Temple University Press, 1995), 82.

69. Gay Wilentz, *Binding Cultures: Black Women Writers in Africa and the Diaspora* (Bloomington: Indiana University Press, 1992), 96–98.

70. Toni Cade Bambara, *The Salt Eaters* (New York: Vintage, 1981), 246.

71. Morrison, "Rootedness," 342.

72. Gayl Caldwell, "Author Toni Morrison Discusses Her Latest Novel *Beloved*" (1987), reprinted in Taylor-Guthrie, *Conversations with Toni Morrison*, 226–27.

73. Holloway, *Moorings and Metaphors*, 31; hereafter cited parenthetically.

74. Charles Johnson, *Faith and the Good Thing* (New York: Viking, 1974), 16; hereafter cited parenthetically.

75. Pryse, "Zora Neale Hurston, Alice Walker, and the 'Ancient Power' of Black Women."

76. For two-well known discussions of the ways in which print technology isolates and heightens the visual sense, see Marshall McLuhan, *The Gutenberg Galaxy: The Making of Typographic Man* (Toronto: University of Toronto Press, 1962); and Walter J. Ong, *Orality and Literacy: The Technologizing of the Word* (New York: Methuen, 1982).

77. Bambara, *Salt Eaters*, 19.

78. Marilyn Sanders Mobley, "Call and Response: Voice, Community, and Dialogic Structures in Toni Morrison's *Song of Solomon*," in Smith, *New Essays on "Song of Solomon,"* 56–58.

79. Joyce Ann Joyce, *Warriors, Conjurers and Priests: Defining African-Centered Literary Criticism* (Chicago: Third World Press, 1994), 42.

80. Jocelyn Hazelwood Donlon, "Hearing Is Believing: Southern Racial Communities and Strategies of Story-Listening in Gloria Naylor and Lee Smith," *Twentieth Century Literature* 41, no. 4 (spring 1995): 25–27. Gary Storhoff similarly argues that in a "speakerly text" such as *Mama Day*, "the distinction between the writer's authority and the speaker's set of communal values ... is mitigated, if not erased." Storhoff, "'The Only Voice Is Your Own': Gloria Naylor's Revision of *The Tempest*," *African American Review* 29, no. 1 (spring 1995): 35, 36.

81. Holloway's argument that literary texts by black men privilege vision over voice is not supported by textual evidence. Among the texts Holloway cites to substantiate her argument is Jean Toomer's *Cane*, in which, according to Holloway, "insistent visual elements" establish the primacy of the present, as compared to the past, which black women's texts evoke through orality (*Moorings and Metaphors*, 37). But sound and song thoroughly permeate *Cane*, forming the vehicles through which Toomer tries to capture a southern folk culture in the process of disappearing into the past. Barbara Bowen suggestively analyzes the oral/aural elements in *Cane* as crucial to its elegiac depiction of a passing folk mode of cultural authority. Bowen, "Untroubled Voice: Call and Response in *Cane*," in Gates, *Black Literature and Literary Theory*, 187–203.

82. Benston, "Re-Weaving the 'Ulysses Scene,'" 90,100.

83. Joyce Irene Middleton, "From Orality to Literacy: Oral Memory in Toni Morrison's *Song of Solomon*," in Smith, *New Essays on "Song of Solomon,"* 33; hereafter cited parenthetically.

84. Susan Meisenhelder, "'The Whole Picture' in Gloria Naylor's *Mama Day*," *African American Review* 27, no. 3 (1993): 405–19.

85. The quoted phrase is from Linda Krumholz, "Dead Teachers: Rituals of Manhood and Rituals of Reading in *Song of Solomon*," *Modern Fiction Studies* 39, nos. 3/4 (1993): 561. For psychoanalytic accounts of the preoedipal language evoked in the hunt scene, see Marianne Hirsch, "'Knowing Their Names': Toni Morrison's *Song of Solomon*," in Smith, *New Essays on "Song of Solomon,"* 86; Benston, "Re-Weaving the 'Ulysses Scene,'" 94; Deborah Clarke, "'What There Was before Language': Preliteracy in Toni Morrison's *Song of Solomon*," in *Anxious Power: Reading, Writing, and Ambivalence in Narrative by Women*, ed. Carol Singley and Susan Elizabeth Sweeney (Albany: SUNY Press, 1993), 275–76.

86. Sherley Anne Williams, *Dessa Rose* (New York: Berkley Books, 1986), ix.

87. Walter Benjamin, *Illuminations*, trans. Harry Zohn (New York: Schocken Books, 1968), 101.

88. I should note that Morrison includes a counterexample of southern naming in which sign and referent do not match: King Walker "was nothing like his name suggested" (274).

89. The quoted phrases are from *Song of Solomon*, 333.

90. My account of literal and metaphorical modes of reading is indebted to Hirsch's excellent discussion of the tension between literal and symbolic discourse in *Song of Solomon*, in "'Knowing Their Names': Toni Morrison's *Song of Solomon*." Shifting the Lacanian terms of Hirsch's argument, I regard the novel's vacillation between literal and metaphorical modes of reading as symptomatic of its contradictory claims to representing racial community.

91. Morrison, "Rootedness," 339.

92. Caldwell, "Author Toni Morrison Discusses Her Latest Novel *Beloved*," 243.

93. Mel Watkins, "Talk with Toni Morrison" (1977), reprinted in Taylor-Guthrie, *Conversations with Toni Morrison*, 46. Also see Nellie Y. McKay, "An Interview with Toni Morrison," in the same collection, 153.

94. Walker, "Black Writer and the Southern Experience," 17.

95. Toni Morrison, "Memory, Creation, and Writing," *Thought* 59 (December 1984): 388; hereafter cited parenthetically. On Morrison's ambivalence toward literature, specifically as it plays out in *Song of Solomon*, see Jan Stryz, "Inscribing an Origin in *Song of Solomon*," *Studies in American Fiction* 19, no. 1 (spring 1991): 31–40.

96. John Brenkman, "Politics and Form in *Song of Solomon*," *Social Text* 39 (summer 1994): 75. Brenkman's essay is valuable for my purposes in this chapter in that it sharply identifies the various rifts and tensions–between vernacular and literature, magical romance and novel, community and public–that shape Morrison's novel. However, I am unconvinced by the conclusions Brenkman draws about Morrison's treatment of these categories. Brenkman argues that *Song of Solomon* ultimately transposes the magical romance onto a novelistic register (of tragic realism) that serves to disqualify the magical mode. For Brenkman, the supersession of magical romance by the novelistic mode signifies a transition from racial community to the modern public sphere. But it is difficult to see how the conclusion of the novel, with its magical image of surrendering to the air, illustrates a realist overwriting of the magical mode. At best, the ambiguity of this scene suggests that the novel does not resolve the tension between its magical and literary modes. In virtually all of Morrison's novels, the passage from vernacular to literary modes, and from racial community to modern public, is captured in elegiac rather than ironic tones.

97. Toni Morrison, "Introduction: Friday on the Potomac," in *Race-ing Justice, Engendering Power: Essays on Anita Hill, Clarence Thomas, and the Construction of Social Reality*, ed. Toni Morrison (New York: Pantheon, 1992), xii; hereafter cited parenthetically.

98. Among the works that can be taken as illustrative of the New Black Aesthetic movement are Rita Dove, *Through the Ivory Gate* (New York: Vintage, 1992); Gerald Early, ed., *Lure and Loathing: Essays on Race, Identity, and the Ambivalence of Assimilation* (New York: Penguin, 1993); Trey Ellis, "The New Black Aesthetic," *Callaloo* 12, no. 1 (winter 1989): 233–43; and Ellis, *Platitudes* (New York: Vintage, 1998); Nelson George, *Urban Romance* (New York: Putnam's, 1993); Lisa Jones, *Bulletproof Diva* (New York: Doubleday, 1994); Jake Lamar, *Bourgeois Blues* (New York: Penguin, 1992); Itabari Njeri, *Every Good-bye Ain't Gone* (New York: Vintage, 1991); Gayle Pemberton, *The Hottest Water in Chicago: Notes of a Native Daughter* (New York: Doubleday, 1992); Darryl Pinckney, *High Cotton* (New York: Penguin, 1992); and Brent Wade, *Company Man* (Chapel Hill: Algonquin Books, 1992).

99. Greg Tate, "Cult-Nats Meet Freaky-Deke: The Return of the Black Aesthetic" (1986), reprinted in *Flyboy in the Buttermilk* (New York: Simon and Schuster, 1992), 200.

100. Morrison, "Memory, Creation, and Writing," 389.

101. Reginald McKnight, "Confessions of a Wannabe Negro," in Early, *Lure and Loathing*, 107.

102. Pinckney, *High Cotton*, 29, 134.

103. Ellis satirizes those African-Americans who "affect a 'superblackness' and try to dream themselves back to the ghetto" ("New Black Aesthetic," 235; hereafter cited parenthetically).

104. McKnight, "Confessions of a Wannabe Negro," 106.

105. Ellis, "New Black Aesthetic," 235; McKnight, "Confessions of a Wannabe Negro," 103–4.

106. For a more detailed critique of Ellis's manifesto, see Madhu Dubey, "Postmodernism as Postnationalism? Racial Representation in U.S. Black Cultural Studies," *New Formations* 45 (winter 2001–2): 150–68.

Chapter Five

1. M. Christine Boyer uses the term *netropolis* in *CyberCities: Visual Perception in the Age of Electronic Communication* (New York: Princeton Architectural Press, 1996), 18, 228–29. On *teletopia,* see Paul Virilio, "Third Interval: A Critical Transition," in *Rethinking Technologies,* ed. Verena Andermatt Conley (Minneapolis: University of Minnesota Press, 1993), 4; and on *cyburbia,* see Michael Sorkin, introduction to *Variations on a Theme Park: The New American City and the End of Public Space,* ed. Michael Sorkin (New York: Hill and Wang, 1992), xii.

2. On the technological determinism of contemporary debates on print and electronic texts, see Geoffrey Nunberg, introduction to *The Future of the Book,* ed. Geoffrey Nunberg (Berkeley and Los Angeles: University of California Press, 1996), 9; and Ilana Snyder, "Beyond the Hype: Reassessing Hypertext," in *Page to Screen: Taking Literacy into the Electronic Era,* ed. Ilana Snyder (London and New York: Routledge, 1998), 129–31.

3. Paul Duguid uses the term *liberation technology* in "Material Matters: The Past and Future of the Book," in Nunberg, *Future of the Book,* 73.

4. Samuel R. Delany, *Stars in My Pocket Like Grains of Sand* (New York: Bantam, 1984), was published the same year as William Gibson's *Neuromancer* (New York: Ace, 1984), the novel to which we owe the coinage *cyberspace.* All further references to *Stars in My Pocket* are parenthetically cited.

5. Samuel R. Delany, *Silent Interviews* (Hanover, N.H.: Wesleyan University Press, 1994), 171; hereafter cited parenthetically in the text as *SI.*

6. Darko Suvin, "SF and the Novum," in *The Technological Imagination: Theories and Fictions,* ed. Teresa de Lauretis, Andreas Huyssen, and Kathleen Woodward (Madison, Wis.: Coda Press, 1980), 156.

7. This is the argument made by Scott Bukatman, *Terminal Identity: The Virtual Subject in Postmodern Science Fiction* (Durham, N.C.: Duke University Press, 1993).

8. On this, see Nan Ellin, *Postmodern Urbanism* (New York: Blackwell, 1996), 45, 253.

9. Melvin Webber, "Urban Place and Nonplace Urban Realm," in *Explorations into Urban Structure,* ed. Melvin Webber (Philadelphia: University of Pennsylvania Press, 1964).

10. Melvin Webber, "Order in Diversity: Community without Propinquity," in *Cities and Space: The Future Use of Land,* ed. Lowdon Wingo Jr. (Baltimore: Johns Hopkins University Press, 1963), 42.

11. See Edward Soja, "Inside Exopolis: Scenes from Orange County," in Sorkin, *Variations on a Theme Park,* 94–122.

12. Manuel Castells, *The Informational City* (Cambridge, Mass.: Blackwell, 1989), 126–71.

13. Boyer, *CyberCities,* 242. William J. Mitchell offers a rare, level-headed account of the impact of information technologies on urban form, arguing that place-based forms of urbanity are being transformed but not eradicated. See Mitchell, *e-topia* (Cambridge: MIT Press, 1999).

14. For a sharp critique of the pervasive use of spatial metaphors in postmodern social theory, see Michael Keith and Steve Pile, "Introduction Part 1: The Politics of Place," in *Place and the Politics of Identity,* ed. Michael Keith and Steve Pile (London and New York: Routledge, 1993), 1–34.

15. See Ellin, *Postmodern Urbanism,* 55–68.

16. M. Christine Boyer, "Cities for Sale: Merchandising History at South Street Seaport," in Sorkin, *Variations on a Theme Park,* 191.

17. Sorkin, introduction to *Variations on a Theme Park*, xiii–xiv. On the hyperreality of postmodern cities, also see John Hannigan, *Fantasy City: Pleasure and Profit in the Postmodern Metropolis* (New York: Routledge, 1998).

18. Fredric Jameson, "Progress versus Utopia; or, Can We Imagine the Future?" *Science-Fiction Studies* 9, no. 2 (July 1982): 152–53.

19. Guy Debord, *Society of the Spectacle* (Detroit: Black and Red, 1983).

20. Margot Lovejoy, *Postmodern Currents: Art and Artists in the Age of Electronic Media* (Englewood Cliffs, N.J.: Prentice-Hall, 1997), 154–60.

21. Soja, "Inside Exopolis," 121–22.

22. Ibid., 122.

23. Michael Heim, *The Metaphysics of Virtual Reality* (New York: Oxford University Press, 1993), 103; hereafter cited parenthetically.

24. Richard Kearney, *The Wake of Imagination: Toward a Postmodern Culture* (Minneapolis: University of Minnesota Press, 1988), 162, 365.

25. Jacques Derrida, *Of Grammatology,* trans. Gayatri Chakravorty Spivak (Baltimore: Johns Hopkins University Press, 1976), 22. Michael Heim is quite frank about wanting to reinstate embodied presence, and, in fact, he openly announces this in the title of his book, *The Metaphysics of Virtual Reality.*

26. Iris Marion Young, "The Ideal of Community and the Politics of Difference," *Social Theory and Practice* 12, no. 1 (spring 1986): 15.

27. Boyer, *CyberCities,* 229; hereafter cited parenthetically.

28. Gibson, *Neuromancer,* 5.

29. Virilio, "Third Interval," 5, 9.

30. Donna Haraway is the best-known postmodern political theorist who staunchly resists organicism. See Haraway, "A Cyborg Manifesto: Science, Technology, and Socialist-Feminism in the Late Twentieth Century," in *Simians, Cyborgs, and Women: The Reinvention of Nature* (New York: Routledge, 1991), 149–81. But Haraway ends up falling prey to the inverse temptation of technological determinism. In the finest gloss on the Cyborg Manifesto I have encountered, Samuel R. Delany writes that Haraway seems to assume that metaphors are "radical in themselves" and that political critique "simply and uncritically falls out of technology." See Delany, "Reading at Work," in *Longer Views: Extended Essays* (Hanover, N.H.: Wesleyan University Press, 1996), 114.

31. Also see David Crane's analysis of "the connection between blackness and ethical realness" in 1990s films about cyberspace. Crane, *"In Medias* Race: Filmic Representation, Networked Communication, and Racial Intermediation," in *Race in Cyberspace,* ed. Beth E. Kolko, Lisa Nakamura, and Gilbert B. Rodman (New York: Routledge, 2000), 87–115.

32. David Harvey, *Justice, Nature, and the Geography of Difference* (Cambridge, Mass.: Blackwell, 1996), 96.

33. Saskia Sassen makes this point in *The Global City* (Princeton: Princeton University Press, 1991), 19, 330.

34. Ibid., 217–38; Castells, *Informational City,* 187.

35. Castells, *Informational City,* 204–5. Also see Janet L. Abu-Lughod, *New York, Chicago, Los Angeles: America's Global Cities* (Minneapolis: Minnesota University Press, 1999), 293–307.

36. Castells, *Informational City,* 227.

37. My discussion of the structures and processes of the informational city is indebted to David Harvey's formulation of the principles of the dialectical process, *Justice, Nature, and the Geography of Difference,* 48–57.

38. Sassen, *Global City,* 22–34. Also see Saskia Sassen, "Whose City Is It? Globalization and the Formation of New Claims," in *Cities and Citizenship,* ed. James Holston (Durham, N.C.: Duke University Press, 1999), 179–84. On the uneven development of the new technologies, see Andrew Gillespie and Kevin Robins, "Geographical Inequalities: The Spatial

Bias of the New Communications Technologies," in *The Information Gap,* ed. Marsha Seifert, George Gerbner, and Janice Fisher (New York: Oxford University Press, 1989), 7–18. For other discussions of the contradictory processes of de- and re-centralization being brought about by information technologies, and of the spatial, social, and economic polarizations that characterize postmodern cities, see Edward Soja, "Postmodern Urbanization: The Six Restructurings of Los Angeles," in *Postmodern Cities and Spaces,* ed. Sophie Watson and Katherine Gibson (Cambridge, Mass.: Blackwell, 1995), 131–34; Tim Hall, *Urban Geography* (New York: Routledge, 1998), 41–55; Sharon Zukin, "The Postmodern Debate over Urban Form," *Theory, Culture and Society* 5 (1988): 434; Philip Cooke, "Modernity, Postmodernity and the City," *Theory, Culture and Society* 5 (1988): 483–86; and Castells, *Informational City,* chap. 4.

39. Castells, *Informational City,* 150.

40. Sassen, "Whose City Is It?" 187.

41. Castells describes these political shifts in terms of a transition from the "welfare state" to the "warfare state" (*Informational City,* 229–306). Also see Abu-Lughod, *New York, Chicago, Los Angeles,* 275–79.

42. On the tension between cultural values embedded in place and the abstract space of flows, as well as on the simultaneous trends toward globalization and tribalization in postmodern culture, see Castells, *Informational City,* 348–53.

43. Webber, "Urban Place and Nonplace Urban Realm," 120. For other discussions of postmodern cities as webs and networks, see Manuel Castells, *The Rise of the Network Society* (Cambridge, Mass.: Blackwell, 1996), 470–71; Soja, "Inside Exopolis," 97; Boyer, *CyberCities,* 18. The term *heterotopia,* initially used by Michel Foucault in "Of Other Spaces," *Diacritics* 16, no. 1 (spring 1986): 24, has acquired great currency in writings on postmodern urbanism. Explanations and critiques of current uses of this term may be found in Edward Soja, "Heterotopologies: A Remembrance of Other Spaces in the Citadel-LA," and Benjamin Genocchio, "Discourse, Discontinuity, Difference: The Question of 'Other' Spaces," both included in Watson and Gibson, *Postmodern Cities and Spaces.*

44. On these metaphors for postmodern cities, see Ellin, *Postmodern Urbanism,* 91, 258.

45. Boyer argues that metaphors of the postmodern city as an inclusive network are attempts to contain the "voices from other times and different spaces [that] are beginning to emerge and disturb the supposed unity" of modernism (*CyberCities,* 19).

46. The most celebrated modernist elaboration of this ideal is Jane Jacobs, *The Death and Life of Great American Cities* (New York: Random House, 1961). For an astute critique of the racial homogeneity of Jacobs's modernist ideal of urban diversity, see Marshall Berman, *All That Is Solid Melts into Air: The Experience of Modernity* (New York: Penguin, 1982). As Berman points out, with all of Jacobs's commitment to a vibrant and heterogeneous street life, there are "no blacks on her block" (324).

47. For example, see Teresa L. Ebert, "The Convergence of Postmodern Innovative Fiction and Science Fiction," *Poetics Today* 1, no. 4 (1980): 91–104. Damien Broderick, *Reading by Starlight: Postmodern Science Fiction* (London and New York: Routledge, 1995), and Bukatman, *Terminal Identity,* also read Delany's science fiction as postmodernist.

48. Fred Pfeil, *Another Tale to Tell: Politics and Narrative in Postmodern Culture* (New York: Verso, 1990), 87.

49. Samuel R. Delany, afterword to *Stars in My Pocket Like Grains of Sand* (New York: Bantam, 1990), 384.

50. Delany argues that in reading science fiction texts, "we will pay particular attention to the rhetorical figures by which differences between our world and the world of the story are suggested." Delany, "Some Reflections on SF Criticism," *Science-Fiction Studies* 8, no. 3 (November 1981): 236.

51. See Heim, *Metaphysics of Virtual Reality,* 82.

52. "But what distinguishes the worst architect from the best of bees is that the architect builds the cell in his mind before he constructs it in wax." Karl Marx, *Capital* (New York: Penguin, 1976), 1:284.

53. See Krishan Kumar's characterization of the postmodern "ecotopia," in *Utopia and Anti-Utopia in Modern Times* (New York: Blackwell, 1987), 406–14.

54. N. Katherine Hayles argues that "much of what we call postmodernism is a response to the separation of text from context that information technology makes possible." Hayles, "Text Out of Context: Situating Postmodernism Within an Information Society," *Discourse* 9 (1987): 24–36.

55. For example, see Russell Blackford, "Debased and Lascivious: Samuel R. Delany's *Stars in My Pocket Like Grains of Sand,*" in *Ash of Stars: On the Writing of Samuel R. Delany,* ed. James Sallis (Jackson: University Press of Mississippi, 1996), 27.

56. Fredric Jameson, *Postmodernism, or, The Cultural Logic of Late Capitalism* (Durham, N.C.: Duke University Press, 1994), 37–38.

57. David Harvey, *The Condition of Postmodernity* (Cambridge, Mass.: Blackwell, 1990), 293–306; Castells, *Informational City,* 350–51.

58. George P. Landow, "What's a Critic to Do? Critical Theory in the Age of Hypertext," in *Hyper/Text/Theory,* ed. George P. Landow (Baltimore: Johns Hopkins University Press, 1994). 1. Landow's observation is echoed by many influential theorists of electronic textuality, including Richard Lanham and Jay Bolter, both of whom contend that hypertext represents a fulfillment of poststructuralist conceptions of textuality and that electronic text and postmodern literary theory alike call into question the hidden cultural assumptions of print technology. See Richard Lanham, *The Electronic Word: Democracy, Technology, and the Arts* (Chicago: University of Chicago Press, 1993), 156; and Jay David Bolter, *Writing Space: The Computer, Hypertext, and the History of Writing* (Hillsdale, N.J.: Lawrence Erlbaum Associates, 1991), 161–62. Certain poststructuralist theorists–especially Barthes and Derrida–are repeatedly invoked in postmodern discourses on electronic textuality. Although there are many points of convergence (on intertextuality, dissemination of meanings, etc.), it is important to note the modernist lineage of most poststructuralist theorists of textuality, whose "mandarin" writing practices and aesthetic tastes clearly set them apart from the more populist proponents of electronic textuality. On this, see Andreas Huyssen, *After the Great Divide: Modernism, Mass Culture, Postmodernism* (Bloomington: Indiana University Press, 1986), 206–16.

59. Patrick Bazin, "Toward Metareading," in Nunberg, *Future of the Book,* 159.

60. Carla Hesse, "Books in Time," in Nunberg, *Future of the Book,* 22.

61. This is Jay Bolter's phrase (*Writing Space,* 2). Also see George P. Landow's argument that "we have already moved far enough beyond the book" that we are in a position to "decenter the book" and perceive it "as technology." Landow, "Twenty Minutes into the Future, or How Are We Moving beyond the Book?" in Nunberg, *Future of the Book,* 214.

62. On the distinctions between reader–author relations in print and electronic texts, see Lanham, *Electronic Word,* 5–6, 129. Lanham argues that electronic technology offers customized forms of reading appropriate to different readers, in contrast to "print's one-size-fits-all approach" (129). Also see Bolter, *Writing Space,* 8, 128; John Slatin, "Reading Hypertext: Order and Coherence in a New Medium," in *Hypermedia and Literary Studies,* ed. Paul Delaney and George P. Landow (Cambridge: MIT Press, 1991), 158; Martin E. Rosenberg, "Physics and Hypertext: Liberation and Complicity in Art and Pedagogy," in Landow, *Hyper/Text/Theory,* 273; Myron C. Tuman, *Word Perfect: Literacy in the Computer Age* (Pittsburgh: University of Pittsburgh Press, 1992), 63–66.

63. Bazin, "Toward Metareading," 159.

64. Ibid., 163.

65. Duguid, "Material Matters," 75. On the cultural and ideological attributes implicit in print technology and in the thingness of the book, see Bolter, *Writing Space,* 4–5, 7, 85, 87, 151–52; Lanham, *Electronic Word,* 73–74; Regis Debray, "The Book as Symbolic Object," in Nunberg, *Future of the Book,* 144; Bazin, "Toward Metareading," 159; Stuart Moulthrop, "Rhizome and Resistance: Hypertext and the Dreams of a New Culture," in Landow, *Hyper/Text/Theory,* 302–3.

66. Landow, "What's a Critic to Do?" 6.

67. Roland Barthes, "From Work to Text," trans. Josue Harari, in *Textual Strategies,* ed. Josue Harari (Ithaca, N.Y.: Cornell University Press, 1979), 77.

68. See Bolter, *Writing Space,* 151–52; Hesse, "Books in Time," 21–33.

69. Slatin, "Reading Hypertext," 155.

70. I am alluding to Jacques Derrida's description of text as "a differential network, a fabric of traces referring endlessly to something other than itself, to other differential traces." Derrida, "Living On," in *Deconstruction and Criticism,* ed. James Hulbart (New York: Seabury Press, 1979), 84.

71. Sven Birkerts, *The Gutenberg Elegies: The Fate of Reading in an Electronic Age* (New York: Fawcett Columbine, 1994); Neil Postman, *Amusing Ourselves to Death* (New York: Penguin, 1985).

72. Joseph J. Corn, epilogue to *Imagining Tomorrow: History, Technology and the American Future* (Cambridge: MIT Press, 1986), 227. For a useful critical overview of the polarized positions taken in recent debates on electronic textuality, see Snyder, "Beyond the Hype," 125–43. Snyder accurately points out that even the postmodern side of this debate smuggles in the modernist assumption that technology can function as an autonomous agent of social change; while questioning other modern meta-narratives, proponents of electronic technology still subscribe to the "grand narrative of technology-as-progress" (129).

73. Samuel R. Delany, "Generic Protocols: Science Fiction and Mundane," in de Lauretis, Huyssen, and Woodward, *Technological Imagination,* 187.

74. On the divergent institutional histories of science fiction and literature, also see Samuel R. Delany, "Reflections on Historical Models in Modern English Language Science Fiction," *Science-Fiction Studies* 7, no. 2 (1980): 135, 146; Samuel R. Delany, "Science Fiction and 'Literature'–Or, the Conscience of the King," in *Starboard Wine,* by Samuel R. Delany (New York: Dragon Press, 1984), 81–100.

75. Delany often tends to treat as equivalent the categories of modern humanism, aesthetic modernism, and the discipline of literature–a reduction that serves powerful polemical purposes. Obversely, Delany identifies poststructuralist theories of textuality with postmodernism, on the grounds of their shared antihumanism.

76. Landow writes of the "denatured physicality" of electronic text ("What's a Critic to Do?" 4).

77. Landow, "Twenty Minutes into the Future," 216–18.

78. Lanham, *Electronic Word,* x–xi.

79. Marshall McLuhan, *The Gutenberg Galaxy: The Making of Typographic Man* (Toronto: University of Toronto Press, 1962), 72; Walter J. Ong, *Orality and Literacy: The Technologizing of the Word* (New York: Methuen, 1982), 136.

80. Hesse, "Books in Time," 32.

81. Alvin Kernan, *The Death of Literature* (New Haven: Yale University Press, 1990). On the shifting conceptions of literacy brought about by the shift from print to electronic technology, see Robert Pattison, *On Literacy: The Politics of the Word from Homer to the Age of Rock* (New York: Oxford University Press, 1982); Tuman, *Word Perfect,* 16–27; Lanham, *Electronic Word,* esp. "The Electronic Word: Literary Study and the Digital Revolution," 2–28; Johndan Johnson-Eilola, "Living on the Surface: Learning in the Age of Global Communication Networks," and Gunther Kress, "Visual and Verbal Modes of Representation in Electronically Mediated Communication: The Potentials of New Forms of Text," both included in Snyder, *Page to Screen,* 185–210 and 53–79, respectively.

82. This psychological-depth model of print literacy is discussed and defended at length in Birkerts, *Gutenberg Elegies,* 74–92.

83. Lanham overstates these claims in *The Electronic Word,* asserting that electronic technology is "democratizing education in all the arts" and can "enfranchise non-native speaking minorities within the world of letters" (10). Advocates of electronic technology often cash in on the challenges to the Western literary canon initiated by racial minorities during the

1960s, seldom substantiating the claim that these challenges support the electronic assault on print technology.

84. See Tuman, *Word Perfect,* 18, 25. Also see Patrick Bazin's argument that practices of literacy associated with electronic technology replace the print aesthetics of depth with a pragmatics of the interface ("Toward Metareading," 164).

85. Delany, "Reading at Work," 98.

86. Derrida, *Of Grammatology,* 69.

87. Gloria Naylor, *Mama Day* (New York: Random House, 1988), 228.

88. On virtual reality as a medium of sensory immersion, see N. Katherine Hayles, "The Seductions of Cyberspace," in Conley, *Rethinking Technologies,* 175; Michael Benedikt, "Cyberspace: Some Proposals," in *Cyberspace: First Steps,* ed. Michael Benedikt (Cambridge: MIT Press, 1991), 190–91.

89. Derrida, *Of Grammatology,* 127.

90. Ibid., 112.

91. Heim, *Metaphysics of Virtual Reality,* 109, 114.

92. Delany, "Generic Protocols," 181.

93. Samuel R. Delany, "The Gestation of Genres: Literature, Fiction, Romance, Science Fiction, Fantasy," in *Intersections: Fantasy and Science Fiction,* ed. George E. Slusser and Eric S. Rabkin (Carbondale: Southern Illinois University Press, 1987), 72.

94. Derrida, *Of Grammatology,* 163.

95. For example, see Bolter, *Writing Space,* 199–203.

96. Tuman, *Word Perfect,* 62.

97. Broderick, *Reading by Starlight,* 149.

98. Delany, "Generic Protocols," 185.

99. Ibid., 177–78; Delany, *Silent Interviews,* 30–31.

100. Delany, "Generic Protocols," 185.

101. See Samuel R. Delany, "About Five Thousand Seven Hundred and Fifty Words," in *The Jewel-Hinged Jaw: Notes on the Language of Science Fiction* (New York: Dragon Press, 1977), 46; and Delany, "Science Fiction and Literature," in *Starboard Wine,* 88–89.

102. Delany, "Generic Protocols," 177.

103. Ibid., 180–81.

104. Teresa de Lauretis, "Signs of Wa(o)nder," in de Lauretis, Huyssen, and Woodward, *Technological Imagination,* 164, 168–69.

105. Delany is well aware of his own tendency to overstate the distinctions between science fiction and literature. In "The Gestation of Genres," he recalls Joanna Russ's remark about his obsessive efforts to pin down the specificity of science fiction: "Worrying about the purity of the genres is like worrying about the purity of the races." Delany writes in response, "I'm afraid I may just be the proof, in both cases, that the horse is already well out of the barn" (64). Delany admits that "Genres are not pure. They come to us, always already mixed" (73).

106. The difficulty of this reading process is clear from the misreadings that result when readers isolate one or the other element of the double movement that Delany's writing requires us to perform. This is why de Lauretis can argue that Delany's theory of science fiction restores reference to language, and Damien Broderick can make the contrary claim that Delany's writing often verges on a "disabling worship of the text" (*Reading by Starlight,* 158).

107. Ibid., 156, 70. For an excellent discussion of science fiction as a peculiar "species of realism," see J. Timothy Bagwell, "Science Fiction and the Semiotics of Realism," in Slusser and Rabkin, *Intersections,* 36–47.

108. Delany, "Reflection on Historical Models in Modern English Language Science Fiction," 147.

109. Derrida, *Of Grammatology,* 101–40.

110. Samuel R. Delany, *Times Square Red, Times Square Blue* (New York: New York University Press, 1999), 127; hereafter cited parenthetically.

111. Young, "Ideal of Community and the Politics of Difference," 302, 318.

ris Marion Young, *Justice and the Politics of Difference* (Princeton: Princeton Uni-
ss, 1990), chaps. 4 and 5; hereafter cited parenthetically.

Zygmunt Bauman, *Postmodern Ethics* (Cambridge, Mass.: Blackwell, 1993), 8, 39;
___ cited parenthetically.

114. James Alan McPherson, "A Region Not Home: The View from Exile," in *The
Prevailing South: Life and Politics in a Changing Region,* ed. Dudley Clendinen (Atlanta:
Longstreet Press, 1998), 202.

Afterword

1. Toni Morrison, "City Limits, Village Values: Concepts of the Neighborhood in Black
Fiction," in *Literature and the Urban Experience,* ed. Michael C. Jaye and Ann Chalmers
Watts (New Brunswick, N.J.: Rutgers University Press, 1981), 37; hereafter cited parentheti-
cally.

2. Toni Morrison, "Rootedness: The Ancestor as Foundation," in *Black Women Writers
(1950–1980),* ed. Mari Evans (New York: Anchor, 1984).

3. For a more detailed analysis of Morrison's theory of the novel, as spelled out in "Rootedness" and "City Limits, Village Values," see Madhu Dubey, "Narration and Migration:
Jazz and Vernacular Theories of Black Women's Fiction," *American Literary History* 10,
no. 2 (summer 1998): 291–316; and Dubey, "The Politics of Genre in *Beloved,*" *Novel: A
Forum on Fiction* 32, no. 2 (spring 1999): 187–206.

4. Samuel R. Delany writes of his book *Times Square Red, Times Square Blue* (New York:
New York University Press, 1999) that the "polemical passion here is forward-looking, not
nostalgic" (xv).

5. Colson Whitehead, *The Intuitionist* (New York: Anchor, 1999), 230; hereafter cited
parenthetically.

6. Paul Gilroy, *The Black Atlantic: Modernity and Double Consciousness* (Cambridge:
Harvard University Press, 1993), 36.

7. Gloria Naylor, *Mama Day* (New York: Random House, 1988), 228.

8. Whitehead, *Intuitionist,* 255.

Index

accumulation, 18, 24, 60, 71
affirmative action, 30, 184
Africa, John, 73
African-American cultural studies, 21, 28, 31–40, 100–102
African-American intellectuals, 24, 29, 31, 35–39, 40, 88
African-American middle class, 5, 27–28, 38, 76, 133, 266n.55
African American Review, 156
African-American studies, 5, 7, 14, 19–31, 24, 32, 256n.74
Agger, Ben, 3, 13
agrarian ideal, 34, 66, 72, 147, 156
Alexander, Elizabeth, 257n.8
ancestor, 67, 158, 167, 173, 218–19, 235
ancestry, tropes of, 75–76
Anderson, Benedict, 3
Anderson, Elijah, 246n.34
Animal Locomotion (Muybridge), 110
anthology, 50, 65
antiphony (call and response), 42, 119
anti-urbanism, 235, 238
Anzaldua, Gloria, 23
Arac, Jonathan, 19
Arcadian ideal, 71, 82, 163, 255n.41
Artaud, Antonin, 89, 90
Atlanta, 151
Auletta, Ken, 26
aurality, 102
authenticity, 9, 31, 32, 34, 38, 115, 144, 146, 156, 183–84, 193, 218, 237

Baker, Houston, Jr., 101, 102, 130, 131, 154–55, 157, 166–67, 169, 170, 250n.98, 256n.74, 257n.8
Bambara, Toni Cade, 28, 167, 169, 237, 243n.3
Banner-Haley, Charles, 44
Baraka, Amiri, 38–39

Barthes, Roland, 111, 112, 114, 212, 273n.58
Bartley, Numan, 266n.43
Bauman, Zygmunt, 24, 231–32, 250n.89
Bazin, Patrick, 212, 275n.84
Beloved (Morrison), 44, 174, 243n.3
Benjamin, Walter, 115, 177
Benston, Kimberly, 171
Bentham, Jeremy, 107
Berger, John, 113, 122, 135, 260n.58
Berman, Marshall, 272n.46
Berube, Michael, 31
"bio-politics," 102
Birkerts, Sven, 213
Black Aesthetic, The (Gayle), 33
Black Arts movement, 33, 43, 155, 265n.42
Black Power movement, 19, 30
Black Southern Voices (anthology), 155
blues, 42, 133
Bluest Eye, The (Morrison), 4, 75, 142, 244n.11
body, 8, 9, 100, 102, 116–18, 124–25, 126–27, 133–36, 137, 193, 194–195, 204
Bolter, Jay, 273n.58
book, tropes of, 2, 5, 6, 50, 54, 56, 77, 78, 80, 138, 141–42, 146–47, 169, 174, 181, 214–16, 240–41. *See also* printed book
Book of Thoth, 47, 50–52, 53, 240
Bowen, Barbara, 268n.81
Boyer, M. Christine, 62, 189, 193–94, 195, 197, 198, 272n.45
Boynton, Robert, 31
Bradley, David, 10, 243n.3
Brenkman, John, 182–83, 269n.96
Broderick, Damien, 226, 275n.106
Brothers and Keepers (Wideman), 87
Butler, Judith, 102, 112
Butler, Octavia, 2, 62, 80, 95, 105, 227.
See also *Parable of the Sower*

call and response, 42, 119
camera, 52, 106, 110, 113–14, 120, 128–29, 140, 190. *See also* photography
Campbell, Bebe Moore, 28
canonization, 4, 9, 10, 43, 89–90, 144, 213, 217, 237
capitalism, 17, 22, 24, 60, 66–67, 103, 115, 201, 208
capitalist restructuring, 18, 20, 24, 25–26, 58, 148–51, 196, 197, 208
capital relocation, 25, 148
Carby, Hazel, 144, 154, 157
Cartesian perspective, 109, 113, 128
Castells, Manuel, 72, 189, 196, 197, 208
Cayton, Horace, 27
Cheatwood, Kiarri, 156, 163
cinema, 13, 114, 260n.63
City of Quartz (Davis), 105–6
Civil Rights movement, 4–5, 13, 19, 20, 24, 26, 28, 151–52, 184, 200, 265n.25
civility, 193, 233
class divisions, intra-racial, 27–29, 30, 35, 51, 76–77, 87–88, 158, 159, 160, 162, 164, 184
Clausen, Jan, 93
Cobb, James, 148
colonialism, 21
commodification, 77, 109, 116–18, 133–36, 154
commodity culture, 37, 51, 79, 80, 83, 84, 97, 101, 104, 164, 175, 212
commodity fetishism, 103, 108, 122–25, 127, 131, 134–36, 142, 192
community, 2–3, 19, 67, 75, 108, 149, 152, 168, 231, 235, 236, 254n.33. *See also* organic community; racial community; urban community
community development programs, 26, 30, 58
Comolli, Jean-Louis, 259n.50
computer literacy, 98
conjurer-critic, 170
conjuring, 42, 166–70, 181–82
consumption, 58–59, 60–61, 73, 80, 83–84, 104, 123–24, 162, 163–64
contextualism, 189, 206
Coser, Stelamaris, 167
cosmopolitanism, 46, 149–50, 151, 198
Crary, Jonathan, 259n.39
Crenshaw, Kimberle, 112
Crisis, The, 28
critical regionalism, 189
Cross, Malcolm, 104
Cruse, Harold, 30
cultural capital, 8, 9, 12, 40, 43, 185
"cultural dominant," 21–22, 24
cultural politics, 9–10, 21–24, 32–40, 45–46, 101–2, 149, 163, 184–85, 208, 215
cultural studies, 8–10, 11–12, 14, 20–22, 28, 31–40, 43, 90, 100–102, 130, 189

cultural value, 9, 12, 13, 80, 164–65, 166, 208–9
cyberspace, 189, 193–94, 195, 204
cyborg, 194, 198, 203, 209

dance, 50
Davis, Mike, 57, 63–64, 105–6, 107, 116, 126, 128, 258n.35
Dawson, Michael, 29
Debord, Guy, 101, 102–3, 118, 126, 128, 131, 257n.2
de Certeau, Michel, 83–84
deconstruction, 11, 42, 170, 200
deindustrialization, 25–26, 156
Delaney, Paul, 263n.7
Delany, Samuel, 2, 11–12, 46, 50, 99, 144–45, 167, 186, 187, 199, 213–14, 221, 223–27, 227–28, 229, 230–31, 231–33, 271n.30, 272n.50, 274n.75, 275n.105. See also *Stars in My Pocket Like Grains of Sand*
de Lauretis, Teresa, 225, 275n.106
Derrida, Jacques, 193, 218, 229–30, 273n.58, 274n.70
desegregation, 30, 150–51
Deutsche, Rosalyn, 62, 63
differences, 7–10, 19–24, 32–34, 87, 101, 103–4, 198–99, 228, 230–33, 237
digital technologies, 3, 190–91, 206, 212
disabled body, 194
Disch, Robert, 96
Donlon, Jocelyn, 170
doubling, 114, 115, 117, 119–20, 134–35, 220
Douglass, Frederick, 4, 40–42
Dove, Rita, 184
Drake, St. Clair, 27
Du Bois, W. E. B., 27, 35–36, 37, 41–42, 88, 249n.71
Dumm, Thomas, 106–7
dystopia, 57, 60, 66, 86, 188, 203, 206–7

Ebony, 28
Economies of Signs and Space (Lash and Urry), 7–8
ecotopias, 255n.40
edge city, 189
egalitarianism, 231–33
Egerton, John, 148, 267n.59
electoral participation, 30
electronic surveillance, 106, 107, 115
electronic technologies, 2, 3, 10, 11, 37, 55, 84, 85, 90, 98, 105, 106, 129, 186–87, 189, 191, 192–93, 196, 207, 212, 214, 217
electronic text, 186, 211–17, 273n.58, 274n.75
Ellis, Trey, 2, 32, 146–47, 157, 158, 183, 184–85, 269n.103
Ellison, Ralph, 40–42, 100

Emmanuel, James, 33
employment structure, 25, 86, 150, 159, 196
Essence, 28
essentialism, 10, 32, 33, 35, 39, 47, 200, 209, 211
exchange value, 69, 80, 103, 115, 116, 118, 123–24, 126–27, 132, 175, 225
exopolis, 189

face-to-face communication, 71, 81, 147, 151–52, 154, 159, 160, 168, 192–93, 195, 198, 204, 218, 227, 229–30, 231, 232
Faith and the Good Thing (Charles Johnson), 2, 168–69, 181–82
family, 64–65, 67–68, 75–76, 209–11
fanzines, 214
Fauset, Jessie, 42
Featherstone, Mike, 24
feminist politics, 20, 21, 32–33
fetishism, 8, 51, 61–62, 100, 103, 104, 108, 120–21, 122, 123, 126, 137, 195, 214, 260n.71
folk culture, 3, 34, 51, 79, 154–55, 163, 181. *See also* southern folk aesthetic
Fordism, 18, 24, 212
formalism, 10, 11, 42, 47–48, 49, 227–28
Forrest, Leon, 237
"Fortress L.A.," 57, 106, 128
Foster, Hal, 103, 257n.13
Foucault, Michel, 2, 23, 106, 272n.43
Fox, Robert Elliott, 251n.107
Frazier, Franklin, 27
funk, rhetoric of, 75
Future of the Race, The (West and Gates), 36, 249n.71

Gaines, Ernest, 243n.3
Gaines, Kevin, 249n.74
garden city ideal, 73, 74
gated communities, 57–58, 60–61, 197
Gates, Henry Louis, Jr., 4, 6, 29, 36, 37, 39, 40–41, 47, 49, 249n.71
Gayle, Addison, 47, 155
gay rights movement, 200
Genovese, Eugene, 149, 150, 151
gentrification, 59, 104
Gibson, Richard, 261n.77
Gibson, William, 194
Gilroy, Paul, 21, 101–2, 239
Glassey, Donald, 73, 81, 82
golden age of the ghetto, 28, 158, 238, 254n.29
Gómez-Peña, Guillermo, 23
graffiti, 131
Great Books, 217
Griffin, Farah, 152, 265n.25
Grossman, Susan, 230–31
growth ideology, 30, 58, 60–62, 64

guerilla theater, 90
Guillory, John, 43

Halliday, George, 101, 112, 257n.8
Haraway, Donna, 271n.30
Harlem, 45, 59, 60, 63, 235
Harlem Renaissance, 4, 265n.42
Harper, Frances, 42
Harper, Phillip Brian, 7, 21
Hartwell, David, 226
Harvey, David, 7, 18, 20–21, 58, 61, 149, 195, 208, 243n.5
Haug, Wolfgang Fritz, 123–24, 126
Havard, William, 147, 151
Hayles, Katherine, 273n.54
Heim, Michael, 192, 193, 194, 195, 219, 220, 271n.25
Herron, Carolivia, 237
heterotopia, 198, 272n.43
Hindery, Michael A., 254n.33
hip-hop culture, 8, 10, 101–2, 244n.19. *See also* rap music
Hirsch, Marianne, 178, 269n.90
historical materialism, 11, 46, 224, 233
history, 21, 46, 129, 136, 145, 165, 174, 201, 209, 224, 230
Hobson, Fred, 151, 267n.59
Hogue, Lawrence, 10, 32–33
Holloway, Karla, 167, 168, 169–70, 173, 268n.81
"home," 21, 68, 116, 118, 152, 254n.36
homelessness, 59, 62, 63
homology, 18
hooks, bell, 7, 8, 14, 20, 22, 23, 32, 33–34, 38, 68, 250n.104
Hooper, Barbara, 32, 33
Hopkins, Pauline, 42
humanism, 21, 24, 33, 37, 43, 55, 89, 96, 215, 217, 220, 221, 232, 239, 274n.75
Hurston, Zora Neale, 40–41, 144, 146, 265n.42
Huyssen, Andreas, 2, 36, 51
hyperreality, 8, 192–93
hypertext, 186, 187, 211, 213, 215, 273n.58

identity politics, 31, 32, 33, 46
I'll Take My Stand, 147
illusion, 110, 112–13, 121, 123–24, 131, 192, 204–5
immersion narratives, 41
immigration, 150
industrial boom, 13, 148, 150, 152
industrial restructuring, 24, 25, 26, 61, 148, 162–63
information city, 188–90, 193–94, 195, 196–99, 203
information economy, 194, 196
information processing, 105, 199

information technologies, 3, 186, 189,
    190–92, 194, 195–96, 197, 203–4, 206,
    207, 218, 219, 230–31
integration, 27, 145, 154, 183, 184, 237
"internal colony" model, 90
intuition, 239–40
Intuitionist, The (Whitehead), 1–2, 238–41
Irigaray, Luce, 124, 125

Jackson, Jerome, 95
Jacobs, Jane, 272n.46
Jacoby, Russell, 31
James, Joy, 40, 44, 249n.74
Jameson, Fredric, 7, 8, 18, 20, 21–22, 23, 24,
    191, 201, 207–8, 255n.42
Jay, Martin, 109
jazz (music), 133, 134, 142–43, 262n.93
Jazz (Morrison), 2, 15, 78, 99, 100, 109,
    130, 131–43, 167, 177, 262n.92
Jenks, Chris, 114, 254n.27, 261n.78
Jim Crow South, 160, 164–65
Johnson, Charles, 2, 168–69, 181, 239
Johnson, James Weldon, 41, 88
Jones, Gayl, 174, 237, 243n.3
Jones, Jacqueline, 157, 163
Jones, Jacquie, 117
Jones, LeRoi. *See* Baraka, Amiri
Joyce, Joyce Ann, 170

Katz, Michael, 27, 64
Kearney, Richard, 192–93, 194, 195
Keith, Michael, 104
Kelley, Robin, 39, 245n.8, 254n.29
Kenan, Randall, 80, 243n.3
Kernan, Alvin, 243n.9
Kerner Commission Report on Civil
    Disorders, 5, 199
Killens, John Oliver, 33, 155–56
Kilson, Martin, 29
King, Rodney, 101, 108, 111–12,
    256n.56
Koch, Edward, 59–60
Kroll, Jack, 92
Kuhn, Annette, 122
Kumar, Kishan, 255n.40

"lag-time spaces," 62, 195, 197, 253n.20
Landow, George P., 211, 212, 213, 273nn.
    58, 61
Langer, Peter, 253n.13
language, 11, 172, 177, 223, 224–26, 229
Lanham, Richard, 90, 213, 215, 273nn. 58,
    62, 274n.83
Lash, Scott, 7–8
Leapheart, Vincent, 73
Lemann, Nicholas, 26
Levitas, Ruth, 255n.41
Lewis, Earl, 266n.48
"liberation technology," 187, 213
listening, 15, 146, 170–85, 217, 218, 219

literacy, 2, 3, 6, 40, 42, 55–56, 62, 77, 78,
    84–88, 96–98, 217, 220, 238–39. *See also*
    print culture
literary imagination, 91–92, 95, 120–21, 131,
    145, 165, 181
literary value, 15, 42–44, 77, 89, 91–93, 98,
    100, 181
literature, 6, 13–14, 38–39, 40–54, 89–95,
    146, 182–83, 213, 214, 216–17, 219,
    221, 223–24, 236
localism, 20, 21, 68–69, 147, 149–50,
    151–52, 206–7
Locke, Alain, 4
Logan, John, 69
Los Angeles, 57–58, 105–6, 108, 258n.27
Loury, Glenn, 29, 39
Lovejoy, Margot, 191
Lubiano, Wahneema, 7, 21, 248n.63,
    267n.65
Lugones, Maria, 23
Lyotard, Jean-François, 19

magic, 52, 146, 166–69, 179–81
Major, Clarence, 44
Mama Day (Naylor), 2, 15, 49, 71, 144,
    145–46, 146, 158, 159, 160–61, 163,
    165–83
Manhattan, 59, 63
manuscript, 77–81, 83, 97
mapping, 62, 174–75, 177
Marable, Manning, 29
margin, 22–23
Marx, Karl, 205
Marx, Leo, 73, 74
Marxism, 11, 12, 22, 32, 192
Marxist urban geography, 20, 24
Massey, Doreen, 20–21
McCone Commission, 258n.35
McDaniel, Antonio, 27
McDowell, Deborah, 136–37
McGee, Patrick, 48
McHale, Brian, 10–11
McKay, Claude, 42
McKinney-Whetstone, Diane, 69
McKnight, Reginald, 183–84, 243n.3
McLuhan, Marshall, 78, 216
McPherson, James Alan, 28, 151, 232
Mebane, Mary, 266n.50
mediation, 3, 9–10, 14, 35, 50, 52–54,
    167–68, 170, 172, 176, 178, 179, 193,
    199, 218, 221, 224–25, 229–30, 232
Meisenhelder, Susan, 171
memory, 118–19, 136, 158, 209
Mercer, Kobena, 40, 45
meta-narratives, 19, 24, 48–49, 238
Middleton, Joyce Irene, 171
migration, 4, 132, 136, 145, 152–53, 154,
    159, 262n.93
migration narratives, 152
Mikics, David, 47

mimesis, 10–11, 165, 224, 225
Mitchell, William J., 270n.13
Mobley, Marilyn Sanders, 170,
    262n.92
Model Cities, 58
modern city, 99–100, 104–5, 106, 115–16,
    186, 189, 190, 240. *See also* urban
    modernity
modernism, 13, 17, 18, 20, 21, 32, 46, 92,
    93, 192, 200, 213–17, 221, 272n.46,
    274n.75
modernization, 18, 20, 145, 148–51, 156,
    159, 160–61, 236, 238
modern politics, 19–20, 21, 32, 45–46, 199,
    231–32
Molotch, Harvey, 69
Morace, Robert, 261n.75
Morrison, Toni, 4, 6, 20–21, 28, 30–31, 38,
    44, 50, 67, 75, 108–9, 131, 146, 153–54,
    158–59, 174, 179, 182, 183, 184, 218,
    227, 235–38, 243n.3, 247n.43, 262n.93.
    See also *Jazz; Song of Solomon*
Mosley, Walter, 44–45
MOVE, 66, 73–75, 81–83, 126–27, 129,
    255n.51
multiculturalism, 183, 184–85
multimedia literacy, 217
Mulvey, Laura, 260n.71
Mumbo Jumbo (Reed), 2, 14, 47–49, 50–52,
    101, 240
Murray, Albert, 265n.29
Murray, Charles, 253n.26
music, 8, 9, 10, 13, 38–39, 44, 101–2,
    130–31, 262n.93
Muybridge, Eadweard, 109–11, 112, 113,
    115–16, 121–22, 125

narrative of ascent, 41
nationalism, black cultural, 32, 33–34, 36,
    42–43, 44, 47, 155
Naylor, Gloria, 50, 146, 227, 239. See also
    Mama Day
Neal, Larry, 38, 39
neo-slave narrative, 174
network, 62, 186, 187, 196, 197, 198, 200,
    207, 208, 212, 272n.45
Neveryóna, or: The Tale of Signs and Cities
    (Delany), 99, 100, 130, 144–45,
    167
New Black Aesthetic, 32, 183–84
Nightingale, Carl, 244n.19
nostalgia, 65–68, 72, 127, 145, 152, 153,
    160–61, 178–79, 188, 193, 227, 238

Ong, Walter, 78, 98, 216
orality vs. visuality, 118–19, 130, 131,
    137–41, 169–73, 216
oral tradition, 3, 6, 9, 38, 39, 41, 42, 50, 77,
    78, 118–19, 146, 154, 166, 169–72, 174,
    176, 236, 237

organic community, 3, 34, 65, 70, 75–76, 81,
    93, 144, 146, 152, 165, 171, 182, 195,
    229, 231, 235, 238
organicism, 10, 11, 34–35, 127, 144,
    169–72, 210, 237
Osiris, 51. *See also* Book of Thoth
otherness, 7, 64, 103, 117, 121, 137, 193,
    195, 200, 218, 219

panopticon, 107
paperback revolution, 214
Parable of the Sower (Butler), 2, 15, 49,
    55–58, 60–64, 66–72, 73–84, 86–87, 91,
    94–99, 210, 239, 255n.41, 256n.61
parody, 47
particularism, 20, 36, 149, 231
pastiche, 47, 189
pastoral, 66–67, 72–74, 76, 156, 165
Patterson, Orlando, 29
Peller, Gary, 112
Penn, William, 72–73, 74
performance, 9, 38, 50, 90, 215, 230
Pfeil, Fred, 200
Philadelphia, 59, 61, 63, 69, 72–73, 116,
    120
Philadelphia Fire (Wideman), 2, 15, 49,
    58–59, 60, 61, 63, 64, 66, 72–76, 81–84,
    87–93, 96, 97, 98, 99, 100, 109, 121,
    122–31, 134, 136, 140, 142, 167, 199,
    210, 255n.50, 261n.77
Phillips, Sarah, 10, 243n.3
photography, 106, 110–11, 112–13, 114,
    115, 122, 126, 140, 190, 191, 259n.50,
    260n.63
Pinckney, Darryl, 92, 184, 243n.3
Platitudes (Ellis), 2, 146–47, 158, 184–85
pluralism, 37, 85, 108, 184–85, 213
Polite, Carlene, 101, 257n.6
political economy, 12–13
political subject, 19, 20, 32, 39, 45–47, 199
politics of difference, 12–13, 19–20, 31–33,
    149, 163, 199, 200–201, 229, 231–33
politikos vs. *ethnos,* 46
popular culture, 14, 31, 36, 37, 44, 49, 50,
    51, 101–2
populism, 14, 35, 37, 39, 43, 50, 213
pornography, 122, 127
Posnock, Ross, 45–47
postindustrial society, 17, 18
Postman, Neil, 213, 261n.75
postmodern city, 15, 56–65, 72, 99–100,
    157, 188, 189, 190, 195, 197–98,
    208–11, 230
postmodern cultural studies, 8, 12, 14, 20,
    35, 43, 90, 189
postmodern ethics, 192–93, 218, 231–32
postmodernism, theories of, 7–9, 19–24
postmodernity, 18
postmodern period, 14, 17–22, 24
postnationalism, 32

poststructuralism, 11, 200, 211, 220–23, 224, 233
Potts, Stephen, 80
poverty, 12, 19, 26–28, 29, 49, 58–59, 62, 64–65, 153, 154, 157, 163, 164, 165
preaching, 38
Preston, Howard, 150
primitivism, 8, 10, 74, 75, 83, 127, 133, 134, 230
print culture, 2, 3–4, 5–6, 14–15, 35–38, 40, 42, 43, 50, 55–56, 84–98, 169, 170, 174, 217
printed book, 3, 5, 6, 11, 40, 50, 54, 56, 77, 78, 96, 97, 131–32, 138, 141–42, 177, 186, 187, 211–13, 241
print readerships, 3, 38, 77, 80, 182–83, 236
Pryse, Marjorie, 169
public intellectuals, 31
public policy, 19, 25–26, 29, 58, 64, 197, 232
public sphere, 3, 4, 31, 40, 183
PUSH (Sapphire), 2, 15, 49, 55–56, 59–60, 60, 62–63, 64, 65–66, 68, 70, 77–78, 81, 85–86, 91, 93–94, 95, 96, 97–98, 98, 210, 239

race riots, 5, 26, 132
racial community, 5–6, 14, 24, 33–35, 41, 77, 78, 119, 144, 146, 153, 156, 157, 158, 160–66, 169–72, 181, 182, 183
racial politics, 20, 21, 29–31, 32–33, 46
racial representation, 5, 10, 15, 23, 24, 31–40, 39–40, 40–54, 85, 92, 101–2, 104
racism, 151–52, 230–31, 239
radical feminism, 32
rap music, 44, 101–2, 130–131. *See also* hip-hop culture
reading, 3, 15, 40, 42, 77, 81, 83–84, 87, 91, 96, 97, 141, 146, 170–85, 212, 216, 217–21, 225–27, 229, 230. *See also* print readerships
real, the, 9, 11, 13, 35, 49–50, 132, 142, 181–82, 192, 195–96, 227
realism, 10–11, 44–45, 47–50, 53, 92–95, 131, 165, 190
Red Summer of 1919, 132
Reed, Adolph, 29–30, 39, 160–61, 165
Reed, Ishmael, 2, 14, 28, 29, 36–37, 40–41, 44, 47–49, 50–52, 53, 101, 239, 240, 250n.92
Reed, John Shelton, 147
referentiality, 3, 11, 49–50, 181–82, 190–91, 205, 218, 223–27
reflection, 18, 47, 95, 168, 180, 181, 224
Reiner, Thomas, 254n.33
representation, 2, 13–14, 17, 20, 110–11, 122, 124–25, 190–92, 227–28. *See also* racial representation
"reproductive underclass," 64
residual, 8–9, 21–24, 147, 161, 163, 195
reterritorializing movements, 208

Reuben (Wideman), 2, 14, 15, 49, 50, 52–53, 99, 100, 109, 112–21, 127, 129, 131, 134, 142, 167, 260n.63
romance of the residual, 8–9, 10, 163
roots metaphor, 67, 68
Rose, Jacqueline, 262n.99
Ross, Andrew, 9, 35
Rowell, Charles, 87, 91–92
rural underclass, 163
Russ, Joanna, 275n.105
Rustbelt, 152, 156

Salt Eaters, The (Bambara), 167, 169, 237
Sapphire, 62, 80, 105, 227. See also *PUSH*
Sassafras, Cypress, and Indigo (Shange), 166–67
Sassen, Saskia, 197
Schmidt, Klaus, 260n.63
science fiction, 44–45, 49, 50, 57, 68, 94, 187–88, 191, 199–200, 201, 203, 213–14, 215, 219, 221, 223–27
Scruggs, Charles, 88, 266n.45
seed metaphor, 67, 68, 74, 80
segregation, 5, 12, 19, 34, 59, 62, 63, 99–100, 104, 109, 145, 150–51, 153, 154, 159, 160, 164–65
semiotics, 7, 12, 57, 100, 103, 104–5, 108, 221–23, 225–26, 228, 229
sexuality, 102, 116–18, 122, 123–24, 127, 133–35, 210–11
Shange, Ntozake, 146, 166–67
Sharpe, William, 104
signification, 47, 80, 219, 220–22, 224, 225–26, 229
signifying, 42
signs, 12, 99, 103, 104, 105, 124, 131, 163, 171, 177, 178, 218–19, 220, 221, 225, 226
simulacra, 192
simulation technologies, 191–92, 195, 203–4, 218
Sister X and the Victims of Foul Play (Polite), 101, 257n.6
Slater, Don, 259n.43
Slatin, John, 213
slave narratives, 4, 21, 40–41, 44, 86, 239, 256n.61
slavery, 20, 21, 174
Smith, Neil, 24, 59
Snyder, Ilana, 274n.72
social science scholarship, 26, 39, 57
"society of the spectacle," 101, 102–3, 118, 126, 131, 191, 257n.2
Soja, Edward, 8, 20, 22–23, 32, 33, 192, 204, 258n.27
Song of Solomon (Morrison), 2, 10, 15, 49, 86, 142, 146, 153, 158, 159, 161, 162–65, 166, 167, 171, 172–73, 175, 177, 178–79, 179, 181–83, 266n.46, 268n.88
Sontag, Susan, 111, 123, 145, 165

Sorkin, Michael, 190
South, 33–34, 142, 148–54, 150, 152–53, 265n.25, 266n.55
southern folk aesthetic, 15, 144–45, 146, 147–52, 154–58, 165–66, 168, 170–85, 217, 218, 240, 265n.42
southern regionalism, 13, 15, 66, 147–52, 156, 163, 165, 208, 232
space of flows, 195, 197, 198, 208
specifying, 42
spectacle, 101, 102–3, 118, 131, 191, 204, 257n.2
Sphinx, 127
Stack, Carol, 152–53
Stars in My Pocket Like Grains of Sand (Delany), 2, 15, 45, 49, 177, 185–88, 190–91, 200, 201–11, 214–23, 225–26, 228–30, 232, 239
Stephanson, Anders, 9, 35, 40
Stepto, Robert, 40, 41–42
Storhoff, Gary, 268n.80
storytelling, 42, 158, 167, 170, 175
structuralism, 42
subjectivity, 17, 19, 20, 21, 45–46, 200, 201, 211, 216, 220, 221
suburbanization, 26
supermarkets, 80, 84
surplus people, 61
surveillance. *See* electronic surveillance

Tagg, John, 106, 115–16
Talented Tenth, 35–38, 249n.71
Talking Book, 40–41, 250n.92
Tate, Greg, 32, 45, 183
technological determinism, 10, 102, 187, 213, 215
technology. *See* electronic technologies; information technologies; visual media
telecommunications, 3, 105, 189, 199
television, 85, 108–9, 111, 112, 129
textuality, 10, 11, 14, 47, 49, 53, 131, 132, 138, 177, 186, 211–13, 215, 217, 220–21, 227–28, 273n.58, 274n.75
theater, 89–90
Their Eyes Were Watching God (Hurston), 40–41
theme parks, 190
"third worldism," Jameson's strategy of, 8, 22
Thirdspace, 8, 22–23
Thomas, Clarence, 30, 108
Thoth, 14, 47–48, 52
Time magazine, 26, 28
Times Square Red, Times Square Blue (Delany), 11–12, 232–33
Toomer, Jean, 268n.81
totality, 18, 19, 32, 47, 62, 198, 208
tradition, 29, 32, 34–35, 40–41, 70, 151, 156–58, 161, 164, 208, 231
translation, 70, 182, 216–17, 228
travel, 208–9, 222–23

tribalism, 46, 198, 237
tribe, 75–76, 153, 235
truth-claims, 13, 47, 49–50, 53, 93–95, 110–12, 121, 131, 142, 166, 179–82, 225–27
Tucker, Lindsey, 167
Tuman, Myron, 213, 221
Tumbling (McKinney-Whetstone), 69

underclass discourses, 5, 7, 9, 26–29, 39, 49, 64, 68, 76, 85, 107–8, 157
undeserving poor, 26
unemployment, 19
uneven development, 8, 9, 23–25, 62, 63, 150, 206–7, 230
Universal Abandon: The Politics of Postmodernism (Ross), 9, 35
universalism, 20, 21, 33, 46, 89, 231–32, 239
uplift ideal, 6, 14, 36, 37, 42, 88–89, 249n.74
urban architecture, 106, 189
urban community, 27–28, 29–32, 65–76, 79, 93, 119, 156, 157, 159
urban community movements, 68–69
urban crisis, 5, 9, 12, 19, 26–27, 29, 34, 49, 62, 76, 107, 127, 131, 156–58, 183, 188, 209–10, 238
urban development, 13, 15, 26, 30, 57–64, 104, 148, 232
urban form, 12, 104–5, 109, 128, 186, 189
urban geography, 20, 189, 197, 258n.27
urbanization, 143, 145, 147, 148, 154, 156, 194, 231, 236, 262n.93
urban modernity, 1–2, 4, 145, 156, 238–41
urban order, 63, 73, 82, 107–8, 127–28, 132–33, 138
urban space, 19, 25, 63, 69, 104–5, 107, 128, 132–33, 196–98
urban studies, 12
urban violence, 58, 61, 101, 107, 108, 132, 134, 199
Urry, John, 7–8
use value, 68, 69, 115, 118, 123–24, 136, 142, 225
utopia, 56, 60, 65–76, 161–62, 188, 203, 204, 206, 232, 240, 241

vernacular culture, 31–32, 34–36, 51, 90, 175, 176, 182–83
vernacular paradigm, 6, 14, 41–43
village ideal, 67, 70, 153, 154, 158, 164, 235, 236, 254n.33
Virilio, Paul, 194
virtual reality, 218, 219, 220
visuality, 100, 102, 118–19, 130–131, 137–41, 169–73, 258n.24
visual media, 100–109, 111–12, 129. *See also* photography; spectacle
Voting Rights Act of 1965, 5
voyeurism, 99, 100, 103, 108–9, 117, 121–30, 135, 138–40, 167, 177, 260n.71

Walker, Alice, 41, 94, 146, 153, 155
Wallace, Michele, 100–101
Wallerstein, Immanuel, 149
Wallock, Leonard, 104–5
War on Poverty, 26
Watkins, Mel, 179
Watts, Jerry, 249n.77
Watts riots, 5, 258n.35
Webber, Melvin, 189, 198
web metaphor, 186, 197, 198, 200, 207–8, 220
Weir, Margaret, 26, 108
welfare reforms, 64
welfare state, 24, 26
West, Cornel, 7, 9, 14, 29, 32, 34–35, 36, 37–38, 39, 40, 44, 49, 50, 249n.71
Whitehead, Colson, 1–2, 238–41
Why the South Matters, 147
Wideman, John Edgar, 14, 15, 49, 50, 57–58, 61, 62, 87–88, 92, 99, 105, 108, 109, 111–12, 167, 218, 243n.3, 254n.36, 256n.56. See also *Philadelphia Fire; Reuben*

Wilentz, Gay, 167
Williams, Brett, 64–65
Williams, Linda, 122, 123
Williams, Raymond, 21–22, 28, 66, 67, 72
Williams, Sherley Anne, 174
Willis, Susan, 158, 161–62, 263n.2
Wilson, Elizabeth, 127
Wilson, Matthew, 255n.50
Wilson, William Julius, 25, 26–28, 29, 30
Wilson-Cartier, Xam, 243n.3
women's movement, 200, 266n.43
word-processing, 184
Wright, Richard, 4, 41, 42, 265n.42
writing, 2, 15, 40–42, 52–53, 78, 80, 83, 87, 88, 95, 99, 100, 131–43, 172, 174, 178, 217–18, 219–20, 224, 230

Young, Iris, 193, 231, 232

zoopraxiscope, 110, 122